MW00813909

Media Stereotypes

This book is part of the Peter Lang Media and Communication list.
Every volume is peer reviewed and meets
the highest quality standards for content and production.

PETER LANG
New York • Bern • Berlin
Brussels • Vienna • Oxford • Warsaw

Media Stereotypes

From Ageism to Xenophobia

Edited by Andrew C. Billings and Scott Parrott

PETER LANG

New York • Bern • Berlin
Brussels • Vienna • Oxford • Warsaw

Library of Congress Cataloging-in-Publication Data

Names: Billings, Andrew C., editor. | Parrott, Scott, editor.
Title: Media stereotypes: from ageism to xenophobia /
edited by Andrew C. Billings and Scott Parrott.
Description: New York: Peter Lang, 2020.
Includes bibliographical references and index.
Identifiers: LCCN 2020020618 (print) | LCCN 2020020619 (ebook)
ISBN 978-1-4331-6667-9 (hardback) | ISBN 978-1-4331-6668-6 (paperback)
ISBN 978-1-4331-6664-8 (ebook pdf)
ISBN 978-1-4331-6665-5 (epub) | ISBN 978-1-4331-6666-2 (mobi)
Subjects: LCSH: Stereotypes (Social psychology) in mass media.
Classification: LCC P96.S74 M44 2020 (print) | LCC P96.S74 (ebook) |
DDC 303.3/85—dc23
LC record available at https://lccn.loc.gov/2020020618
LC ebook record available at https://lccn.loc.gov/2020020619
DOI 10.3726/b15280

Bibliographic information published by **Die Deutsche Nationalbibliothek**.
Die Deutsche Nationalbibliothek lists this publication in the "Deutsche
Nationalbibliografie"; detailed bibliographic data are available
on the Internet at http://dnb.d-nb.de/.

The paper in this book meets the guidelines for permanence and durability
of the Committee on Production Guidelines for Book Longevity
of the Council of Library Resources.

© 2020 Peter Lang Publishing, Inc., New York
80 Broad Street, 5th floor, New York, NY 10004
www.peterlang.com

All rights reserved.
Reprint or reproduction, even partially, in all forms such as microfilm,
xerography, microfiche, microcard, and offset strictly prohibited.

Printed in the United States of America

Table of Contents

Preface

The genesis of this collection emerged through our conversations about media stereotyping, an area of inquiry we believe is entering perhaps its richest period to date: the foundations are established in the literature, theoretical approaches are advancing, and scholars are increasingly turning critical eyes to the representation of social groups via television, film, news, and social media (and those representations' consequences). Despite the burgeoning paradigm, we realized through our conversations with students that our field needed a volume that could serve as a one-stop location for those wishing to understand decades of media stereotyping research. Scholars, whether undergraduate students, graduate students, mid-career or beyond, needed somewhere to turn for an overview of the field, including its methods, theories, and literature. *Media Stereotypes: From Ageism to Xenophobia* was born.

Of course, the most telling factor of any edited book project is whether one can secure key contributors. That's not always easy as highly productive scholars are, quite predictably, in high demand. Here was where the true magic happened for this project: one by one, top scholars in the area of media stereotyping, realizing the need for such a volume, said yes to the prospect of including a chapter. The result is a true state-of-the-field advancement of what we know (as well as what we don't yet know) about a variety of forms of media stereotyping. We are proud of the high quality work our contributors advance here; we hope you enjoy it as well.

We both must thank those contributors here, who worked with tight writing deadlines and always took our feedback in the constructive manner in which it was intended. We also need to thank Peter Lang Publications for their steadfast support of the work, specifically Acquisitions Editor Erika Hendrix, who always responded to our queries promptly and clearly.

We both wish to thank our families for their consistent support and under-standing, as well as our colleagues in the Department of Journalism & Creative Media and the College of Communication & Information Sciences at the University of Alabama. Additionally, Billings wishes to thank the Thompson family, creators of the Ronald Reagan Endowed Chair of Broadcasting at the University, while Parrott wishes to thank the Reese Phifer family, creators of the Phifer Fellowship at UA. Each provided the necessary support to be able to advance this project in the manner it deserved.

Oddly, our dream is to make this book out-of-date in relatively short order. We'd love for these stereotypes to disappear and/or for scholars to advance work to such a degree that our current understanding of media stereotypes would be downright pedestrian. Until then, we present *Media Stereotypes: From Ageism to Xenophobia*, which collectively shows you that the mediated world continues to be a trick mirror that often must be both scruti-nized and opposed.

Andrew Billings
Scott Parrott
Tuscaloosa, Alabama
January 2020

Introduction

The Practice of Studying Media Stereotypes

ANDREW C. BILLINGS
University of Alabama

SCOTT PARROTT
University of Alabama

In 1990, just a few months after its initial debut, the animated television program *The Simpsons* introduced a character that was destined to be—very contradictorily—one of its most beloved, debated, reviled, and ultimately memed and mimicked characters. Indian immigrant and manager of the local Kwik-E-Mart, Apu Nahasapeemapetilon, became a mainstay of the fictional Springfield town. With catchphrases both simplistic ("Thank you, come again") and stereotypical ("Hello, Mr. Homer"), Apu was endearing to some while offensively stereotypical to others (Biswas, 2018). Simmering on the fringe of acceptability for years, Apu became a symbol endemic for race-based stereotypes and microaggressions for some, while being endemic of political correctness run amok for others (Houghton, 2018). Pakistani-American Actor Kumail Nanjiani reported that he was often asked to do the "Apu accent" in auditions (Rao, 2015) and debates roiled with the release of the 2017 documentary *The Problem with Apu*. Three decades of characterization and consumption had still not answered the core questions in this stalwart Simpsons character: Was Apu a media stereotype? Even if so, could he be "grandfathered" into a culture that was less enlightened about such things decades ago?

Is it inaccurate to disproportionately cognitively place Indian immigrants in the role of gas station/convenience store attendant? No—at least it was not in the age when Apu was introduced—according to *New York Times'* Lorch (1992, para. 1) who traced the "immigrant job specialty" of many different ethnic descendants to cultural values and transferrable skills; yes—according to the latest job demographics from the U.S. Department of Labor ("Labor

Force Statistics from the Current Population Survey", 2019). Every aspect of Apu could be debated: yes, Indian immigrants are more likely to struggle with English along with no, not all Indian immigrants remotely exhibited such struggles. The discussion of Apu was said to be about media stereotyping, yet ultimately was about many ancillary tensions within: bias vs. difference, exemplar vs. generalization, representation vs. omission.

In similar ways, discussions over broader stereotypes within media feature the same fault lines. Women represented the majority of professions in areas such as nursing and elementary school teaching, yet it was a stereotype for media to advance narratives making the majority seem like the consensus. Black athletes were disproportionately represented in the NBA, yet it was a stereotype to argue Black people are innately predisposed for success in the game. Even stereotypes that were argued to be positive reduced people to caricature (hence the "supercrip" stereotype of the differentially abled) or inferred reduction of abilities in unrepresented areas (the career-driven Asian strong in math and science could reinforce the lack of interpersonal skills or life-balance harbored within these "strengths"). Considerable deviation could be found between the terms "stereotype," "tendency," "bias," "difference," or a dreaded "-ism" (e.g., sexism, ageism, ableism). Yet the ability to explore the tenets of these differences was beyond the Twittersphere or most colloquial conversations.

Enter this book. Partly because of the need to explore stereotypes in concert rather than in isolation and partly because of the need to represent what stereotypes are—and, hence, the ramifications therein—this book is designed as both a survey (of key theories, methods, and types of studies that collectively represent the investigation of media stereotyping) and reference guide (outlining the seminal works in a variety of related yet distinctive fields). As such, we hope there is insight that can be gleaned for the reader no matter if it is their first or 500th foray into the world of media stereotypes. Each heuristic utilized is debated, yet core agreements have been established within each and will be explored in subsequent sections of this opening chapter.

What Is/Is Not Media Stereotyping?

Given the debate concerning which media representations constitute stereotypes, it would be prudent to conceptually define what "stereotype" means in the research literature. Stereotypes are overgeneralized beliefs about the characteristics, attributes, and/or behavior of social groups. Research from the fields of social and cognitive psychology often provides the foundation for studies concerning media stereotyping, and indeed, these fields have devoted extensive empirical attention to understanding the formation, maintenance, and application of stereotypes (for a review, see Hilton & Von Hippel, 1996). Stereotypes may contain positive (e.g., Southern people are polite) or negative (e.g., obese people are lazy) valences, and each may be problematic because they inform the beliefs, attitudes, and behavior of both ingroup and out-group members. Stereotypes have been described as the byproduct of social categorization, an automatic cognitive process in which humans divide the world into categories, eliciting ingroups and outgroups, "us" versus "them." Similarly, stereotypes have been described as the result of the miserly way in which humans employ our limited cognitive resources, mental shortcuts that help us process information without expending much cognitive effort (see Fiske, 1998). A number of models have been advanced to explain how ste-reotypes are mentally represented (Hilton & Von Hippel, 1996), including an exemplar-based approach in which we store concrete examples of social groups (e.g., Apu as representative of Indian Americans) to a network approach in which concepts are linked in memory via associative pathways, their proximity influencing the likelihood they will be activated and applied (e.g., "conve-nience store clerk" closely associated with "Indian American"). Stereotypes can serve several functions, helping an individual quickly process and interpret information, navigate social norms, or experience a self-esteem boost through downward social comparison with an outgroup member. They can also be problematic. While stereotypes may contain a kernel of truth, as Allport (1988) put it, their overgeneralized nature often renders them inaccurate, misguiding subsequent attitudes and behavior. In this way, stereotypes provide the foun-dation for prejudice and discrimination.

Given this foundation, we conceptually define media stereotypes as <u>medi-ated messages that communicate overgeneralized information about social groups, associating positive or negative characteristics, attributes, and/or behavior with the social group</u>. The mass media perpetuate stereotypes through both *creation* and *reinforcement*, providing audiences novel representations but also perpetuating existing cultural stereotypes concerning social groups. Media stereotypes emerge when news, entertainment, and other programming repeatedly present homogenous messages concerning social groups, increasing the likelihood an audience member will associate a social group with character-istics, attributes, and/or behavior. For example, researchers have examined the representation of mental illness in American television, film, and other media products since the 1950s, and regardless of decade or medium, media have consistently associated mental illness with violent and unpredictable behav-ior. The stereotype pervades everything from news stories, where people with mental illness assault innocent strangers, to children's television programming, where mental illness is a convenient explanation for diabolical behavior.

Sheer frequency is not necessarily a defining factor for media stereotypes, however. Social groups may rarely appear in mainstream media content, but when they do appear, be relegated to roles that reflect and reinforce existing social stereotypes. Take Apu. Indian Americans are largely absent as characters in American media content, and commenters have noted that when they do appear, they often speak with an overly strong accent, work menial jobs (e.g., Apu as convenience store owner), and/or demonstrate social incompetence (e.g., Raj in *The Big Bang Theory*). As Ramasubramanian, Doshi, and Saleem (2017) demonstrated, exposure to such stereotypes may affect the self-esteem of Indian Americans.

Root Causes of Media Stereotyping

While scholars have well-documented media stereotypes within American mass media content, little formal attention has been devoted to the reason stereotypes actually appear. There are hints within the literature, however, suggesting myriad reasons. A number of these potential explanations are represented in Shoemaker and Reese's hierarchy of influences model (2014), which posits that social systems, social institutions, organizational structures, media routines, and individual media practitioners inform the substance of media content.

The mass media, whether news or entertainment, are designed to reach mass audiences, including people from diverse educational, socioeconomic, and cultural backgrounds. Given the economic and ideological desire to reach broad audiences, content creators focus on simplicity of messages. Journalists employ simple wording and brevity, while entertainment writers convey archetypes that are widely and easily understood. One reason stereotypes appear in media content is because they afford simple explanations for complex phenomenon. To illustrate, an entertainment television writer once asked one of the editors, "What is the simplest and quickest way to communicate that a character is a nerd? Put her in glasses." The representation of mental illness provides an illustrative example. The United States witnessed a number of mass shootings in recent years, in which gunmen murdered innocent people for no apparent reason. The murderous behavior elicited questions concerning motive, asking people to comprehend the incomprehensible. As journalists (and society) grappled with the question "Why?" explanations emerged that were both simplistic and rooted in politics, including mental illness, firearm access, and violent video game exposure. While mental illness may certainly factor into a gunman's motivation for assaulting innocent people, news stories generally avoid more complex explanations involving mental health, negative life experiences, the glorification of harmful role models, access to firearms, and bullying. Instead, stories most often associate severe mental illness with mass violence (e.g., McGinty, Webster, Jarlenski, & Barry, 2014).

Gerbner and colleagues (1978) described television as the central cultural arm of U.S. society, the great storyteller sharing homogenous values with diverse audiences. Along these lines, stereotypes appear in media content because they reflect dominant societal norms. For example, U.S. society endorses a so-called thin ideal, defining physical beauty for women as involving a thin body shape (e.g., Harrison, 2000). Magazine producers are motivated by profit (among other factors), and might therefore seek to sell more magazines by highlighting social norms such as the thin ideal, including manipulated images of models on the cover and tips for losing weight centered around eating and exercise. Media content perpetuates the thin ideal, and in doing so, labels as "other" or "unacceptable" heavier body shapes. Mass media also perpetuate anti-fat stereotypes, such as the false notion that people who are overweight are lazy (e.g., Ata & Thompson, 2010).

In addition, stereotypes appear in media content because of professional routines. For example, journalists produce stories by interviewing people and conducting research, yet studies suggest marginalized groups often do not appear in news stories even when they are the subject of the coverage (e.g., Nairn & Coverdale, 2005) and that reporters more often consult elite, official sources such as politicians and CEOs. Given the lack of diversity in America's corporate and government leadership, "elite sources" often translates into "White," "male," "wealthy," and "senior." Researchers have long noted a gender imbalance in sourcing, such that female sources are either missing or relegated to subjects that conform to gender stereotypes (e.g., Armstrong, Boyle, & McLeod, 2012). Similar to routines, stereotypes may appear in the media because a media organization endorses the representation. For example, news coverage concerning immigrants and refugees may differ depending on the news outlet an audience member follows, with one network associating immigrant status with criminality and another network describing immigration as the pursuit of the American dream.

Finally, stereotypes appear in the media because content creators harbor implicit and explicit attitudes concerning the social groups they are representing in print, television, and film. Implicit attitudes are evaluations that people might not necessarily know they have. For example, a football announcer may praise the performance of a black quarterback by focusing on his athletic prowess, while attributing the failures of a white quarterback to his physical shortcomings (e.g., Billings, 2004). Conversely, people are aware of explicit attitudes, in which an individual openly endorses a belief. To illustrate, a news commenter might condemn the acceptance of refugees into the United States by associating refugees with terrorism and disease.

"Pictures in Our Heads": Ramifications of Media Stereotyping

It is important we study media stereotypes because of the potential for mass media to inform the "pictures in our heads," as Lippmann (1922) famously put it, which help us make sense of the world around us. Exposure to media stereotypes (or counter-stereotypes) can affect audience members' beliefs, attitudes, emotions, and behavior toward social groups. The mass media may be especially influential when an individual lacks personal experience with the social group (Schiappa, Gregg, & Hewes, 2006). As highlighted by the chapters in this book, researchers have found stereotypical media exposure affects attitudes concerning everything from social closeness (e.g., mental illness in Chapter 13) to governmental policy (e.g., immigration in Chapter 12). Given the pervasive presence of media in modern life, it is important to note that exposure may influence not only explicit attitudes by informing beliefs, but implicit associations that can operate beyond the individual's conscious awareness. Because most people do not want to appear prejudiced, even when they harbor negative attitudes toward social groups, media researchers have begun to account for implicit attitudes that may provide the foundation for prejudice and discrimination. In a seminal study concerning media stereotypes and implicit attitudes, Brown Givens and Monahan (2005) exposed participants to stereotypical examples of African American women (e.g., mammies, jezebels) before asking participants to rate either an African American or White female job candidate. While exposure did not affect explicit outcomes, stereotype exposure did lead participants to more quickly associate negative words with the African American job candidate, an indicator of increased cognitive association. Other indirect measures of prejudice involve content analyses of reader comments sections, where people provide opinions concerning news topics while under the cloak of anonymity. To illustrate, Gwarjanski and Parrott (2018) found that readers were more likely to express stereotypes and prejudice in the comments section accompanying stereotypical news stories about schizophrenia, compared to counter-stereotypical stories.

In addition to outgroup members, media exposure may affect people who are targeted by media stereotypes. For example, an experiment by Saleem and Ramasubramanian (2019) exposed Muslim American college students to media stereotypes (e.g., terrorism) and counter-stereotypes (e.g., schoolchildren) concerning Muslims. Muslim-American college students who encountered the stereotypical news content subsequently expressed less desire to be accepted by other Americans and greater desire to avoid interaction with other Americans. Similarly, people with mental illness expressed less desire to engage with others following the mass shooting at Virginia Tech because they assumed that news of the tragedy affected people's attitudes concerning mental illness (Hoffner, Fujioka, Cohen, & Seate, 2017). When members of marginalized groups avoid contact, the decision can isolate the individual and carry societal implications. It strips other people of contact with a marginalized out group, which is an important approach to mitigating stereotypes, prejudice, and discrimination (as outlined by Gibson and Thompson in Chapter 1). In addition to such social identity threats, people who are subjected to media stereotypes may internalize stereotypes, experiencing decreased self-esteem or altering their behavior for fear of confirming the misinformation. For example, a famous social psychology experiment had participants play miniature golf on the understanding that (a) success on the course represented an indicator of sports intelligence or (b) it was an indicator of athleticism. White participants performed worse than a control group when the game was described as an indicator of "natural athletic ability," while Black participants underperformed in the "intelligence" condition (Stone, Lynch, Sjomeling, & Darley, 1999).

While research has largely focused on negative outcomes, researchers are increasingly investigating how exposure to counter-stereotypical media content may nurture more prosocial attitudes toward social groups. As reviewed in Chapter 1, the parasocial contact hypothesis suggests that the mass media may afford audience members an opportunity for contact with marginalized groups, which can challenge stereotypes and elicit positive attitudes when the contact is positive. For example, Schiappa et al. (2006) examined the hypothesis using the American television program *Will & Grace*, which featured two prominent gay male characters. The more participants watched the program and parasocially interacted with its characters, the more positive attitudes they expressed toward people who are gay.

Chapter Overview

This book unfolds in a two-fold manner, working from the general (foundations of media stereotyping in Section I) to specific (types of media stereotyping in Section II). In the opening three chapters, the focus is on macro-analyses of theories frequently employed and oft-utilized methods within past studies of media stereotyping. The aim in these opening pieces is to give a sense of how understanding of various media stereotypes work in concert with one another—as well as to delineate areas in which they differ. Forming a plethora of cognitive Venn diagrams, these pieces set the stage for understanding what we tend to talk about when we mention the theories undergirding and the methods analyzing the presence (or lack thereof) of media stereotypes.

The first of these core groundwork chapters is advanced by the team of Rhonda Gibson and Jacob R. Thompson as they advance understanding of key theories as they have been applied to this subfield. Chapter 1 explores the theories that rise to the fore, whether largely the result of content discrepancies, often advanced through the lens of framing, for instance, or the result of effects-based discrepancies, often advanced through theories such as the parasocial contact hypothesis. We opted to open with a chapter on theory simply because these are the communicative lenses in which all other findings must be understood, interpreted, and advanced.

Next, Cory L. Armstrong and Sharon E. Baldinelli use Chapter 2 to explore the wide range of content analyses that inform the field. Arguably the largest collective program of methodological work in this area, content analyses identify what stereotypes are present in current media, providing an appropriate springboard for then understanding what the presence of these stereotypes could mean for various crosshatches of people. Armstrong and Baldinelli articulate the core problems with the characterizations advanced in media, yet end the chapter on a more optimistic tone, advancing a call for also exploring what media gets right—a useful and necessary contrast to draw.

Finally, experiments and outcomes-based studies of media stereotyping become the crux of Chapter 3, where Elizabeth Behm-Morawitz and Andrea Figueroa-Caballero survey the field in this second key methodological regard. Whereas content analyses inform us of the potential impact of problematic stereotyping, experiments allow for causation-based conclusions, showing the ramification of the "pictures in our heads" as they become enacted within public, social, and interpersonal settings.

The remaining eleven chapters then focus more on specific types of media stereotyping that have been uncovered in the past and could be uncovered with greater utility in the future. Each chapter unfolds in a similar manner, advancing each form of media stereotypes in four ways: (a) introducing and creating a warrant for studying given stereotypes surrounding a demographic/social group, (b) establishing how such stereotypes problematically represent a demographic/social group both in the 20th and 21st Centuries, (c) articulating the effects of exposure to these particular stereotypes, and (d) offering robust avenues for future theoretical and methodological investigation. While not at all an exhaustive list of the types of media stereotyping that can and do occur, each of the eleven chapters substantiate the import in exploring how media shape narratives in inordinate, disproportional, and/or problematic manners.

The first of these chapters in Part II is offered from Jennifer Stevens Aubrey and Kun Yan, as they use Chapter 4 to explore one of the deepest of all media stereotyping terrains: gender stereotyping. Offering a systematic longitudinal glance at characterizations based on gender, they show slow yet steady progress, all while acknowledging the considerable work ahead to diminish remaining stereotypes. They begin and end the chapter contending that the largest mechanism for future change involves greater gender diversity in the creation/production roles media entail.

Next, Chapter 5 features the research team of Travis L. Dixon, Kristopher R. Weeks, Melinda Sevilla, and Amanda N. Tolbert as they explore elements of the Black/African-American stereotype. They cover areas where considerable depth has been identified (such as the prevalence of the Black criminal stereotype) yet also touch on numerous singular studies that also serve as touchstones for advancing scholarship in the future.

Race-based stereotypes are also the focus of Chapter 6, zeroing in on stereotypes within Latina/o populations. Dana Mastro and Kevin N. Do advance an argument that, due to a confluence of events that include a consistently growing Latina/o population in America and the rising debate surrounding both legal and illegal immigration, media images are key in understanding and reinterpreting these populations. They argue that "our rapidly changing media environment coupled with new, state-of-the-art research methodologies and techniques suggest that we are at an important inflection point," providing considerable warrant for this statement within the chapter.

Next, Sharon R. Mazzarella explains the problems of youth and age gaps in Chapter 7, particularly focusing on the moral panic that often surrounds the frequent refrain of "kids these days." While surveying considerable work in the area, she then notes a potential wayward sense of direction in this subfield, believing that the "general public and scholars themselves have long been concerned with the effects of a range of mediated artifacts on young people, but the public discourse has failed to raise concerns about the effects of mediated constructions of young people on adult audiences." The need to pair not just content with effects but effects on subgroups (youth vs. adults) is a key contribution within the chapter.

Chapter 8 focuses on the oft-trifurcated world of looks/appearance based on media stereotypes, quite literally showing the influence of framing the good, the bad, and the ugly. Rachel F. Rodgers and Jenna Campagna ably make the case that judging a book by its cover certainly happens in a wide range of media characterizations, yet is much more nuanced than most could presume.

Socioeconomic stereotypes then form the nexus of Chapter 9, with Rebecca Ann Lind showing a variety of differences uncovered between the cash-strapped and the monied, the blue collar and the white collar, and the circumstances that purportedly drive these depictions. The notion of media depicting one deserving one's own hardship/plight is key within the chapter, rarely focusing on the social and historical structures that cause inequities in opportunities. "Class is not dismissed," Lind claims regarding the need for future studies, because of media images that continue to "symbolically annihilate the working class and the poor, or present the bulk of society as an imagined middle class."

LGBTQ communities and the stereotypes within then are advanced by Leigh Moscowitz, as she deftly shows in Chapter 10 which stereotypes overlap (part and parcel of the amalgamation of non-heteronormativity) and which stereotypes are disproportionately levied toward populations within the broader LGBTQ collective. Moscowitz rightly speaks of the false celebrations many have had regarding the increased number of LGBTQ portrayals in media, which are largely the result of an expansive array of media options more than any dramatic rise in mainstream media. Moreover, Moscowitz writes of troubling motifs once these characters are included in narratives, such as the "bury your gays" theme that seems to cause untimely deaths of LGBTQ characters at a much higher rate than others within fictionalized media.

Stephen J. Lind then uses Chapter 11 to till the thorny terrain of religious stereotypes. Showing both Christian-centric and anti-Christian (and broader anti-religion) depictions, Lind makes a case for the need to explore what he terms "religimedia." Quite tellingly, many of his examples are attempts to counter what media producers presumably have as pictures in their own heads about religious people and leaders. Hence, the result is to disproportionately highlight the atypical, whether that involves scandal or troublingly myopic devotion.

Chapter 12 is, arguably, one of the areas America has most grappled with in recent years, with Jennifer Hoewe and Seth P. McCullock outlining the world of media stereotypes as they relate to immigrants and refugees. Noting that many of the modern depictions of these groups are offered through politicized lenses, they contend that studying media portrayals in these areas is crucial as media have the "power to impact individual attitudes and public opinion toward policy directed at immigrants and refugees."

Mental illness (and the related element of mental health disclosures) are the focus of Chapter 13, with Scott Parrott advancing the claim that media depictions tend to focus on the sensationalized rather than, for instance, the 17.3 million Americans experiencing various forms of depression. Instead, partly from a desire for predictable media storylines, schizophrenia and notions of the general "crazy" person move to the fore, providing shock and intense storylines at the expense of accuracy.

Finally, Chapter 14 creates a yin to many of the previous chapters' yang by focusing on positive/counterstereotypes occurring within past and present media. Srivi Ramasubramanian, Asha Winfield, and Emily Riewestahl jointly make the case that the study of positive/counterstereotypes are key to under-standing the full range of media effects in these areas. Arguing for increased media literacy and conversations about differences between stereotypes and demographic trends, the research team highlights that while stereotypes can be seen as "positive" or "counter," these still can imbue negative ramifications on communities within America.

Conclusion

Of course, while we believe these fourteen chapters do yeoman's work in sum-marizing and advancing what we know about media stereotypes as we move into this centuries' third decade, a common theme is that there is still consid-erable work to be done. The most frequent refrain within the volume involves the call for intersectionality studies, rightly seeking to delineate between, for example, a White, blue-collar, male as opposed to a Black, white-collar, female. These intersections are crucial to understanding how one set of stereotypes is enveloped in another, how a Latina woman is portrayed differently as a refugee as opposed to a person with generations of familial history within the United States.

We also readily admit that this book is U.S.-focused and that the increased access to and consumption of international media creates another cross-hatch of images and problems to navigate. Stereotypes are, quite inherently, messy constructs. Our goal in this volume is merely to provide heuristics to consider as scholarship moves into even more byzantine areas. In 2020, the *Simpsons* voice of Apu, Hank Azaria, announced he would no longer voice the character because of the stereotypes it advanced. That is just one small step for progress, yet recognizes an increased cognizance of such problematic images, giving us hope for the future. We hope this volume also helps identify fruitful paths forward.

References

Allport, G. W. (1988). *The nature of prejudice: 25th anniversary edition*. Reading, MA: Addison-Wesley Publishing Company, Inc.

Armstrong, C. L., Boyle, M. P., & McLeod, D. M. (2012). A global trend: How news coverage of protests reinforces gender stereotypes. *Journalism Studies, 13*(4), 633–648.

Ata, R. N., & Thompson, J. K. (2010). Weight bias in the media: A review of recent research. *Obesity Facts, 3*(1), 41–46.

Billings, A. C. (2004). Depicting the quarterback in black and white: A content analysis of college and professional football broadcast commentary. *Howard Journal of Communications, 15*(4), 201–210.

Biswas, S. (2018, May 9). 'The Simpsons': Not all Indians think Apu is a racist stereotype. *BBC News*. Retrieved from https://www.bbc.com/news/world-asia-india-44027613.

Brown Givens, S. M., & Monahan, J. L. (2005). Priming mammies, jezebels, and other controlling images: An examination of the influence of mediated stereotypes on perceptions of an African American woman. *Media Psychology, 7*(1), 87–106.

Fiske, S. T. (1998). Stereotyping, prejudice, and discrimination. In D. T. Gilbert, S. T. Fiske, & G. Lindzey (Eds.), *The handbook of social psychology* (pp. 357–411). Boston, MA: McGraw-Hill.

Gerbner, G., Gross, L., Jackson-Beeck, M., Jeffries-Fox, S., & Signorielli, N. (1978). Cultural indicators violence profile no. 9. *Journal of Communication, 28*(3), 176–207.

Gwarjanski, A. R., & Parrott, S. (2018). Schizophrenia in the news: The role of news frames in shaping online reader dialogue about mental illness. *Health Communication, 33*(8), 954–961.

Harrison, K. (2000). The body electric: Thin-ideal media and eating disorders in adolescents. *Journal of Communication, 50*(3), 119–143.

Hilton, J. L., & Von Hippel, W. (1996). Stereotypes. *Annual Review of Psychology, 47*(1), 237–271.

Hoffner, C. A., Fujioka, Y., Cohen, E. L., & Atwell Seate, A. (2017). Perceived media influence, mental illness, and responses to news coverage of a mass shooting. *Psychology of Popular Media Culture, 6*(2), 159–173.

Houghton, R. (2018, December 21). Simpsons actor says Apu backlash is 'political correctness taken toofar'. *Digital Spy*. Retrieved from https://www.digitalspy.com/tv/ustv/a25652475/simpsons-apu-backlash-political-correctness-joe-mantegna/.

"Labor Force Statistics from the Current Population Survey" (2019, Jan. 18). *Bureau of labor statistics*. Retrieved from https://www.bls.gov/cps/cpsaat18.htm.

Lippmann, W. (1922). *Public opinion*. New York, NY: MacMillan Co.

Lorch, D. (1992, January 12). An ethnic road to riches: The immigrant job specialty. *New York Times*. Retrieved from https://www.nytimes.com/1992/01/12/nyregion/an-ethnic-road-to-riches-the-immigrant-job-specialty.html.

McGinty, E. E., Webster, D. W., Jarlenski, M., & Barry, C. L. (2014). News media framing of serious mental illness and gun violence in the United States, 1997–2012. *American Journal of Public Health, 104*(3), 406–413.

Nairn, R. G., & Coverdale, J. H. (2005). People never see us living well: an appraisal of the personal stories about mental illness in a prospective print media sample. *Australian and New Zealand Journal of Psychiatry, 39*(4), 281–287.

Rao, M. (2015, Nov. 13). Let's talk about the Apu accent. *Vulture.* Retrieved from https://www.vulture.com/2015/11/master-of-none-recap-season-1-episode-4.html.

Ramasubramanian, S., Doshi, M. J., & Saleem, M. (2017). Mainstream versus ethnic media: How they shape ethnic pride and self-esteem among ethnic minority audiences. *International Journal of Communication, 11*(21), 1879–1899.

Saleem, M., & Ramasubramanian, S. (2019). Muslim Americans' responses to social identity threats: Effects of media representations and experiences of discrimination. *Media Psychology, 22*(3), 373–393.

Schiappa, E., Gregg, P. B., & Hewes, D. E. (2006). Can one TV show make a difference? Will & Grace and the parasocial contact hypothesis. *Journal of Homosexuality, 51*(4), 15–37.

Shoemaker, P. J., & Reese, S. D. (2014). *Mediating the message in the 21st century: Theories of influence on mass media content* (3rd ed.). New York, NY: Routledge.

Stone, J., Lynch, C. I., Sjomeling, M., & Darley, J. M. (1999). Stereotype threat effects on Black and White athletic performance. *Journal of Personality and Social Psychology, 77*(6), 1213–1227

Section I *Foundations of Media Stereotyping Research*

1 Theories of Media Stereotyping Research

RHONDA GIBSON
University of North Carolina at Chapel Hill

JACOB R. THOMPSON
University of North Carolina at Chapel Hill

Simply put, stereotypes are generalized characteristics we apply to others based on some aspect of their perceived identity, such as race, gender, sexual orientation, age, or country of origin. Journalist Walter Lippmann is often credited for first conceptualizing stereotypes as cognitive structures—"pictures in our heads"—that can account for individuals' biases and misjudgments in their interpretations of the world around them (Schneider, 2004). In his influential book *Public Opinion*, Lippmann (1922) noted that people know about much more than they have experienced firsthand. As he explained, "There is neither time nor opportunity for intimate acquaintance. Instead we notice a trait which marks a well-known type and fill in the rest of the picture by means of the stereotypes we carry about in our heads" (p. 89). These mental images of aspects of life not directly experienced are created based on information provided by others. It should not come as a surprise, then, to learn that news, entertainment, and social media are a common source of the information we use to form stereotypes.

In the century since Lippmann first wrote about stereotypes, they have been conceptualized by scholars in vastly different ways. Some early researchers described them as reflecting culturally derived generalizations related to ethnic groups (Katz & Braly, 1935), whereas others suggested that stereotypes can also emerge from individual personality types (Adorno, Frenkel-Brunswik, Levinson, & Sanford, 1950; Allport, 1954). Although most scholarly work has focused on the damage that stereotypes can do, it is acknowledged that a tendency toward cognitive categorization is a natural and useful approach to dealing with the complexity of our environment. Indeed, much of contemporary social cognition research characterizes stereotypes rather neutrally as abstract knowledge structures or schemas that individuals deploy in information processing and decision-making (Hamilton, 1981), rather than as the "products of corrupt minds and diseased culture" (Schneider, 2004, p. 12). Nonetheless, a discussion of the theories of media stereotype effects cannot ignore the substantial amount of research that links stereotyping to overgeneralizations, prejudice, and discrimination.

It would be impossible for one chapter to examine all theories related to media stereotypes. This chapter focuses more narrowly on key theories from social and cognitive psychology that are useful in predicting and explaining the effects of stereotypes on both ingroup and outgroup members, with an emphasis on those theories that have been tested extensively using mediated content. First, however, we will briefly review an influential contemporary model of stereotype content that provides a cross-cultural conceptualization of the construct.

The Stereotype Content Model

Scholars have proposed dozens of ways to think about stereotypes and differentiate them from similar concepts such as beliefs, attitudes, prejudice, schema, and heuristics. Many of these definitions have incorporated some aspect of ingroup vs. outgroup comparison and often view stereotypes as unidimensional, falling somewhere along a single negative vs. positive continuum. The stereotype content model (SCM), however, argues that stereotypes are "neither univalent nor unidimensional" (Cuddy et al., 2009, p. 3). First proposed in the early 21st Century by a group of four social psychologists (Fiske, Cuddy, Glick, & Xu, 2002), SCM suggests that all group-based stereotypes form along two dimensions: warmth and competence.

The model's creators argue that when assessing members of an outgroup, people are evolutionarily inclined to first evaluate those individuals' intent to either do harm or provide help (the warmth dimension) and then to evaluate the capacity of those individuals to act on that perceived intention (the competence dimension; Cuddy, Fiske, & Glick, 2008). The warmth dimension is the primary one in the model, and its original components have evolved based on challenges and research findings from other scholars. The revised conceptualization of the warmth dimension involves assessments of an outgroup or individual's potential threat *and* competition levels. It is now seen as encompassing trustworthiness and friendliness (Fiske, 2018). The competence dimension has remained more consistent in conceptualization, involving assessments of capability and assertiveness. Multiple experimental studies applying the SCM to both national and international populations have found that the model reliably predicts stereotype content across cultures and contexts (Cuddy et al., 2008; Fiske, 2005; Fiske, 2018; Fiske, Cuddy, & Glick, 2007).

Members of groups that are considered both very warm and very competent, such as members of an individual's ingroup, are more likely to be stereotyped in positive (but still overly generalized) ways, earning admiration and ally status (Fiske et al., 2002). Members of groups that are considered low in both warmth and competence, such as the poor, will be stereotyped negatively, receiving contempt. Perhaps more interesting is how the SCM addresses *ambivalent* stereotypes, which emerge when outgroups are seen by others as skilled in one dimension (either competence or warmth) but lacking in the other. Individuals high in warmth but low in competence face paternalistic, pity-based stereotypes, whereas those low in warmth but high in competence are saddled with envious stereotypes (Fiske et al., 2002).

A widely cited study involving participants from seven European (individualist) and three East Asian (collectivist) nations (N = 1,028) found evidence that societal stereotypes are quite similar across cultures (Cuddy et al., 2009). Data from that project identified three major cross-cultural, cross-groups similarities and only one difference across the 10 non-US nations. Results supported the general notion that perceived warmth and competence reliably differentiate societal group stereotypes and that many outgroups receive ambivalent stereotypes (high on one dimension; low on the other). Likewise, results showed that high status groups stereotypically are considered competent, whereas competitive groups stereotypically are perceived as lacking warmth. The one cross-cultural difference uncovered in the data, however, was that more collectivist cultures do not locate reference groups in the most positive cluster (high-competence/high-warmth), unlike individualist cultures. Overall, the researchers (Cuddy et al., 2009) concluded that the SCM can serve as a pancultural tool for predicting group stereotypes from structural relations with other groups in society and comparing across societies.

Intergroup Contact Theory and the Parasocial Contact Hypothesis

Although it is widely understood that stereotyping is an innate cognitive function useful for dealing with a complex environment, scholars have long sought to identify ways to minimize the prejudice and discrimination that can result from ingroup members' stereotyping of outgroups. Psychologist Gordon Allport (1954), whose research sought to understand and reduce the negative effects of race-based stereotypes, developed the principle of least effort to explain humans' tendency to stereotype, suggesting that individuals value parsimony and generally seek to expend the minimum amount of energy required to meet a goal. However, Allport also hypothesized that if provided with the opportunity to interact face-to-face with members of outgroups, individuals would replace negative cultural stereotypes with more positive individualized assessments. As he succinctly explained in *The Nature of Prejudice* (1954), "contact and acquaintance make for friendliness" (p. 453), which is the essence of the intergroup contact theory or "the contact hypothesis." Allport qualified his assertion, however, suggesting that in-person acquaintance between groups would promote tolerance and acceptance only under certain conditions. He believed that if there were common goals, equal group status, cooperation between groups, and institutional support, contact would lead to target-specific attitude change. That is, negative stereotypical assumptions would be replaced by positive perceptions of the individual. Allport further suggested that these new individual-level positive associations would be subsequently extended to the outgroup as a whole, thus improving intergroup relations. Unless the specified conditions were met, Allport predicted that superficial contact would cause people to revert to stereotypes.

Contact theory has been described as one of social psychology's most successful ideas (Brown, 2000), and a meta-analysis of more than 500 contact studies found substantial support for the theory (Pettigrew & Tropp, 2006), specifically that face-to-face contact between group members significantly reduced prejudice and the more contact groups had, the less prejudice group members reported. The meta-analysis also suggested that it is not necessary for all of Allport's conditions to be present simultaneously for bias to be reduced, although the conditions further enhance the positive effects of contact. The authors present evidence that contact effects generalize beyond the immediate participants in the contact scenario, reducing stereotyping and prejudice toward other members of the outgroup as well. Subsequent research has identified additional conditions that enhance the bias-reducing effects of intergroup contact, such as voluntary participation and intimate interaction, and have noted that online contact can be as valuable as in-person contact (Amichai-Hamburger & McKenna, 2006).

Not long after Allport's (1954) *The Nature of Prejudice* established the contact hypothesis, Horton and Wohl (1956) brought media into the equation by exploring the concepts of parasocial contact and parasocial interaction by suggesting that television and movies can give the illusion of interpersonal contact and lead audience members to develop some degree of interpersonal relationship with a performer. Building upon this notion, years later three scholars (Schiappa, Gregg, & Hewes, 2005) proposed a media equivalent to

Allport's contact hypothesis, which they labeled the parasocial contact hypothesis (PCH). They argued that, "If people process mass-mediated communication in a manner similar to interpersonal interaction, then it is worth exploring whether the socially beneficial functions of intergroup contact have an analogue in para-social contact" (Schiappa et al., 2005, p. 93). They initially reported the results of three studies examining majority group members' level of prejudice toward sexual minorities. In all three studies, parasocial contact was associated with lower levels of stereotyping and prejudice. Moreover, tests of the underlying mechanisms of the PCH were generally supported, suggesting that parasocial contact facilitates positive parasocial responses and changes in beliefs about the attributes of minority group categories. Mediated contact can produce results similar to in-person contact as long as it is adequate in both quantity and quality to allow for the type of judgments that people make with direct interpersonal contact.

Social Identity Theory

Since the early 1970s, much of the theory regarding the formation of stereotypes has been based in a social cognition perspective (Schneider, 2004), allowing scholars to piggyback their work on existing research from both cognitive and social psychology. One such approach is social identity theory, which suggests that people's interactions are driven not only by their personal identity but also by their social identity, which refers to the parts of an individual's self-concept that come from the social groups to which he or she belongs (Tajfel & Turner, 1986).

Similar to Allport's work on the contact hypothesis, social identity theory finds its origins in work on intergroup conflict and behavior in the decades following World War II. While much of the work focused on psychodynamic approaches to authoritarianism and models based on the frustration-aggression hypothesis, some explanations began to focus on group-level dynamics (Hogg, 2016; Tajfel & Turner, 1986). One of these approaches (Sherif, 1966), which would become known as realistic conflict theory, suggests that conflict between groups emerges when their collective goals place them in competition with one another.

Social psychologist Henri Tajfel built on this model by theorizing that categorization alone is enough to induce conflict and stereotyping. Along with his students and colleagues, he conducted several studies of how people categorize and react to categorization. One type of experiment demonstrated that individuals would favor people who are part of their ingroups at the expense of those identified with outgroups, even if the individuals had never met before the experiment and were separated into groups randomly (Doise & Weinberger, 1972; Rabbie & Wilkens 1971; Tajfel, Billig, Bundy, & Flament, 1971).

This work was eventually synthesized into social identity theory, positing that people categorize others into groups and compare their own social groups to others in order to establish social status (Tajfel & Turner, 1979). Motivated to be part of the optimal group in order to raise their social standing and self-esteem, people categorize others as ingroup or outgroup members through stereotyping. In this context, stereotyping occurs when individuals are understood and categorized based on traits they are perceived to share with a social group (Abrams & Hogg, 1990; Hamilton & Sherman, 1994; Tajfel, 1970; Turner, 1982), obscuring individual traits, and leading people to view outgroup members as more similar to each other than they actually are (Tajfel, 1970).

In order for stereotypes to result in meaningful social categorizations, they must be shared beliefs (Hogg & Abrams, 1988). However, the stereotypes do not have to be accurate and can be based upon and reinforced by misconceptions or poor media representations (Mastro, 2003; Mastro, Behm-Morawitz, & Kopacz, 2008; McKinley, Mastro, & Warber, 2014). As a result, media depictions can contribute to social comparisons that affect the social standing and self-esteem of people who identify with these groups and lead others to view them based on a few salient stereotypes rather than based upon personal characteristics.

Initially, it was theorized that people would think of ingroup members in less reductionist and more individualized ways, but empirical findings have been mixed (for an overview, see Brown, 2000). One explanation is that individuals tend to think of ingroup members using stereotypes as well and are motivated to appear as similar as possible to the ideal group member in order to be well-aligned with the positive ingroup traits. Some research suggests that individuals do perceive their ingroups as homogenous in this way, and that as a result those individuals benefit from positive ingroup depictions in the media (Mastro et al., 2008).

Priming and Stereotype Activation

Media priming may well be the most popular theoretical approach to the examination of stereotype processes and effects (Ramasubramanian & Murphy, 2014). The term priming refers to the process through which exposure to an original stimulus, or prime, can influence the way a subsequent stimulus is understood. From early examinations of "perception readiness" (Bruner,

1957) to more contemporary examinations of automaticity, priming research has consistently demonstrated that past experiences influence current perceptions by making certain ideas or concepts more immediately accessible.

Most work on priming is based on models of memory in which concepts are stored as part of a network. Concepts become linked as they are associated with each other, with repeated exposure to the association strengthening the links (e.g. Collins & Loftus, 1975; Price & Tewksbury, 1997; see also overview of potential models and alternative conceptions in Roskos-Ewoldsen, Roskos-Ewoldsen, & Carpentier, 2009). When one concept is activated, as in response to a priming stimulus, related concepts become more accessible and may be more likely to be triggered when an individual comes into contact with a second stimulus. A particularly influential study by Higgins, Rholes, and Jones (1977) demonstrated priming effects by exposing subjects to either positive words ("adventurous," "self-confident") or negative words ("reckless," "conceited") and then having the subjects read a story about a man who behaved in an ambiguous way. Subjects who had been primed with positive traits viewed the man's behavior as much more positive.

Whereas much of the early research concerning media effects focused on priming of violence and political opinions, recent decades have seen interest in how priming relates to stereotypes (Roskos-Ewoldsen et al., 2009). For example, as one is repeatedly exposed to stereotypical depictions of Black men as violent, the concepts of Black men and violence are likely to become linked within memory. When an individual with this link in memory then encounters a Black man, the concept of violence is more accessible, and the individual may be more likely to interpret ambiguous behavior as violent.

The term priming has often been used to describe any context in which exposure to one stimulus has an effect on how a subsequent stimulus will be interpreted. However, most explanations of priming based on network models of memory do not focus on persistent, long-term effects. Depending on the type of priming taking place, empirical studies have demonstrated effects lasting for as little as 700 milliseconds to as long as 20 minutes (Roskos-Ewoldsen et al., 2009). Some models suggest, however, that repeated association can contribute to chronic accessibility of constructs, making them readily available without specific priming (e.g. Price & Tewksbury, 1997). This would be one mechanism through which the processes that prime a particular stereotype could over time lead to more long-term effects. Nevertheless, it is important to distinguish between actual priming and other mechanisms of media influence.

This does not mean that priming has no real-world effects, however. To the contrary, stereotypes can be primed frequently and without conscious realization. Devine's work (1989) has shown that just the presence of a member of a stereotyped group is enough to prime stereotypical representations. Additionally, there is some evidence that priming effects are most significant when the stereotype and subject are congruent (Banaji & Greenwald, 1995; Banaji, Hardin, & Rothman, 1993). Banaji and colleagues (Banaji et al., 1993) found that priming stereotypes more strongly associated with women affected judgments of women without significantly impacting judgments of men. Taken together, these findings suggest that priming effects maintain stereotypes as they are triggered by the presence of stereotyped groups and applied selectively to members of these groups, reinforcing the stereotype.

In addition to shaping the way that individuals interpret the behaviors and characteristics of others, stereotype priming can have adverse effects on how the subjects of harmful stereotypes themselves perform. Work on stereotype threat examines how members of stigmatized groups can underperform in contexts where they feel negative stereotypes are likely to be used to judge their behavior (for example, women often score worse on math assessments when primed to make gender, and by extension stereotypes about women and math, salient; Spencer, Steele, & Quinn, 1999). While the real-world effects and relevance of stereotype threat have been debated, it is generally argued that underperformance results from extra pressure to succeed, threat to self-integrity, or priming of the stereotype directly (Spencer, Logel, & Davies, 2016). While all of these are dependent on the stereotype being made salient, the latter specifically posits that individuals may respond in accordance with relevant stereotypes as an automatic response to priming (Wheeler & Petty, 2001).

Framing Theory

Sociologist Erving Goffman (1974) is credited with pioneering the research method of frame analysis to examine how people's use of conceptual frames to understand objects and events serve to structure their perception of society. Building upon the work of Goffman in a mediated context, Entman (1993) states that to frame is to "select some aspects of a perceived reality and make them more salient in a communicating text, in such a way as to promote a particular problem definition, causal interpretation, moral evaluation, and/or treatment recommendation" (p. 52). Because issues can be viewed in terms of different concerns, which aspects are made salient has a significant impact on one's evaluation of the issue—or group of people—under consideration (Chong & Druckman, 2007). Further, since individuals do not witness most newsworthy events firsthand, they rely on the media to convey stories to them and experience these stories through the frames the media use to convey them (Iyengar & Kinder, 1987).

At the level of media, then, frames consist of the ideas that are emphasized and omitted in the coverage of a topic, promoting a particular interpretation of the issue or individual at hand. At the level of the consumer, frames consist of the schemas, or collection of interconnected concepts that are used to understand an issue, shaping a reader or viewer's perception.

How the media choose to frame a story can have a significant effect on how the story is understood, especially when the audience does not have a strongly developed schema for the frame already. The original framing study by Kahneman and Tversky (1984) showed that simply changing the way a question about what treatment to try was worded could alter the choices that readers made by influencing what concepts were most salient in evaluating the issue. Similarly, Messner and Solomon (1993) found that whether the coverage of boxer Sugar Ray Leonard's domestic violence was understood as a drug problem or an abuse problem was based on what was emphasized by the story's framing.

When journalists use frames to shape their coverage of a story, they are not making decisions in isolation (Gitlin, 1980). Some frames are shared as part of a broader culture. Employing existing issue frames makes a story more digestible by focusing on only certain elements for evaluation. Some of these elements may mark the story as part of a larger pattern, allowing an individual to easily extend their previous assessments of the issue to the new story.

Often the frames employed are based in or contribute to stereotypes. For example, news coverage consistently frames stories about Black athletes in terms of physical capability or natural talent and White athletes in terms of intelligence (Mercurio & Filak, 2010; Ortega & Feagin, 2017). For readers who hold these stereotypes, this places the individual stories within a familiar pattern, making them more accessible. However, this can lead readers to judge issues or people based on incorrect and harmful stereotypes, as well as to establish these stereotypes more firmly as schemas available for future judgments.

Further, while frames may influence an individual's opinion of a story, they are not persuasive arguments designed to change beliefs (Nelson, Oxley, & Clawson, 1997). Instead, frames shape opinion by affecting how much weight is given to different dimensions of an issue. For example, a story that frames gun violence in terms of mental illness as opposed to gun control may lead individuals who do not have strong schemas for assessing issues of gun violence to think of solutions to the issue in terms of mental health rather than laws restricting access to guns. However, this does not mean that their opinion about mental health or restricting gun access has changed—just that that more weight is given to the mental health dimension.

Notably, frames are not always accepted wholesale. Sometimes individuals have strong existing cognitive schema that lead them to question or reject the frames they encounter elsewhere (Feagin, 2013; Tewksbury, Jones, Peske, Raymond, & Vig, 2000). For example, individuals who are conscious and skeptical of racial stereotypes might push back against frames that explain Black athletes' success primarily in terms of biology or natural talent. Still, repeated exposure to stereotypical frames over time can lead individuals to adopt particular schemas related to subgroups of people, and as a result these frames become common across a given culture. When these schemas involve stereotypes, they can lead to biased assessments of members of outgroups and issues such as social welfare, gun violence, and criminal justice reform.

Cultivation Theory

We will close our discussion of the theories of stereotypes with one of the most commonly studied theories of media influence (Bryant & Miron, 2004): cultivation theory. Cultivation suggests that television is the primary storyteller in American society; thus, it has a substantial impact on audience members' perception of individuals and groups within society (Gerbner & Gross, 1976). Television, with its visual and auditory storytelling and engaging mass-produced narratives, captures people's attention in ways other media cannot. Cultivation is specifically concerned with the long-term effects of television viewing, and a key concept developed within the theory is that of "mainstreaming," in which heavier television viewers are more likely to rely on what they have seen on television when making social judgments and decisions in real-life. Light viewers, on the other hand, are more likely to learn information from sources other than television and thus hold less television-consistent worldviews. Gerbner and Gross (1976) suggest that, "The substance of the consciousness cultivated by TV is not so much specific attitudes and opinions as more basic assumptions about the 'facts' of life and standards of judgment on which conclusions are based" (p. 175). Thus, a primary cultural function of television content is to set and normalize social assumptions and hierarchies and to cultivate among viewers a resistance to change (Gerbner, Gross, Jackson-Beeck, Jeffries-Fox, & Signorielli, 1978).

Research testing the cultivation perspective suggests that long-term exposure to media content can lead to distorted perceptions of reality and increased formation and deployment of stereotypical beliefs (Gerbner, Gross, Morgan, Signorielli, & Shanahan, 2002; Ramasubramanian & Murphy, 2014). Cultivation effects are compounded by the ubiquity of stereotypical television portrayals of underrepresented minorities. Characters who embody stereotypes related to gender, race, age, and sexuality have dominated U.S. news and enter-tainment media throughout history (Adams-Bass, Stevenson, & Kotzin, 2014; Alwood, 1996; Bogle, 2001; Collins, 2011; Gibson, 2018). These repetitive stereotypical portrayals of underrepresented minorities are more likely to be accepted as valid by heavy television viewers and subsequently influence racial attitudes (Fujioka, 1999; Lee, Bichard, Irey, Walt, & Carlson, 2009). Such effects may be strongest for those who have low levels of direct contact with members of other races (Armstrong, Neuendorf, & Brentar, 1992).

Specifically, research related to stereotypes and cultivation effects found that heavy (as compared to light) television viewers are more likely to hold stereotypical attitudes related to women, racial and sexual minorities, women, and individuals with mental illnesses (Armstrong et al., 1992; Busselle & Crandall, 2002; Gerbner, Gross, Jackson-Beeck, Jeffries-Fox, & Signorielli, 1980; Gerbner et al., 2002; Punyanunt-Carter, 2008; Ward, 2002). For example, children who are heavy consumers of television have been shown to believe gender-based stereotypes as their viewership of gender-stereotyped shows increased (Thompson & Zerbinos, 1997) and to believe that boys should be dominant, assertive, and powerful, given the fact that male televi-sion characters regularly exhibit these qualities (Martins & Harrison, 2012). Similarly, women who viewed gender stereotypical commercials are more likely to conform to those stereotypes and be less likely to show confidence in public speaking than were women shown commercials defying gender stereo-types (Jennings-Walstedt, Geis, & Brown, 1980). These real-world stereotypi-cal assessments, referred to as first-order effects, can also influence subsequent beliefs, values, and inclination to support public policy (second-order effects), thus expanding the influence of television-cultivated stereotypes.

Transformations in the way people watch television may actually be enhancing the likelihood that cultivation effects occur. The proliferation of online streaming services such as Netflix and HBO Go allows viewers to watch their favorite series whenever they choose instead of having to wait for a new episode to air once a week and also provides endless recommendations for similar content. That has led to people binge-watching shows, sometimes con-suming an entire season or more in one sitting. Research from Krongard and Tsay-Vogel (2019) has shown that the more hours viewers spend watching online original series from streaming services—shows that tend to have high levels of violence—the more likely they are to see the world as a mean and scary place. It follows, then, that viewers who prefer television genres that contain heavily stereotyped content would easily be able to consume large quantities of this content at will, increasing the likelihood that they would make subsequent social judgments based on the stereotypes they have viewed.

Conclusion

As noted in the introduction, the theories addressed in this chapter are among those most commonly used to guide research into the formation and effects of media stereotypes, and their predictions have been supported and refined by substantial empirical research. To recap, the SCM suggests that, regardless of context and culture, group-based stereotypes form along two dimensions: warmth and competence. Research testing the intergroup contact theory and PCH has demonstrated that stereotyping and prejudice can be lessened by in-person or mediated contact with counter-stereotypical individuals.

Social identity theory explains how individuals, based on how they identify with social groups in any given situation, perceive and interact with members of outgroups. Priming shows how past exposure to mediated stereotypical content can influence current social judgments by making certain ideas more immediately accessible, whereas framing theory explains how stereotypical depictions of groups made salient by frequent inclusion in media messages can influence the ways that those groups are perceived by others. Lastly, cultivation theory suggests that a heavy diet of stereotypical television content can lead individuals to rely on those stereotypes when making social judgments in reality.

References

Abrams, D., & Hogg, M. A. (1990). Social identification, self-categorization and social influence. *European Review of Social Psychology*, 1(1), 195–228. https://doi.org/10.1080/14792779108401862

Adams-Bass, V. N., Stevenson, H. C., & Kotzin, D. S. (2014). Measuring the meaning of Black media stereotypes and their relationship to the racial identity, Black history knowledge, and racial socialization of African American youth. *Journal of Black Studies*, 45, 367–395. https://doi.org/10.1177/0021934714530396

Adorno, T. W., Frenkel-Brunswik, E., Levinson, D. J., & Sanford, R. N. (1950). *The authoritarian personality*. Oxford, England: Harpers.

Allport, G. (1954). *The nature of prejudice*. Oxford, England: Addison-Wesley.

Alwood, E. (1996). *Straight news: Gays, lesbians, and the news media*. New York, NY: Columbia University Press.

Amichai-Hamburger, Y., & McKenna, K. Y. (2006). The contact hypothesis reconsidered: Interacting via the internet. *Journal of Computer-Mediated Communication*, 11, 825–843. https://doi.org/10.1111/j.1083-6101.2006.00037.x

Armstrong, B., Neuendorf, K., & Brentar, J. (1992). TV entertainment, news, and racial perceptions of college students. *Journal of Communication*, 42, 153–176.

Banaji, M. R., & Greenwald, A. G. (1995). Implicit gender stereotyping in judgments of fame. *Journal of Personality and Social Psychology, 68*(2), 181–198. https://doi.org/10.1037/0022-3514.68.2.181

Banaji, M. R., Hardin, C., & Rothman, A. J. (1993). Implicit stereotyping in person judgment. *Journal of Personality and Social Psychology, 65*(2), 272–281. https://doi.org/10.1037/0022-3514.65.2.272

Bogle, D. (2001). *Toms, coons, mulattoes, mammies & bucks: An interpretive history of Blacks in American films* (4th ed.). New York, NY: Continuum International Publishing Group.

Brown, R. J. (2000). *Group processes: Dynamics within and between groups* (2nd ed.). Oxford: Blackwell.

Bruner, J. S. (1957). On perceptual readiness. *Psychological Review, 64*, 123–152. http://dx.doi.org/10.1037/h0043805

Bryant, J., & Miron, D. (2004). Theory and research in mass communication. *Journal of Communication, 54*, 662–704. doi: 10.1093/joc/54.4.662

Busselle, R. W., & Crandall, H. (2002). Television viewing and perceptions about race differences in socioeconomic success. *Journal of Broadcasting & Electronic Media, 46(2)*, 265–282. https://doi.org/10.1207/s15506878jobem4602_6

Chong, D., & Druckman, J. N. (2007). Framing theory. *Annual Review of Political Science, 10*(1), 103–126. https://doi.org/10.1146/annurev.polisci.10.072805.103054

Collins, A. M., & Loftus, E. F. (1975). A spreading-activation theory of semantic processing. *Psychological Review, 82*, 407–428. http://dx.doi.org/10.1037/0033-295X.82.6.407

Collins, R. L. (2011). Content analysis of gender roles in media: Where are we now and where should we go? *Sex Roles, 64*, 290–298. doi: 10.1007/s11199-010-9929-5

Cuddy, A. J. C., Fiske, S. T., & Glick, P. (2008). Warmth and competence as universal dimensions of social perception: The stereotype content model and the BIAS map. In M. P. Zanna (Ed.), *Advances in experimental social psychology* (pp. 61–149). New York, NY: Academic Press.

Cuddy, A. J. C., Fiske, S. T., Kwan, V. S. Y., Glick, P., Demoulin, S., Leyens, J-P., ... Ziegler, R. (2009). Stereotype content model across cultures: Towards universal similarities and some differences. *British Journal of Social Psychology, 48*, 1–33. doi: 10.1348/014466608X314935.

Devine, P. G. (1989). Stereotypes and prejudice: Their automatic and controlled components. *Journal of Personality and Social Psychology, 56*(1), 5–18. https://doi.org/10.1037/0022-3514.56.1.5

Doise, W., & Weinberger, M. (1972). Représentations masculines dans différentes situations de rencontres mixtes. *Bulletin de Psychologie, XXVI, 26*(305), 649–657.

Entman, R. M. (1993). Framing: Toward clarification of a fractured paradigm. *Journal of Communication, 43*(4), 51–58. https://doi.org/10.1111/j.1460-2466.1993.tb01304.x

Feagin, J. R. (2013). *The white racial frame. Centuries of racial framing and counter-framing* (2nd ed.). New York: Routledge.

Fiske, S. T. (2005). Social cognition and the normality of prejudgment. In J. F. Dovidio, P. Glick, & L. A. Rudman (Eds.), *On the nature of prejudice* (pp. 36–53). Malden, MA: Blackwell Publishing.

Fiske, S. T. (2018). Stereotype content: Warmth and competence endure. *Current Directions in Psychological Science, 27,* 67–73. https://doi.org/10.1177/0963721417738825

Fiske, S. T., Cuddy, A. J. C., & Glick, P. (2007). Universal dimensions of social cognition: Warmth, then competence. *Trends in Cognitive Science, 11,* 77–83. http://dx.doi.org/10.1016/j.tics.2006.11.005

Fiske, S. T., Cuddy, A. J. C., Glick, P., & Xu, J. (2002). A model of (often mixed) stereotype content: Competence and warmth respectively follow from perceived status and competition. *Journal of Personality and Social Psychology, 82,* 878–902. http://dx.doi.org/10.1037/0022-3514.82.6.878

Fujioka, Y. (1999). Television portrayals and African-American stereotypes: Examination of television effects when direct contact is lacking. *Journalism and Mass Communication Quarterly, 76,* 52–75. https://doi.org/10.1177/107769909907600105

Gerbner, G., & Gross, L. (1976). Living with television: The violence profile. *Journal of Communication, 26,* 173–199. https://doi.org/10.1111/j.1460-2466.1976.tb01397.x

Gerbner, G., Gross, L., Jackson-Beeck, M., Jeffries-Fox, S., & Signorielli, N. (1978). Cultural indicators violence profile No. 9. *Journal of Communication, 28,* 176–207. doi: 10.1111/j.1460-2466.1978.tb01646.x

Gerbner, G., Gross, L., Morgan, M., Signorielli, N., & Shanahan, J. (2002). Growing up with television: Cultivation processes. In J. Bryant & D. Zillmann (Eds.), *Media effects: Advances in theory and research* (pp. 43–67). Mahwah, NJ: Lawrence Erlbaum.

Gerbner, G., Gross, L., Signorielli, N., & Morgan, M. (1980). Aging with television: Image on television drama and conceptions of social reality. *Journal of Communication, 30,* 37–47. doi: 10.1111/j.1460-2466.1980.tb01766.x

Gibson, R. (2018). *Same-sex marriage and social media: How online networks accelerated the marriage equality movement.* London: Routledge.

Goffman, E. (1974). *Frame analysis: An essay on the organization of experience.* Boston, MA: Northeastern University Press.

Gitlin, T. (1980). *The whole world is watching: Mass media in the making and unmaking of the new left.* Berkeley: University of California Press.

Hamilton, D. L. (Ed.). (1981). *Cognitive processes in stereotyping and intergroup behavior.* Hillsdale, NJ: Erlbaum.

Hamilton, D. L., & Sherman, J. W. (1994). Stereotypes. In R. S. Wyer & T. K. Srull (Eds.), *Handbook of social cognition: Basic processes; Applications* (pp. 1–68). Hillsdale, NJ: Lawrence Erlbaum.

Higgins, E. T., Rholes, W. S., & Jones, C. R. (1977). Category accessibility and impression formation. *Journal of Experimental Social Psychology, 13*(2), 141–154. https://doi.org/10.1016/S0022-1031(77)80007-3

Hogg, M. A. (2016). Social identity theory. In D. J. Christie (Ed.), *Understanding peace and conflict through social identity theory—Contemporary global perspectives* (pp. xv–xx). https://doi.org/10.1007/978-3-319-29869-6

Hogg, M. A., & Abrams, D. (1988). *Social identifications: A social psychology of intergroup relations and group processes.* Florence, KY: Taylor & Francis.

Horton, D., & Wohl, R. R. (1956). Mass communication and para-social interaction. *Psychiatry: Journal for the Study of Interpersonal Processes, 19,* 215–229.

Iyengar, S., & Kinder, D. R. (1987). *News that matters: Television and American opinion.* Chicago, IL: University of Chicago Press.

Jennings-Walstedt, J., Geis, F. L., & Brown, V. (1980). Influence of television commercials on women's self-confidence and independent judgment. *Journal of Personality and Social Psychology, 38,* 203–210. http://dx.doi.org/10.1037/0022-3514.38.2.203

Kahneman, D., & Tversky, A. (1984). Choices, values, and frames. *American Psychologist, 39*(4), 341–350. https://doi.org/10.1037/0003-066X.39.4.341

Katz, D., & Braly, K. (1935). Racial prejudice and racial stereotypes. *Journal of Abnormal and Social Psychology, 30,* 175–193.

Krongard, S., & Tsay-Vogel, M. (2019). Online original TV series: Examining portrayals of violence in popular binge-watched programs and social reality perceptions. *Psychology of Popular Media.* https://doi.org/10.1037/ppm0000224

Lee, M. J., Bichard, S. L., Irey, M. S., Walt, H. M., & Carlson, A. J. (2009). Television viewing and ethnic stereotypes: Do college students form stereotypical perceptions of ethnic groups as a result of heavy television consumption? *Howard Journal of Communications, 20,* 95–110. https://doi.org/10.1080/10646170802665281

Lippmann, W. (1922). *Public opinion.* New York: Harcourt, Brace and Company.

Martins, N., & Harrison, K. (2012). Racial and gender differences in the relationship between children's television use and self-esteem. *Communication Research, 39,* 338–357. doi: 10.1177/0093650211401376

Mastro, D. E. (2003). A social identity approach to understanding the impact of television messages. *Communication Monographs, 70*(2), 98–113. https://doi.org/10.1080/0363775032000133764

Mastro, D. E., Behm-Morawitz, E., & Kopacz, M. A. (2008). Exposure to television portrayals of Latinos: The implications of aversive racism and social identity theory. *Human Communication Research, 34*(1), 1–27. https://doi.org/10.1111/j.1468-2958.2007.00311

McKinley, C. J., Mastro, D., & Warber, K. M. (2014). Social identity theory as a framework for understanding the effects of exposure to positive media images of self and others on intergroup outcomes. *International Journal of Communication, 8*(1), 1049–1068.

Mercurio, E., & Filak, V. F. (2010). Roughing the passer: The framing of black and white quarterbacks prior to the NFL draft. *Howard Journal of Communications, 21*(1), 56–71. https://doi.org/10.1080/10646170903501328

Messner, M. A., & Solomon, W. S. (1993). Outside the frame: Newspaper coverage of the sugar Ray Leonard wife abuse story. *Sociology of Sport Journal, 10*, 119–134. https://doi.org/10.1123/ssj.10.2.119

Nelson, T. E., Oxley, Z. M., & Clawson, R. A. (1997). Toward a psychology of framing effects. *Political Behavior, 19*, 221–246.

Ortega, F. J., & Feagin, J. R. (2017). Framing: The undying white racial frame. In C. P. Campbell (Ed.), *Routledge companion to race and media* (pp. 19–30). New York: Routledge. https://doi.org/10.4324/9781315143460-3

Pettigrew, T. F., & Tropp, L. R. (2006). A meta-analytic test of intergroup contact theory. *Journal of Personality and Social Psychology, 90*, 751–783. doi: 10.1037/0022-3514.90.5.751

Price, V., & Tewksbury, D. (1997). News values and public opinion: A theoretical account of priming and framing. In G. Barnett & F. J. Boster (Eds.), *Progress in communication sciences: Advances in persuasion* (pp. 173–212). New York: Ablex.

Punyanunt-Carter, N. M. (2008). The perceived realism of African American portrayals on television. *Howard Journal of Communications, 19*, 241–257. doi: 10.1080/10646170802218263

Rabbie, J. M., & Wilkens, G. (1971). Intergroup competition and its effect on intragroup and intergroup relations. *European Journal of Social Psychology, 1*, 215–234. https://doi.org/10.1002/ejsp.2420010205

Ramasubramanian, S., & Murphy, C. J. (2014). Experimental studies of media stereotyping effects. In M. Webster & J. Sell (Eds.), *Laboratory experiments in the social sciences* (pp. 385–402). London: Elsevier.

Roskos-Ewoldsen, D. R., Roskos-Ewoldsen, B., & Carpentier, F. R. D. (2009). Media priming: An updated synthesis. In *Media effects: Advances in theory and research* (pp. 74–93). Mahweh, NJ: Lawrence Erlbaum Associates.

Schiappa, E., Gregg, P. B., & Hewes, D. E. (2005). The parasocial contact hypothesis. *Communication Monographs, 72*, 92–115. doi: 10.1080/0363775052000342544

Schneider, D. J. (2004). *The psychology of stereotyping*. New York: The Guilford Press.

Sherif, M. (1966). *Group conflict and cooperation: Their social psychology*. London, UK: Routledge.

Spencer, S. J., Logel, C., & Davies, P. (2016). Stereotype threat. *Annual Review of Psychology, 67*, 415–437. https://doi.org/10.1146/annurev-psych-073115-103235

Spencer, S. J., Steele, C. M., & Quinn, D. M. (1999). Stereotype threat and women's math performance. *Journal of Experimental Social Psychology, 1*, 4–28. https://doi.org/10.1006/jesp.1998.1373

Tajfel, H. (1970). Experiments in intergroup discrimination. *Scientific American, 223*(5), 96–102. https://doi.org/10.1038/scientificamerican1170-96

Tajfel, H., Billig, M. G., Bundy, R. P., & Flament, C. (1971). Social categorization and intergroup behaviour. *European Journal of Social Psychology, 1*, 149–178. https://doi.org/10.1002/ejsp.2420010202

Tajfel, H., & Turner, J. (1979). An integrative theory of intergroup conflict. *The Social Psychology of Intergroup Relations.* https://doi.org/10.1016/S0065-2601(05)37005-5

Tajfel, H., & Turner, J. C. (1986). The social identity theory of intergroup behavior psychology of intergroup relations. In *Political psychology: Key readings in social psychology.* https://doi.org/10.1111/j.1751-9004.2007.00066.x

Tewksbury, D., Jones, J., Peske, M. W., Raymond, A., & Vig, W. (2000). The interaction of news and advocate frames: Manipulating audience perceptions of a local public policy issue. *Journalism and Mass Communication Quarterly, 77*(4), 804–829. https://doi.org/10.1177/107769900007700406

Thompson, T., & Zerbinos, E. (1997). Television cartoons: Do children notice it's a boy's world? *Sex Roles, 37,* 415–432.

Turner, J. C. (1982). Toward a cognitive redefinition of the social group. In Henri Tajfel (Ed.), *Social Identity and Intergroup Relations* (pp. 15–40). Cambridge: Cambridge University Press.

Ward, L. M. (2002). Does television exposure affect emerging adults attitudes and assumptions about sexual relationships? Correlational and experimental confirmation. *Journal of Youth and Adolescence, 31,* 1–15. http://dx.doi.org/10.1023/A:1014068031532

Wheeler, C. S., & Petty, R. E. (2001). The effects of stereotype activation on behavior: A review of possible mechanisms. *Psychological Bulletin, 127*(6), 797–826. https://doi.org/10.1037//0033-2909.127.6.797

2 Consumption Junction: Content Analytic Media Stereotyping Studies

CORY L. ARMSTRONG
University of Alabama

SHARON E. BALDINELLI
University of Alabama

In 2003, the first author of this piece developed an online survey examining how news reporters and editors have defined and employed "content for women." The phrase was intentionally vague to allow for potentially broad interpretations. Editors responded that they believe women's news includes topics such as wedding announcements, gardening, cooking and healthcare-related topics (Armstrong, 2006). The findings of that study are indicative of the types of stereotypical assumptions often given to (and for) women. But let us not stop there: as this book will highlight in great detail, generalized assumptions are also made about men and their ranking on a macho-meter; Latinos and their saucy views of sexuality; Blacks and their supposed inclination toward crime; Asians with their perceived propensity to succeed at math. Further, what about expected norms for various age groups, religious affiliations and disabilities? These are issues that may often be best examined using the methodological approach of content analysis, the focus of this chapter.

What is most telling about the 2003 study is that it represents what media personnel—in this case news organizations—assume about their audiences. These gatekeepers are responsible for much of the content being shown to consumers through various mass media, including news, scripted and unscripted television, streaming content, and much social media. The content created and distributed by those producers is creating and reinforcing damaging stereotypes to consumers. When media provide stereotypical portrayals without offering context for the representation, consumers often focus on characteristics that perpetuate these narrow ideas. Another common approach by media is to just ignore some segments of the population within distributed content, which suggests that diversity in people and populations are more homogeneous than in actual society. The ramifications of this issue often result in a warped view of social reality (see Gamson, Crouteau, Hoynes, & Sasson, 1992).

Therefore, this chapter is on media content and how scholars have examined and studied the type of stereotyping often conveyed in media. Media producers are trained to use labels and categories (e.g., race, age and gender) to help easily classify subjects and individuals, allowing consumers to then focus on the details of the event or story. This often results in stereotypical portrayals being created, reinforced and extended within beliefs of media consumers. In this way, media are providing overly simplified portrayals and eliminating individuality, reducing people to generalized categories that often do not define their individuality accurately.

Before moving forward, we posit a definition for content analysis and how we approach it within this chapter. Content analysis is a systematic count of empirical information, such as symbols, word usage/patterns, framing concepts, word count(s), and even nonverbal gestures which then can be applied to both quantitative and qualitative items. In media, content analysis methodologies are applied to sources such as newspaper articles, movies, advertisements, social media, and more. The rest of this chapter will briefly examine the common theoretical frameworks that have been employed in content analyses of stereotypes, followed by the unique and frequently used codes employed to tackle content analyses. We will then examine the most intriguing and interesting findings within stereotypical content studies, followed by some discussion of how a content analysis involving stereotypes might work. We will complete the chapter discussing some strategies for those who wish to further this knowledge base through content analysis methodology, including a discussion of places to pursue next with research on media stereotyping using content analysis.

Common Conceptual Frameworks Employed in Content Analysis Research

Most effective research projects begin with a clear research question followed by a selection of the most appropriate methodology to answer that question. With our focus on how stereotypes have been studied using content analysis, we note that certain theoretical frameworks frequently appear within these studies. Scholars have linked content to theories ranging from microlevel psychological impacts to macrolevel societal influences. Below we provide a brief overview of how some of these frameworks directly relate to content analyses.

Framing

Framing theory offers social science conceptual ways to interpret and understand how viewers process and understand situations and events (Goffman, 1974). In media, this view is a dimension of how media consumers make sense of events which they are watching unfold through different sources. This conceptual framework suggests that media take a focus of interest with a topic or idea and make portions of it more (or less) salient. When considering framing-based content analyses, researchers examine how a subject is selected, amplified, or excluded and if the audience's perception of the subject was potentially affected by the viewpoint presented (Price, Tewksbury, & Powers, 1997; Stone & Socia, 2019). Similarly, framing can examine exclusionary and neglected frames, or views that are not present in media content (Misener, 2012).

Social Constructionism

Through media framing research, findings indicate that an individual's construction of reality is often biased from their own immediate experience of reality (Fink & Kensicki, 2002; Funkhouser, 1973; Tuchman, 1978), a bias potentially stemming from outside influences, including media portrayals. One way that people learn about people and groups that are different than them is through media—television shows, news accounts, nonfiction stories or social media posts. These media portrayals can provide windows into those who are different—and can shape one's worldviews in various ways, creating a shared norm or reality (Prot et al., 2014). This socially constructed reality becomes an acceptable definition of concepts and ideals.

Symbolic Annihilation

The term *symbolic annihilation* refers to the concept that an item, person or subject is removed from a position of power based on outside influences, such as representations in media (Fink & Kensicki, 2002). As it relates to stereotypes, we consider how repeated portrayals of homogenous individuals cause the symbolic annihilation of certain social groups. In particular, scholars argue that media portray women and minorities in distorted and trivialized ways, making them tangential to the story being told, or—in the extreme—completely missing from the media events (Tuchman, 1978). The lack of diversity among media portrayals have caused the marginalization of women and minorities by the media through the underrepresentation of stories available in magazines, newspaper articles, and airtime.

Cultivation

Cultivation theory exemplifies the idea that significant television viewing creates a reality based on what is consumed through program and format choices. Originally, George Gerbner connected the idea to violence shown during television programming (Gerbner, 1998; Juarez, Kallis, & Xu, 2016). The classic example from Gerbner's work is that the more violent content that consumers watch on television, the more the viewer may believe that their regular life has similar levels of violence in it, known as the "mean world" syndrome. Scholars suggest that similar principles can apply to stereotypes: The typecasts viewers see in media are potentially carried over into their own attitudes and belief systems about people and how they make parallels within their own world.

Social Cognitive

Albert Bandura (2001) applied social cognitive theory (SCT) to media, helping explain how representations in media can teach audiences about ideas, issues and people. The primary goal of SCT is to illustrate how individuals are not shaped by inner or external stimuli, but rather by triadic reciprocity, or interrelations between personal, environmental and behavioral determinants (Bandura, 1986). SCT plays a critical role in how media exposure creates learning paths by the audience. In other words, what the audience consumes is often assigned to real-world models (Sink & Mastro, 2017). Stereotypes, such as gender and race, can be directly affected through this lens.

Hegemonic Masculinity

The practice of accepting and pushing forward the belief that masculinity is requisite to power over femininity in society plays out repeatedly in many forums: education, business practices and political arenas (Sink & Mastro, 2017). Marginalization is also found in pay gaps (Sink & Mastro, 2017), as well as in media representations, oft referred to as *hegemonic masculinity*. Because roles in media for women are often created to be weaker than men's roles or created to be supporting roles instead of leading roles, media venues reinforce this attitude (Signiorelli, 2009). In addition, most media outlets are operated predominantly by men, further supporting hegemonic masculine culture (Connell & Messerschmidt, 2005).

Common Codes in Content Analyses of Stereotyping

The process of content analysis involves developing guidelines, called codebooks, to provide shared understandings of the content for analysis. Using the theoretical frameworks outlined above, scholars have developed and tested multiple coding schemes to operationalize their concepts. We will talk more about that process later in the chapter, but first, we want to highlight some common themes that have developed within stereotyping studies. Most stereotyping work includes some level of categorization. For example, scholars regularly code for gender/sex, race/ethnicity, age, occupation and education (e.g., Signorielli, 2009). These codes are often operationalized through a binary of male or female for gender; White, minority or non-White for race; and high school or college graduate or not, for education (Behm-Morawitz, 2017; Signorielli, 2009). These common categorizations often appear in the literature when the focus is on a particular stereotype that is either exacerbated or mitigated by race, gender or education.

Aside from the categorization of demographic information, scholars have attempted to measure stereotyping through indicators that capture nuances among groups. Perhaps the most frequently used coding scheme for stereotyping—gender or otherwise—is attributed to Goffman (1974) and his seminal gender display study in advertising. He proposed five areas to compare male and female portrayals:

1. The Feminine Touch, which looks at hands—the delicate and nurturing women's touch, compared to powerful male hand postures;
2. Ritualization of Subordination, which demonstrates passive and demure female poses in media, when compared to men;
3. Licensed Withdrawal, which suggests a noticeable difference in the way men and women engage with the world around them in media, with women less connected to media and audiences;
4. Infantilization, in which girls and women are portrayed in the same way, with little difference in relationships between men and women in advertising, regardless of age; and
5. Codes of Masculinity, which focuses on power and assertion—attributes generally given only to men, leaving women in significantly subordinate roles.

Over the years, scholars have adapted these codes in various ways. Scholars have added categories such as "function ranking," where a judgment is made over a shared task and who has control of the task (Döring & Pöschl, 2006) as well as self-subordination and face ratio (Xu & Armstrong, 2019). Elements such as these provide much-needed context when comparing various media characterizations.

Context is also important when considering the sheer number of portrayals in media. As discussed earlier, one must consider not only the frequency of the representation, but the valence or tone of the portrayal. The old adage that any news is good news does not hold when it comes to depictions. As consumers repeatedly see higher frequencies of Whites in authority roles and Blacks as criminals, they are more likely to reinforce this belief in reality. Therefore, one could argue that the invisibility of certain social groups may be less harmful than repeated negative portrayals.

In examining this idea, scholars use content analyses to evaluate the egregiousness of stereotypical portrayals by examining the context for the portrayals and evaluating the tone/valence of the portrayal. Zurbriggen and Sherman (2010) compared race and gender portrayals in the 2008 presidential primary campaign, which included both Barack Obama and Hillary Clinton. They coded for an overall valence of the candidate's portrayal, along with the valence of appearance codes, including "noticeably unattractive," infantilization and size (referring back to Goffman's coding schemes). They also coded for racism and sexism—defined by them as advancing or reinforcing gender or racist stereotypes.

Scholars have also attempted to break down the categories within the general demographic measures to learn more about how stereotypical portrayals are reinforced in media. For example, Signorielli (2009) defined job portrayals in primetime television by prestige—high paying and status were deemed prestigious jobs—finding that regardless of the diversity of the cast, most jobs were of either neutral prestige or prestigious in nature, suggesting that many industrial or blue-collar jobs are rarely seen in media portrayals, which is not indicative of the labor force. As Lind will highlight more specifically in Chapter 9, in 2018, the U.S. Bureau of Labor Statistics reported that 14.3 percent of all jobs are in office support, 8.5 percent are in food service, and 9.8 in service/retail jobs, totaling 32.6 percent of all jobs. In effect, the media are portraying 6.3 percent of jobs in management and professional jobs with higher prestige than the fields in which more individuals are employed ("Employment by detailed occupations," 2019).

In terms of gender, researchers have focused on the connection of women to men within the portrayal. More specifically, when women are portrayed—particularly in the political realm—they are connected in some way to men. For example, Zurbriggen and Sherman (2010) coded for the presence of a spouse in the 2008 presidential campaign; Bill Clinton was more prevalent in editorial cartoons with Hillary than were other spouses in election coverage (Zurbriggen & Sherman, 2010). Other studies have focused on the prevalence of "lifestyle" activities when women are the main characters. When women are the focus of a media portrayal, it seemingly must include references to traditional female gender roles (Grau & Zotos, 2016). While one could argue that having a former president as a spouse is unique, most gender-related scholars would refute that point by noting that Hillary is either qualified to be president or not—connections to Bill would not change her qualifications. Thus, his presence is more about him than her.

Context becomes even more important when considering digital content. With the proliferation of social media, individual posts can be shared to exponential proportions. In those instances, the original context may be lost as the social media posts are shared in various ways. For example, Armstrong, Hull and Saunders (2015) coded the tone of the characterizations of the victim and two perpetrators in a sexual assault involving Ohio high school football players, finding the victim—a 16-year-old girl—was often shown in photos and videos as severely intoxicated and was often blamed for the attack.

One of the more overlooked areas of stereotyping in media content is the conveyance of information about mental illness, which will be explored in this book in Chapter 13. Gwarjanski and Parrott (2018) examined the frequency of "challenge statements" to stereotypical frames of schizophrenia. That was operationalized through coding items including positive statements, successful treatments, challenging stereotypical comments and information about treatment options. This study is one of a few recent examinations of how effective media have been regarding combating or challenging common stereotypical narratives within media content.

Notable Findings

The various coding schemes employed to understand the level of stereotyping in media content have provided some significant findings through decades of research in this area. Race and gender research has found that overall, White men are more frequently and more systematically featured than women and/ or minorities in all areas of media, certainly a vast overrepresentation when compared to actual U.S. Census figures. That is, while men constitute roughly 50 percent of the population, their representations are considerably higher in media content. This domination has lessened throughout the years, but studies have continually found that the disparity in gender and race continues. There are virtually no exceptions.

Given this vast disparity, we choose to focus on the more noteworthy exemplars within research on stereotypes, in an effort to understand the nuances of this research. First, we focus on sports. Examining *Sports Illustrated* images, Fink and Kensicki (2002) found that, when shown, female athletes were generally illustrated in non-sport settings, wearing makeup and casual clothes. They argue that the diametrically different ways that male and female athletes are portrayed feeds into Tuchman's symbolic annihilation theory of women (1978). In particular, that female athletes need to be portrayed in gender-appropriate roles to demonstrate their appeal to a general (read: male) audience. Their discussion—and Hardin, Whiteside, and Ash (2014)—focus on the gender ambivalence argument, that even when focusing on the success and accomplishments that women athletes achieve in their field, the audience needs to be reminded that women are still expected and assumed to be in a subordinate role to men, on and off the field (Hardin et al., 2014).

While much of this chapter has focused on gender stereotypes, other noteworthy issues have been found in terms of sports stereotypes. In perhaps the only study to examine how disability is portrayed in sport textbooks, Hardin and Hardin (2004) found that sports is for able-bodied individuals (Hardin & Hardin, 2004), with no more than 1.5 percent of any single source materials including disabled athletes. In sport textbooks, virtually no information was conveyed about how adaptive athletics supplements other sports at the collegiate or intramural level. Given that this study was completed roughly 15 years ago, before the NCAA's adaptive athletics initiatives, it would be a study ripe for replication ("Student-athletes with disabilities," n.d.). The authors suggest that the invisibility of disabled athletes in physical education textbooks reinforces a hegemonic culture—that disabled athletes are not similar to able-bodied athletes.

Turning to informational media, some studies are making some inroads into challenging stereotypes, according to the findings. For example, in examining coverage of schizophrenia, Gwarjanski and Parrott (2018) found that while stigma frames about the illness often linked to violence or other inaccuracies, roughly 20 percent of news articles included counter-stereotypical information, demonstrating at least a modicum of awareness of media of its important role in educating the public with accurate information.

However, media continue to contribute to this stereotypical issue more frequently than not, often exacerbating the issue. For example, Stone and Socia (2019) examined media coverage of the police shooting of 12-year-old Tamir Rice while holding a toy gun in Cleveland, noting that language choices employed by media suggested culpability by Rice, saying his hold on the gun was "brandishing," "pointing," or "wielding." However, video evidence did not support those descriptions. Two articles used images of a real gun that were similar to the fake weapon Rice was carrying, suggesting a level of callousness and deliberate framing of an issue to more appropriately favor police over victim. Similarly, Tien Vu, Lee, Duong, and Barnett (2018) examined how female leaders in Vietnam were represented, finding them underrepresented when compared to their male counterparts. Journalists surveyed in that country expressed beliefs that male sources had more decisive and authoritative traits, compared to the compassionate views of female sources (Tien Vu et al., 2018).

Speaking of victims, content analysis studies repeatedly find that media revictimize those who report sexual crimes and harassment, particularly for women. The tone of coverage concerning a teenaged victim of sexual assault by two male athletes was more negative when female sources discussed the case and when social media posts were used as sources in news content (Armstrong et al., 2015). These findings suggest that when females come forward with allegations, they are again blamed and accosted publicly through media accounts.

Venturing into other media, many of the same patterns emerge. A 2016 study of visual content of online science education resources for primary schools found men were significantly more likely to be portrayed as working in a "science profession" than women (55 to 30.5 percent), whereas women were significantly more likely to be portrayed in those resources as teachers when compared to men (22.7 to 7.7 percent; Kerkhoven, Russo, Land-Zandstra, Saxena, & Rodenburg, 2016). Also, a study of Indian Muslims in Bollywood movies in 2016 found that they were predominantly portrayed negatively, often as non-patriotic or antagonistic (Umber, Ghauri, & Nawaz, 2018).

Perhaps most telling among these analyses of media stereotyping is a recent study from Choi and Lawallen (2018). This study examined Instagram's user-generated visual content of parents from February 2015 using the hashtag *#children*, focusing on race representations in children's activities and appearance. The study found that following stereotypical patterns, pink was the predominant clothing color of content including girls, while blue was the predominant color of clothing worn by boys. Similarly, content reflected boys more frequently shown in activities outside, while girls were more likely to be shown inside engaging in activities such as reading or listening to music (Choi & Lawallen, 2018). What makes this study unique among these findings is that the content examined was purposefully chosen by parents to showcase their children. They were making the choice to publicly display one of the most time-honored of all gender-related stereotypes.

The question becomes—are the content choices based on individual choices (e.g., the reporter) or societal/industry norms? Grau and Zotos (2016) argue it is both, at least in advertising media. Advertising is geared toward the consumer, suggesting that while ad research has consistently found that men and women are portrayed differently, content is geared toward the targeted recipient/viewer. Often, consumers may not receive ads challenging gender stereotypes, as it challenges beliefs. That is not likely to make the consumer want to purchase or engage with the product.

Conducting a Content Analysis about Media Stereotyping

With the plethora of studies about media stereotyping, scholars have provided several models to mirror for those wishing to study these areas. This section will review some of the specific procedures of content analysis, along with some common pathways that scholars have utilized to navigate these pathways. As in all social science research, the first step in the process is to determine the research question or problem for investigation. For an example, we will focus on male-centered versus female-centered political dramas as a running example throughout this section. Our question will be: *Do differences exist between the way male- and female-led political characters are portrayed in scripted dramas?*

Once the research question is determined, researchers have to consider how the question can be operationalized and measured. In content analysis, there are two ways to consider coding content: manifest or latent content. Manifest content can be defined as material that can easily be observed, or content that most individuals understand with the same shared normative definition. On the other hand, latent content is material that may have implied meaning under the surface and consumers may have different understandings of the same content. It requires judgment to decipher. Riffe, Lacy and Fico (2014) define manifest content as denotative content which is generally easy to see, whereas latent content is connotative content, which often requires interpretation to decipher.

Returning to our example, counting the female and male characters within scenes would constitute manifest content, while latent content could be observed when attempting to code whether the characters were portrayed through their race, age or family life. Clearly, defining and providing examples of how those variables could be measured through content would be key to determining that variable. Coders would be asked to determine what clothing, language, and perhaps visual cues would help provide information about those items. Those would be considered latent content, unless some clear key element stood out in the content.

At this point, it makes sense to talk about how the data collection process works in content analysis. Data come from "coding of content," or turning the images or text into numbers for quantitative data analysis. That data is often created by human coders, who examine the content and provide each item a numeric code, which stands for its meaning for the project. As part of this process, researchers have to develop a codebook or guide to how the content will be examined by coders. This is a coder's "bible," from which they code. The purpose of the coding guide is to provide clear directions to minimize discrepancies among coders, for both manifest, and particularly, for latent, or underlying, content. The coding guide can be used for computer coding as well, although that is generally for manifest content only. Table 2.1 (below) provides a sample coding scheme for our example above. Notice that the more explicit the definitions, the easier it is for multiple coders to follow the guide.

Once the codebook is created, coders must be trained. The goal behind the codebook is to ensure that multiple coders will quantify the content in similar ways. Coders should meet multiple times with the researchers (if they are not the same people) and discuss discrepancies within coding. We cannot stress enough how important this training is for the validity of the coding, particularly for latent content and when thinking of stereotypical content. As discussed in multiple chapters within this book, stereotypes are developed through individual schema and experiences, of which all individuals are unique. The goal of a coding guide is to minimize individual judgments and provide enough examples that coders can agree with the content. This often takes several meetings and conversations.

Once discrepancies are addressed, the numerical content needs to be evaluated for intercoder reliability, or the number of agreements and disagreements among coders. This evaluation includes at least one of a number of possible statistical tests, which take into account the possibility of chance in the coding scheme. The most common of those tests include Krippendorf's *alpha*, Scott's *pi* and Cohen's *kappa*, and their appropriateness depends, in

Table 2.1: Coding Guide Samples

Manifest Content: People
How many ELECTED OFFICIALS are mentioned in the scene? Mentioned means anyone who was discussed or listed in story, whether or not information was attributed to them. Elected officials are those who have been specifically identified as elected, such as Senator Joe Smith or President Nancy Drew. The character MUST have been elected or labeled "President-ELECT" to be considered an elected official.
Latent Content: Valence
In each category below what was the tone of the discussion of the elected official in the story, on a 1–5 scale where 1 is very negative and 5 is very positive? Use 99 if not applicable to story.
A. Knowledge/intelligence—related to the character's job as an elected official.
B. Personal life—refers to a character's personal life, marriage, family etc.

part, on the level of measurement of the variables included. Riffe et al. (2014) offer several insights on this process, including general guidelines on inter-coder reliability numbers for coding and for acceptable statistical results using the various tests listed here.

One final issue to address is the unit of analysis for this type of study. The unit of analysis refers to the piece of content we are interested in studying. This could be any piece of content, depending upon interest. Examples include a word, image, tweet, news story, film, book or medium. For example, Zhou and Bryant (2016) examined the portrayals of Asian women in pornography. They chose "scene" as the unit of analysis, noting that a scene changed if the participants of sex (individuals or groups of individuals) change, or the place changes in a way that resets the situation. For our running example of political dramas, we would likely use episodes to allow for an adequate comparison across an equal amount of content.

Where Should Content Analysts Go from Here?

As this book demonstrates, scholars have researched the impact of stereo-types for several decades, across media, over time and targeting multiple social groups. It begs the question: what avenues are open for future content analy-ses? That is, aside from replicating prior studies with new content or producing longitudinal looks at certain stereotypes, how can others add to our scholarly knowledge about media content and one-dimensional portrayals? We know that despite the heightened awareness of the dangers of stereotyping among media producers, the use of categorical or prejudicial content continues. While women and minorities have been provided more access to employment and laws exist to limit discrimination of many social groups, the diversity of media content continues to be limited. A deluge of media channels and streaming content has not changed the landscape of media content, as it pertains to ste-reotypes. Certainly, a chapter like this must mention the continual consolida-tion of media ownership to a small number of main companies, who continue to churn out and share content across their vast holdings ("Who Owns the Media," n.d.). Still, aside from ownership influences, what are the pressing issues in studying content on media stereotypes?

Perhaps foremost in importance is an examination of digital media—more specifically, social media—to learn more about how stereotypes in content analysis are being translated to the interactive digitized world. Given the pro-liferation of shared content via social media, new coding schemes are needed to determine the best way to examine these venues. However, researchers are challenged in trying to measure the influence of digital content (e.g., rotating video board, news alerts with stereotypical content) on consumers. While content can be available, the level of exposure to quickly changing content may limit the influence of the material. Content can be added and deleted with the click of the mouse, which makes capturing content difficult at times. New technological tools, such as MAXQDA and Crimson Hexagon, can track and capture media content over time, but there are limitations to proprietary content as well.

Similarly, a noticeable shortage within content analysis research is the focus on images within technology. While for years, studies have been conducted on scripted and unscripted television, and even video games; however, a base-level understanding of the kinds of content that can be shared digitally is lacking. As discussed above, preparing a codebook that can be agreed on and employed to examine content is difficult with images and visual elements. Attempting to define and agree upon race via skin color in a visual image is virtually impossible, not to mention the issues of content and face validity issues it poses in research. Perhaps new technology will be able to make inroads in this avenue.

Further, what is the role of digital media customization on media content and exposure? Individuals now have the ability to get "alerts" from their phones about news or entertainment that interests them. Does that customization enhance or reinforce stereotypical views, when prejudicial content is presented? Are the "alerts" impactful, particularly in an age of extreme political polarization when a president tends to tweet this content himself? It seems likely that the alerts will be customized to reinforce existing belief systems—much like selective exposure—but empirical work is needed to confirm this idea.

Now that certain social groups are receiving more attention in scripted and non-scripted media—LGBTQ representations are a clear example as will be outlined by Moscowitz in Chapter 10—more study needs to focus on these areas. In the 2019–2020 television season, 10.2 percent of regular characters were found to be LGBTQ on broadcast television, 47 percent were people of color and with 3.1 percent of people with disabilities (Gay and Lesbian Alliance Against Defamation (GLAAD), 2019). These numbers are at their highest since GLAAD started tracking these figures, but still significantly below national averages for people with disabilities (roughly 12.8 percent, according to GLAAD). However, these figures are based, again, on the frequency of portrayal, without providing the context of the representation. What kinds of representations are these? Ideally, they should run the gamut of being complicated individuals with positive and negative characteristics that make them multidimensional and relatable to viewers and consumers. Further, few, if any, of these representations take into account the intersectionality (for an example, see Purdie-Vaughns & Eibach, 2008) of these subcategories, such as FX's *Pose*, a TV show that examines gay Black men and trans women.

Another issue is the expansion of computer coding for content analysis (e.g., NVivo, Diction, LIWC), which will continue to be a challenge in isolating stereotypes. As we have discussed, there are two facets to studying stereotypes in content analysis: frequency and context. Most computer content analyses are mainly focused on frequency and manifest content, with limited ability to capture context. Software that manages sentiment analysis and word clouds (See Figure 2.1) to develop the kinds of language used to describe social groups and stereotypical information—latent content—might be useful.

However, for the most part, computer programs are limited by their encoding, and it is challenging, at a minimum, to provide context within a computer. That means most content analyses still need to be focused on human coding, or better mechanisms need to be developed to address computer coding. For example, the word cloud in Figure 2.1 provides manifest content of this chapter; however, it cannot interpret the valence of those word choices, which supports the argument for human coders in content analysis.

Perhaps the main bright spot within this quasi-meta-analysis is the few studies that have started to focus on media advocacy, and more studies should look at how media content is challenging existing beliefs and stereotypical content. Gwarjanski and Parrott (2018) coded for positive representations of

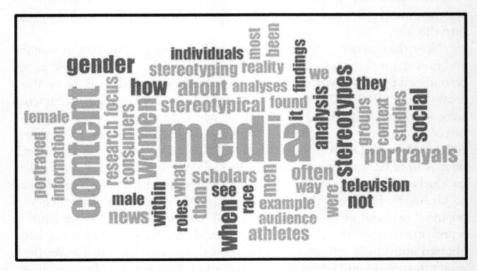

Figure 2.1. Sample Visual Word Cloud of Consumption Junction Chapter Showing Word Frequencies

mental illness, and the final chapter in this book by Ramasubramanian notes more complementary or complex portrayals. More studies should follow this lead, examining content that challenges stereotypes and one-dimensional descriptions.

Conclusion

Within this chapter, the focus has been on common theories and codes within content analyses of stereotypes, along with unique and important findings. What we have learned is that stereotype research through content analysis has gathered a lot of information focusing on how media are getting it wrong. Media often take the easy way out, by choosing narrow and general categorizations to portray individuals. These representations allow individuals to selectively process information without considering the potential flaws of their consumption habits.

At this point, we need to start considering what media are getting right. There are more portrayals, overall, of various social groups. This helps socialization. While much improvement is needed, a greater awareness exists of the importance of diversity in content. As the GLAAD survey noted earlier, the frequency of LGBTQ portrayals has increased (GLAAD, 2019). Supporting those strides through ratings, web clicks and subscriptions is something that consumers can do to reward these positive portrayals. That support may help demonstrate that audience members want more diverse media portrayals—a message that producers need to hear.

References

Armstrong, C. L. (2006). Writing about women: An examination of how content for women is determined in newspapers. *Mass Communication and Society*, 9(4), 447–460. https://doi.org/10.1207/s15327825mcs0904_4

Armstrong, C. L., Hull, K., & Saunders, L. (2015). Victimized on plain sites: Social and alternative media's impact on the Steubenville rape case. *Digital Journalism*, 4(2), 247–265. https://doi.org/10.1080/21670811.2015.1040043

Bandura, A. (1986). *Social foundations of thought and action: A social cognitive theory*. Englewood Cliffs, NJ: Prentice-Hall, Inc.

Bandura, A. (2001). Social cognitive theory: An agentic perspective. *Annual Review of Psychology*, 52, 1–26.

Behm-Morawitz, E. (2017). Examining the intersection of race and gender in video game advertising. *Journal of Marketing Communications*, 23(3), 220–239. https://doi.org/10.1080/13527266.2014.914562

Choi, G. Y., & Lewallen, J. (2018). "Say Instagram, kids!": Examining sharenting and children's digital representations on Instagram. *Howard Journal of Communication, 29*(2), 140–160.

Connell, R. W., & Messerschmidt, J. W. (2005). Hegemonic masculinity: Rethinking the concept. *Gender & Society, 19*(6), 829–859. https://doi.org/10.1177/0891243205278639

Döring, N., & Pöschl, S. (2006). Images of men and women in mobile phone advertisements: A content analysis of advertisements for mobile communication systems in selected popular magazines. *Sex Roles, 55*(3–4), 173–185. https://doi.org/10.1007/s11199-006-9071-6

Employment by detailed occupations. (2019, September 4). Retrieved October 13, 2019, from United States Department of Labor website: https://www.bls.gov/emp/tables/emp-by-detailed-occupation.htm.

Fink, J. S., & Kensicki, L. J. (2002). An imperceptible difference: Visual and textual constructions of femininity in *Sports Illustrated* and *Sports Illustrated for Women*. *Mass Communication and Society, 5*(3), 317–339. https://doi.org/10.1207/S15327825MCS0503_5

Funkhouser, G. R. (1973). The issues of the sixties: An exploratory study in the dynamics of public opinion. *Public Opinion Quarterly, 37*(1), 62–75. https://doi.org/10.1086/268060

Gamson, W. A., Crouteau, D., Hoynes, W., & Sasson, T. (1992). Media images and the social construction of reality. *Annual Review of Sociology, 18*, 373–393.

Gay and Lesbian Alliance Against Defamation (GLAAD). (2019). *Where we are on TV.* Retrieved January 21, 2020 from: https://www.glaad.org/sites/default/files/GLAAD%20WHERE%20WE%20ARE%20ON%20TV%202019%202020.pdf.

Gerbner, G. (1998). Cultivation analysis: An overview. *Mass Communication and Society, 1*(3–4), 175–194. https://doi.org/10.1080/15205436.1998.9677855

Goffman, E. (1974). *Frame analysis: An essay on the organization of experience.* Cambridge, MA: Harvard University Press.

Grau, S. L., & Zotos, Y. C. (2016). Gender stereotypes in advertising: A review of current research. *International Journal of Advertising, 35*(5), 761–770. https://doi.org/10.1080/02650487.2016.1203556

Gwarjanski, A. R., & Parrott, S. (2018). Schizophrenia in the news: The role of news frames in shaping online reader dialogue about mental illness. *Health Communication, 33*(8), 954–961. https://doi.org/10.1080/10410236.2017.1323320

Hardin, B., & Hardin, M. (2004). Distorted pictures: Images of disability in physical education textbooks. *Adapted Physical Activity Quarterly, 21*(4), 399–413. https://doi.org/10.1123/apaq.21.4.399

Hardin, M., Whiteside, E., & Ash, E. (2014). Ambivalence on the front lines? Attitudes toward Title IX and women's sports among Division I sports information directors. *International Review for the Sociology of Sport, 49*(1), 42–64. https://doi.org/10.1177/1012690212450646

Juarez, A. V. O., Kallis, R., & Xu, Y. (2016). Evolution of the Disney princess: From damsel in distress to damsel of distress. *Journal of Communications Media Studies, 8*, 54–71.

Kerkhoven, A. H., Russo, P., Land-Zandstra, A. M., Saxena, A., & Rodenburg, F. J. (2016). Gender stereotypes in science education resources: A visual content analysis. *PLOS ONE, 11*(11), e0165037.

Misener, L. (2012). A media frames analysis of the legacy discourse for the 2010 Winter Paralympic Games. *Communication & Sport, 1*(4), 342–364.

Purdie-Vaughns, V., & Eibach, R. P. (2008). Intersectional invisibility: The distinctive advantages and disadvantages of multiple subordinate-group identities. *Sex Roles, 59*, 377–391.

Price, V., Tewksbury, D., & Powers, E. (1997). Switching trains of thought: The impact of news frames on readers' cognitive responses. *Communication Research, 24*(5), 481–506.

Prot, S., Gentile, D. A., Anderson, C. A., Suzuki, K., Swing, E., Lim, K. M., . . . Lam, B. C. P. (2014). Long-term relations among prosocial-media use, empathy, and prosocial behavior. *Psychological Science, 25*(2), 358–368. https://doi.org/10.1177/0956797613503854

Riffe, D., Lacy, S., & Fico, F. (2014). *Analyzing media messages* (3rd ed.). New York: Routledge.

Signorielli, N. (2009). Race and sex in prime time: A look at occupations and occupational prestige. *Mass Communication and Society, 12*(3), 332–352. https://doi.org/10.1080/15205430802478693

Sink, A., & Mastro, D. (2017). Depictions of gender on primetime television: A quantitative content analysis. *Mass Communication and Society, 20*(1), 3–22. https://doi.org/10.1080/15205436.2016.1212243

Stone, R., & Socia, K. M. (2019). Boy with toy or Black Male with gun: An analysis of online news articles covering the shooting of Tamir Rice. *Race and Justice, 9*(3), 330–358. https://doi.org/10.1177/2153368716689594

Student-athletes with disabilities. (n.d.). Retrieved October 12, 2019, from NCAA website: http://www.ncaa.org/about/resources/inclusion/student-athletes-disabilities.

Tien Vu, H., Lee, T-T., Duong, H. T., and Barnett, B. (2018). Gendering leadership in Vietnamese media: A role-congruity study on news content and journalists' perception of female and male leaders. *Journalism & Mass Communication Quarterly, 95*(3), 565–587.

Tuchman, G. (1978). *Making news: A study in the construction of reality.* New York: Free Press.

Umber, S., Ghauri, M. J., & Nawaz, H. (2018). Exploring the image of Muslims in India. *South Asian Studies, 33*(2), 475–490.

Who Owns the Media. (n.d.). *FreePress.Net.* Retrieved from https://www.freepress.net/issues/media-control/media-consolidation/who-owns-media

Xu, Q., & Armstrong, C. L. (2019). #SELFIES at the 2016 Rio Olympics: Comparing self-representations of male and female athletes from the U.S. and China. *Journal of*

Broadcasting & Electronic Media, *63*(2), 322–338. https://doi.org/10.1080/08838
    151.2019.1621138

Zhou, Y., & Bryant, P. (2016). Lotus blossom or dragon lady: A content analysis of "Asian
    Women" online pornography. *Sexuality & Culture*, *20*, 1083–1100.

Zurbriggen, E. L., & Sherman, A. M. (2010). Race and gender in the 2008 U.S.
    Presidential Election: A content analysis of editorial cartoons: Race and gender in
    2008 election. *Analyses of Social Issues and Public Policy*, *10*(1), 223–247. https://doi.
    org/10.1111/j.1530-2415.2010.01211.x

3 Experiments & Outcomes-Based Study of Media Stereotyping

ELIZABETH BEHM-MORAWITZ
University of Missouri

ANDREA FIGUEROA-CABALLERO
University of Missouri

A growing area of scholarship examines the effects of stereotypical portrayals of underrepresented and stigmatized groups in the media on people's cognitions, emotions, and behaviors. Specifically, researchers have undertaken the weighty task of isolating and examining the effects of exposure to media stereotyping in news, entertainment, and social media on people's responses to marginalized groups. This line of research has been established over the past two decades and continues to evolve with changes in the media environment. This work is not without challenges, including the pitfalls of self-report measures and participant social desirability. In this chapter, we discuss the types of outcomes studied, the primary approaches to using experimental design to study the effects of media stereotyping, as well as some future directions for empirical examination. Examples of media psychology scholarship exemplifying these methodological techniques will be overviewed throughout the chapter.

Outcome-based media stereotyping research provides evidence of the influence of both stereotypical and counter-stereotypical representations of social groups in the media on individuals. Whereas content and textual analysis approaches are used to examine the presence (and absence) of stereotyping in media content, experiments are used to establish the causality of exposure to media stereotyping on effects on media users. To begin, what types of effects are studied? The effects of exposure to media stereotyping largely fall into the following categories: short-term, long-term, cognitive (e.g., attitudinal), affective, and behavioral (Bryant & Thompson, 2002). Counter-stereotyping, indirect, conditional, and transactional effects are also reviewed as growing areas of media stereotyping outcome-based research.

Cognitive, Affective, and Behavioral Outcomes of Media Stereotyping

Experimental media stereotyping research has primarily documented various cognitive outcomes of exposure to stereotypical media portrayals of underrepresented or stigmatized groups of people. Employing social identity theory, Tajfel and Turner (1986) characterize these stereotyped groups as 'outgroups,' or marginalized social groups, that experience undue prejudicial treatment in society, limiting their access to equitable treatment and opportunities. Most commonly, media stereotyping research examines the effects of stereotypical media portrayals of social groups on individuals' attitudes and beliefs about these groups as well as policies affecting these groups (e.g., affirmative action in the United States). In line with Tajfel and Turner's research, Mastro (2003) applied this social identity theory framework to understanding the effects of television portrayals of Latinos/as on viewers' perceptions of this racial/ethnic group, hypothesizing that media stereotypes contribute to the development and maintenance of prejudicial beliefs about marginalized groups in order to maintain self-esteem of dominant group members and because these stereotypic portrayals may conform to the status quo. The results of Mastro's (2003) research demonstrated increased privileging of Whites over Latinos after exposure to stereotypical presentations of Latino characters as criminal in entertainment television programming. Experimental research can help to uncover the roles media stereotyping plays in affecting attitudes and beliefs about various social groups.

A growing body of research provides evidence that exposure to media stereotypes predicts prejudicial judgments of minority racial/ethnic groups (e.g., Brown Givens & Monahan, 2005; Figueroa-Caballero & Mastro, 2018; Ford, 1997; Fujioka, 1999; Mastro, Behm-Morawitz, & Ortiz, 2007; Mastro & Tropp, 2004; Oliver, Jackson, Moses, & Dangerfield, 2004; Valentino, 1999; See Chapters 5 and 6 in this volume), women (e.g., Aubrey & Harrison, 2004; Behm-Morawitz & Mastro, 2009; Dill & Thill, 2007; Kilbourne, 1990; Yao, Mahood, & Linz, 2010; See Chapter 4 in this volume), religious groups (e.g., Riles, Behm-Morawitz, Shin, Funk, 2019; Saleem, Prot, Anderson, & Lemieux, 2017; See Chapter 11 in this volume), mental illness (Gwarjanski & Parrott, 2018; Riles, 2018; See chapter 13 in this volume), and sexual minorities (e.g., Calzo & Ward, 2009; Sink, Mastro, & Dragojevic, 2018; See Chapter 10 in this volume), among other stereotypes (See Chapters 7, 8, 9, and 12 in this volume for an overview). Earlier work, such as Ford's (1997) study exposing White college students to stereotypical comedy skits about African Americans, demonstrated a link between media stereotyping and prejudicial beliefs about racial/ethnic minority groups. More recent work has replicated findings of early research as well as examined effects of media stereotyping on ingroup and self-stereotyping (e.g., Ortiz & Thompson, 2019) and effects of intersectional stereotyping—wherein multiple stigmatized identities come together or intersect in a media portrayal—to affect media users' perceptions of social group identities (Dill-Shackleford et al., 2017; Wigger, 2019).

Research has also examined the effects of media stereotyping on affective, or emotional, responses to marginalized groups. Exposure to negative stereotypes has led to decreased empathy for (Johnson, Olivo, Gibson, Reed, & Ashburn-Nardo, 2009) and increased emotional responses to (e.g., Behm-Morawitz, Hoffswell, & Chen, 2016; Fujioka, 2005; Riggle, Ellis, & Crawford, 1996; Riles et al., 2019) marginalized groups. For example, in an earlier study by Riggle and colleagues (1996), exposure to a positive documentary film about the life of a gay man resulted in greater negative emotions and disturbance in low-prejudiced viewers when they thought about how others may unfairly negatively perceive homosexuals. Likewise, Richeson and Pollydore (2002) found that Black college students exposed to positive portrayals of Black television characters interacting with White characters caused increased anxiety, in comparison to when Black characters acted in stereotypical, expected ways (e.g., "clownish" and using slang) amongst White characters. Research has also demonstrated that White audiences exhibit greater feelings of threat (e.g., fear) when exposed to stereotypical violent representations of minority groups (e.g., Behm-Morawitz et al., 2016; Dixon, 2007).

Lastly, a smaller set of studies has examined the effects of media stereotyping on prejudicial and helping behaviors, or more commonly, behavioral intentions. From a spreading activation perspective (Collins & Loftus, 1975), media stereotyping may shape perceptions which guide subsequent judgments and behavioral responses to social groups. In application, experimental research has examined behavior and behavioral intentions in creative ways to uncover prejudice following exposure to media stereotyping. For example, behavioral intention has been measured frequently by having participants deliver sentencing recommendations as if they were a jury member, after viewing race-based depictions of criminals in news media (e.g., Dixon, 2007; Ford, 1997; Mastro, Lapinski, Kopacz, & Behm-Morawitz, 2009). Other researchers have used more direct self-report measures of antisocial behavioral intentions, such as Yao et al.'s (2010) study demonstrating that exposure to a sexually-explicit and gender stereotypical video game portrayal resulted in male players' greater reported intentions to behave in sexually aggressive and inappropriate ways toward women.

Short- and Long-Term Effects of Media Stereotyping

Most experimental designs are used to study short-term effects of media stereotyping on outcomes. Short-term effects are evidenced in the influence of media exposure or media interaction on an individual over a short period of time, typically right after exposure to or interaction with media content. These effects may include cognitive outcomes, such as attitude or belief change after media viewing or interaction. For example, Armstrong, Neuendorf, and Brentar (1992) found that short-term exposure to television news and dramas had differential effects on White college students' beliefs about the socioeconomic status of African Americans. Exposure to news resulted in belief in the lower socioeconomic status, whereas exposure to dramas predicted belief in the higher socioeconomic status of African Americans.

Long-term effects of media stereotyping have also been established, although this type of research is less common than short-term effects experiments and introduces additional challenges. Long-term effects are lasting effects of exposure to media stereotyping over a longer period of time such as one month. However, the vast majority of media stereotyping studies utilize long-term exposure to stereotyped media portrayals as a media usage variable that is employed to explore correlational, rather than causal, relationships with stereotyping outcomes. For example, Dill, Brown, and Collins (2008) demonstrate that long-term exposure to sexually explicit and violent video games correlated with greater rape myth acceptance and tolerance of sexual harassment. Most often, scholars note in the limitations and future directions section the need for more research into long-term media stereotyping effects. For now, it is hypothesized that the evidenced short-term effects of media stereotyping may be indicative of longer lasting, cumulative effects of exposure on cognitive and behavioral outcomes.

Indirect, Conditional, and Transactional Effects of Media Stereotyping

Valkenburg, Peter, and Walther (2016) also point out that media effects can be indirect, conditional, and transactional. First, an "indirect effect is one in which the influence of an independent variable (e.g., media use) on other variables (e.g., outcomes of media use) works via its influence on one or more intervening (mediating) variables" (Valkenburg et al., 2016, p. 324). In the case of media stereotyping, exposure to the stereotype would predict an intervening variable, which, in turn, would predict an outcome variable. Recent research has advanced understanding of cognitive processes predictive of media stereotyping outcomes. For example, Arendt (2019) found that the process of negation (i.e. active cognitive disbelief in the stereotype during exposure) partially mediated the relationship between exposure to more blatant negative stereotypes of a marginalized group on individuals' subsequent beliefs about that group. In other words, greater cognitive disbelief in the accuracy of the stereotype reduced the effect of the media portrayal on individual perceptions of the stereotyped group.

Second, conditional effects emerge when a third variable moderates the effect of media stereotyping, such that the effect becomes stronger or weaker—or changes direction—depending on individual or situational variables. Traditionally, much of the research has examined individual differences, such as how trait dispositions and demographics influence the relationship between exposure to media stereotyping and subsequent effects. For example, Johnson, Adams, Hall, and Ashbum (1997) found that participant gender moderated the relationship between exposure to Black violent criminal depictions and dispositional judgments of blame. Beyond such individual demographic and trait differences, there are cognitive processing differences that account for moderation effects. For example, past research suggests that media stereotypes that are perceived to be moderately discrepant from one's own cognitions about the depicted group are more likely to be internalized and fit into one's existing schemata, whereas highly discrepant media portrayals are less likely to be fluidly processed (Valkenburg & Peter, 2013).

Third, transactional effects examine the reciprocal effects of media use and media outcomes, such that media use habits (i.e. in the present case, exposure to and interaction with stereotypical representations) influence stereotyping outcomes (e.g., attitudes and behavior), which in turn affect the future selection or proclivity for certain types of media content. Slater (2015) describes this as a reinforcement effect, where exposure to media stereotyping may reinforce preference for such stereotypical media content. In other words, there is a cyclical relationship between our media use patterns and media stereotyping outcomes. Little research has explored such outcomes of media stereotyping due to the complexity of measuring this feedback loop and the challenges of establishing causal, directional relationships between media use habits, exposure to particular content, and continued preference for particular types of content.

Counter-Stereotypes

It is worthy to note that media stereotyping experiments also examine the outcomes of exposure to counter-stereotypes and positive stereotypes. See Chapter 14 of this volume for a complete overview. Most notably, this research (e.g., Holt, 2013; Ramasubramanian, 2007; Richeson & Pollydore,

2002) explores the potential for positive, atypical representations of marginalized and stigmatized groups to counteract negative perceptions and produce more favorable responses. These experimental studies empirically examine the potential effects of positive media portrayals on prosocial attitudes, favorable beliefs, and policy support for marginalized groups.

Researchers have exposed participants to counter-stereotypical media portrayals of marginalized groups and compared the effects of this exposure to no-exposure and/or stereotypical portrayal exposure groups (e.g., Ramasubramanian, 2011). In some cases, participants have been presented with an additional stimulus (e.g., a news story about a criminal) following the counter-stereotypical exposure to examine the effects of the positive portrayal on subsequent judgments about media content and issues that affect marginalized groups. In other studies, an intervention is used to help train participants to view media more critically. For example, Ramasubramanian (2007) exposed participants to an informative video about media literacy, critical media viewing, and media stereotypes before exposing them to either stereotypical negative or counter-stereotypical positive portrayals of African Americans and Asian Indians. The exposure to the media literacy video diminished implicit stereotyping of the marginalized groups after viewing the counter-stereotypical portrayals. This demonstrates the potential utility in the use of media literacy training in conjunction with positive counter-stereotypical media content for decreasing stereotyping of marginalized groups.

Experimental Design for the Study of Media Stereotyping

Empirical examinations of the effects of exposure to media stereotyping, such as those reviewed above, have largely been conducted using laboratory studies and online experiments to assess short-term effects on cognitions (e.g., attitudes and beliefs). As noted by Ramasubramanian and Murphy (2014), laboratory experiments "along with statistical advances in modeling techniques have enhanced the ability of media psychologists to systematically investigate the message features, situational contexts, and audience characteristics that influence cause–effect relationships between stereotypical media content and audience outcomes" (p. 386). The hallmark of laboratory experiments is increased control in isolating the cause (media stereotyping) on particular effects (cognitions, attitudes, and behaviors). The majority of the studies reviewed in this chapter utilize experimental design to account for the unique contributions that exposure to, or interaction with, media stereotypes may have on bias that ultimately may impact the real-world experiences of marginalized groups.

There are limitations, however, in experimenters' reliance on self-report measures of bias (e.g., Modern Racism Scale, McConahay, 1983). For example, participants who encounter questions concerning prejudice might lean toward providing socially desirable responses. Therefore, researchers have used measures of both explicit (i.e. self-report) attitudes and implicit association tests to gauge outcomes following exposure to media stereotypes.

Implicit Measures of Bias

Perhaps one of the most common tests of implicit bias is the Implicit Association Test (IAT). The goal of the IAT is to assess the true extent of an individual's level of bias, such as racial bias (Greenwald, McGhee, & Schwartz, 1998). Social desirability can drive people to censor their prejudicial attitudes in research studies to appear more egalitarian. Thus, a measurement of implicit bias is advantageous because it taps into people's unconscious bias despite social norms or pressure to appear politically correct. The IAT, however, has been criticized as a measure of implicit bias because it has failed to be used consistently in predicting behaviors (Oswald, Mitchell, Blanton, Jaccard, & Tetlock, 2013). Nevertheless, the IAT has proven a useful measurement in experimental design as a 'state measure' of implicit bias to test whether an experimental manipulation affects implicit attitudes in the short-term following exposure to a stimulus (Forscher et al., 2019), in the present case of a media stereotype. The use of tests such as the IAT to measure automatic bias is advantageous to triangulate with self-report measures. For example, Hinman, Burmeister, Kiefner-Burmeister, Borushok, and Carels (2015) examined the effects of exposure to stereotypical depictions of obese people on weight bias. They used two forms of the IAT to measure implicit weight bias to triangulate with self-report measures, specifically the Multidimensional Body Self-Relations Questionnaire, Overweight Preoccupation Scale, Appearance Orientation Scale, Fear of Fat Scale, and the Anti-fat Attitudes Scale. Their research demonstrates a significant association between exposure to media stereotyping, implicit bias, and self-report attitudinal and belief measures.

Interactive Media and Stereotyping

As referenced at times throughout this chapter, outcomes of media stereotyping are derived from interaction with media, not just exposure to media content. Video games, virtual reality, the Internet, and social media have broadened the contexts in which a person may encounter, or even create, media stereotyping and counter-stereotyping. This has introduced interactive and immersive media to media stereotyping experimental designs. For instance, in the context of gender, video game research has established a link between embodying a stereotypically sexualized female avatar with decreased egalitarian gender attitudes (Behm-Morawitz & Mastro, 2009) and greater self-objectification and rape myth acceptance (Fox, Ralston, Cooper, & Jones, 2015; Yao et al., 2010). In immersive contexts, such as video games, media users can embody—not simply view—stereotypical portrayals in the form of avatars (or digital character representations). Behm-Morawitz, Pennell, and Speno (2016) examined the short-term cognitive effects of embodying an outgroup racial/ethnic avatar on White college students' race-based attitudes. Virtual embodiment of an outgroup member resulted in greater liking and more positive attitudes toward the outgroup, in comparison to participants who embodied a same-race avatar.

In the world of social media, interactive features include the sharing of posts, commenting on posts, social endorsement of content through favoriting and likes, and, of course, the creation of original posts. This adds complexity to social media stereotyping empirical work, as the need to account for interactive elements of the media platforms is necessary to accurately assess the effects of these media experiences. In fact, Cirucci (2013) argues that the methods used to study video game effects could and should be similarly applied to studying effects of social media. Specifically, Cirucci argues that social media and video games alike contribute to the construction of identity and social reality through digital interaction and self-representation. In the context of media stereotyping, video games, virtual reality, and social media share the potential experience of virtual embodiment and exploration of the self in the context of others in digital spaces.

At the most basic level, however, research indicates that well-recognized social stereotypes are often reflected in online spaces, including social media such as Facebook. Rose et al. (2012) found that a sample of Facebook photos were gender-role conforming and representative of common gender stereotypes, such as men as independent and women as dependent. Moreover, Döring, Reif, and Poeschl (2016) examined women's selfies on Instagram and found that the social media images were even more highly gender stereotypical than depictions of women in popular magazines. The effects of exposure to social media content may be explained in part through its highly personalized and interactive nature. Dixon (2016) argues that social media use may serve as a powerful reinforcement of pre-existing stereotypes due to selective exposure to online content that confirms an individual's beliefs. Further, Turetsky and Riddle (2018) posit that social media and Internet use promote echo chambers of thought "that amplify homogenous perspectives" (p. 163) and perpetuate racial stereotypes.

Experimental research in the arena of the effects of social media use on stereotypical attitudes, beliefs, and behaviors is scant, and most research is correlational or qualitative in nature. However, a solid foundation of work is building in this area with research on incivility in political social media discussions. For example, Wang and Silva (2018) examined the use of stereotypes in users' content production and responses in political debates on Facebook. The reliance on stereotypes to insult and mock outgroup members, or those they disagreed with, was evident.

Future Directions in Experimental Design and Media Stereotyping

As indicated by the work reviewed above, research exploring the deleterious effects that stereotypical media depictions of marginalized groups can have on media users has undoubtedly made significant strides over the last several decades. However, despite the valuable insight this work has provided, there are still ways in which this body of work is limited in its ability to speak to the breadth of potential cognitive, affective, and behavioral effects of exposure to media stereotypes.

One limitation is experimental media stereotyping research's overuse of non-representative student samples (Ramasubramanian & Murphy, 2014), despite strong evidence that these students are, in many ways, extreme cultural outliers (Henrich, Heine, & Norenzayan, 2010). Though this critique can and has been applied to most quantitative communication research (Basil, 1996), it has been levied less frequently at experimental studies due to the nature of approach. In other words, historically it has been much easier (and less expensive) to get students to come to a laboratory and take part in an experiment than other members of the general public (Clifford & Jerit, 2014). However, with the emergence of platforms (e.g., Qualtrics) that allow for experiments to take place online, this limitation has become less of an issue.

These platforms and other services allow for greater variety in subject pools (e.g., CloudResearch), which also mitigates another limitation of extant media stereotyping studies—the use of majority group only samples (e.g., White, heterosexual, etc.; Ramasubramanian & Murphy, 2014). Of course, these services also present new quandaries for researchers as to the loss of control they have in their experimental designs (Clifford & Jerit, 2014) and the overuse of participants recruited through online crowdsourcing sites like Amazon Mechanical Turk (McInnis, Cosley, Nam, & Leshed, 2016). Thus, though this provides a further avenue for experimental research with broader populations, media stereotyping scholars must contend with a new set of inherent limitations.

As noted above, extant research examining the relationship between the media, stereotypes, and a host of consequential outcomes has relied heavily on the use of self-report measures. This practice has continued despite (a) apparent issues regarding social desirability effects (Paulhus & Vazire, 2007) and (b) the emergence of more objective research tools (Ravaja, 2004). Concerning the latter point, there has been a general lack of enthusiasm as to the use of psychophysiological measures to assess media stereotyping effects. This is particularly surprising because such measures have been readily taken up not only within other communication subdisciplines (e.g., Afifi et al., 2018), but also because much of the psychophysiological work conducted within the field of communication generally emerges from research on media effects (Potter & Bolls, 2012), relying on media theories such as the limited capacity model of motivated mediated message processing (LC4MP; Alhabash, Almutairi, Lou, & Kim, 2019; Lang, 2000).

The scarcity of studies marrying media stereotyping effects and psychophysiological measures can perhaps be partially explained by a lack of knowledge among researchers as to how these measures might be particularly helpful when it comes to outcomes of interest such as prejudice, discrimination, etc. Put simply, much of this research has focused on questions related to attention, arousal, information processing, and emotion within the context of media use and exposure (see Ravaja, 2004 for a review); these concepts are central to any study of media effects, but are often not the final outcomes media stereotyping in which researchers are interested. However, research in the field of social psychology has evinced the value of psychophysiological measures when examining stereotyping and prejudice. Of particular interest to media stereotyping scholars is how these measures have been found to differ in key ways from self-report measures. For instance, O'Handley, Blair, and Hoskin (2017) found that irrespective of an individual's self-reported level of homophobia, exposure to images in which same-sex couples display affection manifested in increased salivary alpha-amylase responses—a biomarker that has been associated with disgust and prejudice responses. Similarly, Cikara and Fiske (2012) found that exposure to images featuring a negative event (e.g., getting soaked by a taxi driving through a puddle) resulted in contrasting findings between the self-reported affect response and the physiological response (zygomaticus major activation measured via facial electromyography [EMG]) depending on whether the outgroup member elicited feelings of envy. Specifically, they hypothesized (and their findings supported) that feelings of envy would result in positive affect in response to the outgroup members' misfortune but that social desirability bias would result in a null relationship between the self-reported affective response and the physiological response. In sum, these studies indicate that self-report measures designed to assess feelings toward outgroups might not be appropriately or accurately capturing this outcome and perhaps should be paired with physiological measures to do so.

Another promising avenue in which physiological measures can provide greater insight relates to threat and threat appraisals within media content. Specifically, it has been established that marginalized groups are often depicted as threatening in the media (Dixon & Williams, 2015) and that exposure to these threatening images can have negative consequences (Figueroa-Caballero & Mastro, 2018). However, research indicates that intergroup threat is multifaceted, such that distinct types of threat (e.g., physical, economic, cultural/moral) or the level at which the threat is appraised (e.g., individual or group level) can result in unique affective, behavioral, and cognitive consequences (Cottrell & Neuberg, 2005; Stephan, Ybarra, & Rios Morrison, 2009). For example, Davis and Stephan (2011) used EMG to assess differential muscle activation associated with anger and fear (i.e., the left corrugator supercilia and the left medial frontalis, respectively) and responses to group- and individual-level threatening content. In addition, physiological research also points to expanding the concept of threat to include groups that might not necessarily be considered threatening, but rather stigmatized. For example, Blascovich, Mendes, Hunter, Lickel, and Kowai-Bell (2001) found that interactions with members of stigmatized groups (e.g., those with facial birthmarks) resulted in similar cardiovascular reactivity responses to those facing a threat. In other words, from a media stereotyping standpoint, perhaps groups argued to be historically portrayed in a non-threatening but problematic fashion are evoking similar responses to groups typically characterized as threatening. In sum, the use of psychophysiological measures to study the effect of media stereotypes on audiences has been largely absent. However, the work reviewed above indicates not only its utility for media stereotype researchers, but also new and promising avenues for us to explore.

Conclusion

The goal of the current chapter was to outline not only the range of outcomes that have been explored within experimental research focused on stereotyping and media effects, but also the potential approaches that have been—or could be—used to mitigate the shortcomings of this methodology. Overall, it is clear that the use of experimental design over the past few decades has contributed greatly to the body of work examining the effects of stereotypical representations of marginalized identities on majority audiences. However, in relative terms, the study of these relationships is still in its infancy. Consequently, the continued study of the mechanisms underlying these deleterious effects is paramount.

References

Afifi, T. D., Davis, S., Merrill, A. F., Coveleski, S., Denes, A., & Shahnazi, A. F. (2018). Couples' communication about financial uncertainty following the Great Recession and its association with stress, mental health and divorce proneness. *Journal of Family and Economic Issues, 39*, 205–219. https://doi.org/10.1007/s10834-017-9560-5

Alhabash, S., Almutairi, N., Lou, C., & Kim, W. (2019). Pathways to virality: Psychophysiological responses preceding likes, shares, comments, and status updates on Facebook. *Media Psychology, 22*, 196–216.

Arendt, F. (2019). Investigating the negation of media stereotypes: Ability and motivation as moderators. *Journal of Media Psychology: Theories, Methods, and Applications, 31*, 48–54.

Armstrong, G. B., Neuendorf, K. A., & Brentar, J. E. (1992). TV entertainment, news, and racial perceptions of college students. *Journal of Communication, 42*, 153–176.

Aubrey, J. S., & Harrison, K. (2004). The gender-role content of children's favorite television programsand its links to their gender-related perceptions. *Media Psychology, 6*, 111–146.

Basil, M. D. (1996). Standpoint: The use of student samples in communication research. *Journal of Broadcasting & Electronic Media, 40*, 431–440.

Behm-Morawitz, E., Hoffswell, J., & Chen, S. W. (2016). The virtual threat effect: A test of competing explanations for the effects of racial stereotyping in video games on players' cognitions. *Cyberpsychology, Behavior and Social Networking, 19*, 308–313.

Behm-Morawitz, E., & Mastro, D. (2009). The effects of the sexualization of female video game characters on gender stereotyping and female self-concept. *Sex Roles, 61*, 808–823.

Behm-Morawitz, E., Pennell, H., & Speno, A. G. (2016). The effects of virtual racial embodiment in a gaming app on reducing prejudice. *Communication Monographs*, 396–418. http://dx.doi.org/10.1080/03637751.2015.1128556

Blascovich, J., Mendes, W. B., Hunter, S. B., Lickel, B., & Kowai-Bell, N. (2001). Perceiver threat in social interactions with stigmatized others. *Journal of Personality and Social Psychology, 80*, 253–267.

Brown Givens, S. M., & Monahan, J. L. (2005). Priming mammies, jezebels, and other controlling images: An examination of the influence of mediated stereotypes on perceptions of an African American woman. *Media Psychology, 7*, 87–106.

Bryant, J., & Thompson, S. (Eds.), (2002). *Fundamentals of media effects.* Boston, MA: McGraw-Hill.

Calzo, J. P., & Ward, L. M. (2009). Media exposure and viewers' attitudes toward homosexuality: Evidence for mainstreaming or resonance? *Journal of Broadcasting & Electronic Media, 53,* 280–299.

Cikara, M., & Fiske, S. T. (2012). Stereotypes and schadenfreude: Affective and physiological markers of pleasure at outgroup misfortunes. *Social Psychological and Personality Science, 3,* 63–71. https://doi.org/10.1177/1948550611409245

Cirucci, A. M. (2013). First person paparazzi: Why social media should be studied more like video games. *Telematics and Informatics, 30,* 47–59.

Clifford, S., & Jerit, J. (2014). Is there a cost to convenience? An experimental comparison of data quality in laboratory and online studies. *Journal of Experimental Political Science, 1,* 120–131. https://doi.org/10.1017/xps.2014.5

Collins, A. M., & Loftus, E. F. (1975). A spreading-activation theory of semantic processing. *Psychological Review, 82,* 407–428.

Cottrell, C. A., & Neuberg, S. L. (2005). Different emotional reactions to different groups: A sociofunctional threat-based approach to "prejudice." *Journal of Personality and Social Psychology, 88,* 770–789. https://doi.org/10.1037/0022-3514.88.5.770

Davis, M., & Stephan, W. (2011). Electromyographic analyses of responses to intergroup threat: Responses to intergroup threat. *Journal of Applied Social Psychology, 41,* 196–218. https://doi.org/10.1111/j.1559-1816.2010.00709.x

Dill, K. E., Brown, B. P., & Collins, M. A. (2008). Effects of exposure to sex-stereotyped video game characters on tolerance of sexual harassment. *Journal of Experimental Social Psychology, 44,* 1402–1408.

Dill, K. E., & Thill, K. P. (2007). Video game characters and the socialization of gender roles: Young people's perceptions mirror sexist media depictions. *Sex Roles, 57,* 851–864.

Dill-Shackleford, K. E., Ramasubramanian, S., Behm-Morawitz, E., Scharrer, E., Burgess, M. C. R., & Lemish, D. (2017). Social group stories in the media and child development. *Pediatrics, 140,* S157–S161.

Dixon, T. L. (2007). Black criminals and white officers: The effects of racially misrepresenting law breakers and law defenders on television news. *Media Psychology, 10,* 270–291.

Dixon, T. L. (2016). Understanding how the Internet and social media accelerate racial stereotyping and social division: The socially mediated stereotyping model. In R. A. Lind (Ed.), *Race and gender in electronic media: Content, context, culture.* New York, NY: Routledge.

Dixon, T. L., & Williams, C. L. (2015). The changing misrepresentation of race and crime on network and cable news: Race and crime on network and cable news. *Journal of Communication, 65,* 24–39. https://doi.org/10.1111/jcom.12133

Döring, N., Reif, A., & Poeschl, S. (2016). How gender-stereotypical are selfies? A content analysis and comparison with magazine adverts. *Computers in Human Behavior, 55,* 955–962.

Figueroa-Caballero, A., & Mastro, D. (2018). Examining the effects of news coverage linking undocumented immigrants with criminality: Policy and punitive implications. *Communication Monographs*. doi: 10.1080/03637751.2018.1505049

Ford, T. E. (1997). Effects of stereotypical television portrayals of African-Americans on person perception. *Social Psychology Quarterly, 60*, 266–275.

Forscher, P. S., Lai, C. K., Axt, J. R., Ebersole, C. R., Herman, M., Devine, P. G., & Nosek, B. A. (2019). A meta-analysis of procedures to change implicit measures. *Journal of Personality & Social Psychology, 117*, 522–559.

Fox, J., Ralston, R. A., Cooper, C. K., & Jones, K. A. (2015). Sexualized avatars lead to women's self-objectification and acceptance of rape myths. *Psychology of Women Quarterly, 39*, 349–362. doi: 10.1177/0361684314553578

Fujioka, Y. (1999). Television portrayals and African-American stereotypes: Examination of television effects when direct contact is lacking. *Journalism & Mass Communication Quarterly, 76*, 52–75.

Fujioka, Y. (2005). Emotional TV viewing and minority audience: How Mexican Americans process and evaluate TV news about in-group members. *Communication Research, 32*, 566–593.

Greenwald, A. G., McGhee, D. E., & Schwartz, J. L. K. (1998). Measuring individual differences in implicit cognition: The implicit association test. *Journal of Personality and Social Psychology, 74*, 1464–1480. doi: 10.1037/0022-3514.74.6.1464

Gwarjanski, A. R., & Parrott, S. (2018). Schizophrenia in the news: The role of news frames in shaping online reader dialogue about mental illness. *Health Communication, 33*, 954–961.

Henrich, J., Heine, S. J., & Norenzayan, A. (2010). The weirdest people in the world? *Behavioral and Brain Sciences, 33*, 61–83. https://doi.org/10.1017/S0140525X0999152X

Hinman, N. G., Burmeister, J. M., Kiefner-Burmeister, A., Borushok, J. E., & Carels, R. A. (2015). Stereotypical portrayals of obesity and the expression of implicit weight bias. *Body Image, 12C*, 32–35. 10.1016/j.bodyim.2014.09.002.

Holt, L. F. (2013). Writing the wrong: Can counter-stereotypes offset negative media messages about African Americans? *Journalism & Mass Communication Quarterly, 90*, 108–125.

Johnson, J. D., Adams, M. S., Hall, W., & Ashbum, L. (1997). Race, media, and violence: Differential racial effects of exposure to violent news stories. *Basic and Applied Social Psychology, 19*, 81–90.

Johnson, J. D., Olivo, N., Gibson, N., Reed, W., & Ashburn-Nardo, L. (2009). Priming media stereotypes reduces support for social welfare policies: The mediating role of empathy. *Personality and Social Psychology Bulletin, 4*, 463–476.

Kilbourne, W. E. (1990). Female stereotyping in advertising: An experiment on male–female perceptions of leadership. *Journalism Quarterly, 67*, 25–31.

Lang, A. (2000). The limited capacity model of mediated message processing. *Journal of Communication, 50*, 46–70.

Mastro, D., Lapinski, M. K., Kopacz, M. A., & Behm-Morawitz, E. (2009). The influence of exposure to depictions of race and crime in TV news on viewer's social judgments. *Journal of Broadcasting & Electronic Media, 53,* 615–635.

Mastro, D. E. (2003). A social identity approach to understanding the impact of television messages. *Communication Monographs, 70,* 98–113.

Mastro, D. E., Behm-Morawitz, E., & Ortiz, M. (2007). The cultivation of social perceptions of Latinos: A mental models approach. *Media Psychology, 9,* 347–365.

Mastro, D. E., & Tropp, L. R. (2004). The effects of interracial contact, attitudes, and stereotypical portrayals on evaluations of Black television sitcom characters. *Communication Research Reports, 21,* 119–129.

McConahay, J. B. (1983). Modern racism and modern discrimination: The effects of race, racial attitudes, and context on simulated hiring decisions. *Personality and Social Psychology Bulletin, 9,* 551–558.

McInnis, B., Cosley, D., Nam, C., & Leshed, G. (2016). Taking a HIT: Designing around rejection, mistrust, risk, and workers' experiences in Amazon Mechanical Turk. *Proceedings of the 2016 CHI Conference on Human Factors in Computing Systems— CHI '16,* 2271–2282. https://doi.org/10.1145/2858036.2858539

O'Handley, B. M., Blair, K. L., & Hoskin, R. A. (2017). What do two men kissing and a bucket of maggots have in common? Heterosexual men's indistinguishable salivary α-amylase responses to photos of two men kissing and disgusting images. *Psychology & Sexuality, 8,* 173–188.

Oliver, M. B., Jackson, R. L., 2nd, Moses, N. N., & Dangerfield, C. L. (2004). The face of crime: Viewers' memory of race-related facial features of individuals pictured in the news. *Journal of Communication, 54,* 88–104.

Ortiz, R. R., & Thompson, B. A. (2019, online first). Sorority see, sorority do: How social identity and media engagement relate to in-group stereotyping and self-stereotyping. *Psychology of Popular Media Culture.* Available from https://psycnet.apa.org/record/2019-15475-001?doi=1.

Oswald, F. L., Mitchell, G., Blanton, H., Jaccard, J., & Tetlock, P. E. (2013). Predicting ethnic and racial discrimination: A meta-analysis of IAT criterion studies. *Journal of Personality and Social Psychology, 105,* 171–192.

Paulhus, D. L., & Vazire, S. (2007). The self-report method. In R. W. Robins, R. C. Fraley, & R. F. Krueger (Eds.), *Handbook of research methods in personality psychology* (pp. 224–239). New York: Guilford Press.

Potter, R. F., & Bolls, P. D. (2012). *Psychophysiological measurement and meaning: Cognitive and emotional processing of media.* New York: Routledge.

Ramasubramanian, S. (2007). Media-based strategies to reduce racial stereotypes activated by news stories. *Journalism & Mass Communication Quarterly, 84,* 249–264.

Ramasubramanian, S. (2011). The impact of stereotypical versus counterstereotypical media exemplars on racial attitudes, causal attributions, and support for affirmative action. *Communication Research, 38,* 497–516.

Ramasubramanian, S., & Murphy, C. J. (2014). Experimental studies of media stereotyping effects. In *Laboratory experiments in the social sciences* (pp. 385–402). https://doi.org/10.1016/B978-0-12-404681-8.00017-0

Ravaja, N. (2004). Contributions of psychophysiology to media research: Review and recommendations. *Media Psychology, 6,* 193–235.

Richeson, J. A., & Pollydore, C.-A. (2002). Affective reactions of African American students to stereotypical and counterstereotypical images of Blacks in the media. *Journal of Black Psychology, 28,* 261–275.

Riggle, E. D. B., Ellis, A. L., & Crawford, A. M. (1996). The impact of "media contact" on attitudes toward gay men. *Journal of Homosexuality, 3,* 55–69.

Riles, J., Behm-Morawitz, E., Shin, H., Funk, M. (2019). The effect of news peril-type on social inclinations: A social group comparison. *Journalism & Mass Communication Quarterly.* Advanced Online Access.

Riles, J. M. (2018). The social effect of exposure to mental illness media portrayals: Influencing interpersonal interaction intentions. *Psychology of Popular Media Culture.* Advanced Online Access.

Rose, J., Mackey-Kallis, S., Shyles, L., Barry, K., Biagini, D., Hart, C., & Jack, L. (2012). Face it: The impact of gender on social media images. *Communication Quarterly, 60,* 588–607.

Saleem, M., Prot, S., Anderson, C. A., & Lemieux, A. F. (2017). Exposure to Muslims in media and support for public policies harming Muslims. *Communication Research, 44,* 841–869.

Sink, A., Mastro, D., & Dragojevic, M. (2018). Competent or warm? A stereotype content model approach to understanding perceptions of masculine and effeminate gay television characters. *Journalism & Mass Communication Quarterly, 95,* 588–606.

Slater, M. D. (2015). Reinforcing spirals model: Conceptualizing the relationship between media content exposure and the development and maintenance of attitudes. *Media Psychology, 18,* 370–395.

Stephan, W. G., Ybarra, O., & Rios Morrison, K. (2009). Intergroup threat theory. In T. D. Nelson (Ed.), *Handbook of prejudice, stereotyping, and discrimination* (pp. 43–61). New York: Psychology Press.

Tajfel, H., & Turner, J. C. (1986). The social identity theory of intergroup behavior. In S. Worchel & W. G. Austin (Eds.), *Psychology of intergroup relations* (pp. 7–24). Chicago, IL: Nelson-Hall.

Turetsky, K. M., & Riddle, T. A. (2018). Porous chambers, echoes of valence and stereotypes: A network analysis of online news coverage interconnectedness following a nationally polarizing race-related event. *Social Psychological and Personality Science, 9,* 163–175.

Valentino, N. A. (1999). Crime news and the priming of racial attitudes during evaluations of the president. *Public Opinion Quarterly, 63,* 293–320.

Valkenburg, P. M., & Peter, J. (2013). The differential susceptibility to media effects model. *Journal of Communication, 63,* 221–243.

Valkenburg, P., Peter, J., & Walther, J. (2016). Media effects: Theory and research. *Annual Review of Psychology, 67*, 315–338. doi: 10.1146/annurev-psych-122414-033608

Wang, M. Y., & Silva, D. E. (2018). A slap or a jab: An experiment on viewing uncivil political discussions on Facebook. *Computers in Human Behavior, 81*, 73–83.

Wigger, I. (2019, online first). Anti-Muslim racism and the racialisation of sexual violence: 'Intersectional stereotyping' in mass media representations of male Muslim migrants in Germany. *Culture and Religion*. doi: 10.1080/14755610.2019.1658609

Yao, M. Z., Mahood, C., & Linz, D. (2010). Sexual priming, gender stereotyping, and likelihood to sexually harass: Examining the cognitive effects of playing a sexually-explicit video game. *Sex Roles, 62*, 77–88.

Section II   Forms of Media Stereotyping

4 Gender-Based Media Stereotypes and Their Effects on Audiences: The More Gender Changes, the More Media Representation Stays the Same

Jennifer Stevens Aubrey
University of Arizona

Kun Yan
University of Arizona

In 2018, Frances McDormand ended her Oscar acceptance speech with just two words: "inclusion rider" (Kilkenny, 2018). Backstage, McDormand explained that an inclusion rider is a clause that actors can put into their contracts insisting on gender and racial diversity in hiring on movie and television sets. From whom did this idea originate? Communication scholar Stacy Smith, director of University of Southern California's Media, Diversity and Social Change Initiative, wrote about a then-called "equity rider" in 2014. In response to the dismal male-to-female ratios of characters in the top films from 2013, she suggested that actors could exercise their power on behalf of women and girls to procure a more gender-diverse "onscreen demography reflecting a population comprised of 50 percent women and girls. In other words, reality" (Smith, 2014, para 4–5). Indeed, when women are involved with media production, there tends to be more gender diversity onscreen (Smith, Choueiti, & Pieper, 2016).

Recent events, such as the introduction of the inclusion rider into the cultural vernacular as well as the #metoo and the Time's Up movements, raise hope that long-standing gender stereotypes in the media will finally see some cracks in their foundations. However, it takes a while for Hollywood to react to current events, and it takes even longer for research to track those changes.

Considering that gender stereotypes are deeply embedded in our society, breaking down these barriers and achieving gender equality in the media world is "painfully slow" (Lemish & Götz, 2017, p. 9). Indeed, after reviewing the research literature, we conclude that we are a way off from documenting fundamental change in the portrayals of gender stereotypes across mainstream screen media.

Thus, in light of current events, it is important to gauge the state of the literature on gender-based stereotypes in screen media and their effects on audiences. In the following, we review the content analytic literature with an eye toward drawing similarities and contrasts between stereotypes in the 20th Century versus the 21st Century. Then, we investigate the effects of gender-based stereotypes, using the social cognition of stereotypes theoretical perspective as our foundation. Our discussion focuses on the effects of media exposure on gender-based stereotypes in four major domains: occupations, traits, sexualization and idealization, and hypermasculinity. Finally, we offer suggestions for future methodological and theoretical directions.

Gender-Based Stereotypes in the Media

Although the number of men and women are fairly equal in the United States (U.S. Census Bureau, 2015), media still present a primarily male-dominated world (Hust & Brown, 2008). Research from the middle of the 20th Century found two-thirds of major characters in films and TV dramas to be male (Head, 1954; Jones, 1942). Content analytic studies from the 1970s found approximately 30% of characters were female (Greenberg, 1980; McNeil, 1975). From research published in the 1980s–1990s, the proportion of female characters on television were 40% (e.g., Davis, 1990; Elasmar, Haswegawa, & Brain, 1999; Lauzen & Dozier, 1999). That proportion seems to be holding steady. Today, the ratio of male lead characters to female lead characters across television, advertising, and movies is 2 to 1 (Geena Davis Institute on Gender in Media, 2019a). Male characters are also more likely to hold starring roles, and they enjoy more screen time and speaking time. Although women are more likely to be represented in certain genres such as comedies, an overarching theme across genres is that men dominate the representation. In this section, we first review the common stereotypes depicted in the media, focusing on the domains of occupations, traits, the sexualization and idealization of bodies, and hypermasculinity, and then track their changes in the 21st Century.

20th Century Gender Stereotypes

In the 20th Century, the representation of occupational roles in the media was reliably gender stereotypical, with women being disproportionately depicted at home, in secondary roles, and as subordinates. In the 1970s, only 9% of women in advertisements had working roles, which contrasted with the fact that women actually accounted for 33% of the full-time workers at the time (Courtney & Lockeretz, 1971). By the end of the 20th Century about 50% of female characters were portrayed as having an occupation (Glascock, 2001), but in comparison to men, they were in lower-paying jobs, and they were more likely to be supervisees and domestics, not executives and leaders (Greenberg & Collette, 1997).

In terms of traits, exemplified by *Leave it to Beaver* or *Father Knows Best*, male characters in the 1950s and 1960s' programs were typically depicted as dominant, active, and adventurous, whereas female characters were dependent, nursing, passive, and affectionate. Although there are scattered depictions of females with nontraditional traits (e.g., Lucy Ricardo in *Love Lucy*, Ellie Mae Clampett in *The Beverly Hillbillies*; Vande Berg, 1991), more progressive changes seem to occur around the 1980s. Researchers discovered that female cartoon characters demonstrated more independence, competence, and assertiveness after the 1980s (Thompson & Zerbinos, 1995), and female characters such as Mary Beth Lacey in *Cagney & Lacey* in the 1980s presented both masculine and feminine traits (Vande Berg, 1991).

Media are also notorious for sexualizing female characters. A content analytic study found that about one in five popular songs from the 1940s–1970s treated women as sex objects, and mentions of women's body parts increased during the same time period (Cooper, 1985). The findings are not surprising considering that it was an era in which more than 90% of the lyrics sampled were written by men. In addition, women were usually idealized onscreen; they tended to conform to strict appearance standards of attractiveness, youth, and perfection. In one study of advertising spanning from the 1950s until the mid-1990s, independent judges agreed that more than 95% of the women in advertisements were attractive (Paff & Lakner, 1997).

So far we have focused on stereotypes for women, but what stereotypes pervaded the portrayal of men in the 20th Century? Hegemonic masculinity, featured by men being urbane, patriarchal, strong, and decisive, was a dominant stereotypical depiction of men over the 1940s and 1950s, but these depictions evolved into stereotypes of hypermasculinity in the 1990s. Men who are portrayed as stereotypically hypermasculine advocate violence and emotional toughness. However, the trend of hypermasculinity did not evolve linearly throughout all media. For example, a content analysis of 24 top police and detective series demonstrated that male characters adhering to the hyper-masculine role declined between the 1950s and the 1980s, but they increased profoundly in the 1990s (Scharrer, 2012). Indeed, in the 1980s and 1990s, masculinity was negotiated, reconstructed, and underwent "the initial throes of incorporating feminism into its structuring cultural ideology" (Lotz, 2014, p. 20). First introduced by Alan Alda's *M*A*S*H* character and Jim Rockford in *The Rockford Files*, an alternative portrayal of men on television—masculinity with feminist consciousness—developed in the 1980s, but become less explicit in the 1990s.

Stereotypes in the 21st Century

To examine changes in stereotypes, we relied on content analyses that were longitudinal in nature (examining changes in stereotypes over time) or that used a comparison approach (contrasting one time period to another). Based on our review of these studies, we found that some stereotypical portrayals (e.g., occupations) have declined in the 21st Century, while other stereotypes (e.g., sexualization and idealization) have either remained the same or actually *strengthened* in certain genres.

Changes in Gender-Based Stereotypes

Portrayals of occupations have progressed past the stereotypical housewives of the mid-20th Century. Longitudinal studies show that women are more likely to engage in nontraditional activities (e.g., playing sports or purchasing a car) in Super Bowl ads (Hatzithomas, Boutsouki, & Ziamou, 2016) than in previous decades. However, in G-rated movies, male characters were more likely to be shown in traditionally masculine occupations (e.g., firefighter, U.S. president), whereas female characters were more likely to be shown in traditionally feminine occupations (e.g., dancer, seamstress; Geena Davis Institute on Gender in Media, 2019a). And despite current efforts to increase the representation of women in Science, Technology, Engineering, and Mathematics (STEM) careers, there are twice as many male adult scientists as female adult scientists in children's television science series, and the majority of female adult scientists are portrayed in secondary, decorative roles, such as lab assistants or students (Long et al., 2010).

In terms of gender-typed traits, the media seem to circulate contradicting messages, encouraging women to be feminine and masculine at the same time. For instance, a longitudinal study on action heroines in movies indicates that heroines, exemplified by *Alien*'s Ellen Ripley and *Terminator*'s Sarah

Connor, have challenged gender norms in movies because they participate in the main action of the movie and exhibit violent behaviors when necessary. However, these female action characters still adhere to other traditionally feminine traits in that they are often submissive to the main male hero of the movie and are often romantically involved with or interested in the male hero (Gilpatric, 2010).

The mediated stereotypes that support the sexualization of women and girls are still holding strong, but a proliferation of content analyses on these topics have revealed some variance observed across genres. Longitudinal studies suggested a decrease in sexualized portrayals in TV ads (Fowler & Thomas, 2015) and video games (Lynch, Tompkins, Van Driel, & Fritz, 2016). However, a decline in the sexualization stereotype does not apply to music videos (Aubrey & Frisby, 2011). A longitudinal study on music videos from 1995 to 2016 found sexualized gestures, pose, and facial expression increased over the 20 years (Karsay, Matthes, Buchsteiner, & Grosser, 2019). Similarly, there is little progress regarding the depiction of idealization onscreen in the 21st Century. Indeed, 86% of male characters in television ads conformed to the mesomorphic muscular body type in 2008, a significant increase from 76% in 2003 (Fowler & Thomas, 2015). An investigation of MTV docusoaps between 2004–2011 found that the most popular body types were conspicuously thin and curvaceously thin for female characters and the mesomorphic V-shape for male characters, indicating that body shapes onscreen were idealistic rather than realistic (Flynn, Park, Morin, & Stana, 2015).

Last, the stereotypical portrayal of masculinity has also changed in the 21st Century. Compared to female characters, men tend to lack emotional intelligence and to demonstrate more aggression (Scharrer, 2012). In primetime television, male characters are more likely to be verbally and physically aggressive, bullies, and dominant in interactions compared to female characters (Sink & Mastro, 2017). Drawing from a sample of television adolescent-oriented shows, Roberts' (2019) content analysis of two indicators of toxic masculinity—aggression and avoidance of femininity—found that at least one of these themes occurred within 37% of scenes on adolescent television shows, showing that such portrayals are not single-case examples but rather often permeating the entire script.

Effects of Media Exposure on Gender-Based Stereotypes

A valid next question is: does media exposure to gender stereotypes reliably predict audiences' endorsement of these stereotypes? The general answer to this question is yes. For example, a recent meta-analysis revealed a link between media exposure and endorsement of gender stereotypes for both male and female children and adults observed in studies that employed both survey and experimental methods (Oppliger, 2007).

Social Cognition and Stereotype Development

To understand how media exposure helps to build stereotypes and then to activate them for use at later times, the social cognition literature offers the most cogent explanation. Social cognition reflects the cognitive underpinnings of stereotypes, including how they are formed, reinforced, and then later applied in everyday scenarios. In its most basic terms, a stereotype is a schema containing a person's knowledge, beliefs, and expectancies about members of a social group. Based on the neoassociationistic model of memory (Berkowitz, 1984), memory is a complex collection of semantic networks, with each network consisting of nodes representing thoughts, feelings, and action tendencies—all linked through associative pathways. A stereotype is composed of interconnected "nodes" representing attributes, thoughts, feelings, and behaviors with social groups, including gender. By attaching certain attributes or behaviors (e.g., nurturing, nurturance) to a certain social group (e.g., women), a stereotype is formed through the creation of links between the nodes. The encoding of stereotypes occurs through a variety of sources, including through personal experiences and through mediated exposure to portrayals of members of the social group. By repetitively portraying men and women in predictable ways (e.g., women are nurturing; men are aggressive), media exposure helps people attach certain attributes and features with men versus women. To the extent that these patterns are observed in their own lives, connections between the node of gender and gender stereotypical attributes will become even stronger. Consequently, it becomes easier for individuals to expect traits of the social group when presented with only one member of a social group. Members of a social group are expected to behave in a certain way, but if they do not, they violate people's encoded norms, which can create discomfort. For example, the stereotype of Muslim women is that they are oppressed, subdued, and deferential to men, but if they do speak their minds, such as the case with outspoken U.S. Representatives Rashida Tlaib (D-MI) and Ilhan Omar (D-MN), many will react with discomfort, disdain, sometimes even outrage, for violating the stereotype (Boustany, 2019).

The premise of priming is that when people hear, see, or read stimuli, ideas sharing similar meanings are activated for a short time afterward and are used to process subsequent stimuli (Ewoldsen & Rhodes, 2020). The activation of nodes in the network model is based on environmental input, such as media stimuli, or the spread of activation from related nodes. The ability of a media depiction to prime a certain concept in memory occurs when it exceeds an activation threshold for the concept. Some concepts will need very little provocation to become accessible; others will require a more intense (typically measured in frequency or duration) stimulus to exceed the activation threshold. Once activated, the schema can affect how we perceive subsequent stimuli; we are more likely to interpret incoming information to be congruent with activated schema. For example, activating stereotypes about gender will increase the probability that subsequent ambiguous scenarios will be judged as gender stereotypical.

Priming is conceived as a short-term media effect; as our thoughts change, so do the activated nodes in the semantic network (Ewoldsen & Rhodes, 2020). However, as certain nodes get repeatedly and frequently activated (e.g., housewife) and attached to a certain social group (e.g., women), the more likely that connection will become chronically accessible. For example, a study that tested the difference between chronic and temporary accessibility on gender stereotype activation showed that a media prime (i.e., stereotypic advertising of women as housewives) only caused participants to generate more stereotypical evaluations of an ambiguous woman when they were low in the tendency to stereotype in the first place (Johar, Moreau, & Schwarz, 2003). For those who were already high in the tendency to stereotype, the prime was redundant with their already highly accessible beliefs about women as they did not need the media to make these stereotypes temporarily accessible because they were already chronically accessible.

Thus, to review, the media have three main influences on stereotypes of social groups. First, stereotypes can be established, formed, and reinforced through media exposure. Second, the media can activate our already encoded stereotypes in the short term, which causes us to interpret incoming stimuli or situations in line with this stereotype. Third, the more that the media reinforce already existing stereotypes of a social group, the more chronically accessible the stereotype becomes. Thus, rather than focusing on the longevity of each activation, this chapter explores a more important question: how often is the stereotype of the social group activated? If people are constantly reminded of the fundamental differences between men and women, especially in ways that conform to traditional stereotypes, it will be easier for audience members to automatically and implicitly rely on their encoded stereotypes.

Empirical Research Documenting Effects of Gender-Based Stereotypes

Clearly, a comprehensive review of all media effects studies on gender-based stereotypes is beyond the scope of this chapter. In reviewing the empirical research, we focused on media effects on the four domains of stereotype that were reviewed in the previous section: occupations, gendered traits, sexualization and idealization, and masculinity.

Effects of Media Exposure on Gender-Based Beliefs about Occupations

Gender-based media portrayals about occupations are likely to at least partially inform expectations about what kinds of work are appropriate for men versus women. These stereotypes are especially salient for children and adolescents as they start to imagine themselves in the workforce. As young as fifth and sixth grade, media exposure seems to guide occupational preferences. Wroblewski and Huston (1987) found that girls who watched a greater proportion of traditional television programs and few nontraditional programs were more likely to express interest in occupations stereotyped for women on TV (e.g., secretary, model) than girls with other viewing patterns. Also, girls who watched more of the nontraditional programs were less likely to consider female-typed occupations and more likely to consider male-typed ones (e.g., private detective, insurance salesperson).

One important framework to understand the effects of gender-based stereotypes in all of these main media effects areas is stereotype threat. When persons of a stigmatized group feel that they are at threat of being reduced to a negative stereotype of their social group, the resulting disruptive state can undermine performance and aspirations in the stereotype-relevant domain (Davies, Spencer, Quinn, & Gerhardstein, 2002, see Chapter 5 for a discussion of stereotype threat in the domain of racial stereotypes). Davies and colleagues found that gender-stereotypic television ads led to outcomes in line with stereotype threat among undergraduate women. First, women for whom the activated gender stereotype was self-relevant underperformed on a subsequent math test (Davies et al., 2002). Second, exposure to the stereotypic commercials led women taking an aptitude test to avoid math items in favor of verbal items (Davies et al., 2002), to indicate less interest in quantitative educational/vocational options and more interest in verbal fields, and to express less interest in leadership tasks (Davies, Spencer, & Steele, 2005).

In response to these detrimental (albeit short-term) impacts on women, there is typically a call for more and varied media representations of women in counter-stereotypic roles, such as STEM professionals or as leaders (Geena Davis Institute on Gender in Media, 2019b). However, if women do not perceive that these counter-stereotypic role models actually disconfirm the stereotype that they are meant to contradict, there might be a boomerang effect on aspirations. For example, Hoyt and Simon (2011) found that undergraduate women's exposure to elite female leaders (e.g., Ruth Bader Ginsburg, Connie

Chung) before engaging in a leadership task reported lower levels of perceived performance, greater task difficulty, and greater feelings of inferiority compared to women exposed to outstanding male role models and those in the control condition. This was likely because these "superstar" women (p. 145) were perceived to be so elite that their successes did not make the participants' own prospects for leadership seem attainable. Indeed, a follow-up study corroborated this impact of top-level female leaders by revealing the comparatively less positive influence of these role models on leadership aspirations relative to mid-level female leaders (operationalized as people in the same careers but who were earlier in their careers).

Effects of Media Exposure on Beliefs about Feminine and Masculine Traits

Media play a significant role in the formation and reinforcement of gender norms (i.e., expectations aligned with embodying a certain gender). Thus, exposure to media that portrays women and men in gender-traditional roles reinforce the traditional norms which women and men are supposed to adhere. In childhood, the media serve to build these norms. For example, first and second graders' most-preferred TV programs were related to their beliefs about what attributes are important for men to have (Aubrey & Harrison, 2004); holding a stronger preference for male-stereotypical TV content was associated with attributing greater importance of boys' being good at telling jokes and being hardworking.

Media effects research has also examined the effects of media portrayals that simultaneously reinforce *and* subvert traditional gender roles. For example, Taylor and Setters (2011) examined the effects of exposure to female protagonists who both embody stereotypically masculine traits of aggression and assertiveness and who also conform to stereotypical conceptions of female beauty. Consistent with the "super woman" ideal in which women are expected to be highly achieving in both masculine and feminine domains, female undergraduate students who viewed clips featuring an aggressive and attractive female protagonist reported a greater endorsement of stereotypically masculine and feminine gender-role expectations for women. More specifically, compared to those who viewed the clips of aggressive heroines who were not attractive, women reported stronger feminine gender-role expectations for women after viewing the clips of aggressive and attractive heroines. Thus, the heroines violating the norm of attractiveness seemed to prime the importance of femininity. However, this presents a double-edged sword because typically women who are judged to be feminine are also more likely to be judged as incompetent (Fiske, Cuddy, Glick, & Xu, 2002). This association might explain the findings of a similar experiment in which it was found that women who played a video game from the perspective of a sexualized character (Lara Croft) reported less female self-efficacy than women who played the same game from the perspective of a non-sexualized Lara Croft (Behm-Morawitz & Mastro, 2009).

Effects of Media Exposure on Gender-Based Beliefs about Sexualization and Idealization

One of the most consistent themes of Western media is that women are val-ued primarily for their bodies, primarily existing as sexual objects for others' sexual use. In kind, both men and women who consume media saturated with such themes tend to agree with this notion that women are sexual objects (e.g., Ward & Friedman, 2006). Moreover, exposure to sexualizing media also affects self-views, as it is associated with self-objectification, the internalized view of the self as an object to be looked at by others (see Karsay, Knoll, & Matthes, 2018, for meta-analysis). This link is especially disconcerting because self-objectification is, in turn, related to a host of detrimental outcomes, including depression, eating disorders, and sexual dysfunction. Moreover, a substantial literature base supports the idea that the idealization of both male and female bodies in the media predicts the internalization of body ideals, which is related to body image disturbance (see Barlett, Vowells, & Saucier, 2008; Grabe, Ward, & Hyde, 2008, for meta-analyses). For example, early adolescents' exposure to popular tween television programs (e.g., *Big Time Rush*, *Jessie*) positively predicted the internalization of the ideals of attractive-ness, which, in turn, led to dysfunctional appearance beliefs, defined as the degree to which adolescents equate their self-worth with their physical appear-ance (Trekels & Eggermont, 2017).

In line with spreading activation, exposure to sexualization in the media can spread to other semantically-related beliefs. For example, Ward and Friedman (2006) found that adolescents who were exposed to television clips portraying the notion that women are sexual objects were more likely to endorse general gender-role stereotypes, such as "swearing is worse for a girl than a boy." Similarly, Driesmans, Vandenbosch, and Eggermont (2015) found that playing a videogame with a sexualized female character posi-tively predicted adolescents' acceptance of rape myths and tolerance for sex-ual harassment. Mainstream pornography also contains high levels of female objectification and regularly features sexually aggressive behaviors, both verbal and physical, targeting the female actors, who often respond with pleasure

(Bridges, Wosnitzer, Scharrer, Sun, & Liberman, 2010; Fritz & Paul, 2017). Consequently, pornography consumption is linked with more lax perceptions of sexual violence and rape myth acceptance (Foubert, Brosi, & Bannon, 2011; Fritz & Paul, 2017).

Effects of Media Exposure on Gender-Based Beliefs about Masculinity

Because media effects research is dominated by a focus on femininity and female stereotypes, there is a comparative dearth of research examining media influence on stereotypes of masculinity. Some recent research provides support for the idea that media exposure tends to reinforce notions of traditional masculinity. In one study, sports TV viewing and reality TV viewing were associated with stronger adherence to set of beliefs called "masculinity ideology," which includes emotional control (e.g., "I hate it when people ask me to talk about my feelings"), being a playboy (e.g., "If I could, I would frequently change sexual partners"), and heterosexual self-presentation (e.g., "I would be furious if someone thought I was gay") (Giaccardi, Ward, Seabrook, Manago, & Lippman, 2016). Another correlational study found positive relationships between reading men's lifestyle magazines, perceiving television to be generally realistic, and viewing television in order to learn about the world around them and masculinity ideology (Ward, Merriwether & Caruthers, 2006). Video games (Blackburn & Scharrer, 2019), sitcoms (Scharrer & Blackburn, 2018), crime shows, and sports programing also appear to reinforce masculine role norms.

Experimental work yields similar findings. Scharrer (2005) found that undergraduate men who were exposed to an episode of *The Sopranos*, a television show containing both violence and masculine characters, were more likely to later report agreement with two facets of hypermasculinity: danger as thrilling and violence as manly. A similar experiment based on assigning high school students to play video games that are both sexist *and* violent revealed that playing such games increased masculine beliefs, but only for male participants who were highly identified with the game characters (Gabbiadini, Riva, Andrighetto, Volpato, & Bushman, 2016). Finally, an experiment on another major characteristic of hypermasculinity—emotional stoicism—also found effects of stereotypical media portrayals (Ben-Zeev, Scharnetzki, Chan, & Dennehy, 2012). In the study, male undergraduates who were assigned to view a movie featuring a blatant representation of a male character emotionally withdrawing during a tense conversation were themselves more likely to shy away from facilitating affective communication in a subsequent task compared to a control group.

Theoretical and Methodological Directions for Future Examination

Based on our review of the content analytic and media effects literatures, we offer some future directions for media research on gender stereotypes.

Examining the Role of Counter-Stereotypes in Media Content and Audience Effects

Although we have largely focused on traditional gender stereotypes in the media, we also recognize the increased presence of counter-stereotypes, or gender portrayals that contradict traditional stereotypes (Lemish & Götz, 2017). For example, the increased presence of counter-stereotypes was demonstrated in a recent content analysis of eight popular preschool television shows that showed that characters demonstrated more counter-stereotypical emotions (e.g., men crying) than gender stereotypical emotions (e.g., men expressing anger; Martin, 2017). Another related trend is casting women in male roles, as is the case with Jodi Whittaker as the new Dr. Who or Parker Posey as Dr. Smith in Netflix's reboot of *Lost in Space*, a part played by a male actor in the original series (Nguyen, 2018). Such recasting could challenge viewers to reimagine the gender roles and dynamics of the narrative universe, though this has not been empirically tested, to our knowledge. Results across content analyses of counter-stereotypes are promising; it is nevertheless important to note that television shows that feature counter-stereotypes are more likely to be designed by independent and non-commercial producers and are more likely to appear in specific genres (e.g., children's shows, Lemish & Götz, 2017). Thus, these counter-stereotypical portrayals are more likely "exceptions" than "standards" (Reinhard, Olson, & Kahlenberg, 2017, p. 8).

Nevertheless, as we have argued that media exposure tends to support a belief system of traditional gender roles, it must follow that exposure to media content that is counter-stereotypical will facilitate the acceptance of nontraditional gender norms. After all, based on the social cognition literature, it is a matter of re-wiring associations between nodes so that the stereotypical links get weakened or are never connected in the first place. Research supports this idea in the STEM literature. Ziegler and Stoeger (2008) assigned German high school students to one of three conditions: a film that featured a female role model who conformed to typically feminine characteristics but was not talented at math/science, a film that featured a female role model who did not conform to typically feminine characteristics but was talented at math/science, and a film that featured a female character who was typically feminine and who was talented at math/science. The results suggested that the condition in which the female scientist was portrayed as talented *and* feminine was the most effective among boys and girls who had a high prior interest in math/science. However, among girls who had a low prior interest in math/science, watching either film of the female scientist depressed assessments of their abilities and their intent to pursue math or science.

In light of these findings, it is important to recognize the nuance required for effective counter-stereotypes in the media. The Ziegler and Stoeger (2008) study reminds us that counter-stereotypical portrayals will not be effective if they completely and strongly disconfirm all stereotypical aspects of the social group. Thus, for women, being attractive (i.e., a valued aspect of femininity) but also counter-stereotypical in some other way, such as exhibiting aggressive behavior (Taylor & Setters, 2011) or success in a STEM career (Ziegler & Stoeger, 2008), will likely be more influential to audience members' acceptance of counter-stereotypes than an exemplar that rejects all aspects of femininity. Also, as the Hoyt and Simon (2011) study suggested, it is important to consider the attainability of the counter-stereotype. If the viewer views the counter-stereotypical character as a superstar, that will likely have a deflating effect on the viewer. Thus, female role models who are perceived to "have it all," with perfect careers, family lives, and looks, might not be the best antidote to gender stereotypes. In contrast, if the idea is to inspire the viewer to assimilate to counter-stereotypes, successes must seem attainable.

A Focus on Female Production

Another focus for future research would be an increased attention on who is creating the media content. Perhaps the most reliable way to combat gender stereotypes in the media is to promote more gender diversity in the production of media messages. Women have traditionally been sorely underrepresented in behind-the-scenes production roles of entertainment media. For example, Glascock (2001) found that the disparity between male and female creative personnel, such as producers, directors, writers and creators, was 3.6 to 1. This disparity matters because there is a link between having more women in key decision-making roles on production crews and having more women in the cast. Having a woman director and at least one woman on the writing team produces more female leads, more female characters, and more dialogue for these characters (Lauzen, 2019; Lauzen & Dozier, 1999). Thus, it is imperative for content analyses to not only track the gender stereotypes within media content, but also to relate the portrayals of stereotypes to the representation of gender in media production (see Smith et al., 2016 for an example). Perhaps the findings of these studies will inspire production companies to make concerted efforts to re-balance the number of women placed in creative production roles. For example, the Oprah Winfrey Network's *Queen Sugar* is said to be the first television series in which each episode is helmed by a female director and in which gender parity was achieved with the full production crew (Patten, 2020).

Conclusion

This brings us back to the beginning—to the inclusion rider and other policies and initiatives that encourage behind-the-scenes gender parity in the media industry. As we have seen in this chapter, there has been some progress in gender stereotypes since the start of the 21st Century, but there is still a long way to go. Perhaps the next big step in progress will occur if (or when) women achieve balance in the creative and production roles behind the camera.

References

Aubrey, J. S., & Frisby, C. (2011). Sexual objectification in music videos: A content analysis comparing gender and genre. *Mass Communication & Society*, *14*, 475–501. doi: 10.1080/15205436.2010.513468

Aubrey, J. S., & Harrison, K. (2004). The gender-role content of children's favorite television programs and its links to their gender-related perceptions. *Media Psychology*, *6*, 111–146. doi:10.1207/s1532785xmep0602_1

Barlett, C., Vowels, C., & Saucier, D. (2008). Meta-analyses of the effects of media images on men's body-image concerns. *Journal of Social and Clinical Psychology*, *27*, 279–310. doi: 10.1521/jscp.2008.27.3.279

Behm-Morawitz, E., & Mastro, D. (2009). The effects of the sexualization of female video game characters on gender stereotyping and female self-concept. *Sex Roles*, *61*, 808–823. doi: 10.1007/s11199-009-9683-8

Ben-Zeev, A., Scharnetzki, L., Chan, L., & Dennehy, T. (2012). Hypermasculinity in the media: When men "walk into the fog" to avoid affective communication. *Psychology of Popular Media Culture*, *1*, 53–61. doi: 10.1037/a0027099

Berkowitz, L. (1984). Some effects on thought on anti- and prosocial influence of media events: A cognitive-neoassociationistic analysis. *Psychological Bulletin*, *95*, 410–427. doi: 10.1037/0033-2909.95.3.410

Blackburn, G., & Scharrer, E. (2019). Video game playing and beliefs about masculinity among male and female emerging adults. *Sex Roles, 80*(5–6), 310–324. doi: 10.1007/s11199-018-0934-4

Boustany, N. (2019, May 16). Rep. Tlaib and Omar challenge the trope of modest Muslim women. *Washington Post.* Retrieved from https://www.washingtonpost.com/nation/2019/05/16/reps-tlaib-omar-challenge-trope-modest-muslim-women/.

Bridges, A. J., Wosnitzer, R., Scharrer, E., Sun, C., & Liberman, R. (2010). Aggression and sexual behavior in best-selling pornography videos: A content analysis update. *Violence against Women, 16,* 1065–1085. doi: 10.1177/1077801210382866

Cooper, V. W. (1985). Women in popular music: A quantitative analysis of feminine images over time. *Sex Roles, 13,* 499–506. doi: 10.1007/BF00287756

Courtney, A. E., & Lockeretz, S. W. (1971). A woman's place: An analysis of the roles portrayed by women in magazine advertisements. *Journal of Marketing Research, 8,* 92–95. doi: 10.1177/002224377100800114

Davies, P. G., Spencer, S. J., Quinn, D. M., & Gerhardstein, R. (2002). Consuming images: How television commercials that elicit stereotype threat can restrain women academically and professionally. *Personality and Social Psychology Bulletin, 28,* 1615–1628. doi: 10.1177/014616702237644

Davies, P., Spencer, S., & Steele, C. (2005). Clearing the air: Identity safety moderates the effects of stereotype threat on women's leadership aspirations. *Journal of Personality and Social Psychology, 88,* 276–287. doi: 10.1037/0022-3514.88.2.276

Davis, D. M. (1990). Portrayals of women in prime-time network television: Some demographic characteristics. *Sex Roles, 23,* 325–332. doi: 10.1007/BF00290052

Driesmans, K., Vandenbosch, L., & Eggermont, S. (2015). Playing a videogame with a sexualized female character increases adolescents' rape myth acceptance and tolerance toward sexual harassment. *Games for Health Journal, 4,* 91–94. doi: 10.1089/g4h.2014.0055

Elasmar, M., Hasegawa, K., & Brain, M. (1999). The portrayal of women in U.S. prime time television. *Journal of Broadcasting & Electronic Media, 43,* 20–24. doi: 10.1080/08838159909364472

Ewoldsen, D. R., & Rhodes, N. (2020). Media priming and accessibility. In M. B. Oliver, A. A. Raney, & J. Bryant (Eds.), *Media effects: Advances in theory and research* (4th ed., pp. 83–99). New York, NY: Taylor & Francis.

Fiske, S., Cuddy, A., Glick, P., & Xu, J. (2002). A model of (often mixed) stereotype content: Competence and warmth respectively follow from perceived status and competition. *Journal of Personality and Social Psychology, 82,* 878–902. doi: 10.1037//0022-3514.82.6.87

Flynn, M. A., Park, S. Y., Morin, D. T., & Stana, A. (2015). Anything but real: Body idealization and objectification of MTV docusoap characters. *Sex Roles, 72,* 173–182. doi: 10.1007/s11199-015-0464-2

Foubert, J. D., Brosi, M. W., & Bannon, R. S. (2011). Pornography viewing among fraternity men: Effects of bystander intervention, rape myth acceptance and behavioral

intent to commit sexual assault. *Sexual Addiction & Compulsivity, 18*, 212–231. doi:1
    0.1080/10720162.2011.625552

Fowler, K., & Thomas, V. (2015). A content analysis of male roles in television advertis-
    ing: Do traditional roles still hold? *Journal of Marketing Communications, 21*, 356–
    371. doi: 10.1080/13527266.2013.775178

Fritz, N., & Paul, B. (2017). From orgasms to spanking: A content analysis of the agentic
    and objectifying sexual scripts in feminist, for women, and mainstream pornography.
    Sex Roles, 77, 639–652. doi: 10.1007/s11199-017-0759-6

Gabbiadini, A., Riva, P., Andrighetto, L., Volpato, C., & Bushman, B. J. (2016). Acting
    like a tough guy: Violent-sexist video games, identification with game characters, mas-
    culine beliefs, & empathy for female violence victims. *PLoS ONE, 11*(4), e0152121.
    doi: 10.1371/journal.pone.0152121

Geena Davis Institute on Gender in Media. (2019a). The Geena benchmark report,
    2007–2017. Retrieved from https://seejane.org/research-informs-empowers/
    the-geena-benchmark-report-2007-2017/.

Geena Davis Institute on Gender in Media. (2019b). Rewrite her story: How film and
    media stereotypes affect lives and leadership ambitions of girls and young women.
    Retrieved from https://seejane.org/research-informs-empowers/rewrite-her-story/.

Giaccardi, S., Ward, L. M., Seabrook, R., Manago, A., & Lippman, J. (2016). Media and
    modern manhood: Testing associations between media consumption and young men's
    acceptance of traditional gender ideologies. *Sex Roles, 75*, 151–163. doi: 10.1007/
    s11199-016-0588-z

Gilpatric, K. (2010). Violent female action characters in contemporary American cinema.
    Sex Roles, 62, 734–746. doi: 0.1007/s11199-010-9757-7

Glascock, J. (2001). Gender roles on prime-time network television: Demographics and
    behaviors. *Journal of Broadcasting & Electronic Media, 45*, 656–669. doi: 10.1207/
    s15506878jobem4504_7

Grabe, S., Ward, L., & Hyde, J. (2008). The role of the media in body image concerns
    among women: A meta-analysis of experimental and correlational studies. *Psychological
    Bulletin, 134*, 460–476. doi: 10.1037/0033-2909.134.3.460

Greenberg, B. S. (1980). *Life on television: Content analyses of U.S. drama.* Norwood,
    NJ: Ablex.

Greenberg, B. S., & Collette, L. (1997). The changing faces on TV: A demographic analysis
    of network television's new seasons, 1966–1992. *Journal of Broadcasting & Electronic
    Media, 41*, 1–13. doi: 10.1080/08838159709364386

Hatzithomas, L., Boutsouki, C., & Ziamou, P. (2016). A longitudinal analysis of the
    changing roles of gender in advertising: A content analysis of Super Bowl commer-
    cials. *International Journal of Advertising, 35*, 888–906. doi: 10.1080/02650487.2
    016.1162344

Head, S. (1954). Content analysis of television drama programs. *Quarterly Journal of Film,
    Radio, and Television, 9*, 175–194. doi: 10.1525/fq.1954.9.2.04a00080

Hoyt, C., & Simon, S. (2011). Female leaders: Injurious or inspiring role models for women. *Psychology of Women Quarterly, 35,* 143–157. doi: 10.1177/0361684310385216

Hust, S. J. T., & Brown, J. D. (2008). Gender, media use, and effects. In Calvert, S. L. & Wilson, B. J. (Eds.), *The handbook of children, media, and development* (pp. 98–120). Malden, MA: Blackwell.

Johar, G. V., Moreau, P., & Schwarz, N. (2003). Gender typed advertisements and impression formation: The role of chronic and temporary accessibility. *Journal of Consumer Psychology, 13,* 220–229. doi: 10.1207/S15327663JCP1303_04

Jones, D. (1942). Quantitative analysis of motion picture content. *The Public Opinion Quarterly, 6,* 411–428.

Karsay, K., Knoll, J., & Matthes, J. (2018). Sexualizing media use and self-objectification: A meta-analysis. *Psychology of Women Quarterly, 42,* 9–28. doi: 10.1177/0361684317743019

Karsay, K., Matthes, J., Buchsteiner, L., & Grosser, V. (2019). Increasingly sexy? Sexuality and sexual objectification in popular music videos, 1995–2016. *Psychology of Popular Media Culture, 8,* 346–357. doi: 10.1037/ppm0000221

Kilkenny, K. (2018, March 4). What is an inclusion rider? Frances McDormand's Oscars speech explained. *The Hollywood Reporter.* Retrieved from https://www.hollywoodreporter.com/news/what-is-an-inclusion-rider-frances-mcdormands-oscars-speech-explained-1091532.

Lauzen, M. (2019). *The celluloid ceiling: Behind-the-scenes employment of women on the top 100, 250, and 500 films of 2018.* Center for the Study of Women in Television and Film, San Diego, CA. Retrieved from womenintvfilm.sdsu.edu/wp-content/uploads/2019/01/2018_Celluloid_Ceiling_Report.pdf.

Lauzen, M. M., & Dozier, D. M. (1999). Making a difference in prime time: Women on screen and behind the scenes in the 1995–96 television season. *Journal of Broadcasting & Electronic Media, 43,* 1–19. doi: 10.1080/08838159909364471

Lemish, D., & Götz, M. (2017). *Beyond the stereotypes? Images of boys and girls, and their consequences. The international clearinghouse on children, youth and media, yearbook 2017.* Gothenburg, Sweden: Nordicom.

Long, M., Steinke, J., Applegate, B., Lapinski, M. K., Johnson, M. J., & Ghosh, S. (2010). Portrayals of male and female scientists in television programs popular among middle school-age children. *Science Communication, 32,* 356–382. doi: 10.1177/1075547009357779

Lotz, A. D. (2014). *Cable guys: Television and masculinities in the 21st century.* New York: New York University Press.

Lynch, T., Tompkins, J., Van Driel, I., & Fritz, N. (2016). Sexy, strong, and secondary: A content analysis of female characters in video games across 31 years. *Journal of Communication, 66,* 564–584. doi: 10.1111/jcom.12237

Martin, R. (2017). Gender and emotion stereotypes in children's television. *Journal of Broadcasting & Electronic Media, 61*, 499–517. doi: 10.1080/08838151.2017.1344667

McNeil, J. C. (1975). Feminism, femininity, and the television series: A content analysis. *Journal of Broadcasting, 19*, 259–269. doi: 10.1080/08838157509363786

Nguyen, H. (2018, April 18). Gender flipping on TV: What's gained when a male character is reimagined as female. *Indiewire*. Retrieved from https://www.indiewire.com/2018/04/gender-swap-lost-in-space-elementary-male-to-female-1201954385/.

Oppliger, P. A. (2007). Effects of gender stereotyping on socialization. In R. W. Preiss, B. M. Gayle, N. Burrell, M. Allen, & J. Bryant (Eds.), *Mass media effects research: Advances through meta-analysis* (pp. 199–214). Mahwah, NJ: Lawrence Erlbaum Associates.

Paff, J. L., & Lakner, H. B. (1997). Dress and the female gender role in magazine advertisements of 1950–1994: A content analysis. *Family and Consumer Sciences Research Journal, 26*, 29–58. doi: 10.1177/1077727X970261002

Patten, D. (2020, January 16). Ava DuVernay's 'Cherish the Day' series sets OWN debut dates; Drops final trailer with some Sade. *Deadline*. Retrieved from https://deadline.com/video/ava-duvernay-cherish-the-day-premiere-date-new-trailer-oprah-cicely-tyson-xosha-roquemore-alano-miller-own/.

Reinhard, C. D., Olson, C. J., & Kahlenberg, S. G. (2017). Looking past stereotypes of gender identity and sexuality in children's media. In C. D. Reinhard & C. J. Olson (Eds.), *Heroes, heroines, and everything in between: Challenging gender and sexuality stereotypes in children's entertainment media*. London, UK: Lexington.

Roberts, L. (2019). *Masculinity is for the boys: A content analysis of toxic masculinity on television* (Unpublished master's thesis). University of Arizona, Tucson, AZ.

Scharrer, E. (2005). Hypermasculinity, aggression, and television violence: An experiment. *Media Psychology, 7*, 353–376. doi: 10.1207/S1532785XMEP0704_3

Scharrer, E. (2012). More than "just the facts"?: Portrayals of masculinity in police and detective programs over time. *Howard Journal of Communications, 23*, 88–109. doi: 10.1080/10646175.2012.641882

Scharrer, E., & Blackburn, G. (2018). Cultivating conceptions of masculinity: Television and perceptions of masculine gender role norms. *Mass Communication and Society, 21*(2), 149–177. doi: 10.1080/15205436.2017.1406118

Sink, A., & Mastro, D. (2017). Depictions of gender on primetime television: A quantitative content analysis. *Mass Communication and Society, 20*, 3–22. doi: 10.1080/15205436.2016.1212243

Smith, S. (2014, December 15). Hey, Hollywood: It's time to adopt the NFL's Rooney rule—For women. *The Hollywood Reporter*. Retrieved from https://www.hollywoodreporter.com/news/hey-hollywood-time-adopt-nfls-754659.

Smith, S. L., Choueiti, M., & Pieper, K. (2016, September). *Inequality in 800 popular films: Examining portrayals of gender, race/ethnicity, LGBT, and disability from 2007–2015*. Los Angeles, CA: Annenberg Foundation. Retrieved from https://

annenberg.usc.edu/sites/default/files/2017/04/10/MDSCI_Inequality_in_800_Films_FINAL.pdf.

Taylor, L., & Setters, D. (2011). Watching aggressive, attractive, female protagonists shapes gender roles for women among male and female undergraduate viewers. *Sex Roles, 65*, 35–46. doi: 10.1007/s11199-011-9960-1

Thompson, T. L., & Zerbinos, E. (1995). Gender roles in animated cartoons: Has the picture changed in 20 years? *Sex Roles, 32*, 651–673. doi: 10.1007/BF01544217

Trekels, J., & Eggermont, S. (2017). Beauty is good: The appearance culture, the internalization of appearance ideals, and dysfunctional beliefs among tweens. *Human Communication Research, 43*, 173–192. doi: 10.1111/hcre.12100

U.S. Census Bureau. (2015). Age and sex composition in the United States: 2015. Retrieved from https://www.census.gov/data/tables/2015/demo/age-and-sex/2015-age-sex-composition.html.

Vande Berg, L. R. (1991). Using television to teach courses in gender and communication. *Communication Education, 40*, 105–111. doi: 10.1080/03634529109378830

Ward, L., Merriwether, M., & Caruthers, A. (2006). Breasts are for men: Media, masculinity ideologies, and men's beliefs about women's bodies. *Sex Roles, 55*(9–10), 703–714. doi: 10.1007/s11199-006-9125-9

Ward, L. M., & Friedman, K. (2006). Using TV as a guide: Associations between television viewing and adolescents' sexual attitudes and behavior. *Journal of Research on Adolescence, 16*, 133–156. doi: 10.1111/j.1532-7795.2006.00125.x

Wroblewski, R., & Huston, A. C. (1987). Televised occupational stereotypes and their effects on early adolescents: Are they changing? *Journal of Early Adolescence, 7*, 283–297. doi: 10.1177/0272431687073005

Ziegler, A., & Stoeger, H. (2008). Effects of role models from films on short-term ratings of intent, interest, and self-assessment of ability by high school youth: A study of gender-stereotyped academic subjects. *Psychological Reports, 102*, 509–531. doi: 10.2466/pr0.102.2.509-531

5 Black Stereotypes in the Media: A Continuing Problem

KRISTOPHER R. WEEKS
University of Illinois at Urbana-Champaign

TRAVIS L. DIXON
University of Illinois at Urbana-Champaign

AMANDA N. TOLBERT
University of Illinois at Urbana-Champaign

MELINDA SEVILLA
University of Illinois at Urbana-Champaign

Understanding how media affects audiences' perceptions of Black people requires first recognizing that media's ubiquity obscures reality. Gerbner and Gross's (1976) cultivation theory posits heavy exposure to media influences a person's reality perceptions over time. The theory gained popularity in the Communication field (Bryant & Miron, 2004), and the concerns it raised in the 1970s remain to this day (Busselle & Van den Bulk, 2020). Mastro (2015) calls our attention to media's continued role in influencing socio-political perceptions of race and ethnicity: "... it may be difficult for audience members to even recognize the influence of exposure on perceptions of reality" (p. 3).

Race and media scholars seek to understand how media influences audience members' cognitions, attitudes, and behaviors toward Black people. Some scholars borrow inspiration from social identity theory (Tajfel & Turner, 1979, 1986). In the race and media context, the theory suggests audiences compare their racial group to other racial groups based in part on what they see in media. Audience members focus on media depictions that portray their own racial groups in a positive light and other racial groups in a negative light to enhance self-esteem. Other scholars reference prevalent ethnic blame discourses in media. These discourses insinuate minorities are at fault for their own circumstances and society's problems (Dixon & Williams, 2015; Romer,

Jamieson, Riegner, Emori, & Rouson, 1997, p. 24). Both theoretical perspectives suggest stereotypical portrayals exacerbate the gap between racial ingroups and outgroups.

Heightened racial tensions within the United States in the past decade suggest that we need to examine the current race and media literature. This chapter provides a review of the quantitative social scientific literature regarding the dissemination and impact of Black stereotypes. Although a few Black stereotypes subsided, Black representations in many media platforms remain largely problematic. In this chapter, we outline current research in race and media. The first section discusses improvements in Black representation. The second section addresses the current problems in Black representation. The third section summarizes how Black (mis)representation affects audiences. The last section offers suggestions for future research.

Black Stereotype Diminishment

Unlike chapter 14's focus on overt positive stereotypes in media, this chapter addresses the extent to which negative Black stereotypes in media have diminished. We first discuss prime-time television's generally improved portrayal of Black characters and then follow with a description of more balanced criminal depictions.

Improved Prime-Time Entertainment Television Representation

Ongoing research suggests Black stereotypes' prevalence varies by media platform. In this section, we focus on where Black representations appear to be improving. Some areas demonstrate only minor improvement. However, identifying these areas allows us to recognize the platforms in need of reform.

Content analyses determined Black people appear in a moderately positive light on primetime national television. Tukachinsky, Mastro, and Yarchi (2015) determined a marked increase in generally positive depictions occurred between 2003–2005. Signorielli (2009) found that, between 2000–2008, Black men and women were represented at a proportional rate to their respective populations in the United States. However, Black people most often appeared in situation comedies. This finding suggests Black characters often assume satirical roles, limiting Black character respectability.

Monk-Turner and colleagues' (2010) analysis of prime-time television assessed social indicators related to success and acceptable behavior. Whereas 52% of Black people appeared smart, only 43% of White people appeared smart. Yet, 15% of Black people were rated as dumb, and less than 4% of White people received the same rating. Although Black characters have a higher chance of exhibiting above average and below average intelligence, White characters are likelier to exhibit average intelligence. In addition, while 67% of Black characters lived middle-income lives, 74% of White characters lived the same life. Furthermore, no significant difference was found between Black, White, and Latino aggression and laziness levels. In addition, Tukachinsky et al. (2015) found that, from 1988–2008, 55% of Black characters assumed a highly professional status. The researchers also determined almost 77% of Black characters displayed likable qualities.

Research also examined the sexualization of Black people on television. One study found hyper-sexual depictions occurred much less frequently in Black (7.6%) than Latino portrayals (24.1%; Monk-Turner, Heiserman, Johnson, Cotton, & Jackson, 2010). This finding coincides with research that assessed racial differences in primetime advertising. Messineo (2008) discovered that, in 2002, Black characters appeared in marital relationships more often on mainstream network broadcasts than on the Black Entertainment Television (BET) channel. Mainstream advertisements sexually objectified Black characters much less often than BET advertisements. The researchers reference Collin's (1991) explanation for this phenomenon. BET's founders did not seek to influence social norms or political policies. From a macro-structural perspective, given the media industry's capitalistic motives and tendency to protect the dominant majority, BET opted to sexualize Black women to both generate profit and avoid conflict with media's dominant forces. Yet, ironically, these depictions reinforce the notion that Black women are sexually desirable and worthy of romantic engagement in a White-dominated society (Alexander, 1999).

Mentioned later on, media often overlook the impoverished Black elderly, but advertisers also recognize the spending power of the non-impoverished Black elderly. Brooks, Bichard, and Craig (2016) analyzed the frequency of mature adult depictions in Super Bowl commercials spanning 2010–2014. Although only 1% of mature characters were Asian or Hispanic, 12% were Black.

Signs of Balanced Crime Depictions

Depictions that associate Black people with crime and violence marginalize the Black population. Within this context, some signs of improvement exist, but first, consider Dixon and Linz's (2000a) analysis of local television news programs from 1995 to 1996 aired in Southern California (Dixon & Linz, 2000a). Black perpetrators were depicted more often than Black police officers and White perpetrators were depicted less often than White police officers. In other words, while Black people appeared to disrupt law and order,

White people appeared to maintain it. However, when compared to data published by the California Department of Justice (California Department of Justice, 1998a, 1998b), the actual Black arrest rate (21%) was significantly lower than the rate at which they were depicted as perpetrators in local news (37%). Conversely, the actual White arrest rate (28%) was higher than the rate they were depicted as perpetrators in local news (21%). Furthermore, in felony cases, Black perpetrators were depicted at 2.46 times the rate of White perpetrators.

Dixon (2017b) replicated the study and assessed local television news content from 2008–2012. The study did not find a significant difference between the rate of reported Black arrests and rate of depicted Black perpetrators in news. It also found the rate of Black officers in service matched the rate of Black officer depictions. However, local news overrepresented White officers. Such overrepresentation implies White people still assume the most responsibility for maintaining law and order.

Even so, a closer examination suggests the law and order frame does not dominate crime news. Potterf and Pohl (2018) analyzed 23 national newspapers to determine how news media framed the context of Michael Brown's death in Ferguson, Missouri. The study compared the occurrence of law and order narratives that supported law enforcement to the occurrence of social justice narratives that supported the victims. While 21.4% of the stories utilized a law and order frame, 50% utilized a social justice frame. The study did not compare these findings to news coverage of a nationally recognized White victim of a police shooting. However, Dixon and Linz (2000b) found local news in Los Angeles and Orange counties depicted Black homicide victims at an accurate rate. These findings suggest Black victimization receives reasonable attention.

Crime fiction on television also exhibits a potential shift toward racially balanced crime depictions. Parrott and Parrott's (2015) analysis of fictional television crime programming from 2010–2013 found Black male characters were no more likely than White male characters to perpetrate a violent act. However, White women were more likely to be victimized at a greater rate than White men, Black women, and Black men. Hence, while Black victims might receive reasonable attention, they may not receive attention comparable to White women.

Although some media arenas publish accurate and respectable Black depictions, they may simultaneously depict White people in an overly positive manner. Hence, gaps between Black and White depictions persist. The following section presents evidence that, despite the accurate and respectable

Black depictions discussed in this section, other problematic Black depictions remain.

Problematic Representations

We have identified a number of problematic representations that persist despite the progress noted above. There continues to be problems of aggression and crime. There are numerous "dumb" athlete stereotypes promoted in the media. Persistent stereotypes of Black poverty and gendered portrayals remain. We elaborate below.

Aggression and Crime

Glascock and Preston-Schreck's (2018) focus on primetime reality television programming in 2013 uncovers a telling pattern regarding verbal aggression. Male and female Black characters were overrepresented as verbal aggressors and victims of verbal aggression when compared to other racial and ethnic groups. Such depictions endorse the notion that Black people are threatening and irrational. Furthermore, these depictions suggest that, to interact with Black people, one must also engage in threatening and irrational acts. The study also found Black women were most likely to assume both aggressor and victim roles, obscuring the difference between Black female independence and Black female aggression.

Recent news depictions also tie Black families to criminal behavior. Dixon (2017a) investigated Black family depictions in news across national newspapers, cable television news networks, and national broadcast news programming. The study analyzed news stories that identified perpetrators' relationship to their families. Of those criminals depicted, 37% were Black family members. However, when compared to FBI crime data (U.S. Department of Justice, 2015), Black people account for only 26% of arrests. In comparison, White family members accounted for 28% of depicted perpetrators. But, in actuality, White people accounted for 67% of arrests. The study suggests news sources depict Black families as sources of social instability and White families as sources of social stability. In other words, while White families appear to meet social ideals, Black families appear to fit the broken home stereotype.

Mastro, Blecha, and Atwell Seate (2011) investigated news articles regarding criminal athletes from *The Los Angeles Times, The New York Times,* and *USA Today* from 2005 to 2007. The proportion of Black criminal athletes depicted in these newspapers exceeded the proportion of Black athletes in their respective sports. These newspapers also provided higher levels of explicit details about the crime for Black criminals than for White criminals. Furthermore, in comparison to White athlete criminal stories, the newspapers were more accusatory toward Black athlete criminals, used a respectful tone less often, and situated their crimes in broader social contexts (known as thematic framing; see Iyengar, 1991) less often. In other words, these newspapers suggested White athletes were less responsible for their crimes than Black athletes. In addition, news stories adopted a supportive narrative for victims of Black athlete crime more often than for victims of White athlete crime.

Physically Strong, but Unwise Athletes

Beyond criminal stereotypes, media depict Black athletes in other problematic ways. Quick, Lambert, and Josey (2016) studied television news programming coverage of Major League Baseball (MLB) steroid scandals. All players studied generally received negative coverage. However, Mark McGuire, a White player, received the most favorable coverage, including references to steroid use for rehabilitative purposes. Barry Bonds, a Black player, received the least sympathetic coverage. The authors suggest news producers stereotyped Bonds as having natural physical talent and strength (see also Billings, 2004; Rada & Wulfemeyer, 2005). Therefore, Bonds's steroid use was reprehensible because it enhanced his perceived natural advantage.

Rada and Wulfemeyer (2005) also determined sports media invoke the natural advantage stereotype. An analysis of announcer commentary during the NCAA Division 1-A football season in 1998 and March Madness season in 1999 found Black athletes received more positive comments about their physical attributes than White athletes. In addition, Byrd and Ustler (2007) found *Sports Illustrated*, from 2002–2004, referenced Black quarterbacks' positive physical qualities 66 times and negative physical qualities three times. In comparison, the magazine referenced White quarterbacks' positive physical qualities 19 times and negative physical qualities 7 times. Mercurio and Filak (2010) found, from 1998 to 2007, *Sports Illustrated* generally characterized Black NFL quarterback draftees as physically capable and their White counterparts as unathletic.

Otherwise, White athletes generally receive more positive comments and less negative comments than Black athletes. In Rada and Wulfemeyer's (2005) study, White athletes received compliments about their character and intellect more than Black athletes. Also, Black athletes received more criticism about their intelligence. Announcers referenced positive White personal interest stories more often than Black personal interest stories. Negative interest stories were referenced more often for Black athletes than White athletes. In Mercurio and Filak's (2010) *Sports Illustrated* study, intelligence and strong mental ability were attributed to White quarterbacks. Black quarterbacks were depicted as lacking intelligence. Angelini, Billings, MacArthur, Bissell, and Smith (2014) found NBC commentators for the 2012 London Olympic games offered more positive comments about White athlete intellect than Black athlete intellect. Interestingly, these researchers also found White Olympic athletes received both more positive comments and negative comments about their physical ability than Black Olympic athletes. Black athletes received both more positive and negative comments about their athlete experience level than White athletes. In this context, the commentators' narratives suggest audience members should pay close attention to White athletes' ability to overcome their physical barriers and Black athletes' ability to overcome decision-making problems.

Butterworth (2007) critically analyzed sports news stories that tracked the MLB home-run race between Mark McGuire and Sammy Sosa, a Dominican, in 1998. Although Latino, Sosa was characterized as a happy coon, likely due to his dark skin. The happy coon Black stereotype refers to a humorously inane man (Jackson, 2006). While McGuire was described as a prototypical American hero, Sosa was considered McGuire's sidekick who was "just happy to be along for the ride" (Butterworth, 2007, p. 238).

Indeed, there are instances when Black and White athletes receive equivalently favorable treatment. However, other problems may undergird these situations. Lewis, Bell, Billings, and Brown (2020) analyzed ESPN's coverage of National Signing Day (NSD), a player recruitment event for college football teams, from 2015–2018. The researchers compared the frequency of comments Black and White players received based on four variables: athletic success, athletic failure, personality, and physicality. No significant difference was found across these variables. However, White sportscasters voiced 98% of all comments and 86.4% of comments about Black athletes. Also, the commentators generally did not describe the Black athletes in counter-stereotypical ways. The commentators rarely mentioned intelligence. In addition, while White athletes received run-of-the-mill compliments about their physicality, "... Black athletes were referenced as a 'beast of an athlete,' 'road-grader,' 'different animal,' and bell cow" (Lewis et al., 2020, p. 9).

Still Poor

Media also tend to misrepresent Black poverty. Gilens (1996) conducted a content analysis on major US news magazine images published from 1988 to 1992 to assess how media represent Black poverty. During this timeframe, 28% of people depicted as poor were Black. However, the study determined that in about 62% of cases where a picture associated a person with poverty, the person was Black. Not only were Black people overrepresented as poor, they were also disproportionately cast in unsympathetic roles. For example, the Black elderly poor, a sympathetic group, constituted less than 1% of the depictions found by the study. Yet, during this time, the Black elderly poor constituted 11% of the overall poor population. Although depicted as the poor majority, only 40% of employment programs and 17% of Medicaid ads depicted Black people. Readers may correlate poverty with Black people, yet not associate jobs programs with Black people.

One might wonder if these depictions improved after the 1996 Welfare Reform Act. Van Doorn (2015) analyzed stories on poverty from *Time, Newsweek* and *U.S. News and World Report* published from 1992 to 2010 to determine if welfare reform efforts during the 1990s influenced media's general Black poverty narrative. Overall, 52% of people associated with poverty were Black, indicating a minor shift toward an accurate depiction of Black poverty. However, an exaggerated narrative of Black welfare dependence persisted, suggesting welfare reform did not influence media's reporting habits. Nevertheless, during times of economic prosperity, Black people (56%) were associated with welfare more often than White people (33%). Conversely, during times of economic decline, 53% of cases comprised White depictions and 34% comprised Black depictions. The Black elderly were rarely mentioned in both scenarios. Within the family context, Dixon (2017a) found both newspapers and national news television reports overrepresent Black families (59% of depicted poor families reported; 27% of actual poor families are Black) and underrepresent White families (17% of depicted poor families reported; 66% of actual poor families are White).

Gender and Sexuality

Generally, music videos objectify women. Frisby and Aubrey (2012) analyzed music videos of the top ten songs on Billboard's "Hot 100" list from 2007–2008. Female artists reveal more body parts, dress more provocatively, engage in sexually suggestive dances, and appear more attractive than male artists. In the R&B and hip-hop genres, generally associated with people of color, women cast as extras were more likely to engage in sexually suggestive dance and serve as visual decoration than pop and country genres.

A follow-up study analyzed the top ten "Hot 100" songs from 2006–2010 (Frisby & Aubrey, 2012). Only lead female artist music videos were analyzed. Black women dressed provocatively more often than White women. However, sexualized dance occurrences in R & B and hip-hop music videos did not significantly differ from pop or country videos. Although Black women remained sexually objectified in music videos more often than White women, this difference subsided when only comparing lead artists.

Researchers argue advertisers favor Eurocentric features. Baker (2005) found that in both Black-oriented and White-oriented magazines, Black women most often sported straight hair. Furthermore, in White-oriented magazines, Black women were more likely to have light skin tone than dark skin tone and more likely to have a thin figure than a curvy figure. Also, in an analysis of fitness, fashion, and sexually themed magazines from 2011–2012, Schug, Alt, Lu, Gosin, and Fay (2017) found Black women underrepresented in these outlets. These patterns suggest magazines and advertisers believe White and Asian women better represent fitness, fashion, and sexual themes than Black women.

Some research also addresses non-heterosexual Black depictions. Paceley and Flynn (2012) found the racial depiction rate of LGBT victims of bullying in mainstream news vastly overrepresented the White (94.4%) and male (96.7%) population. Only 3% of unique bullying victims were transgender. Hence, while news outlets occasionally recognized Black victims and female victims, White male victims received repeated coverage, pushing the other groups into obscurity. In male gay-oriented blogs, Grimm and Schwartz (2017) found that Black men appeared more muscular than any other racial group, suggesting a hypermasculine standard of Black gay male beauty. These hypermasculine depictions may make it difficult for readers to imagine Black gay males as bullying victims.

Media often undermine the idea that Black men successfully execute social leadership roles. Across two studies, Bailey (2006) observed, in both Black-oriented and White-oriented magazines, advertisements most often associated Black men with clothing, shoes, and accessories. In the first study, within magazines that targeted Black youth (*The Source, Vibe, and XXL*), 75.2% of Black males were associated with these products. In the second study, within magazines that appeal to a mainstream audience (*Ebony, Essence, GQ, and SPIN*), 17.4% of Black male depictions occurred in context to the aforementioned products. The authors suggest ads tailored to Black youth do not promote Black male leadership. Additionally, Dixon (2017a) found mainstream news across major newspapers and television news programs overrepresented the frequency of Black father absenteeism (or unavailability). Thus, stereotypes associated with Black male irresponsibility persist.

Effects of Black (Mis)representations

Researchers have increasingly sought to go beyond simply documenting depictions of African Americans and have instead begun to work on trying to investigate the potential effects of these stereotypes on media consumers. We outline several of these areas below including Black criminality in the news and in video games. We also assess the extent to which perceptions of support might be influenced by these depictions. We end with discussions of victim/lifestyle matters and ingroup effects.

Black Criminals in News

A notable relationship exists between repeated media exposure to the Black criminal stereotype and audiences' perceptions of and attitudes about criminal justice. Dixon (2006) found viewers who pay close attention to crime news that overrepresents Black criminals are susceptible to perceptual and attitudinal changes. These viewers consider Black and race-unidentified suspects more culpable (or responsible and guilty) for their alleged crimes than their White counterparts. Also, viewers who endorse (or believe in the veracity of) Black stereotypes express greater support for the death penalty when exposed to crime news involving Black or unidentified suspects. Furthermore, Dixon and Maddox (2005) found Black and dark-skinned perpetrators are more emotionally unsettling to heavy news consumers than Black and light-skinned perpetrators. These viewers also express more favorability toward victims of dark-skinned perpetrators than toward other victims. In addition, regardless of news consumption behavior, Black and dark-skinned perpetrators are the most memorable perpetrators to viewers. Furthermore, a high frequency of exposure to Black criminal news in a short time period increases viewers' perception that racially nondescript criminals are culpable for their crimes (Hurley, Jensen, Weaver, & Dixon, 2015). In other words, Black criminal overrepresentation encourages viewers to assume a suspect is Black when the suspect's actual race is unknown. However, when minority viewers are exposed to overrepresented Black crime, their support for police declines.

Black Criminals in Video Games

Black criminal stereotypes in video games also influence video game players' cognition and behavior. Yang, Gibson, Lueke, Huesmann, and Bushman (2014) asked White experiment participants to use a Black or White avatar in either a violent or nonviolent video game. The study found gamers who assumed a Black avatar in a violent video expressed the most negative implicit and explicit attitudes toward Black people. In a subsequent study, the participants only played a violent video game. Participants who played as a Black avatar implicitly associated Black people with weapons (such as firearms) more often than White avatar participants. Furthermore, Black avatar participants exhibited higher aggression. Increased implicit associations that linked Black people to weapons were related to increased aggression incidences. A similar implicit association observation was found in Cicchirillo's (2015) study. Both Black and White players who used a violent Black avatar associated negative words with Black people and positive words with White people faster than those who used a White avatar. In addition, Dill and Burgess (2012) found exposure to Black thug video game characters decreased participants' likelihood to vote for and support a Black politician. Exposure to Black professional video game characters produced an opposite effect, increasing the likelihood participants would vote for and support a Black politician.

Undeserving of Support

Researchers discovered a link between exposure to the Black criminal stereotype and perceptions of Black people's deservingness of government support. An experiment that compared the effects of different Black victim images from Hurricane Katrina in New Orleans produced ironic, but expected results (Johnson, Olivo, Gibson, Reed, & Ashburn-Nardo, 2009). The study recruited only White participants. One participant group saw Black hurricane victims taking food and other objects from stores. Another group saw Black people walking in the devastated city. A control group did not see any images. The group that saw the Black people taking items from stores expressed the least empathy for the victims and the least policy support for Black evacuees. These images represented the stereotypical act of "looting" to these participants. Yet, these images most clearly depicted these victims' desperate need for government support.

Ramasubramanian (2010) also discovered when White viewers perceive increased levels of Black criminality and laziness on television, their stereotypical beliefs about Black criminality and laziness respectively increase. Interestingly, viewers do not associate the criminal stereotype belief with hostile feelings. Instead, increased belief in criminal stereotypes leads to a decrease in support for affirmative action policies and an increased belief in the laziness stereotype. Increased beliefs about Black laziness increased hostile feelings toward Black people. In turn, stronger hostile feelings also contributed to decreased support for affirmative action. Ramasubramanian (2010) argues the Black criminality stereotype feeds into the perception that Black people are unmotivated, irresponsible, and undeserving of public support.

Victim Lifestyle Matters

Crime victims' perceived lifestyle also influences audiences' perceptions about both victims and perpetrators. As observed by Dukes and Gaither (2017), viewers judge Black male shooting victims who exhibit stereotypical life-styles more harshly than counter-stereotypical Black male shooting victims. Stereotypical victims receive more blame and less sympathy from viewers than what counter-stereotypical victims receive. Viewers' sympathy, ability to understand, and ability to identify with the shooter's behavior increases when viewers are exposed to a stereotypical victim. All three variables increase slightly when the shooter is White. A counter-stereotypical victim also increases the likelihood a viewer will recommend a harsh indictment for shooters.

Ingroup Effects

When exposed to negative Black representations in prime time television, Black viewers' warm feelings and favorable characterizations of Black people decrease (Tukachinsky, Mastro, & Yarchi, 2017). However, Black adolescents who watch majority-Black films report a higher incidence of aggression, alcohol use, and sexual activity than those who watch mainstream films (Bleakley et al., 2017). Mainstream media reduce adolescents' endorsement of mainstream gender roles and Black-oriented media increase endorsement of the strong Black woman role (Anyiwo, Ward, Fletcher, & Rowley, 2018). Therefore, while mainstream media affect perceptions about ingroup attitudes, Black-oriented media relate to Black behavioral learning.

Monahan, Shtrulis, and Givens (2005) discovered exposure to Black female stereotypes influenced experiment participants' perception of Black women's suitability for jobs related to housekeeping, sex appeal, and low-wage temporary work. When exposed to a stereotypical welfare queen (characterized as poor, with many children, and living on government aid), participants believed a fictional Black female seeking employment was most fitting for low-wage temporary work. However, exposure to the mammy (a stout, dark-skinned, and stern domestic worker) and jezebel (an attractive Black woman with an excessive sexual appetite) stereotypes did not influence perceived job suitability for the fictional Black female. One might surmise economic-based stereotypes about women tend to produce more powerful effects than stereotypes linked to maternity and sexuality.

Future Research Directions

Although stereotypical Black portrayals are decreasing in some arenas, these portrayals are prevalent and alarmingly perpetual in others. In either case, we cannot ignore the nuances uncovered by race and media researchers. Preparing general audiences to view media in a nuanced manner presents a daunting but feasible task. Scharrer and Ramasubramanian (2015) argue media literacy programs teach young viewers to use analytical and critical tools that deconstruct media messages yet, for these tools to work, young viewers must learn how to develop their own critiques instead of adopting critiques prescribed by educators. A grounded and practical approach to media analysis makes it possible for audiences to appreciate, understand, and act upon the shaded distinctions discussed in this chapter.

Media may also contribute to bridging the racial divide. Oliver et al. (2015) found inspiring content increased viewers' feelings of connection to humanity. In turn, viewers felt a greater sense of connectedness with racial and ethnic outgroups and reported an increase in positive attitudes toward these groups. These findings highlight the potential for prosocial media to invoke emotions that promote positive racial attitudes.

Most research addressed in this chapter assumes an institutionalized top-down approach to mediated communication. In other words, the studies examine mass messages created by large organizations that are transmitted to mass audiences. However, we are now called upon to account for the heightened interactivity, increased selectivity, and improved sharing capabilities brought about by new media. We might consider how a transmitted stereotypical or counter-stereotypical Black meme influences both sender and receiver. We might also expand our investigations to content realms previously unimaginable. For example, On December 12, 2019, a cursory search for the term "police brutality" yielded approximately, 2,560,000 hits on the Google Video service. The term "street fight" yielded 112,000,000 hits on the same service. Such violence may appear in social media users' content feed. Some users actively seek out this content on platforms such as YouTube, LiveLeaks, and WorldstarHipHop. Respective to the Black criminal stereotype, future research could uncover whether heavy exposure to real violence differs from heavy exposure to fictional or news-mediated violence.

Sundar and Limperos (2013) note evolving technologies challenges us to assess the psychological needs media users seek to fulfill. As options for content and interactivity increase, the ability for users to fulfill previously unattainable desires also increases. Furthermore, Knobloch-Westerwick, Westerwick, and Sude (2020) argue media effects scholars should integrate selective exposure methodologies and theoretical frameworks into their research. Media selection facilitates a dynamic process that influences self-concept and affectual state based on users' situational needs, according to Knobloch-Westerwick's Selective Exposure Self- and Affect-Management Model (SESAM) (2015).

A rigid top-down examination primarily addresses the following question: *How do Black media stereotypes influence audiences?* But when we also regard the complexities involved with a bottom-up approach, new questions arise: *Why, where, and how are media users finding stereotypic and counter-stereotypic content? What happens when users' expected effects do or do not occur?* These two questions recognize that both media users and Black stereotypic content are free to migrate from mainstream sources to media realms not yet accounted for by researchers.

Conclusion

Although stereotypic Black portrayals have diminished in some media arenas, the media landscape stands to benefit from much improvement. In some cases, Black people are blatantly stereotyped. In other cases, Black portrayals are subtly skewed. Repeated exposure to both scenarios reinforce biased perceptions about Black people. Not all Black portrayals need to be counter-stereotypical. However, at the very least, the diversity of Black depictions in media should reflect real-world data. To this end, momentum exists. But much work still exists for researchers, educators, and media professionals to break media's addiction to Black stereotypes. This addiction, found within media's micro and macro structures, is fueled by hegemonic pressure. Without further intervention, we should expect that this addiction will persist into new media's evolution and beyond.

References

Alexander, S. (1999). The gender role paradox in youth culture: An analysis of women in music videos. *Michigan Sociological Review, 13*, 46–64. Retrieved from https://www.michigansociology.org/michigan-sociological-review.

Angelini, J. R., Billings, A. C., MacArthur, P. J., Bissell, K., & Smith, L. R. (2014). Competing separately, medaling equally: Racial depictions of athletes in NBC's primetime broadcast of the 2012 London Olympic Games. *Howard Journal of Communications, 25*(2), 115–133. doi: 10.1080/10646175.2014.888380

Anyiwo, N., Ward, L. M., Fletcher, K. D., & Rowley, S. (2018). Black adolescents' television usage and endorsement of mainstream gender roles and the strong Black woman schema. *Journal of Black Psychology, 44*(4), 371–397.

Bailey, A. A. (2006). A year in the life of the African-American male in advertising: A content analysis. *Journal of Advertising, 35*(1), 83–104. doi: 10.2753/JOA0091-3367350106

Baker, C. N. (2005). Images of women's sexuality in advertisements: A content analysis of Black-and White-oriented women's and men's magazines. *Sex Roles, 52*(1–2), 13–27. doi: 10.1007/s11199-005-1190-y

Billings, A. C. (2004). Depicting the quarterback in Black and White: A content analysis of college and professional football broadcast commentary. *Howard Journal of Communications, 15*(4), 201–210. doi: 10.1080/10646170490521158

Bleakley, A., Ellithorpe, M. E., Hennessy, M., Jamieson, P. E., Khurana, A., & Weitz, I. (2017). Risky movies, risky behaviors, and ethnic identity among Black adolescents. *Social Science & Medicine, 195*, 131–137. doi: 10.1016/j.socscimed.2017.10.024

Brooks, M. E., Bichard, S., & Craig, C. (2016). What's the score?: A content analysis of mature adults in Super Bowl commercials. *Howard Journal of Communications, 27*(4), 347–366. doi: 10.1080/10646175.2016.1206046

Bryant, J., & Miron, D. (2004). Theory and research in mass communication. *Journal of Communication, 54*(4), 662–704. doi: 10.1111/j.1460-2466.2004.tb02650.x

Busselle, R., & Van den Bulk, J. (2020). Cultivation theory, media, stories, processes and reality. In M. B. Oliver, A. Rainey, & J. Bryant (Eds.), *Media effects: Advances in theory and research* (4th ed., pp. 69–82). New York: Routledge.

Butterworth, M. L. (2007). Race in "The Race": Mark McGwire, Sammy Sosa, and heroic constructions of whiteness. *Critical Studies in Media Communication, 24*(3), 228–244. doi: 10.1080/07393180701520926

Byrd, J., & Utsler, M. (2007). Is stereotypical coverage of African-American athletes as "dead as disco"?: An analysis of NFL quarterbacks in the pages of Sports Illustrated. *Journal of Sports Media, 2*(1), 1–28. doi: 10.1353/jsm.0.0002

California Department of Justice. (1998a). *Criminal justice profile, 1997: Los Angeles & Orange County.* Retrieved from Sacramento, CA: Division of Law Enforcement, Bureau of Criminal Information and Analysis, Law Enforcement Information Center.

California Department of Justice. (1998b). *Supplementary report of the criminal justice profile, 1997: Los Angeles & Orange County.* Retrieved from Sacramento, CA: Division of Law Enforcement, Bureau of Criminal Information and Analysis, Law Enforcement Information Center.

Cicchirillo, V. (2015). Priming stereotypical associations: Violent video games and African American depictions. *Communication Research Reports, 32*(2), 122–131. doi: 10.1080/08824096.2015.1016148

Collins, P. (1991). *Black Feminist thought: Knowledge, consciousness and the politics of empowerment.* New York: Routledge.

Dill, K. E., & Burgess, M. C. R. (2012). Influence of Black masculinity game exemplars on social judgments. *Simulation & Gaming, 44*(4), 562–585. doi: 10.1177/1046878112449958

Dixon, T. L. (2006). Psychological reactions to crime news portrayals of Black criminals: Understanding the moderating roles of prior news viewing and stereotype endorsement. *Communication Monographs, 73*(2), 162–187. doi: 10.1080/03637750600690643

Dixon, T. L. (2017a). A dangerous distortion of our families: Representations of families, by race, in news and opinion media. Retrieved from https://colorofchange.org/dangerousdistortion/.

Dixon, T. L. (2017b). Good guys are still always in White?: Positive change and continued misrepresentation of race and crime on local television news. *Communication Research, 44*(6), 775–792. doi: 10.1177/0093650215579223

Dixon, T. L., & Linz, D. G. (2000a). Overrepresentation and underrepresentation of African Americans and Latinos as lawbreakers on television news. *Journal of Communication, 50*(2), 131–154. doi: 10.1111/j.1460-2466.2000.tb02845.x

Dixon, T. L., & Linz, D. G. (2000b). Race and the misrepresentation of victimization on local television news. *Communication Research, 27*(5), 547–573. doi: 10.1177/009365000027005001

Dixon, T. L., & Maddox, K. B. (2005). Skin tone, crime news, and social reality judgments: Priming the stereotype of the dark and dangerous black criminal. *Journal of Applied Social Psychology, 35*(8), 1555–1570. doi: 10.1111/j.1559-1816.2005.tb02184.x

Dixon, T. L., & Williams, C. L. (2015). The changing misrepresentation of race and crime on network and cable news. *Journal of Communication, 65*(1), 24–39. doi: 10.1111/jcom.12133

Dukes, K. N., & Gaither, S. E. (2017). Black racial stereotypes and victim blaming: Implications for media coverage and criminal proceedings in cases of police violence against racial and ethnic minorities. *Journal of Social Issues, 73*(4), 789–807. doi: 10.1111/josi.12248

Frisby, C. M., & Aubrey, J. S. (2012). Race and genre in the use of sexual objectification in female artists' music videos. *Howard Journal of Communications, 23*(1), 66–87. doi: 10.1080/10646175.2012.641880

Gerbner, G., & Gross, L. (1976). Living with television: The violence profile. *Journal of Communication, 26*(2), 173–199. doi: 10.1111/j.1460-2466.1976.tb01397.x

Gilens, M. (1996). "Race coding" and white opposition to welfare. *The American Political Science Review, 90*(3), 593–604. doi: 10.2307/2082611

Glascock, J., & Preston-Schreck, C. (2018). Verbal aggression, race, and sex on reality TV: Is this really the way it is? *Journal of Broadcasting & Electronic Media, 62*(3), 427–444. doi: 10.1080/08838151.2018.1451859

Grimm, J., & Schwartz, J. (2017). Body image and race on gay male-targeted blogs. *Howard Journal of Communications, 28*(4), 323–338. doi: 10.1080/10646175.2017.1300967

Hurley, R., Jensen, J. J., Weaver, A., & Dixon, T. L. (2015). Viewer ethnicity matters: Black crime in TV news and its impact on decisions regarding public policy. *Journal of Social Issues, 71*(1), 155–170. doi: 10.1111/josi.12102

Iyengar, S. (1991). *Is anyone responsible?: How television frames political issues.* Chicago, IL: University of Chicago Press. doi: 10.7208/chicago/9780226388533.001.0001

Jackson, R. L. (2006). *Scripting the Black masculine body: Identity, discourse, and racial politics in popular media.* Albany: State University of New York Press.

Johnson, J. D., Olivo, N., Gibson, N., Reed, W., & Ashburn-Nardo, L. (2009). Priming media stereotypes reduces support for social welfare policies: The mediating role of empathy. *Personality and Social Psychology Bulletin*, 35(4), 463–476. doi: 10.1177/0146167208329856

Knobloch-Westerwick, S. (2015). The selective exposure self- and affect-management (SESAM) model: Applications in the realms of race, politics, and health. *Communication Research*, 42(7), 959–985. doi: 10.1177/0093650214539173

Knobloch-Westerwick, S., Westerwick, A., & Sude, D. (2020). Media choice and selective exposure. In M. B. Oliver, A. Raney, & J. Bryant (Eds.), *Media effects: Advances in theory and research* (pp. 146–162). New York: Routledge.

Lewis, M., Bell, T., Billings, A. C., & Brown, K. A. (2020, in press). White sportscasters, Black athletes: Race and ESPN's coverage of college football's National Signing Day. *The Howard Journal of Communications*.

Mastro, D. (2015). Why the media's role in issues of race and ethnicity should be in the spotlight. *Journal of Social Issues*, 71(1), 1–16. doi: 10.1111/josi.12093

Mastro, D., Blecha, E., & Atwell Seate, A. (2011). Characterizations of criminal athletes: A systematic examination of sports news depictions of race and crime. *Journal of Broadcasting & Electronic Media*, 55(4), 526–542. doi: 10.1080/08838151.2011 .620664

Mercurio, E., & Filak, V. F. (2010). Roughing the passer: The framing of Black and White quarterbacks prior to the NFL draft. *The Howard Journal of Communications*, 21(1), 56–71. doi: 10.1080/10646170903501328

Messineo, M. J. (2008). Does advertising on Black entertainment television portray more positive gender representations compared to broadcast networks? *Sex Roles*, 59(9–10), 752–764. doi: 10.1007/s11199-008-9470-y

Monahan, J. L., Shtrulis, I., & Givens, S. B. (2005). Priming welfare queens and other stereotypes: The transference of media images into interpersonal contexts. *Communication Research Reports*, 22(3), 199–205. doi: 10.1080/00036810500207014

Monk-Turner, E., Heiserman, M., Johnson, C., Cotton, V., & Jackson, M. (2010). The portrayal of racial minorities on prime time television: A replication of the Mastro and Greenberg study a decade later. *Studies in Popular Culture*, 32(2), 101–114. doi: 10.2307/23416158

Oliver, M. B., Kim, K., Hoewe, J., Chung, M.-Y., Ash, E., Woolley, J. K., & Shade, D. D. (2015). Media-induced elevation as a means of enhancing feelings of intergroup connectedness. *Journal of Social Issues*, 71(1), 106–122. doi: 10.1111/josi.12099

Paceley, M. S., & Flynn, K. (2012). Media representations of bullying toward queer youth: Gender, race, and age discrepancies. *Journal of LGBT Youth*, 9(4), 340–356. doi: 10.1080/19361

Parrott, S., & Parrott, C. T. (2015). US television's "mean world" for White women: The portrayal of gender and race on fictional crime dramas. *Sex Roles*, 73(1–2), 70–82. doi: 10.1007/s11199-015-0505-x

Potterf, J. E., & Pohl, J. R. (2018). A Black teen, a White cop, and a city in turmoil: analyzing newspaper reports on Ferguson, Missouri and the death of Michael Brown. *Journal of Contemporary Criminal Justice*, 34(4), 421–441. doi: 10.1177/1043986218787732

Quick, B. L., White Lambert, N. J., & Josey, C. S. (2016). A two-study investigation into how television news frames the steroid scandal in major league baseball and fans' support for Bonds, McGwire, and Palmeiro's pending induction into the Baseball Hall of Fame. *Communication Research, 43*(1), 73–108. doi: 10.1177/0093650214558253

Rada, J. A., & Wulfemeyer, K. T. (2005). Color coded: Racial descriptors in television coverage of intercollegiate sports. *Journal of Broadcasting & Electronic Media, 49*(1), 65–85. doi: 10.1207/s15506878jobem4901_5

Ramasubramanian, S. (2010). Television viewing, racial attitudes, and policy preferences: Exploring the role of social identity and intergroup emotions in influencing support for affirmative action. *Communication Monographs, 77*(1), 102–120.

Romer, D., Jamieson, K. H., Riegner, C., Emori, M., & Rouson, B. (1997). Blame discourse versus realistic conflict as explanations of ethnic tension in urban neighborhoods. *Political Communication, 14*(3), 273–291. doi: 10.1080/105846097199326

Scharrer, E., & Ramasubramanian, S. (2015). Intervening in the media's influence on stereotypes of race and ethnicity: The role of media literacy education. *Journal of Social Issues, 71*(1), 171–185. doi: 10.1111/josi.12103

Schug, J., Alt, N. P., Lu, P. S., Gosin, M., & Fay, J. L. (2017). Gendered race in mass media: Invisibility of Asian men and Black women in popular magazines. *Psychology of Popular Media Culture, 6*(3), 222–236. doi: 10.1037/ppm0000096

Signorielli, N. (2009). Minorities representation in prime time: 2000 to 2008. *Communication Research Reports, 26*(4), 323–336. doi: 10.1080/08824090903293619

Sundar, S. S., & Limperos, A. M. (2013). Uses and grats 2.0: New gratifications for new media. *Journal of Broadcasting & Electronic Media, 57*(4), 504–525. doi: 10.1080/08838151.2013.845827

Tajfel, H., & Turner, J. C. (1979). An integrative theory of intergroup conflict. In W. G. Austin & S. Worchel (Eds.), *The social psychology of intergroup relations* (pp. 33–47). Monterey, CA: Brooks/Cole.

Tajfel, H., & Turner, J. C. (1986). The social identity theory of intergroup behavior. In S. Worchel & W. G. Austin (Eds.), *Psychology of intergroup relations* (pp. 7–24). Chicago, IL: Nelson-Hall.

Tukachinsky, R., Mastro, D., & Yarchi, M. (2015). Documenting portrayals of race/ethnicity on primetime television over a 20-year span and their association with national-level racial/ethnic attitudes. *Journal of Social Issues, 71*, 17–38. doi: 10.1111/josi.12094

Tukachinsky, R., Mastro, D., & Yarchi, M. (2017). The effect of prime time television ethnic/racial stereotypes on Latino and Black Americans: A longitudinal national level study. *Journal of Broadcasting & Electronic Media, 61*(3), 538–556. doi: 10.1080/08838151.2017.1344669

U.S. Department of Justice. (2015). Uniform crime reports for the United States. Retrieved from https://ucr.fbi.gov/crime-in-the-u.s/2015/crime-in-the-u.s.-2015/persons-arrested/persons-arrested.

van Doorn, B. W. (2015). Pre-and post-welfare reform media portrayals of poverty in the United States: The continuing importance of race and ethnicity. *Politics & Policy*, 43(1), 142–162. doi: 10.1111/polp.12107

Yang, G. S., Gibson, B., Lueke, A. K., Huesmann, L. R., & Bushman, B. J. (2014). Effects of avatar race in violent video games on racial attitudes and aggression. *Social Psychological and Personality Science*, 5(6), 698–704. doi: 10.1177/1948550614528008

6 Stereotypes of Latina/o Populations

DANA MASTRO
University of California, Santa Barbara

KEVIN N. DO
University of California, Santa Barbara

According to the most recent data released by the Federal Bureau of Investigation, hate crimes targeting Latinos increased by approximately 14% last year and are up a staggering 41% since 2016 (Kaleem, 2019). This alarming spike in violence and aggression toward Latinos is perhaps unsurprising when considering that our current socio-political environment is characterized by vitriolic social media posts and inflammatory news coverage of race-related issues and policies, often promoted by the U.S. President at the time of this writing (e.g., Edwards & Rushin, 2018). Although few underserved groups are spared from this increasingly caustic and incendiary rhetoric, Latinos face a uniquely threatening form of attention in this context. Not only does *news* coverage featuring Latinos focus nearly exclusively on crime in the context of undocumented immigration/immigrants (Dixon & Williams, 2015) but *entertainment* media also persistently define Latinos within a narrow set of stereotypical and oftentimes disparaging characterizations, although this is not exclusively the case (see Mastro & Sink, 2017). Among non-Latino audiences (e.g., Whites), exposure to these types of depictions is associated with a wide range of real-world cognitive, affective, and behavioral responses toward Latinos in society, in a manner consistent with the representation. Exposure has additionally been found to impact group- and self-perceptions among Latino audiences. The current chapter provides a comprehensive review of this body of scholarship, including: (a) existing quantitative content analyses documenting portrayals of Latinos across media platforms and genres, (b) empirical research investigating the effects of exposure to these characterizations on Latino and non-Latino consumers and (c) avenues for future research addressing Latina/o media stereotyping.

Representations of Latinos in the Media: Past and Present

Historically, representations of Latinos in U.S. media served to reflect the socio-political interests of European-Americans (e.g., Garcia Berumen, 1995; Wilson, Gutiérrez, & Chao, 2013). Dating back to the earliest print media accounts of the westward expansion of U.S. settlers in the 1800s, Latinos—Mexicans, in particular—were predominately described as a cruel and violent threat to the interests of European Americans, which were focused on territorial gain and the removal of non-White inhabitants. Across popular literature and in print news, Mexicans were represented as violent, unclean, unintelligent, and lazy, with the Mexican culture debased as foreign and inhuman. Descriptions such as these arguably functioned to rationalize and excuse the treatment of Mexicans in the region during the United States' pursuit of manifest destiny. It was from this foundation that the earliest film depictions of Latinos emerged.

Film. Images of Latinos in the early days of cinema took their cue from the stereotypic representations established in print (Garcia Berumen, 1995; Wilson et al., 2013). Although scarcely portrayed on screen, Latinos often served as the foil to their White counterparts in film; accentuating the preeminence of these White characters (Ramírez Berg, 2002). As detailed by Ramírez Berg (2002), these include representations as villainous criminals, childish buffoons, and sex objects. For men, the criminal stereotype (el bandido) embodies emotional volatility, cruelty, and dishonesty, alongside a disheveled, dirty appearance and heavy accent. The female equivalent (the harlot) to this dangerous figure is not only violent, unstable, and hot-tempered but also sexually insatiable. In roles as buffoons, Latinas/os are objects of derision; present on screen for the amusement of others. These characters, both female and male, are one-dimensional, childlike, foolish, simple-minded, unintelligent, and speak in bumbling English. Finally, when depicted as sex objects (i.e., dark lady and Latin lover), Latinas/os are primarily defined by their erotic appeal and sexual magnetism, with little ambition beyond sensual gratification.

Certainly, there is variation in the extent to which each of these (sometimes overlapping) characterizations might be seen as wholly detrimental or explicitly negative. Further, many of these more egregious caricatures have been sanitized over the decades. At the same time, there is no denying that Latinos have largely been reduced to a handful of stereotypic roles in this medium. Recent research suggests that little has changed in this regard (see Smith et al., 2019). As Smith and colleagues' (2019) content analysis of 1,200 top grossing movies from 2007–2018 indicates, Latinos in film today are both underrepresented (in a mere 3% of films & constituting 4.5% of speaking characters) and constrained to stereotypic attributes aligned with criminality and sexualization. Putting this into perspective, this level of representation in film is a sixth of what representations would look like if Latinos were presented at a rate proportional to the U.S. population. Additionally, their results indicate that current cinematic depictions portray Latinos as poor and in low status jobs which require minimal/no education (Smith et al., 2019). Thus, although a handful of Latino superstars can be pointed to as notable exceptions to the cinematic archetypes typically assigned to this group, Smith et al. (2019) ultimately conclude that Hollywood has offered "no meaningful change" in the overarching representations of Latinos in film in decades.

Broadcast, cable, and digital television. Portrayals of Latinos on television parallel many of the patterns and themes found in film (Mastro & Sink, 2017). Consistent with long-standing depictions on the big screen, Latinos on television have faced persistent underrepresentation and relegation to roles associated with criminality, sexualization, derision, and subordination. Beginning in the 1950s, the television landscape offered U.S. audiences images of bandido-like characters and Latin lovers in several popular programs (Wilson et al., 2013). However, a less egregious presentation of these long-standing cinematic stereotypes was often offered in the TV programming of this era. Although the bandit figures portrayed in this content were at times wholly representative of the archetype discussed in film, heroic outlaws more akin to Robin Hood than the unhinged villains seen in the movies also were presented. Further, Latin lover roles frequently displayed respectable attributes alongside the more stereotypic hot-tempered sensuousness that typifies this media trope. Notably, this decade (i.e., 1950s) is the only period of time during which the proportion of Latino characters on television was comparable to that of the U.S. population (Mastro & Sink, 2017).

The 1960s–1990s saw a decline in the both the proportional representation and quality of Latino depictions on television (Mastro & Sink, 2017; Wilson et al., 2013). On average, shows during these decades offered more distasteful portrayals of Latinos, centering on roles as ridiculed buffoons with accents, villainous criminals, or romanticized Latin lovers. Although some notable exceptions emerged in these decades, particularly in terms of representations in law enforcement, the roles occupied by Latinos on TV were predominately tied to ridicule, romance, and crime.

From the 2000s through today, a more varied set of multidimensional roles has emerged alongside a continued reliance on stereotypes regarding sexuality, criminality, as well as social and/or economic subordination (e.g., maids & blue-collar workers; see Mastro & Sink, 2017; Negrón-Muntaner,

2014; Tukachinsky, Mastro, &, Yarchi, 2015). At the same time, Latinos seem trapped in the periphery on TV, in secondary or nonrecurring roles (Mastro & Behm-Morawitz, 2005). Further, some scholarship has found that many of the advances in contemporary characterizations have emerged for Latinas only, with little progress being made for Latinos (Negrón-Muntaner, 2014). Yet, the dominant feature associated with roles for Latinas remains sexuality and eroticism (Tukachinsky et al., 2015). Indeed, over the last two decades the sexualization of Latinas has increased on TV while their professional status has decreased. Thus, it appears there are a handful of respectable, complex, stand-out roles in some shows and genres (e.g., the character Andy Herrera in ABC's *Station 19* and Amy Sosa in NBC's *Superstore*), but with trivial changes in the overall pattern of depictions of Latinos across the contemporary TV landscape.

In terms of current numeric representation, not only are Latinos under-represented on TV compared with other underserved groups, but they are also presented at a rate well below their proportion of the U.S. population at 18.3% (U.S. Census, 2018). Today, Latinos comprise 6.2% of characters on broadcast entertainment shows, 5.3% of characters on cable, and 7.2% of roles on digital outlets such as Hulu, YouTube, and Amazon (Hunt, Ramón, & Tran, 2019). It is also important to note that despite some notable examples of ethnically targeted, or niche, television programming that centers on particular racial/ethnic groups (e.g., *Fresh Off the Boat*, *Blackish*), television programs that primarily highlight Latino characters have largely been neglected. Simply put, the gap between the proportion of Latinos on TV and in the U.S. population has worsened over time.

News. Latinos are also virtually absent in the news, with representation in only 2–5% of news stories (Akdenizli, Dionne, Kaplan, Rosenstiel, & Suro, 2008; Hispanics in the News, 2009; Sui & Paul, 2017). Within this coverage, Latinos are rarely seen as experts or authorities (see Sui & Paul, 2017). Instead, there is a near singular focus on crime, particularly in the context of immigration (e.g., Dixon & Williams, 2015; Stewart, Pitts, & Osborne, 2011). Recent quantitative analyses of this coverage indicate that Latinos are grossly overrep-resented as immigrants compared with U.S. Department of Justice statistics, on both network and cable news (Dixon & Williams, 2015) as well as in print newspapers (Sui & Paul, 2017). Moreover, nearly all undocumented immigrant crime suspects depicted in the news are Latino (99%); a rate that again pro-foundly exceeds real-world estimates from the U.S. Department of Homeland Security (Dixon & Williams, 2015). Similarly, Wei and Lin's (2016) analysis of nearly 441,000 print news articles spanning 1997–2014 found that Latinos were only referenced in approximately 3% of stories and that the bulk of this coverage was centered on illicit behavior and undocumented immigration, particularly from Mexico. Further, themes of unwillingness to conform to the purported "U.S. way of life" and messages describing immigrants as a threat to the safety of U.S. citizens were additionally common. Thus, Latinos, particularly Mexicans, when covered in the news, are nearly exclusively represented as criminals and undocumented immigrants (see Hoewe, Chapter 12 in this volume, for more on stereotypes of immigrants and refugees).

The specific language (i.e., classes of words) used in immigration news also has been examined using a linguistic category model approach (LCM: Semin & Fiedler, 1988). According to LCM, people's behaviors are described using four classes of words that occur on a spectrum from concrete to abstract. Specifically, advantageous ingroup behaviors and unfavorable outgroup behaviors are communicated using abstract language, which implicitly suggest dispositional (i.e., stable) attributions. Conversely, unfavorable ingroup behaviors and auspicious outgroup behaviors are characterized with concrete language, which evoke situational attributions (Fiedler, Nickel, Asbeck, & Pagel, 2003; Maass, Salvi, Arcuri, & Semin, 1989). This linguistic tendency sustains stereotypes without overtly revealing prejudice or discrimination (Carpenter & Radhakrishnan, 2002; Maass et al., 1989). The research testing this model in the context of media messages indicates that variations in language known to reinforce stereotypes exist in news content (Dragojevic, Sink, & Mastro, 2017; Mastro, Tukachinsky, Behm-Morawitz, & Blecha, 2014). Indeed, these studies find that unsympathetic, negative coverage of immigration from Mexico is likely to utilize linguistic patterns that promote stable, dispositional attributions about immigrants (i.e., abstract language). In other words, the language structure used in this news coverage reflects a linguistic intergroup bias (i.e., Maass et al., 1989), whether or not deliberately, which has been demonstrated to perpetuate stereotypes and promote prejudice.

Altogether, the news presents a uniform and menacing image when it comes to Latinos that mischaracterizes the overwhelming body of empirical data on immigration patterns and crime statistics (e.g., Ousey & Kubrin, 2009). This creates a multi-pronged expansion of stereotypes: Latinos are exclusively Mexican; Mexicans are undocumented immigrants; undocumented immigrants are criminals who are a threat to the safety, economic well-being, and norms/values of U.S. citizens.

Videogames. Little is documented regarding the presence and quality of Latinos beyond the traditional media platforms. Given the interactive affordances offered by videogames, the lack of insight into the ways that Latinos are presented in this medium is potentially problematic. Indeed, the active role that users assume when playing videogames has led scholars to argue that players are not merely observing racial/ethnic stereotypes and interracial dynamics but also reproducing and enacting "socially prescribed and technologically mediated notions of race" (Everett & Watkins, 2008, p. 149). Accordingly, how Latino characters are represented in videogames as well as the extent, constraints, and context of their playability are meaningful.

Generally, the research in this domain reveals a pattern of underrepresentation consistent with more long-standing/traditional media forms. For example, in their 2001 analysis of top selling videogames, Glaubke and associates (2001) found that Latinos comprised only 2% of all videogame characters and 5% of playable characters. Notably, and distinct from trends in film and on television, these characters were exclusively male and appeared only in sports games. Dill, Gentile, Richter, Dill (2005) also examined top selling videogames, this time revealing that 11% of main characters and 0% of secondary characters were Latino. Alternatively, Williams and colleagues (2009) found no Latino primary characters in videogames, with Latinos appearing only as secondary characters. Specifically, their analyses indicated that across all characters appearing in these games, Latinos constituted only 1.61% to 1.7% of games rated "Everyone," "E10" and "Teen" and 7.59% of games rated "Mature" by the Entertainment Software Rating Board. In a more recent analysis, Burgess, Dill, Stermer, Burgess, and Brown (2011) found that aliens and other creatures were more commonly occurring characters in videogames than Latinos, who represented 3.6% of characters. In these roles, Latinos (along with other racial/ethnic groups) were more aggressive and violent than their White counterparts and more likely to be portrayed as athletes.

Social media and user-generated content. Customizable websites like Facebook and user-generated platforms such as YouTube present challenges for researchers when it comes to identifying and coding content as well as capturing generalizable samples. As such, the manner in which these media offerings are explored often deviates from best practices in quantitative content analyses. Nonetheless, the few studies that examine racial/ethnic representations in online environments provide important but tentative insight into how and when Latinos are characterized.

In their analysis of news tweets from the Twitter accounts of 59 top circulation English-language newspapers, Sui and Paul (2019) determined that the presence of Latinos in this content varied depending on the size of the Latino audience and the ethnicity of the journalists. Overall, tweets about Latinos were infrequent; however, the trivial rate of representation was not inconsistent with the rate at which any groups, including Whites, were reflected in this content. At the same time, Latino visibility in tweets was significantly larger for papers with larger Latino audiences and with Latino reporters. The quality and content of these social media messages was not evaluated.

Representations of Latinos in a convenience sample of YouTube videos also have been examined (Guo & Harlow, 2014). This research reveals that the vast majority of videos (99%) reinforced ethnic stereotypes about Latinos, with only one video challenging them. Among these stereotypic characterizations, female sexualization was most common (69% of videos), followed by criminality (20%). These patterns parallel those found in legacy media forms such as television and film.

Effects of Exposure on Latina/o Audiences

Given the often unfavorable characterizations identified in these content analytic investigations across time and platforms, it is reasonable to focus attention on the potential for exposure to have a harmful effect on Latino audiences. Although empirical tests are limited, they cautiously suggest that media use can affect the emotions, self-concept, and esteem of Latino consumers as well as impact perceptions about the treatment of Latinos in society (e.g., Ortiz & Behm-Morawitz, 2015; Rivadeneyra, Ward, & Gordon, 2007).

Experimental research has demonstrated that viewing negative stereotypes of Mexican Americans in film can have a harmful impact on the state emotions and self-esteem of Mexican American viewers, even when audiences find the content to be entertaining (Schmader, Block, & Lickel, 2015). Specifically, Schmader and colleagues' (2015) research indicates that viewing demeaning stereotypes of Mexican Americans can evoke shame, guilt, and anger in Mexican American viewers as well as damage self-esteem, varying in relation to different aspects of group identity. Moreover, their findings suggest that such exposure can even harm Mexican Americans' implicit attitudes toward their ethnic group. In the same vein, research finds that watching unsympathetic news coverage about Latinos reduces ratings of Latino entitativity among Mexican Americans, a concept which speaks to perceptions of the group's unity, coherence, and the linked nature of the group's collective well-being (Atwell Seate & Mastro, 2015). Finally, Martinez and Ramasubramanian's (2015) experimental test of Latino responses to stereotypical comedy offers additional insights into this relationship. Their results suggest that Latinos with high ethnic identification (vs. those with low identification) were more likely to negatively evaluate stereotypical humor from White comedians; in this case, the content was judged to be less enjoyable.

Although the number of experimental studies testing the implications of exposure to unfavorable characterizations of Latinos on self- and group-perceptions is small, together they reveal a harmful environment for Latino audiences. However, experimental studies also have assessed the psychological benefits of exposure to auspicious representations on Latino audiences. For example, McKinley and associates' (2014, Study 1) research cautiously indicates that exposure to popular Latino celebrities can enhance appearance and social self-esteem, underscoring the importance of favorable media models.

The association between media use and outcomes for Latino consumers has also been explored in survey examinations, but with somewhat less consistent results. In a repeated, cross-sectional national level analysis of the relationship between media depictions of Latinos over a 20-year period and concomitant attitudes about one's Latino ingroup in the U.S., Tukachinsky and colleagues (2017) found that higher numbers of professional representations of Latinos on TV were associated with positive ingroup attitudes about one's Latino ingroup in society, whereas higher numbers of sexualized Latino TV characterizations were related to less favorable views about one's ingroup. Similarly, Rivadeneyra et al.'s (2007) data indicate that watching TV and movies, listening to music, and reading magazines had a negative effect on numerous dimensions of Latino adolescents' self-esteem, particularly for those who were highly identified with their ethnicity and actively engaged with media. Alternatively, Subervi-Velez and Necochea's (1990) survey results revealed no relationship between television viewing and Latino elementary school children's self-concept. However, given the limited number of Latinos on TV at the time of their study, the authors reasonably concluded that there may have been too few Latino characters available in the content to assure exposure based on the overall consumption measures used in the design.

In a more specific test of the factors implicated in this context, survey studies also have explored emotional responses to immigration news coverage on Latino consumers. This work indicates that U.S. Latino news users may feel group shame or anger in response to immigration news and that the particular emotional response is associated with distinct, group-based outcomes (Figueroa-Caballero & Mastro, 2019a). In particular, shame promotes distancing from one's Latino ingroup, affiliating with one's broader American identity, as well as greater support for harsh immigration policy. On the other hand, experiencing anger (in response to the prejudicial treatment of their group in news accounts), prompts greater affiliation with the Latino ingroup and less support for severe immigration policies. Given the uniform framing of immigration as a Mexican issue, it is not unexpected that Mexican Americans (vs. non-Mexican Latinos) were also more likely to withdraw from or psychologically distance themselves from the group and the immigration message and perceive that this coverage depicts negative beliefs that are held about their group in U.S. society. Findings from Ortiz and Behm-Morawitz (2015) support this conclusion, suggesting that as English-language television consumption increases, perceptions of prejudice and discrimination against Mexican Americans in the U.S. also increases.

Thus, it appears that media use can contribute to Latino audience members' feelings and cognitions about themselves and their group (in a manner consistent with the frequency and quality of the message) as well as perceptions about value and treatment of their group in society. However, given the limited number of studies and inconsistencies across results, such an interpretation should be considered with caution.

Media selection and avoidance. As the findings reported to this point reveal, the media environment is a challenging one for Latino users, as the ability to find content that favorably represents the group is limited (at least in English-language media) and the consequences of exposure are linked to the quality of these messages. Thus, the simple decision to use media presents a trial for Latinos that White audiences do not experience (see Abrams, Eveland, & Giles, 2003). As a result, it is theorized that Latinos (and racial/ethnic groups, generally) must cautiously navigate the media landscape to avoid harming their group identity; making selections to support group perceptions and avoiding content that would damage it. In one test of this assertion, Abrams and Giles (2009) surveyed Latinos regarding their television use and their ethnic group perceptions. Their results revealed that Latinos who were highly identified with their ethnicity were selective in choosing or avoiding media content to support group identity needs which, in turn, affected perceptions of their ingroup's status, standing, power, and support in the broader socio-structural environment (i.e., group vitality perceptions).

Effects of Exposure on non-Latino Audiences

Considering the overarching messages about Latinos in the news and across entertainment media, much scholarship has focused on the potential for media use to damage interethnic relations in society and negatively affect non-Latinos' (particularly Whites') perceptions about and behaviors toward Latinos. Indeed, the majority of the research in this domain has focused on stereotyping, prejudice, and discrimination among White media users. Consistently, this research has found, in both experimental and survey based designs, that both long-term and short-term exposure to depictions of Latinos in the media can influence: (a) the development of stereotypes about Latinos, (b) feelings toward Latinos, (c) behaviors and behavioral intentions toward Latinos, and (d) policy preference affecting Latinos.

Cognitions. A handful of studies have been conducted which demonstrate that exposure to media's representations of Latinos contribute to the development and maintenance of real-world stereotypes about Latinos. For example, Mastro, Behm-Morawitz, and Ortiz (2007) found that the more Whites watched television, the greater the influence of TV on their views about Latinos, such that evaluations reflected the TV version of reality of Latinos as criminal, lazy, and uneducated. This was particularly the case when consumers had limited real-world closeness with Latinos, producing greater reliance on televised messages when constructing social judgments. Tukachinsky and colleagues' (2015) data offer additional support for this relationship. They used multi-level modeling to test the relationship between TV representations of Latinos over a 22-year period and national-level attitudes about Latinos during the same period. Results revealed that representations of Latinos as professional contributed to positive attitudes towards Latinos in society, whereas hyper-sexualized depictions were associated with negative attitudes towards Latinos. Similarly, McLaughlin and colleagues (2018) found that increased exposure to depictions of hot-tempered, sexualized Latinas was associated with increased stereotyping of Latinas as "spit-fires" (particularly among conservative male viewers). Together, these findings cautiously suggest that the way that the media depicts Latinos plays a meaningful role in the formation of perceptions about them in society.

Emotions. Media exposure can additionally impact emotional responses to Latinos, affecting a range of interethnic outcomes. For example, Atwell Seate and Mastro (2016) experimentally tested the influence of viewing threatening immigration news coverage on Whites' emotions. Their results indicated that exposure to the commonly occurring news narrative that Mexican immigrants are a threat to the U.S. elicited contempt among Whites, producing both active and passive harming behaviors. Specifically, this emotional response prompted unfavorable policy preferences toward Latinos and resulted in sharing unsympathetic immigration messages about Latinos. Importantly, the extent to which viewers identified with their White ingroup moderated this relationship, such that more pronounced effects occurred for highly identified individuals. Results supporting this association were yielded by Schmader et al. (2015), who found that Whites who were higher in racial pride experienced more positive emotions in response to exposure to overtly stereotypical depictions of Mexicans in the media.

Interethnic dynamics. The persistent pairing of Latinos with negative stereotypes in the media has additionally been found to impact group-based social comparison processes (i.e., White-Latino). For example, experimental evidence indicates that for Whites who are highly identified with their race, exposure to unfavorable media representations of Latinos prompts downward social comparisons which advantage Whites (Mastro, 2003). In other words, for White media users whose identity is meaningfully defined by their race, viewing negative Latino stereotypes provides an opportunity for judging this group to be inferior, supporting Whites' self-concept. Notably, such stereotype-based responses and the subsequent boost to esteem (among Whites who identify strongly with their racial ingroup) have been found to be more pronounced when the context offers sufficient ambiguity for the reaction to be considered unconnected with ethnicity/race (Mastro et al., 2008). Further, research indicates that exposure to unfavorable depictions of Latinos in the media not only generates unfavorable stereotyping of Latinos but also prompts decreased support for public policies supportive of Latinos (Mastro & Kopacz, 2006) and encourages harsher criminal sentencing of Latinos (Figueroa-Caballero & Mastro, 2019b).

Prosocial outcomes. It is important to recognize that just as negative media stereotypes can elicit unfavorable ethnicity/race-related outcomes, auspicious outcomes also can emerge when messages offer constructive, respectable characterizations of Latinos. Indeed, media content that provides favorable depictions of Latinos can decrease stereotyping and improve perceptions of Latinos along a number of dimensions (e.g., Mastro & Tukachinsky, 2011, see also Ramasubramanian, Chapter 14, in this volume). Further, media messages that disconfirm or counter stereotypes can also reduce stereotypical perceptions and prejudice (Ramasubramanian, 2007, 2015). Research additionally indicates that although constructive media, generally, is essential, characterizations that are seen as representative or prototypical of the group and that embody recognized and valued attributes of Latinos are most effective in producing prosocial outcomes (Mastro & Tukachinsky, 2011). Ultimately, constructive and favorable portrayals are likely to encourage more harmonious intergroup dynamics in society as well as provide important benefits to ingroup identity among Latino audiences.

Future Theoretical and Methodological Directions

The capital intensive nature of our media industries means that they are slow to deviate from successful narratives and messages. As a consequence, it is clear from the research detailed in this chapter that stereotypes endure in this content. One underutilized method for navigating the implications of this reality is media literacy (see Potter, 2010 for review). As Potter (2010, pp. 684–685) articulates, "the purpose of media literacy interventions is to target a potential negative media effect and to either inoculate people against such an effect occurring or to counter the already existing negative effect." With this in mind, media literacy campaigns may be useful tools in the context of media stereotypes, which pervade platforms, genres, and time. Although such efforts have rarely been applied to stereotyping, prejudice, and discrimination (cf., Erba, Chen, & Kang, 2019; Ramasubramanian & Oliver, 2007; Ramasubramanian, 2007), the approach can be employed in an effort to reduce stereotyping and prejudice stemming from media use as well as to improve attitudes and beliefs about racial/ethnic groups. In one such attempt, Erba et al. (2019) investigated how different types of media literacy interventions affect audiences' perceptions of stereotypical media images of Latinos. Specifically, interventions designed to encourage audiences to think critically about media production practices and how they may affect audiences' perceptions of social groups (i.e., critical media literacy) were found to improve Whites' attitudes toward Latinos, in the short term. Interventions focused on acknowledging media's stereotypes about racial groups and their role in perpetuating and potentially challenging them (i.e., stereotype media literacy) improved short- and long-term attitudes toward Latinos. Neither approach, however, reduced stereotypical beliefs. Nonetheless, the potential for targeted efforts that build on previous successful interventions is a real and promising possibility for mitigating potentially adverse effects of exposure on both Latino and non-Latino audiences.

Internet and media customization. Many have also looked to new technology as a potential salve or even panacea for the failings in our traditional media environment. Regrettably, most would agree that the internet and associated technologies have failed to deliver on their potential to serve as a liberating technology, with little evidence that they have democratized media or opened access to previously marginalized groups. Instead, behemoth technology companies dominate our online experiences, creating an environment that scarcely differs from traditional mainstream media (e.g., Kim, 2012; Papacharissi, 2002). Although the internet provides a space for user-generated content, the professionally-generated content produced by these large technology companies dominates user experiences (Kim, 2012; Papacharissi, 2002). Further, online algorithms (e.g., recommendation systems and popularity-based filters) commonly prioritize this professional content, thereby attracting a disproportionate number of users and overshadowing user-generated options (Kim, 2012; Napoli, 2011; Papacharissi, 2002). As a result, the internet has become an environment filled with content produced and distributed in large part by massive technology and media corporations, with search results and shares setting the norm for what is considered popular, important, or even what is trending across both old and new media (Kim, 2012).

Unsurprisingly then, representations of marginalized groups on the internet (e.g., Guo & Harlow, 2014) often fail to differ from those found in more traditional media such as film and television (e.g., Tukachinsky et al., 2015).

Nonetheless, an infinite array of websites and affordances exist, which allow for highly distinct and specialized experiences, depending on the user. As such, this environment should not be uniformly dismissed. Instead, research designed to understand our customized environment is needed. Indeed, users play an active role in choosing, removing, organizing, and editing media content to their liking; developing tailored content that meets their unique preferences, needs, and interest (Kang & Sundar, 2016). Consequently, research efforts must adapt to keep pace with the reality of our dynamic online lives. A notable example can be seen in the innovative "screenomics" framework which captures users' continuously changing screens and devices as well as interactions with the content, at constant intervals over time (Reeves et al., 2019). Developed by a team of researchers at Stanford University, this pioneering technique provides a comprehensive record of users' screen behavior, including movement from screen to screen, images, texts, purchases, and any other activity performed on the devices we use. Certainly, analyzing data of this kind represents a labor- and skill-intensive activity, yet it is possibly the closest we have come to understanding what our personalized media lives encompass. This type of approach can provide unique insights into both: (a) if and how Latinos use media to sustain, bolster and protect identity and also (b) whether and how non-Latinos' perceptions about and treatment of Latinos are shaped by their mediated lives.

Additional methodological directions. It is certainly clear that issues tied to race/ethnicity, identity, and intergroup relations can be fraught; complicating efforts to examine the role of media in this context. Researchers not only face challenges identifying and measuring when and how stereotypes and biases are operating but also encounter obstacles in compelling participants to acknowledge them. Given this, physiological (e.g., EMG, ECG), neurocognitive (e.g., fMRI) and biosocial approaches (e.g., cortisol activity) have emerged as meaningful steps forward in addressing these complications. These approaches take the perspective that a person's biological responses to the social environment can offer objective and uncorrupted feedback on outcomes such as stress, fear, anger, sadness, disgust, happiness, adaptability, disordered tendencies, aggression, cognitive immersion, and beyond (e.g., Horan & Afifi, 2014; Turner, Huskey, & Weber, 2019). Although numerous indicators of biological processes exist that can be implemented to assess varying biological and physiological responses, an increasingly utilized biomarker in communication is the hormone cortisol, which is an indicator of stress and anxiety levels (e.g., Nabi, Prestin, & So, 2016). Given that cortisol is reactive to stressful situations as well as regulated in the human body in a circadian rhythmic pattern, it can be examined either through responsiveness to stressful situations (i.e., acute stress) or a person's standard daily circadian patterns (i.e., chronic stress) (Mayeux, 2004; Smyth, Hucklebridge, Thorn, Evans, & Clow, 2013). This presents meaningful possibilities for scholars examining intersections of media, race/ethnicity, identity, and interracial relations, as it allows researchers to directly, sensitively, and accurately gauge both one-time and cumulative effects of media use in this context.

Although such approaches can be time and labor intensive as well as costly, measuring physiological responses and biomarkers may provide substantial benefits including: (a) circumventing participant bias and (b) providing biological reactions that individuals may otherwise be unaware of (Horan & Afifi, 2014; Mayeux, 2004). When partnered with self-report measures, these approaches can increase the robustness of findings, allowing for a more comprehensive understanding of how media users respond to race-related media content. Indeed, this may even yield more substantial effect sizes than commonly found in media effects research. Of course, the utility of these approaches should not be overstated. However, they present significant advances to the scholarship that warrant increased use and attention.

Conclusion

Altogether, it seems fair to assert that the scholarship in this context reveals an unwelcoming picture when it comes to the implications of exposure to media stereotypes of Latino populations, as we know it. This is all the more crucial in a contemporary political landscape where the basic safety and welfare of underserved groups can become quickly jeopardized. At the same time, our rapidly changing media environment coupled with new, state-of-the-art research methodologies and techniques suggest that we are at an important inflection point, which may allow for rapid change and innovation in both understanding and testing the implications of our idiosyncratic, digital lives in the context of media and Latinos. It is essential, then, that such empirical evidence move beyond academic print toward actionable efforts aimed at education as well as a wide range of socially constructive outcomes.

References

Abrams, J. R., Eveland, W. P., & Giles, H. (2003). The effects of television on group vitality: Can television empower nondominant groups?. *Annals of the International Communication Association, 27*, 193–219.
Abrams, J. R., & Giles, H. (2009). Hispanic television activity: Is it related to vitality perceptions? *Communication Research Reports, 26*(3), 247–252.

Akdenizli, B., Dionne, E. J., Kaplan, M., Rosenstiel, T., & Suro, R. (2008). *Democracy in the age of new media: A report on the media and the immigration debate*. The Brookings Institution and the University of Southern California Annenberg School for Communication. https://www.brookings.edu/wp-content/uploads/2012/04/0925_immigration_dionne.pdf.

Atwell Seate, A., & Mastro, D. (2015). The effect of media exposure on perceptions of group entitativity: A preliminary investigation. *Communication Research Reports, 32*, 29–34.

Atwell Seate, A., & Mastro, D. (2016). Media's influence on immigration attitudes: An intergroup threat theory approach, *Communication Monographs, 83*, 194–213.

Burgess, M. R., Dill, K. E., Stermer, S., Burgess, S. R., & Brown, B. P. (2011). Playing with prejudice: The prevalence and consequences of racial stereotypes in video games. *Media Psychology, 14*, 289–311.

Carpenter, S., & Radhakrishnan, P. (2002). The relation between allocentrism and perceptions of ingroups. *Personality and Social Psychology Bulletin, 28*(11), 1528–1537.

Dill, K., Gentile, D., Richter, W., & Dill, J. (2005). Violence, sex, race and age in popular videogames. In E. Cole and J. Daniel (Eds.), *Featuring females: Feminist analysis of the media* (pp. 115–30). Washington, DC: American Psychological Association.

Dixon, T. L., & Williams, C. L. (2015). The changing misrepresentation of race and crime on network and cable news. *Journal of Communication, 65*, 24–39. doi: 10.1111/jcom.12133

Dragojevic, M., Sink, A., & Mastro, D. (2017). Evidence of linguistic intergroup bias in US print news coverage of immigration. *Journal of Language and Social Psychology, 36*, 462–472.

Edwards, G., & Rushin, S. (2018, January 14). The effect of President Trump's election on hate crimes. Social Science Research Network. http://dx.doi.org/10.2139/ssrn.3102652

Erba, J., Chen, Y., & Kang, H. (2019). Using media literacy to counter stereotypical images of Blacks and Latinos at a Predominantly White University. *Howard Journal of Communications, 30*(1), 1–22.

Everett, A., & Watkins, S. C. (2008). The power of play: The portrayal and performance of race in video games. In K. Salen (Eds.), *The ecology of games: Connecting youth, games, and learning* (pp. 141–164). Cambridge, MA: MIT Press.

Fiedler, K., Nickel, S., Asbeck, J., & Pagel, U. (2003). Mood and the generation effect. *Cognition and Emotion, 17*(4), 585–608.

Figueroa-Caballero, A., & Mastro, D. (2019a). Does watching this make me feel ashamed or angry? An examination of Latino Americans' responses to immigration coverage. *Journal of Cross-Cultural Psychology, 50*, 937–954.

Figueroa-Caballero, A., & Mastro, D. (2019b). Examining the effects of news coverage linking undocumented immigrants with criminality: Policy and punitive implications. *Communication Monographs, 86*, 46–67.

Garcia Berumen, F. J. (1995). *The Chicano/Hispanic image in American film*. New York, NY: Vantage Press.

Glaubke, C., Miller, P., Parker, M., & Espejo, E. (2001). Fair play? Violence, gender and race in video games. Children Now. Retrieved from https://files.eric.ed.gov/fulltext/ED463092.pdf.

Guo, L., & Harlow, S. (2014). User-generated racism: An analysis of stereotypes of African Americans, Latinos, and Asians in YouTube videos. *Howard Journal of Communications, 25*(3), 281–302.

Hispanics in the News. (2009, December 31). https://www.journalism.org/2009/12/07/hispanics-news/.

Horan, S. M., & Afifi, T. D. (2014). Advancing instructional communication: Integrating a biosocial approach. *Communication Education, 63*(4), 383–404.

Hunt, D., Ramón, A., & Tran, M. (2019). *Hollywood diversity report 2019: Old story, new beginning*. UCLA College of Social Sciences. Retrieved from https://social-sciences.ucla.edu/wp-content/uploads/2019/02/UCLA-Hollywood-Diversity-Report-2019-2-21-2019.pdf.

Kaleem, J. (2019, November 12). Latinos and transgender people see big increases in hate crimes, FBI reports. *Los Angeles Times*. https://www.latimes.com/world-nation/story/2019-11-12/hate-crimes-fbi-2018.

Kang, H., & Sundar, S. S. (2016). When self is the source: Effects of media customization on message processing. *Media Psychology, 19*(4), 561–588.

Kim, J. (2012). The institutionalization of YouTube: From user-generated content to professionally generated content. *Media, Culture & Society, 34*, 53–67.

Maass, A., Salvi, D., Arcuri, L., & Semin, G. R. (1989). Language use in intergroup contexts: The linguistic intergroup bias. *Journal of Personality and Social Psychology, 57*, 981–993.

Martinez, A., & Ramasubramanian, S. (2015). Latino audiences, racial/ethnic identification, and responses to stereotypical comedy. *Mass Communication & Society, 18*, 209–229.

Mastro, D. (2003). A social identity approach to understanding the impact of television messages. *Communication Monographs, 70*(2), 98–113.

Mastro, D., & Behm-Morawitz, E. (2005). Latino representation on primetime television. *Journalism and Mass Communication Quarterly, 82*, 110–130.

Mastro, D., Behm-Morawitz, E., & Kopacz, M. (2008). Exposure to TV portrayals of Latinos: The implications of aversive racism and social identity theory. *Human Communication Research, 34*, 1–27.

Mastro, D., Behm-Morawitz, E., & Ortiz, M. (2007). The cultivation of social perceptions of Latinos: A mental models approach. *Media Psychology, 9*(2), 347–365.

Mastro, D., & Kopacz, M. (2006). Media representations of race, prototypicality, and policy reasoning: An application of self-categorization theory. *Journal of Broadcasting & Electronic Media, 50*, 305–322.

Mastro, D., & Sink, A. (2017). Portrayals of Latinos in the media and the effects of exposure on Latino & non-Latino audiences. In. R. Lind (Ed.), *Race and gender in electronic media: Content, context, culture* (pp. 144–160). New York, NY: Routledge Press.

Mastro, D., & Tukachinsky, R. (2011). Exemplar versus prototype-based processing of mediacontent and the influence on racial/ethnic evaluations. *Journal of Communication, 61*, 916–937.

Mastro, D., Tukachinsky, R., Behm-Morawitz, E., & Blecha, E. (2014). News coverage of immigration: The influence of exposure to linguistic bias in the news on consumer's racial/ethnic cognitions. *Communication Quarterly, 62*, 135–154.

Mayeux, R. (2004). Biomarkers: Potential uses and limitations. *NeroRx: The Journal of the American Society for Experimental NeroTherapeutics, 1*, 182–188.

McKinley, C., Mastro, D., & Warber, K. (2014). Social identity theory as a framework for understanding the effects of exposure to positive media images of self and other on intergroup outcomes. *International Journal of Communication, 8*, 1049–1068.

McLaughlin, B., Rodriguez, R., Dunn, J., Martinez, J. (2018). Stereotyped identification: How identifying with fictional Latina characters increases acceptance and stereotyping. *Mass Communication and Society, 21*, 585–605.

Nabi, R. L., Prestin, A., & So, J. (2016). Could watching TV be good for you? Examining how media consumption patterns relate to salivary cortisol. *Health Communication, 31*(11), 1345–1355.

Napoli, P. M. (2011). *Audience evolution: New technologies and the transformation of media audiences.* New York, NY: Columbia University Press.

Negrón-Muntaner, F. (2014). *The Latino media gap. A report on the state of Latinos in U.S. media.* Center for the Study of Ethnicity and Race, Columbia University. https://ecfsapi.fcc.gov/file/7522909797.pdf.

Ortiz, M., & Behm-Morawitz, E. (2015). Latinos' perceptions of intergroup relations in the United States: The cultivation of group-based attitudes and beliefs from English- and Spanish-language television. *Journal of Social Issues, 71*(1), 90–105.

Ousey, G. C., & Kubrin, C. E. (2009). Exploring the Connection between Immigration and Violent Crime Rates in U.S. Cities, 1980–2000. *Social Problems, 56*, 447–473. https://doi.org/10.1525/sp.2009.56.3.447

Papacharissi, Z. (2002). The virtual sphere: The Internet as a public sphere. *New Media & Society, 4*(1), 9–27.

Potter, J. (2010). The state of media literacy, *Journal of Broadcasting & Electronic Media, 54*, 675–696.

Ramasubramanian, S. (2007). Media-based strategies to reduce racial stereotypes activated by news stories. *Journalism & Mass Communication Quarterly, 84*, 249–264.

Ramasubramanian, S. (2011). The impact of stereotypical versus counterstereotypical media exemplars on racial attitudes, causal attributions, and support for affirmative action. *Communication Research, 38*(4), 497–516.

Ramasubramanian, S. (2015). Using celebrity news stories to effectively reduce racial/ethnic prejudice. *Journal of Social Issues, 71*, 123–138.

Ramasubramanian, S., & Oliver, M. B. (2007). Activating and suppressing hostile and benevolent racism: Evidence for comparative media stereotyping. *Media Psychology, 9*, 623–646.

Ramírez Berg, C. (2002). *Latino images in film.* Austin: University of Texas Press.

Reeves, B., Ram, N., Robinson, T. N., Cummings, J. J., Giles, C. L., Pan, J., ... Yeykelis, L. (2019). Screenomics: A framework to capture and analyze personal life experiences and the ways that technology shapes them. *Human–Computer Interaction, 0,* 1–52. doi: 10.1080/07370024.2019.1578652

Rivadeneyra, R., Ward, L. M., & Gordon, M. (2007). Distorted reflections: Media exposure and Latino adolescents' conception of self. *Media Psychology, 9*(2). 261–290.

Schmader, T., Block, K., & Lickel, B. (2015). Social identity threat in response to stereotypic film portrayals: Effects on self-conscious emotion and implicit ingroup attitudes. *Journal of Social Issues, 75*(1), 73–89.

Semin, G. R., & Fiedler, K. (1988). The cognitive functions of linguistic categories in describing persons: Social cognition and language. *Journal of Personality and Social Psychology, 54*(4), 558–568.

Smith, S. L., Choueiti, M., Pieper, K., Yao, K., Case, A., & Choi, A. (2019). *Inequality in 1,200 popular films: Examining portrayals of gender, race/ethnicity, LGBTQ & Disability from 2007 to 2018.* Annenberg Foundation and USC Annenberg Inclusion Initiative. http://assets.uscannenberg.org/docs/aii-inequality-report-2019-09-03.pdf.

Smyth, N., Huckelbridge, F., Thorn, L., Evans, P., & Clow, A. (2013). Salivary cortisol as a biomarker in social science research. *Social and Personality Psychology Compass, 7*(9), 605–625.

Stewart, C., Pitts, M., & Osborne, H. (2011). Mediated intergroup conflict: The discursive construction of "illegal immigrants" in a regional U.S. newspaper. *Journal of Language and Social Psychology, 30*, 8–27.

Subervi-Vélez, F. A., & Necochea, J. (1990). Television viewing and self-concept among Hispanic children—A pilot study. *Howard Journal of Communications, 2*(3), 315–329.

Sui, M., & Paul, N. (2017). Latino portrayals in local news media: Underrepresentation, negative stereotypes, and institutional predictors of coverage. *Journal of Intercultural Communication Research, 46,* 273–294.

Sui, M., & Paul, N. (2019). Latinos in Twitter news: The effects of newsroom and audience diversity on the visibility of Latinos on Twitter. *Howard Journal of Communications, 31,* 50–70.

Tukachinsky, R., Mastro, D., & Yarchi, M. (2015). Documenting portrayals of race/ethnicity on primetime television over a 20-year span and their association with national-level racial/ethnic attitudes. *Journal of Social Issues, 71*, 17–38.

Tukachinsky, R., Mastro, D., & Yarchi, M. (2017). The effect of prime time television ethnic/racial stereotypes on Latino and Black Americans: A longitudinal national level study. *Journal of Broadcasting & Electronic Media, 61*(3), 538–556.

Turner, B., Huskey, R., & Weber, R. (2019). Charting a future for fMRI in communication science. *Communication Methods and Measures, 13*, 1–18.

U.S. Census. (2018). Quick facts: United States. https://www.census.gov/quickfacts/fact/table/US/RHI725218.

Wei, K., & Lin, Y. R. (2016). The evolution of Latino threat narrative from 1997 to 2014. In *IConference 2016 Proceedings*. Philadelphia, PA: Drexel University.

Williams, D., Martins, N., Consalvo, M., & Ivory, J. D. (2009). The virtual census: Representations of gender, race and age in video games. *New Media & Society, 11*, 815–834.

Wilson, C., Gutiérrez, F., & Chao, L. (2013). *Racism, sexism, and the Media*. Thousand Oaks, CA: Sage.

7 Constructing Youth: Stereotyping Young People

SHARON R. MAZZARELLA
James Madison University

I teach a class on youth culture at James Madison University where I begin our unit on generations by having students search Google news for "Millennials." That's it, just "Millennials." Without exception, the headlines are never positive, with most proclaiming Millennials to be "lazy," "burnouts," "miserable," and so financially illiterate that they spend money on "avocado toast" rather than saving to buy a home (Horowitz, 2017). Most interesting are the wide range of industries, products, and practices Millennials have been accused of "killing" (yes, that is the word used in headlines)—from canned tuna to paper napkins, from chain restaurants to mayonnaise—as demonstrated by the following sample headlines:

- " 'Psychologically scarred' millennials are killing countless industries from napkins to Applebee's" (Taylor, 2017)
- "Millennials are killing canned tuna, but the industry is fighting back" (Lucas, 2018)
- "How millennials eat: Are they killing beer, American cheese and canned tuna?" (Yue, 2019)

But what exactly is a Millennial, and are these headlines really relevant for the topic of this chapter? While the average person in the general public, not to mention many in the media and the academy, continue to refer to teenagers and college students as "Millennials," the Pew Research Center reminds us that the oldest Millennials are today nearing 40. In fact, Pew identifies Millennials as anyone born between 1981–1996 (roughly aged 24–39 now; Dimock, 2019). Yet, as SurveyMonkey CEO Zander Lurie (2019, para. 2) reminds us, "We've used 'millennial' as a synonym for 'young person' for so long that it's easy to forget that every generation graduates, gets jobs, and grows up like those before them."

So, while Millennials themselves may no longer accurately be called "youth," it is the fact that the label "Millennial" tends to be used by older adults to mean "young person" that makes the term relevant for this chapter. Yet the public discourse has been shifting in the past year or so to include "Generation Z" in the mix. According to the Pew Research Center, this new generation is currently defined as anyone born starting in 1997. While earlier Pew reports purposely did not use a name to refer to this generation, its most recent report in January 2019 (Dimock) finally jumped on the bandwagon and referred to them as "Generation Z" since the label had "taken hold in popular culture and journalism" (Dimock, 2019, para. 6).

So if Millennials were the poster children for industry-killing, avocado-toast-eating, financially illiterate youth, do Gen Zers fare any better? Yes, Generation Z is sometimes proclaimed as killing something in news article titles:

- "Gen Z is leading an evolution in shopping that could kill brands as we know them" (Hanbury, 2019)
- "Millennials have taken down dozens of industries—but it looks like Gen Z will be the ones to hurt Facebook" (Abadi, 2018)

However, they are also covered as bringing about more positive changes (although many would argue that killing Facebook itself would be a positive change). For example, in an article titled "How Gen Z is redefining the rock star CEO," Lurie (2019, subheading) prophesizes "that young people's protests and preferences will make racist, sexist, narcissistic leaders focused only on profit a thing of the past."

Whether optimistic or negative, more likely the latter, news coverage of Millennials and Generation Z demonstrates the flaws in lumping together millions of individuals into a single, homogenously-defined age cohort, while ignoring other demographic differences *within* the group (Costanza, 2018). So while "people love talking about generations" (Seemiller & Grace 2019, p. xxi), Costanza (2018, para. 22) reminds us that generational labels "perpetuate stereotyping." Moreover, I would argue such labels, and the news coverage employing them, have been typical of the "representational politics" behind media (particularly news) constructions of youth for decades (Giroux, 1998, p. 28). According to Stern and Odland (2017), "for at least the past 50 years, representations of teenagers" for example "in American news media have been scant, narrowly focused and largely negative" (p. 507)—in fact, as I will demonstrate in this chapter, one could say the news media *stereotype* the young. Following from pioneering Cultural Studies scholar Stuart Hall (1997), however, I use the language of "representation" in this chapter rather than "stereotypes," although the two concepts are certainly related.

While there is a smaller body of scholarship examining the representation of young people in more entertainment-focused media, the work on news media is quite extensive and of great significance since newspapers, television, and radio news have been documented as attracting an older generation of readers, viewers, and listeners (Berr, 2018; Conaghan, 2017; Falk, 2015; Gallivan, 2010). So, the question for this chapter then is how has the news media in the U.S. represented youth for an audience of predominantly older adults? Before returning to that question, it is imperative first to understand two key components contributing to the coverage: (1) the fact that "youth" is a construct that is often discussed within (2) the broader public discourse of moral panic.

Youth as a Cultural Construct

While there have always been people who are younger than others, the way a given culture *thinks* about its younger members evolves over time and often conflicts with the way other cultures think about their young. As Projansky (2014) reminds us, childhood is "discursively produced and historically and socially specific" (p. 19). Moreover, this discursive construct, according to Spigel (1993, p. 259), is "a pleasing image that adults need in order to sustain their own identities. Childhood is the difference against which adults define themselves." Yet while the cultural construct of youth works toward defining adult identities, according to Giroux (1996, p. 10), it also "has become indeterminate, alien, and sometimes hazardous to the public eye."

In the United States, how we think about youth evolved significantly over the past century and a half. Prior to the late 19th and early 20th Centuries, children were not considered as a distinct social group (and the term "teenager" didn't even enter the public lexicon until the middle of the 20th Century). During earlier times, children were considered miniature adults who, in all but upper-class White families, had delegated and gendered roles within the family structure and livelihood. As the decades characterized by industrialization and urbanization progressed, childhood itself evolved to be considered a carefree time of innocence—a life stage characterized by the need for proper molding and protection by parents, newly established public schooling laws, and child-protection legislation among other initiatives (see for example, Spigel, 1993, Wartella & Mazzarella, 1990). According to Spigel (1993), since the beginning "of industrialization, children have been conceptualized as blank slates upon whom parents 'write' their culture" (p. 261).

Giroux (2000, p. 5) argues that this "myth of childhood innocence" continues to this day to be at the heart of adult concerns about youth. Children are either innocents needing to be protected by adults, or little monsters who are no longer the innocents we need them to be. Before going further, however, it is imperative to acknowledge that not all children have been afforded this presumption of innocence. Roberts (1997), for example, asserts that the Western construction of youth as innocent does not hold for Black children. This is especially pronounced when it comes to the perception of youth violence (Giroux, 2000) and childhood sexual innocence (Fields, 2005). Moreover, the ideological code of innocence was found at work throughout the 19th Century when the culture worked to link "innocence to whiteness through the body of the child" (Bernstein, 2011, p. 6). As Egan notes, this "socio-historical legacy" of childhood innocence has worked to "support dubious social policies" particularly when related to race and class inequalities (p. 25). Moreover, I would argue, it has factored extensively into news coverage of young people to be discussed shortly.

Moral Panic Discourse

Given the cultural construction of childhood/youth as innocent (at least *some* children/youth), it is not surprising youth behavior and perceived transgressions have been fodder for a range of moral panics cycling over the decades. Whether it be concerns about the perceived link between juvenile delinquency and comic books in the 1950s, the fears that videogames led to school shootings in the 1990s, or the current outrage over digital technology and youth sexting, adult anxiety about "kids these days" has been a staple of the generation gap discourse (Mazzarella, 2018). Originally defined by Cohen (1980, p. 9) as occurring when "a condition, episode, person or group of persons emerges to become defined as a threat to societal values and interests," more recent scholars have refined this definition. Springhall (1998, p. 4), for example, demonstrated that moral panics typically include media coverage that is an out-of-proportion overreaction. Taking this one step further, McRobbie and Thornton (1995) contend that moral panics have morphed from the sporadic events described by Cohen to "the way in which daily events are brought to the attention of the public" (p. 560). Moral panics, they argue, are used by politicians, the corporate world, and the media for their own gains and to control the public. As I have documented elsewhere, the news media traditionally have played a dramatic role in the perpetuation of moral panics about young people (Mazzarella, 2018).

One component typical of news coverage of youth both in general and in cases of moral panic is the absence of youth voices in stories about them. Numerous studies document that journalists rarely quote from the young people who are the subject of their stories, preferring instead to quote from various adult officials including academics, child advocates, law enforcement, educators, media industry representatives, and so on (e.g., Children Now, 2001; Egan, 2013; Mazzarella & Pecora, 2007; Stern & Odland, 2017). Such sources provide, for a readership made up of other adults, an adult perspective on youth, the latter of whom Grossberg (1994) labels "the most silenced population in society" (p. 25). Given the lack of control young people have over their representations in *traditional* media, it is imperative to critically examine these representations.

Media Representations of Youth in the 1990s

Based on her analysis of news coverage of young people in the Canadian Press, Faucher (2009) concludes that "the prevailing image of young people who break the law morphs over the course of the twentieth century from naughty kids who need guidance to evil young men and women who are to be held accountable for their misbehaviour" (p. 439). We can look at numerous examples of mediated constructions of youth in every decade of the 20th Century (Sternheimer, 2006) such as Robert and Helen Lynd's 1929 classic *Middletown: A Study in Modern American Culture* in which Middletown adults complained vociferously about youth "nowadays" (as cited in Sternheimer, 2006). Yet nowhere have the negative representations and stereotypes been more pronounced than during the 1990s—a time of intense conservative backlash that targeted youth in general and youth of color in particular (Braxton, 2016; Males, 1999). At the time, a range of high-profile scholars including Henry Giroux, Henry Jenkins, Mike Males, and Donna Gaines exposed what Giroux then labeled the media's "essentialist representation of youth" (1996, p. 36) that was characterized by what he saw as a "mean-spirited discourse" (1996, p. 30), much of it grounded in a rhetoric of (lost) innocence and moral panic. News coverage of young people (predominantly defined as teenagers) in the 1990s centered extensively on violence, criminality, and/or victimization. A report for the Frameworks Institute (Amundson, Lichter, & Lichter, 2005) documented that 1 out of 12 stories on local television news in 1999 addressed something to do with young people. In fact, the three most frequently covered topics were youth as perpetrators or victims—perpetrators

138

SHARON R. MAZZARELLA

of crime, victims of crime, victims of accidents (such as car crashes). Not surprisingly the remaining stories were likely to be other risky behaviors such as substance use (Amundson et al., 2005). Moreover, they pointed out that such stories tended to be more "episodic" in their focus on *specific* events rather than "thematic," or providing bigger picture context or linking an event to broader issues affecting the young such as poverty, racism, reduction in school funding, and the like. While one could easily point out that the news covers other age groups similarly as victims and/or villains, Males (1999) reminds us that one difference in coverage of youth is proportion. The amount of coverage of young people in these ways far exceeds the real-life incidences of youth in these roles.

Obviously, the extensive coverage of the 1999 Columbine High School shooting factored into this broader discourse with scholars examining the coverage's contribution to representations of *some* youth as "sick/deviant" outsiders (Consalvo, 2003), transitioning "America's suburban youth into an exotic new species to be observed, feared, hated, and controlled," (Frymer, 2009, p. 1389) as well as contributing to "the myth of the juvenile superpredator" (Muschert, 2007, p. 351). Consalvo's (2003) work on news coverage of White masculinity and Columbine powerfully demonstrated that what the news coverage left out was equally as important as what it included. Specifically, while constructing the two perpetrators as "sick" and "deviant," the coverage did not look bigger picture at such contributing factors as Whiteness, privilege, hegemonic masculinity, school culture, and more. The coverage, she argued, "did not allow for more complex discussions of masculinity and its role in school culture. Hierarchic conventions within masculinity and within school culture were reinscribed more deeply into news values concerning proper criminals and ways to cover crime" (p. 41). This relates directly to Amundson et al.'s (2005) finding that much news coverage of youth is episodic, shying away from bigger picture issues. It is bad kids, not structural inequalities, at fault.

But the focus on 1990s youth as " 'thugs,' 'animals,' drive-by shoot-outs, gangsters and teenage crack moms rocking in the free world, jock gang rapists, parricide perps, low math and science scorers, zombies without morals" (Gaines, 1994, p. 231) cannot be solely attributed to Columbine. Even before Columbine, Giroux (1996) bemoaned the way in which "headlines proliferate[d] like dispatches from a combat zone, frequently coupling youth and violence in the interest of promoting a new kind of commonsense relationship" (p. 27). Moreover, a year before Columbine, Austin and Willard (1998) described "atrocity tales appearing in newspaper headlines, on magazine covers, and in television newscasts ask[ing] us, with alarming regularity, to see young people as animalistic, alien Others" (p. 1).

In his compelling and aptly-named 1999 book *Framing Youth*, Males declared young people to be "the officially designated scapegoat of the 1990s" (p. 288). For example, in his study of the *Los Angeles Times*, Males documented that "media reporting on youth murder and violence as a policy issue was *triple* what youths' contribution to violence arrests would warrant, *five times* more than youths' contribution to the volume of homicide merited, and *nine times* more than adult violence as an issue" (p. 281). This disproportionate coverage was even more pronounced when looking specifically at youth of color. For example, as discussed in Chapter 5 of this volume, Dixon and Azocar (2006) found that Los Angeles area television coverage of youth in the mid-1990s was more likely to portray African American and Latino "juveniles" as crime perpetrators (p. 154).

While there were distinct differences in news coverage of youth of color and White youth, there were also differences based on biological sex. Despite a small number of articles mentioning violent girls such as "girl gangs" in the 1990s, Norma Pecora and I found that the vast majority of U.S. newspaper articles about girls during the mid- to late-1990s framed them as *vulnerable* to a host of internalizing problems (low self-esteem, eating disorders, problematic body image, and so on; Mazzarella & Pecora, 2007). The argument was that girls were in "crisis," and that it was up to adults to "save" them (Mazzarella & Pecora, 2007).

As the 1990s segued into the new century, Sternheimer (2006) set out to debunk a range of "common complaints" (p. 3) at the root of early 21st Century news coverage of young people from "kids are rude and annoying" (p. 3), to "kids are lazy, greedy, and self-centered" (p. 5), to "kids are at risk and in danger" (p. 6). While she documented the news media's role in contributing to these stereotyped complaints, she also reminded us that most are rooted in each succeeding generation's complaints about "kids these days" (p. 152).

While decrying the media's biased coverage of "youth," many late-20th Century youth scholars mentioned earlier in this chapter (e.g., Giroux, Grossberg, Males) perpetuated the flaws of early clinical and academic work on youth by failing to address the differences in news constructions of female versus male youth. Similarly, *rarely* were raced and classed differences in representation discussed. Yet, as will be discussed in the next two sections, it is imperative for scholars to move to more intersectional approaches when studying mediated representations of young people. Coverage varies by race, sexuality, gender identity, and more. In the next section I look at more recent representations of young people by focusing on three subtopics—(1) girls and girlhoods, (2) missing children, and (3) youth online—all of which demonstrate the predominant 21st Century mediated stereotype of youth as victims.

21st Century Media Representations

As discussed in the previous section, 1990s news coverage of youth focused both on criminalization and victimization. More recent coverage, however, plays up the victimization stereotype, particularly when related to girls.

Constructing Girls

While 1990s scholarship on news coverage of youth focused primarily on the undifferentiated category of "youth," over the past two decades, more and more scholars have turned their attention specifically to news coverage of girls and girlhoods (e.g., Fyfe, 2014; Mazzarella, 2020; Projansky, 2014; Thiel-Stern, 2014), including reminding us of the need to look at how youth and gender *intersect* with race, class, sexuality, ability and other axes of identity. For example, in her analysis of news coverage of girls in Canada and the U.S., Fyfe (2014) argues that media "risk discourses depict girls as unsympathetic victims and offenders in cases where they are deemed to have failed to perform heteronormative, white femininity" (p. 51).

This construction of a singular, vulnerable, White girl has been documented by Projansky's (2014) analysis of *Time, Newsweek,* & *People* magazine covers from 1994–2012. On the most basic level, her analysis reveals a glaring overrepresentation of White cover girls, and that such girls are often constructed as "innocent and vulnerable." Girls of color, however, are rarely portrayed in these ways, further evidencing the public discourse that it is only some girls who are deserving of protection. For example, Projansky (2014) reveals that she had to look to the alternative press to find coverage of the 2003 murder of Sakia Gunn, a 15-year-old queer African American girl killed by a stranger at a bus stop in Trenton, New Jersey. Moreover, what national coverage did exist downplayed the role Gunn's "sexuality and gender presentation" (p. 163) played in her attacker's motives.

My own research extends and supports Projansky's findings (Mazzarella, 2020). For example, in revising my previously mentioned article, "Girls in Crisis," (Mazzarella & Pecora, 2007), I critique how Norma Pecora and I analyzed the coverage in that we focused almost exclusively on deconstructing journalistic decisions made in framing the girls who were covered, but we failed to address who the coverage omitted—notably girls of color, working-class girls, girls with disabilities, LGBTQ+ girls, immigrant girls, and a range of axes of identity that intersect with the subject position of "girl." In my more recent analysis (Mazzarella, 2020) of 25 years of *Time* magazine coverage of girls and girls' lives, I document a continuing definition of *"the girl"* as White and middle class as well as an ongoing emphasis on girls' bodies as troublesome—defined by a focus on dieting, self-mutilation, victimization, compulsive tanning, sexualization, and so on. Nowhere has this been more apparent than in the way the news media cover the phenomenon of early puberty in girls. My research (2020) reveals that newspapers frame the phenomenon as one in which (some) girls' bodies transgress culturally prescribed dictates of childhood innocence. Whether it be early puberty, teen pregnancy, or girls' use of social media, my recent research (2020) documents a moral panic discourse grounded in fears of girls growing up too fast. Yet, again, however, the girls in the various news sources analyzed tend to be overwhelmingly White, presumably middle class, heterosexual, and cisgender. In other words, only some girls are constructed as worthy of concern and protection (Mazzarella, 2020).

Constructing Missing Children

A growing area of scholarship in recent years has focused on the news media's construction of "missing children," a topic that traditionally has received extensive news coverage. Scholars have documented dramatic and disturbing differences in the race, gender, and/or social class of those missing children who are the subject of news coverage (Duvall & Moscowitz, 2016; Min & Feaster, 2007; Moscowitz & Duvall, 2011; Simmons & Woods, 2015; Sommers, 2017). For example, Min and Feaster's (2007) analysis of 2005–2007 TV news coverage documented a significant underrepresentation of missing African American children in comparison with actual statistics. A replication of that study by Simmons and Woods (2015) of news coverage from 1987—2011 also found "African American missing children, as well as kids of other minority groups, are significantly underrepresented in national television news stories" (p. 244) when compared to real-world statistics.

Focusing specifically on news coverage of child kidnappings, multiple studies by Duvall and Moscowitz have further exposed the stereotyping of which children are deemed both innocent and worthy of attention (Duvall & Moscowitz, 2016; Moscowitz & Duvall, 2011) as well as documenting the ongoing existence of what journalist Gwen Ifel called "Missing White Woman Syndrome" (Duvall & Moscowitz, 2016; Sommers, 2017). In their content analysis of over 200 newspaper articles published from 2000–2003, Moscowitz and Duvall (2011) identified "clear patterns" (p. 158) in the gender and class of kidnapped youth deemed worthy of coverage. "Though statistically rare," they concluded, "the news media disproportionately covered stories of young Caucasian girls being snatched from their middle- to upper-class homes by male strangers, manufacturing a nationwide epidemic" (Moscowitz & Duvall, 2011, p. 147). Following up with a series of in-depth critical/cultural case studies of news coverage of child abductions between 2002 and 2012, Duvall and Moscowitz (2016) uncovered a troubling pattern of gendered, raced, and classed biases behind *which* child abductions are/are not covered and *which* children are constructed as innocent victims. These studies are important as they work to construct stereotypes of which children are deemed innocent and worthy of our attention, concern, and protection. What does it mean for the tens of thousands of missing children and teens when the lion's share of the coverage goes to a handful of conventionally attractive, heteronormative, often blonde, well-off, White girls such as Elizabeth Smart and Natalee Holloway?

Constructing Youth Online

According to the Pew Research Center, nine in ten U.S. teens report going online daily with 45% reporting they are online "almost constantly" (Anderson & Jiang, 2018). Moreover, 95% of teens surveyed have or have access to a smartphone. In a media landscape dominated by smartphones and social media, adults' overriding concern about the relationship between young people and media has shifted. Where earlier moral panics were grounded in a fear about what the content of various technologies was doing to youth, now the panic centers on what youth are doing with these technologies—chatting with potential predators, divulging private information, cyberbullying, sexting, and more. Yet while young people are constructed as more active agents in their engagement with social media, they are still constructed as vulnerable. In their extensive analysis of 2013–2014 U.S. newspaper, magazine, and online coverage of teens and "social media" specifically, Stern and Odland (2017) documented coverage steeped in an ideology of "dysfunction and danger" (p. 517). According to the authors, social media was constructed in part as a "dangerous place for teens," a location responsible for "fueling problematic teen behaviors and practices." Simultaneously, the coverage ignored, even "undermined," more positive stories about teens and social media (p. 511). Stern and Odland (2017) also noted that the coverage did not address race, ethnicity, gender, and other differences in teens' use of social media. Much in the way "millennials" or "Generation Z" has been constructed, Stern and Odland found that teens online were "presented as a uniform group of like-minded and like-acting people" such that "real teenagers' extensive diversity was obscured" (p. 512).

In my own research on how journalists (in this case book authors) talk about girls and social media (Mazzarella, 2020), I document the stereotyping of girls as simultaneously aware of, yet powerless over, the effects of digital technology. Moreover, this feeds into a broader protectionist narrative, justifying the need for adult intervention to protect vulnerable girls. Similarly in her study of news coverage of young people's use of social networking site

MySpace in the mid-2000s, Thiel-Stern (2009) found newspapers stereotyped girls on MySpace as "stupid," "naïve," "helpless victims" (p. 35) online while boys were constructed as "active agents who seize upon the technology in order to become more violent" (p. 35). According to Thiel-Stern, "these discourses" reinforced "a moral panic and extending stereotypes about girls and boys, and about technology" (p. 20). Updating her work to include news coverage of girls online in general and during the first decade of the 21st Century, Thiel-Stern (2014) found that "most of this reportage continues to foster and perpetuate gender-related crises related to teen girls' use of the Internet and to social media in particular . . . that subtly (or not so subtly) suggests the Internet is no place for a girl" (p. 172). This is especially pronounced in news coverage of sexting—"the transfer of nude or semi-nude pictures or videos between mobile devices" (Draper, 2012, p. 221). It is a discourse grounded in a dystopian technological determinism (boyd, 2014; Draper, 2012). In her research on news coverage of sexting, Draper (2012) exposed the media's role in perpetuating a panic about how young people use the Internet and/or mobile phones. Draper's findings document that girls, in particular heterosexual girls, are constructed as being "the primary victims of technology"—a stereotype that obscures the benefits of digital technologies for girls (p. 233) and further stereotypes girls as victims.

Effects

Despite the often stereotyped, exaggerated, and narrowly constructed coverage of the young, studies of the effects of the coverage are lacking. I would argue that is because the general public and scholars themselves have long been concerned with the effects of a range of mediated artifacts on young people, but the public discourse has failed to raise concerns about the effects of mediated constructions of young people on adult audiences. In one such analysis for the Frameworks Institute, Abrun and Grady (2001) argued that general television representations of youth rely on a narrow range of "scripts," a dependence which "contributes to an impoverishment of people's understanding of youth" (p. 2). Moreover, they argue that "local news is especially damaging in its reinforcement of narrow and negative stereotypes." (p. 2). It should be noted that they focus specifically on local news since they found youth to be all-but-absent from national news coverage. More specifically, Abrun and Grady (2001) argue that local news coverage promotes a "spectator stance" that does not contribute to any sense of empathy and "tends to separate" teens "from the rest of society." (p. 4). As a result, they conclude: "The public conversation set up by the news in general and local news in particular tends to remain at a low level of discourse, with a negative impact on the public's perception of teens. In this public conversation the fate of 'teens' is to be personalized, stereotyped, and exaggerated" (p. 6).

Theoretical and Methodological Directions for Future Examination: Moving Toward Intersectionality

Throughout this chapter, I have discussed the need for evolving the study of this topic away from just "youth," "children," "teenagers," "adolescents," "Millennials," as singular entities and acknowledging that the lived experiences, public discourse about, and media representations of the young vary along a range of axes of identity. Scholars examining mediated representations (stereotyping) of young people need to incorporate a more intersectional perspective in our analyses. Introduced in the 1980s by legal scholar Kimberlé Crenshaw (2018), the concept of intersectionality argues that the intersection of one's various identities (e.g., race, biological sex, class, gender identity, ability, and so on) cannot be examined separately, but rather are entwined, particularly when related to intersecting oppressions. (For example, young, trans women/girls of color are brutalized or killed with alarming frequency, yet those stories don't generate headlines, or when they do, the stories are often framed within a traditional gender binary discourse; Baker-Plummer, 2013.) With its roots in Black feminism and Critical Race Theory (Carbado, Crenshaw, Mays, & Tomlinson, 2013, p. 304) and originally applied to understanding how the intersections of race and sex contributed to the discrimination against African American women in the workforce (Crenshaw, 2018), intersectionality has since proven to be a fertile and robust approach for analyzing the ways identities intersect in the world and in mediated representations. It is time for youth media studies scholars to incorporate intersectionality into their work so that we no longer assume that "youth is youth."

References

Abadi, M. (2018, January 19). Millennials have taken down dozens of industries—But it looks like Gen Z will be the ones to hurt Facebook. *Business Insider*. Retrieved December 26, 2019 from https://www.businessinsider.com/generation-z-facebook-2018-1.

Abrun, A., & Grady, J. (2001). *Aliens in the living room: How TV shapes our understanding of "teens."* The Frameworks Institute. Retrieved December 26, 2019 from https://www.frameworksinstitute.org/assets/files/PDF/youth_TV_understanding.pdf.

Amundson, D. R., Lichter, L. S., & Lichter, S. R. (2005). *What's the matter with kids today? Television coverage of adolescents in America.* The Frameworks Institute. Retrieved

December 26, 2019 from https://pdfs.semanticscholar.org/9ca3/f73f71af4a72147d9c156a8ad63acd0d6275.pdf.

Anderson, M., & Jiang, J. (2018, May 31). *Teens, social media & technology 2018.* Pew Research Center. Retrieved December 26, 2019 from https://www.pewresearch.org/internet/2018/05/31/teens-social-media-technology-2018/.

Austin, J., & Willard, M. N. (1998). Introduction: Angels of history, demons of culture. In J. Austin & M. N. Willard (Eds.), *Generations of youth: Youth cultures and history in twentieth-century America* (pp. 1–20). New York: New York University Press.

Barker-Plummer, B. (2013). Fixing Gwen: News and the mediation of (trans) gender challenges. *Feminist Media Studies, 13*(4), 710–724. https://doi.org/10.1080/14680777.2012.679289

Bernstein, R. (2011). *Racial innocence: Performing American childhood from slavery to civil rights.* New York: New York University Press.

Berr, J. (2018, March 2). Has CNN discovered 'The Fountain Of Youth' in cable news? *Forbes.* Retrieved January 4, 2020 from https://www.forbes.com/sites/jonathan-berr/2018/03/02/has-cnn-discovered-the-fountain-of-youth-in-cable-news/#3ff-888be6a7a.

boyd, d. (2014). *It's complicated: The social lives of networked teens.* New Haven, CT: Yale University Press.

Braxton, E. (2016). Youth leadership for social justice: Past and present. In J. Conner & S. M. Rosen (Eds.), *Contemporary youth activism: Advancing social justice in the United States* (pp. 25–38). Santa Barbara, CA: Praeger.

Carbado, D. W., Crenshaw, K. W., Mays, V. M., & Tomlinson, B. (2013). Intersectionality: Mapping the movements of a theory. *Du Bois Review, 10*(2), 303–312. doi: 10.10170S1742058X13000349

Children Now. (2001, October). *The local television news media's picture of children.* Retrieved from http://publications.childrennow.org/assets/pdf/cmp/newsmedia/news-media-pic-01.pdf.

Cohen, S. (1980). *Folk devils and moral panics: The creation of the mods and rockers.* New York: St Martin's.

Conaghan, J. (2017, May 17). Young, old, and in between: Media age shows newspaper platforms well-distributed. *News Media Alliance.* Retrieved from https://www.news-mediaalliance.org/age-newspaper-readers-platforms/.

Consalvo, M. (2003). The monsters next door: Media constructions of boys and masculinity. *Feminist Media Studies, 3*(1), 27–45. doi: 0.1080/1468077032000080112

Costanza, D. (2018, April 13). Can we please stop talking about generations as if they are a thing? *Slate.* Retrieved January 32, 2020 from https://slate.com/technology/2018/04/the-evidence-behind-generations-is-lacking.html.

Crenshaw, K. (2018). Demarginalizing the intersection of race and sex: A Black feminist critique of antidiscrimination doctrine, feminist theory, and antiracist politics [1989]. In K. Bartlett & R. Kennedy (Eds.), *Feminist legal theory: Readings in law and gender* (pp. 57–80). New York: Routledge.

Dimock, M. (2019, January 17). *Defining generations: Where Millennials end and Generation Z begins.* Pew Research Center. Retrieved 12/26/19 from https://www. pewresearch.org/fact-tank/2019/01/17/where-millennials-end-and-generation-z-begins/.

Dixon, T. L., & Azocar, C. L. (2006). The representation of juvenile offenders by race on Los Angeles area television news. *The Howard Journal of Communications, 17*(2), 143–161. https://doi.org/10.1080/10646170600656896

Draper, N. R. A. (2012). Is your teen at risk? Discourses of adolescent sexting in United States television news. *Journal of Children and Media, 6*(2), 221–236. doi: 10.1080/17482798.2011.587147.

Duvall, S. S., & Moscowitz, L. (2016). *Snatched: Child abductions in U.S. news media.* New York: Peter Lang.

Egan, D. R. (2013). *Becoming sexual: A critical appraisal of the sexualisation of girls.* Cambridge, UK: Polity Press.

Falk, T. (2015, October 16). Drop in younger listeners makes dent in NPR news audience. *Current.* Retrieved January 4, 2020 from https://current.org/2015/10/drop-in-younger-listeners-makes-dent-in-npr-news-audience/.

Faucher, C. (2009). Fear and loathing in the news: A qualitative analysis of Canadian print news coverage of youthful offending in the Twentieth Century. *Journal of Youth Studies, 12*(4), 439–456. https://doi.org/10.1080/13676260902897426

Fields, J. (2005). "Children having children": Race, innocence, and sexuality education. *Social Problems, 52*(4), 549–571. http://dx.doi.org/10.1525/sp.2005.52.4.549

Frymer, B. (2009). The media spectacle of Columbine: Alienated youth as an object of fear *American Behavioral Scientist, 52*(10), 1387–1404. doi: 10.1177/0002764209332554

Fyfe, A. (2014). News and the social construction of risky girls. *Girlhood Studies, 7*(1), 45–64. doi: 10.3167/ghs.2014.070105

Gaines, D. (1994). Border crossing in the U.S.A. In A. Ross & T. Rose (Eds.), *Microphone fiends: Youth music & youth culture* (pp. 227–234). New York: Routledge.

Gallivan, M. (2010, May 4). Median ages across NPR platforms. *NPR.* Retrieved January 4, 2020 from https://www.npr.org/sections/gofigure/2010/04/05/125578017/median-ages-across-npr-platforms.

Giroux, H. A. (1996). *Fugitive cultures: Race, violence, and youth.* New York: Routledge.

Giroux, H. A. (1998). Teenage sexuality, body politics, and the pedagogy of display. In J. S. Epstein (Ed.), *Youth culture: Identity in a postmodern world* (pp. 24–55). Malden, MA: Blackwell.

Giroux, H. A. (2000). *Stealing innocence: Corporate culture's war on children.* New York: Palgrave.

Grossberg, L. (1994). The political status of youth and youth culture. In J. S. Epstein (Ed.), *Adolescents and their music: If it's too loud, you're too old* (pp. 25–46). New York: Garland.

Hall, S. (1997). The work of representation. In S. Hall (Ed.), *Representation: Cultural representations and signifying practices* (pp. 13–74). London: Sage.

Hanbury, M. (2019, n.d.). Gen Z is leading an evolution in shopping that could kill brands as we know them. *Business Insider.* Retrieved December 26, 2019 from https://www.businessinsider.com/gen-z-shopping-habits-kill-brands-2019-7.

Horowitz, J. (2017, May 15). Millionaire to millennials: Lay off the avocado toast if you want a house. *CNN Money.* Retrieved from https://money.cnn.com/2017/05/15/news/millennials-home-buying-avocado-toast/index.html.

Lucas, A. (2018, December 3). Millennials are killing canned tuna, but the industry is fighting back. *CNBC.* Retrieved from https://www.cnbc.com/2018/12/03/millennials-are-killing-canned-tuna-but-the-industry-is-fighting-back.html.

Lurie, Z. (2019, December 19). How Gen Z is redefining the rock star CEO. *FastCompany.* Retrieved from https://www.fastcompany.com/90444539/how-gen-z-is-redefining-the-rockstar-ceo.

Males, M. A. (1999). *Framing youth: 10 myths about the next generation.* Monroe, ME: Common Courage Press.

McRobbie, A., & Thornton, S. L. (1995). Rethinking "moral panic" for multi-mediated social worlds. *The British Journal of Sociology, 46*(4), 559–574. doi: 10.2307/591571

Mazzarella, S. R. (2018). Why is everybody always pickin' on youth? Moral panics about youth, media, and culture. In N. A. Jennings & S. R. Mazzarella (Eds.), *20 questions about youth and media (revised edition)* (pp. 37–47). New York: Peter Lang.

Mazzarella, S. R. (2020). *Girls, moral panic, and news media: Troublesome bodies.* New York Routledge.

Mazzarella, S. R., & Pecora, N. (2007). Girls in crisis: Newspaper framing of adolescent girls. *Journal of Communication Inquiry, 31*(1), 6–27. doi 10.1177/0196859906294712.

Min, S., & Feaster, J. C. (2007). Missing children in national news coverage: Racial and gender representations of missing children cases. *Communication Research Reports, 27*(3), 207–216. doi: 10.1080/08824091003776289

Moscowitz, L., & Duvall, S. (2011). Every parent's worst nightmare. *Journal of Children and Media, 5*(2), 147–163. doi: 10.1080/17482798.2011.558267

Muschert, G. W. (2007). The Columbine victims and the myth of the juvenile super-predator. *Youth Violence and Juvenile Justice, 5*(4), 351–366. https://doi.org/10.1177/1541204006296173

Projansky, S. (2014). *Spectacular girls: Media fascination & celebrity culture.* New York: New York University Press.

Roberts, D. (1997). *Killing the Black body: Race, reproduction, and the meaning of liberty.* New York: Vintage Books.

Seemiller, C., & Grace, M. (2019). *Generation Z: A century in the making.* London: Routledge.

Simmons, C., & Woods, J. (2015). The overrepresentation of White missing children in national television news. *Communication Research Reports, 32*(3), 239–245. https://doi.org/10.1080/08824096.2015.1052898

Sommers, Z. (2017). Missing White woman syndrome: An empirical analysis of race and gender disparities in online news coverage of missing persons. *Journal of Criminal Law & Criminology, 106*(2), 275–314.

Spigel, L. (1993). Seducing the innocent: Childhood and television in postwar America. In W. S. Solomon & R. W. McChesney (Eds.), *Ruthless criticism: New perspectives in U.S. communication history* (pp. 259–290). Minneapolis: University of Minnesota Press.

Springhall, J. (1998). *Youth, popular culture and moral panics: Penny gaffs to gangsta rap, 1830–1996.* New York: St. Martins.

Stern, S. R., & Odland, S. B. (2017). Constructing dysfunction: News coverage of teenagers and social media. *Mass Communication and Society, 20*(4), 505–525. https://doi.org/10.1080/15205436.2016.1274765

Sternheimer, K. (2006). *Kids these days: Facts and fictions about today's youth.* Lanham, MD: Rowman & Littlefield Publishers.

Taylor, K. (2017, October 31). "Psychologically scarred" millennials are killing countless industries from napkins to Applebee's—Here are the businesses they like the least. *Business Insider.* Retrieved from https://www.businessinsider.com/millennials-are-killing-list-2017-8.

Thiel-Stern, S. (2009). Femininity out of control on the Internet: A critical analysis of media representations of gender, youth, and MySpace.com in international news discourses. *Girlhood Studies, 2*(1), 20–39. https://doi.org/10.3167/ghs.2009.020103

Thiel-Stern, S. (2014). *From the dance hall to Facebook: Teen girls, mass media, and moral panic in the United States, 1905–2010.* Amherst: University of Massachusetts Press.

Wartella, E., & Mazzarella, S. R. (1990). A historical comparison of children's use of leisure time. In R. Butsch (Ed.), *For fun and profit: The transformation of leisure into consumption* (pp. 173–194). Philadelphia, PA: Temple University Press.

Yue, F. (2019, August 26). How millennials eat: Are they killing beer, American cheese and canned tuna? *USA TODAY.* Retrieved from https://www.usatoday.com/story/money/2019/08/26/millennial-eating-decisions-healthy-convenience-social-elements/2072794001/.

8 Stereotypes Based on Looks/ Appearance: "Beautiful Is Good"

Rachel F. Rodgers
Northeastern University

Jenna Campagna
Northeastern University

Appearance- and attractiveness-based stereotypes have long existed, and may be simplistically summarized as "beautiful is good" stereotypes. While social understandings of beauty may have changed, the overwhelmingly positive stereotypes that accompany the current definitions of beauty, and parallel negative ones that accompany what is deemed unattractive, have endured (Feingold, 1992). Contemporary Western society maintains a strong focus on physical appearance with unrealistic and narrow appearance standards that are predominantly focused on extreme thinness combined with muscle tone among women (Hesse-Biber, 1996; Tiggemann & Zaccardo, 2015), and a muscular and mesomorphic body shape for men (Boyd & Murnen, 2017). These standards are intricately linked to a number of for-profit industries and systems of power and social capital that serve to maintain them. As a consequence, the discrimination faced by numerous individuals on the basis of these appearance stereotypes has far reaching consequences at the societal level, as well as for the individuals themselves. Indeed, attractiveness-based stereotypes are associated with inequities in terms of education, professional advancement, compensation, access to health care, and at an individual level, mental and even physical health (Eagly, Ashmore, Makhijani, & Longo, 1991; Feingold, 1992; Pearl & Puhl, 2018). Given this impact, attractiveness stereotypes have been the subject of much investigation since the 1970s, and a robust body of research has emerged (Cash, 1990; Cash, & Kilcullen, 1985). The aim here is to review and present some of these findings, describing the evolution of attractiveness stereotypes as well as their impact, and outlining future directions for investigation.

How Attractiveness Stereotypes Are Problematic

Stereotypes of the Past; Less Present Now

Previous portrayals of physical beauty and attractiveness and their accompanying stereotypes have in many ways resembled contemporary ones, although some historical variations have existed. Among the unvarying characteristics are symmetry and the importance of certain proportions such as waist-to-hip ratio (Furnham, Dias, & McClelland, 1998; Morrison, Bain, Pattison, & Whyte-Smith, 2018). Indeed, a low waist-to-hip ratio, as indicated by a small waist with proportionately larger hips, was a feature found across a variety of figures that were deemed to be attractive, regardless of body and breast size, suggesting the importance of symmetry as a beauty ideal (Furnham et al., 1998). In contrast, preferences and stereotypes associated with body size have varied somewhat widely throughout time. A frequently cited example includes the rounded figures represented in well-known paintings of the Italian renaissance (Swami, Gray, & Furnham, 2006). In more recent times, preferences for slim figures emerged in the 1920s, but then were replaced mid-century by more voluptuous figures yet again. Since the 1960s, however, standards of attractiveness in Western industrialized countries have become increasingly thin. These variations have been tied to social and economic factors. In particular, the preference for fuller figures in the Renaissance is thought to reflect the way that the "good life" signified freedom from physical work and sufficient affluence to afford enough food. In the 1920s, a prosperous period following the first World War, slimness became fashionable as social order started to change and social privilege sought new embodiment. Similar trends have been described related to skin tone for example, with very fair to golden skin tones preferred overall, but very white skin tones or alternately sun-kissed ones bestowed additional value at times when they represented social and economic power (e.g., the release from outside manual labor, lack of opportunity to vacation in sunny places).

Despite these variations in standards of attractiveness, the "Beautiful-is-Good" stereotype has largely prevailed, along with opposite attributions regarding unattractive appearances. While research in this area has dated back a few decades, examples of such stereotypes are found in popular myths or tales, as well as representations of important cultural or religious figures (Hawley, 2002).

21st Century Media: Happiness Is Thin, Muscular, Fair and Youthful

Contemporary media portrays individuals who are disproportionately highly attractive, very lean, and toned, with an emphasis on extreme thinness for women, and hypermuscularity for men (Levine & Murnen, 2009). In addition, traditional media typically features younger individuals with light skin (increasingly golden, but still light) and European features (Cafri, Thompson, & Jacobsen, 2006; Capodilupo, 2015). These individuals are highly unrepresentative, reflecting only a small proportion of the range of physical appearances found among the general population. In addition to this selective portrayal that leads to the promotion of a singular type of appearance as attractive, media images are almost without exception digitally manipulated in ways that render them even more unrealistic: thinner, leaner and more muscular, more symmetrical, and flawless. The "Beautiful-is-Good" stereotype is first implicitly present in the apparent message that some individuals are worthy of representation while others are not. In addition, media also model and reinforce attractiveness stereotypes by presenting narratives consistent with stereotypes around beauty and attractiveness (Ata & Thompson, 2010; Bazzini, Curtin, Joslin, Regan, & Martz, 2010). Thus, media images tell a story in which individuals who are presented as attractive are also professionally successful, engaged in fulfilling and profitable activities, upwardly socially mobile, economically advantaged, popular, romantically successful, and all around living their "best lives." In contrast, individuals who fail to meet social standards of attractiveness are largely absent from the media landscape, and when present, they are portrayed as facing challenges that will hopefully be achieved through, or accompanied by, a positive physical transformation. In this way, media create a visual environment that normalizes extreme attractiveness while constraining attractiveness to a unique type of physique.

Most recently, research attention has shifted to the representations of attractiveness on social media. Given the ability for users to contribute to social media platforms in ways that are not possible in traditional media, it would be possible for a broader range of individuals to be represented and in less stereotypical ways. Overall, however, content analysis of social media portrayals of attractive appearance, for example focusing on content identified through the use of hashtags such as "fitspiration," has revealed a narrow range of body types, including thin and toned women, and highly muscular men with minimal body fat, further reinforcing a specific set of physical features that define what it is attractive (Tiggemann & Zaccardo, 2016). Indeed, the most noticeable contribution of social media so far has been to place an emphasis on muscularity as an important dimension for both men and women (Simpson & Mazzeo, 2017). Thus, attractiveness stereotypes are consistently illustrated throughout media including print and screen. Furthermore, on social media individuals seek to curate their self-presentation in ways that replicate the way the "Beautiful-is-Good" stereotype is constructed in traditional media. Thus, many images posted to social media are similarly unrepresentative, and unrealistic, oftentimes modified to portray individuals embodying appearance ideals as closely as possible in images that convey their individual happiness and success (Rhodes Lonergan et al., 2019). A growing body of research suggests negative consequences of engaging with and contributing to the curated content typical of social media. In a cross-sectional study of adolescent girls, it was found that girls who engaged in specific activities such as taking "selfies" reported significantly higher overevaluation of shape and weight, body dissatisfaction, dietary restraint, and internalization of the thin ideal in comparison to peers who did not engage in these activities (McLean, Paxton, Wertheim, & Masters, 2015). Additionally, among those who posted photos of themselves on social media, higher engagement in manipulation of and investment in these photos, but not higher media exposure, were associated with greater body-related and eating concerns (McLean et al., 2015). Findings such as these are critical in developing an understanding of the nuanced impact social media may have on users and the extent to which emulating beauty ideals by engaging in behaviors such as modifying one's appearance in photos may exacerbate these risks.

The media portray a narrow definition of attractiveness characterized by ultra-thin female figures, lean and muscular male figures, fair skin tones, and European features, and these appearances are stereotypically associated with broad positive outcomes. The value placed on contemporary appearance standards can be understood by considering the extent to which social media users go to great lengths to portray according to these ideals by carefully posing, editing, and curating photo content. Concurrently, appearances that deviate from social standards of attractiveness are associated with negative personal characteristics and outcomes, thus generating equally powerful stereotypes.

Effects of Exposure to Attractiveness Stereotype

The effects and impacts of these media stereotypes can best be understood through theories accounting for the ways in which media representations are internalized and endorsed by individuals, such as cultivation theory (Gerbner, Gross, Morgan, & Signorielli, 1986). Cultivation theory describes the broad macro-level effects of exposure to media messages on the endorsement of the scripts and attitudes that resonate across media contents and platforms. In this way, cultivation theory offers an account for how media-portrayed stereotypes are then reenacted in life and impact inter- and intra-personal processes.

Internalization and Endorsement

As reviewed above, the existence of attractiveness-related stereotypes has been well-established. One of the first consequences of exposure to such stereotypes to consider is the extent to which they are adopted by individuals. This has been explored through both self-report and experimental research aiming to unobtrusively assess attitudes consistent with attractiveness stereotypes. A traditional means of assessing individuals' views of attractiveness involves requiring them to indicate their preference from a range of silhouettes, or more recently, designing them in a 3D program (Crossley, Cornelissen, & Tovée, 2012). Another means, however, of assessing the endorsement of attractiveness stereotypes is through self-report, by measuring internalization of the appearance ideals (Thompson & Stice, 2001). Higher levels of internalization reflect greater endorsement of socially prescribed appearance ideals and belief in their centrality to an individuals' worldview. A robust body of literature has documented the widespread internalization of the thin and muscular ideal, with children (Shapiro, Newcomb, & Loeb, 1997; Spiel, Paxton, & Yager, 2012), adolescents (Tiggemann & Miller, 2010), and adults indicating preferences for thin and muscular figures (Harper & Tiggemann, 2008; Thompson, Schaefer, & Menzel, 2012).

In addition, experimental studies have also begun to provide evidence of implicit attitudes towards thin and muscular physiques, further characterizing the extent to which these stereotypes are present among young adults (Juarascio et al., 2011). Similarly, paradigms assessing visual attention allocation have revealed preferential allocation of visual attention towards thin and muscular figures as compared to figures that are further from attractiveness standards, which is interpreted as indicative of positive attitudes (Rodgers & DuBois, 2016). Thus, both self-report and unobtrusive measures of preferences for thin/lean and muscular physiques support the widespread adoption of social attractiveness standards with regard to weight and shape.

In addition to these stereotypes regarding weight and shape, a number of other dimensions have been highlighted as being elements of stereotypical attractiveness, such as hair (texture, density versus hair loss), and skin tone, as well as physical height (Bond & Cash, 1992; Cash, 1990). Therefore, while weight and shape constitute core elements of attractiveness stereotypes, it is helpful to also consider the presence of more peripheral elements.

As described above, the counterpoint to stereotypes of attractiveness is provided by the existence of corresponding negative stereotypes related to individuals whose physical characteristics are generally considered unattractive. As weight is a dimension to which much social value is attached, one aspect of this is the negative attitudes towards larger bodied individuals, or weight bias. A parallel body of work, investigating the endorsement of positive attractiveness-related stereotypes, has focused on the exploration of negative weight-related stereotypes. Using similar methods such as silhouette choices, it has been shown that children (Holub, 2008; Musher-Eizenmann, Holub, Miller,

Goldstein, & Edward-Leeper, 2004; Spiel et al., 2012), youth (Cramer & Steinwert, 1998; Puhl & Latner, 2007), and adults hold negative attitudes towards higher-weight individuals (Latner, Stunkard, & Wilson, 2012). In addition, self-report measures have been developed that successfully capture the negative stereotypes that individuals endorse related to higher-weight individuals (Greenleaf, Chambliss, Rhea, Martin, & Morrow, 2006; Pearl & Puhl, 2018). Here too, unobtrusive measures of negative weight-related stereotypes and attitudes have been developed (Brochu & Morrison, 2007).

Other, non-weight-related dimensions of physical appearance that may bear negative stereotypes have also been investigated. For example, children have been found to display negative stereotypes related to individuals with visible facial differences and disfigurement (Rumsey, Bull, & Gahagan, 1986). A minor but recurring area of research throughout the previous decades has also centered on stereotypes of negative behaviors, such as criminality, and their association with facial features (Valla, Ceci, & Williams, 2011). Thus, individuals have been shown to hold negative stereotypes related to various aspects of appearance (e.g. Rumsey et al., 1986), although weight has perhaps received the most research attention, likely related to widespread beliefs regarding its controllability.

Intrapersonal Consequences

As described above, the first consequence of the widespread presence of attractiveness stereotypes is their internalization and endorsement by individuals. However, this internalization, in turn, has been shown to be associated with a number of detrimental consequences for individuals particularly in terms of mental and physical health.

The endorsement of stereotypes linked to the thin ideal and the association of positive attributes and expectations with thinness have been shown to be related to decreases in well-being and impairments in psychosocial functioning, including severe mental health concerns. For example, among children and youth, the internalization of the thin ideal has been shown to be cross-sectionally associated with low self-esteem, poor body image, and harmful eating behaviors such as dieting (Damiano, Paxton, Wertheim, McLean, & Gregg, 2015). Furthermore, these attitudes have been shown to be prospectively related to increases in body dissatisfaction, disordered eating, and depression among adolescents (Stice, 2002; Stice & Bearman, 2001; Stice & Whitenton, 2002). Among adults, the endorsement of positive stereotypes associated with thinness has also been associated with detrimental consequences, including eating disorders and depression, as well as a number of risky behaviors for health such as smoking (Stice & Shaw, 2003) and lower levels of physical exercise (Bucchianeri & Neumark-Sztainer, 2014). In addition, individuals have been shown to engage in a number of risky cosmetic surgery procedures to decrease adiposity or increase the shapeliness of body parts such as breasts (Menzel et al., 2011).

Positive stereotypes related to aspects of attractiveness other than weight and shape have also been shown to be associated with negative health behaviors. For example, light skinned individuals have been shown to engage in UV tanning behaviors that carry a high risk for skin cancer due to internalization of appearance ideals (Cafri et al., 2006; Darlow, Heckman, & Munshi, 2016). Conversely, darker skinned individuals have been shown to use skin-lightening products that are equally harmful (Hunter, 2011). Attractiveness stereotypes related to specific facial features such as eyes have been shown to push individuals to engage in cosmetic surgery (Jackson & Chen, 2015).

Similarly, the internalization of negative stereotypes related to higher weight has been shown to be robustly associated with mental health concerns including anxiety, depression, poor body image, and eating disorders, as well as physical health concerns such as metabolic risk (Pearl & Puhl, 2018). Of note, these associations have been found to exist above and beyond any contribution of body weight itself, highlighting that it is indeed the negative stereotypes and attitudes surrounding weight that are driving the association.

Despite the overarching negative effects of the endorsement of attractiveness stereotypes, a number of individual traits have been identified as buffering these effects. Sociocultural theory predicts that the negative effects of attractiveness stereotypes occur through the internalization of these stereotypes and their adoption as personal standards (Thompson, Heinberg, Altabe, & Tantleff-Dunn, 1999). However, these processes may be disrupted by competing beliefs or critical processing skills that buffer individuals from the effects of widespread stereotypes by either making them seem less applicable to oneself specifically, or by highlighting the extent to which such standards are generally unrealistic and unattainable. In this way, for example, ethnic identity has emerged as a buffering dimension against the negative effects of fair and light skinned attractiveness stereotypes. Indeed, sociocultural theory would predict that should attractiveness ideals be perceived as irrelevant to the individual, this would minimize pressure to pursue such ideals (Thompson et al., 1999). Consistent with this, research has revealed that among ethnic minority girls and young women who do not perceive attractiveness ideals as representing them, strong ethnic identity may buffer against internalization of mainstream appearance ideals and their negative effects on body image and well-being (Rakhkovskaya & Warren, 2016; Schooler & Daniels, 2014). In addition,

media literacy, that is the capacity to critically appraise attractiveness stereotypes as unattainable and to question their realism, has been highlighted as
another buffering mechanism (McLean, Paxton, & Wertheim, 2016). Critical
media literacy is posited to protect against the effects of attractiveness stereotypes by increasing an individuals' capacity to challenge them, and to evaluate
the extent to which for-profit systems stand to benefit from these stereotypes
(Mclean et al., 2016). Consistent with this, media literacy has been found to
be associated with lower levels of endorsement of attractiveness stereotypes,
and interventions building media literacy have been successful in supporting
positive body image and well-being (Levine & Murnen, 2009; Mclean et al.,
2016; Rodgers, McLean, & Paxton, 2019).

In sum, a robust body of literature has documented the associations
between internalization of stereotypes related to weight, as well as those
related to other dimensions of physical attractiveness, and mental and physical health outcomes. These data contribute to highlighting the overall detrimental impact of the stereotypes, although some individual factors such as
positive ethnic identity and media literacy may be protective against these
effects. Building on this, below we described the interpersonal and social consequences of these stereotypes.

Interpersonal Consequences

As highlighted by early work in this area (Cash & Kilcullen, 1985), social
norms of attractiveness, and the "Beautiful-is-Good" stereotype in particular, have important interpersonal and social consequences. Increasing research
has expanded our understanding of the different domains and settings across
which these stereotypes have an impact. For example, it has been shown that
more attractive individuals are judged as more intelligent (Ritts, Patterson, &
Tubbs, 1992), more cooperative and competent (Andreoni & Petrie, 2008),
treated more leniently in criminal and civil proceedings (Ahola, Christianson,
& Hellström, 2009), find employment more easily (Hosoda, Stone-Romero,
& Coats, 2003), and earn higher incomes (Frieze, Olson, & Russell, 1991).
In addition to these social advantages, it has also been shown that similar
processes occur online. For example, more help is offered to stereotypically
attractive avatars (Waddell & Ivory, 2015).

In addition to the work documenting the impact of attractiveness stereotypes related to shape and weight on social and interpersonal outcomes,
some research has investigated the presence of similar effects related to other
dimensions of attractiveness. In this way, for example, tan faces have been
shown to be perceived more positively than non-tanned faces (Grant, Gillen,

& Bernstein, 2014), and tanness has been shown to positively influence evaluations of job applicants (Gillen & Bernstein, 2015). Conversely, but consistent with appearance ideals, among African American individuals, lighter skin has been shown to be associated with perceptions of being more successful (Wade & Bielitz, 2005). Regarding age, the endorsement of attractiveness stereotypes may be related to more negative attitudes towards older individuals (Haboush, Warren, & Benuto, 2012). Thus, the impact of attractiveness stereotypes across physical characteristics has been shown to be highly pervasive.

In similar ways to the social privileges and social capital gained by individuals who embody stereotypes of attractiveness, research has documented the discrimination and negative social and interpersonal consequences faced by individuals in larger bodies (Puhl & Heuer, 2009). Over the past decade, the prevalence of weight discrimination has increased by 66% (Andreyeva, Puhl, & Brownell, 2008), and with this insurgence, the ways in which discrimination occur have also grown. Indeed, a well-established body of research shows that weight-based discrimination and prejudice occur across settings, including employment settings insofar as larger bodied individuals face stereotypical attitudes from employers and disadvantages in hiring, wages, promotions, and job termination because of their weight (Roehling, 1999). Similar findings were also reflected in education settings, showing that larger bodied individuals reported experiencing weight bias from instructors from middle school through university settings (Puhl & Heuer, 2009). Relatedly, individuals with larger bodies have also been shown to face discrimination in health-care settings (Pearl, 2018; Puhl & Heuer, 2009). Health-care providers in a range of specialties have been shown to endorse stereotypical assumptions about higher-weight individuals who were frequently perceived as awkward, unattractive, ugly, and noncompliant. The consequences of weight bias on health-care utilization are notable, with larger bodied individuals less likely to undergo age-appropriate screening for breast, cervical, and colorectal cancer, suggesting that weight bias in addition to weight barriers are challenges to accessing appropriate care. Other areas in which larger bodied individuals have been shown to be vulnerable to weight-based discrimination include public accommodations, jury selection, housing, and adoption. Thus, weight-based discrimination is highly pervasive.

Negative social consequences have also been documented among those who deviate from appearance ideals on dimensions other than weight and shape. For example, individuals with a visible difference have reported experiencing relational difficulties, stigmatizing interactions, and discrimination in various settings (see, for example, Van Der Donk, Hunfeld, Passchier, Knegt-Junk, & Nieboer, 1994). These reports are corroborated by experimental evidence of social discrimination and lower levels of help offered to those with visible differences (example Houston & Bull, 1994).

Thus, the social and interpersonal consequences of stereotypes related to physical attractiveness are far reaching and lead to a system of body capital that further reinforces beliefs in such stereotypes.

Systemic and Social Consequences

In addition to the intrapersonal and interpersonal consequences of attractiveness stereotypes, a number of broader effects are noteworthy. Thus, stereotypes linked to weight in particular have implications for access to health care, the identification and treatment of health conditions, and the shaping of policy. For example, systemic weight bias has resulted in insurance premiums being more elevated for individuals of higher weight (Fornhan & Salas, 2013). Similarly, weight bias has contributed to the existence of diagnostic criteria for diseases such as eating disorders that exclude individuals of higher weight, significantly impeding identification and access to care among this group (Forney, Brown, Holland-Carter, Kennedy, & Keel, 2017). Although legislation exists to protect individuals against discrimination related to a number of characteristics (for example gender, or racial/ethnic identity) few legal protections exist against discrimination based on size and weight (Pearl, 2018). In this way, a number of social and institutional level consequences exist related to the pervasive nature of attractiveness stereotypes.

Theoretical and Methodological Directions for Future Examination

A consistent body of evidence has documented the existence of stereotypes related to physical attractiveness, their adoption by individuals, and the consequences that such stereotypes may have for individual well-being as well as interpersonal processes. One important direction of future research is related to the issue of intersectionality and the way in which some individuals who hold identities across several groups that are targeted by appearance stereotypes may face exacerbated consequences. For example, it has been shown that the negative social impact of living in a larger body is greater among women compared to men (Sheets & Ajmere, 2005). This example shows how certain subgroups may be particularly sensitive to the effects of stereotypes linked to physical attractiveness. It is important to note that such subgroups are often related to the structures of power and privilege at the broader societal level. Additional work related to the ways in which certain combined characteristics may drive social and interpersonal consequences of attractiveness stereotypes, and investigating which groups may be most vulnerable to being stereotyped, will be important areas of further research.

A second important direction for future work is to extend our understanding of how disruptive the processes are that perpetuate these stereotypes and account for their negative impacts on individuals. Part of this research should aim to investigate how to decrease the internalization of stereotypes related to physical attractiveness, and the extent to which individuals hold these attitudes. In addition, however, it would be important to investigate specifically how to buffer individuals from the negative impacts on psychological and physical health imposed by these stereotypes. Promising findings have already been generated by work in this area, including the development of individual-level programs capable of decreasing investment in the pursuit of thinness and risk for body image and eating concerns (Guest et al., 2019; Watson et al., 2006). However, more work is needed. In addition, it will be critical to develop our capacity to limit the promotion of stereotypes related to physical attractiveness at the societal level. To date, too little work has targeted these stereotypes within the sociocultural environment. While buffering individuals against their negative effects is important and helpful, decreasing their presence in their environment is another important direction.

Conclusion

In sum, media stereotypes related to appearance and attractiveness are prevalent and have important social, interpersonal, and individual consequences. These effects are best understood using frameworks such as cultivation theory that account for the ways in which media-created narratives and realities are adopted by individuals. Overall, the impact of media-relayed stereotypes related to attractiveness set up a system of appearance capital that advantages those whose appearance is most in line with such representations. Increased efforts aiming to identify and mitigate vulnerabilities to these effects are warranted.

References

Ahola, A. S., Christianson, S. Å., & Hellström, Å. (2009). Justice needs a blindfold: Effects of genderand attractiveness on prison sentences and attributions of personal characteristics in a judicial process. *Psychiatry, Psychology and Law, 16*(sup1), S90–S100. doi: 10.1080/13218710802242011

Andreoni, J., & Petrie, R. (2008). Beauty, gender and stereotypes: Evidence from laboratory experiments. *Journal of Economic Psychology*, *29*(1), 73–93. doi: 10.1016/j.joep.2007.07.008

Andreyeva, T., Puhl, R. M., & Brownell, K. D. (2008). Changes in perceived weight discrimination among Americans: 1995–1996 through 2004–2006. *Obesity (Silver Spring)*, *16*, 1129–1134.

Ata, R. N., & Thompson, J. K. (2010). Weight bias in the media: A review of recent research. *Obesity Facts*, *3*(1), 41–46. doi: 10.1159/000276547

Bazzini, D., Curtin, L., Joslin, S., Regan, S., & Martz, D. (2010). Do animated Disney characters portray and promote the Beauty–Goodness stereotype? *Journal of Applied Social Psychology*, *40*(10), 2687–2709. doi: 10.1111/j.1559-1816.2010.00676.x

Bond, S., & Cash, T. F. (1992). Black beauty: Skin color and body images among African-American college women 1. *Journal of Applied Social Psychology*, *22*(11), 874–888. doi: 10.1111/j.1559-1816.1992.tb00930.x

Boyd, H., & Murnen, S. K. (2017). Thin and sexy vs. muscular and dominant: Prevalence of gendered body ideals in popular dolls and action figures. *Body Image*, *21*, 90–96. doi: 10.1016/j.bodyim.2017.03.003

Brochu, P. M., & Morrison, M. A. (2007). Implicit and explicit prejudice toward overweight and average-weight men and women: Testing their correspondence and relation to behavioral intentions. *The Journal of Social Psychology*, *147*(6), 681–706. doi: 10.3200/SOCP.147.6.681-706

Bucchianeri, M. M., & Neumark-Sztainer, D. R. (2014). Body dissatisfaction: An overlooked public health concern. *Journal of Mental Health*, *13*, 64–69. doi: 10.1108/JPMH-11-2013-0071

Cafri, G., Thompson, J. K., & Jacobsen, P. B. (2006). Appearance reasons for tanning mediate the relationship between media influence and UV exposure and sun protection. *Archives of Dermatology*, *142*(8), 1065–1086.

Capodilupo, C. M. (2015). One size does not fit all: Using variables other than the thin ideal to understand Black women's body image. *Cultural Diversity and Ethnic Minority Psychology*, *21*(2), 268–278. doi: 10.1037/a0037649

Cash, T. F. (1990). Losing hair, losing points?: The effects of male pattern baldness on social impression formation 1. *Journal of Applied Social Psychology*, *20*(2), 154–167. doi: 10.1111/j.1559-1816.1990.tb00404.x

Cash, T. F., & Kilcullen, R. N. (1985). The aye of the beholder: Susceptibility to sexism and beautyism in the evaluation of managerial applicants 1. *Journal of Applied Social Psychology*, *15*(4), 591–605. doi: 10.1111/j.1559-1816.1985.tb00903.x

Cramer, P., & Steinwert, T. (1998). Thin is good, fat is bad: How early does it begin? *Journal of Applied Developmental Psychology*, *19*(3), 429–451. doi: 10.1016/S0193-3973(99)80049-5

Crossley, K. L., Cornelissen, P. L., & Tovée, M. J. (2012). What is an attractive body? Using an interactive 3D program to create the ideal body for you and your partner. *PLoS One*, *7*(11), e50601. doi: 10.1371/journal.pone.0050691

Damiano, S. R., Paxton, S. J., Wertheim, E. H., McLean, S. A., & Gregg, K. J. (2015). Dietary restraint of 5-year-old girls: Associations with internalization of the thin ideal and maternal, media, and peer influences. *International Journal of Eating Disorders*, 48(8), 1166–1169. doi: 10.1002/eat.22432

Darlow, S. D., Heckman, C. J., & Munshi, T. (2016). Tan and thin? Associations between attitudes toward thinness, motives to tan and tanning behaviors in adolescent girls. *Psychology, Health & Medicine*, 21(5), 618–624. doi: 10.1080/13548506.2015.1093643

Eagly, A. H., Ashmore, R. D., Makhijani, M. G., & Longo, L. C. (1991). What is beautiful is good, but ...: A meta-analytic review of research on the physical attractiveness stereotype. *Psychological Bulletin*, 110(1), 109. doi: 10.1037/0033-209.110.1.109

Feingold, A. (1992). Good-looking people are not what we think. *Psychological Bulletin*, 111(2), 304. doi: 10.1037/0033-2909.111.2.304

Forhan, M., & Salas, X. R. (2013). Inequities in healthcare: a review of bias and discrimination in obesity treatment. *Canadian Journal of Diabetes*, 37(3), 205–209. doi: 10.1016/j.jcjd.2013.03.362

Forney, K. J., Brown, T. A., Holland-Carter, L. A., Kennedy, G. A., & Keel, P. K. (2017). Defining "significant weight loss" in atypical anorexia nervosa. *International Journal of Eating Disorders*, 50(8), 952–962. doi: 10.1002/eat.22717

Frieze, I. H., Olson, J. E., & Russell, J. (1991). Attractiveness and income for men and women in management 1. *Journal of Applied Social Psychology*, 21(13), 1039–1057. doi: 10.1111/j.1559-1816.1991.tb00458.x

Furnham, A., Dias, M., & McClelland, A. (1998). The role of body weight, waist-to-hip ratio, and breast size in judgments of female attractiveness. *Sex Roles*, 39(3–4), 311–326. doi: 10.1023/A:1018810723493

Gerbner, G., Gross, L., Morgan, M., & Signorielli, N. (1986). Living with television: The dynamics of the cultivation process. In J. Bryant & D. Zillmann (Eds.), *Perspectives on media effects* (pp. 17–40). Hillsdale, NJ: Erlbaum.

Gillen, M. M., & Bernstein, M. J. (2015). Does tanness mean goodness? Perceptions of tan skin in hiring decisions. *North American Journal of Psychology*, 17(1).

Grant, R. L., Gillen, M. M., & Bernstein, M. J. (2014). The tan bias: perceptions of tan and non-tan Caucasian faces. *Health Behavior and Policy Review*, 1(6), 484–489.

Greenleaf, C., Chambliss, H., Rhea, D. J., Martin, S. B., & Morrow Jr, J. R. (2006). Weight stereotypes and behavioral intentions toward thin and fat peers among White and Hispanic adolescents. *Journal of Adolescent Health*, 39(4), 546–552.

Guest, E., Costa, B., Williamson, H., Meyrick, J., Halliwell, E., & Harcourt, D. (2019). The effectiveness of interventions aiming to promote positive body image in adults: A systematic review. *Body Image*, 30, 10–25. doi: 10.1016/j.bodyim.2019.04.002

Haboush, A., Warren, C. S., & Benuto, L. (2012). Beauty, ethnicity, and age: Does internalization of mainstream media ideals influence attitudes towards older adults?. *Sex roles*, 66(9–10), 668–676. doi: 10.1007/s11199-00-0102-6

Harper, B., & Tiggemann, M. (2008). The effect of thin ideal media images on women's self-objectification, mood, and body image. *Sex Roles, 58*(9–10), 649–657. doi: 10.1007/s11199-007-9379-x

Hawley, R. (2002). The dynamics of beauty in Classical Greece. In *Changing bodies, changing meanings* (pp. 53–70). London: Routledge.

Hesse-Biber, S. (1996). *Am I thin enough yet? the cult of thinness and the commercialization of identity*. New York: Oxford University Press.

Holub, S. C. (2008). Individual differences in the anti-fat attitudes of preschool-children: The importance of perceived body size. *Body Image, 5*(3), 317–321. doi: 10.1016/j.bodyim.2008.03.003

Hosoda, M., Stone-Romero, E. F., & Coats, G. (2003). The effects of physical attractiveness on job-related outcomes: A meta-analysis of experimental studies. *Personnel Psychology, 56*(2), 431–462. doi: 10.1111/j.1744-6570.2003.tb00157.x

Houston, V., & Bull, R. (1994). Do people avoid sitting next to someone who is facially disfigured?. *European Journal of Social Psychology, 24*(2), 279–284. doi: 10.1002/ejsp.2420240205

Hunter, M. L. (2011). Buying racial capital: Skin-bleaching and cosmetic surgery in a globalized world. *The Journal of Pan African Studies, 4*(4), 142–164.

Jackson, T., & Chen, H. (2015). Predictors of cosmetic surgery consideration among young Chinese women and men. *Sex Roles, 73*(5–6), 214–230.

Juarascio, A. S., Forman, E. M., Timko, C. A., Herbert, J. D., Butryn, M., & Lowe, M. (2011). Implicit internalization of the thin ideal as a predictor of increases in weight, body dissatisfaction, and disordered eating. *Eating Behaviors, 12*(3), 207–213. doi: 10.1016/j.eatbeh.2011.04.004

Latner, J. D., Stunkard, A. J., & Wilson, G. T. (2012). Stigmatized students: Age, sex, and ethnicity effects in the stigmatization of obesity. *Obesity Research, 13*(7), 1226–1231. doi: 10.1038/oby.2005.145

Levine, M. P., & Murnen, S. K. (2009). "Everybody knows that mass media are/are not [pick one] a cause of eating disorders": A critical review of evidence for a causal link between media, negative body image, and disordered eating in females. *Journal of Social and Clinical Psychology, 28*(1), 9–42.

McLean, S. A., Paxton, S. J., & Wertheim, E. H. (2016). The role of media literacy in body dissatisfaction and disordered eating: A systematic review. *Body Image, 19*, 9–23. doi: 10.1016/j.bodyim.2016.08.002

McLean, S. A., Paxton, S. J., Wertheim, E. H., & Masters, J. (2015). Photoshopping the selfie: Self photo editing and photo investment are associated with body dissatisfaction in adolescent girls. *International Journal of Eating Disorders, 48*(8), 1132–1140. doi: 10.1002/eat.22449

Menzel, J. E., Sperry, S. L., Small, B., Thompson, J. K., Sarwer, D. B., & Cash, T. F. (2011). Internalization of appearance ideals and cosmetic surgery attitudes: A test of the tripartite influence model of body image. *Sex Roles, 65*(7–8), 469–477. doi: 10.1007/s11199-011-9983-7

Morrison, E. R., Bain, H., Pattison, L., & Whyte-Smith, H. (2018). Something in the way she moves: biological motion, body shape, and attractiveness in women. *Visual Cognition, 26*(6), 405–411.

Musher-Eizenman, D. R., Holub, S. C., Miller, A. B., Goldstein, S. E., & Edwards-Leeper, L. (2004). Body size stigmatization in preschool children: The role of control attributions. *Journal of Pediatric Psychology, 29*(8), 613–620. doi: 10.1093/jpepsy/jsh063

Pearl, R. L. (2018). Weight bias and stigma: public health implications and structural solutions. *Social Issues and Policy Review, 12*(1), 146–182.

Pearl, R. L., & Puhl, R. M. (2018). Weight bias internalization and health: A systematic review. *Obesity Reviews, 19*(8), 1141–1163. doi: 10.1111/obr.12701

Puhl, R. M., & Heuer, C. A. (2009). The stigma of obesity: A review and update. *Obesity, 17*(5), 941–964. doi: 10.1038/oby.2008.636

Puhl, R. M., & Latner, J. D. (2007). Stigma, obesity, and the health of the nation's children. *Psychological Bulletin, 133*(4), 577–580. doi: 10.1037/0033-2909.133.4.557

Rakhkovskaya, L. M., & Warren, C. S. (2016). Sociocultural and identity predictors of body dissatisfaction in ethnically diverse college women. *Body Image, 16*, 32–40. doi: 10.1016/j.bodyim.2015.10.004

Rhodes Lonergan, A., Bussey, K., Mond, J., Brown, O., Griffiths, S., Murray, S. B., & Mitchison, D. (2019). Me, my selfie, and I: The relationship between editing and posting selfies and body dissatisfaction in men and women. *Body Image, 28*, 39–43. doi: 10.1016/j.bodyim.2018.12.001

Ritts, V., Patterson, M. L., & Tubbs, M. E. (1992). Expectations, impressions, and judgments of physically attractive students: A review. *Review of Educational Research, 62*(4), 413–426. doi: 10.3102/00346543062004413

Rodgers, R. F., & DuBois, R. H. (2016). Cognitive biases to appearance-related stimuli in body dissatisfaction: A systematic review. *Clinical Psychology Review, 46*, 1–11. doi: 10.1016/j.cpr.2016.04.006

Rodgers, R. F., McLean, S. A., & Paxton, S. J. (2019). When seeing is not believing: An examination of the mechanisms accounting for the protective effect of media literacy on body image. *Sex Roles, 81*(1–2), 87–96. doi: 10.1007/s11199-018-0973-x

Roehling, M. V. (1999). Weight-based discrimination in employment: Psychological and legal aspects. *Personnel Psychology, 52*(4), 969–1016. doi: 10.1111/j.1744-6570.1999.tb00186.x

Rumsey, N., Bull, R., & Gahagan, D. (1986). A developmental study of children's stereotyping of facially deformed adults. *British Journal of Psychology, 77*(2), 269–274.

Schooler, D., & Daniels, E. A. (2014). "I am not a skinny toothpick and proud of it": Latina adolescents' ethnic identity and responses to mainstream media images. *Body Image, 11*(1), 11–18. doi: 10.1016/j.bodyim.2013.09.001

Shapiro, S., Newcomb, M., & Loeb, T. B. (1997). Fear of fat, dysregulated-restrained eating, and body-esteem: Prevalence and gender differences among eight- to ten-year old children. *Journal of Clinical Child Psychology*, *26*, 358–365. doi: 10.1207/ s15374424jccp2604_4

Sheets, V., & Ajmere, K. (2005). Are romantic partners a source of college students' weight concern? *Eating Behaviors*, *6*(1), 1–9. doi: 10.1016.j.eatbeh.2004.08.008

Simpson, C. C., & Mazzeo, S. E. (2017). Skinny is not enough: A content analysis of fitspiration on Pinterest. *Health Communication*, *32*(5), 560–567. doi: 10.1080/104 10236.2016.1140273.

Spiel, E. C., Paxton, S. J., & Yager, Z. (2012). Weight attitudes in 3-to 5-year-old children: Age differences and cross-sectional predictors. *Body Image*, *9*(4), 524–527. doi: 10.1016/j.bodyim.2012.07.006

Stice, E. (2002). Risk and maintenance factors for eating pathology: A meta-analytic review. *Psychological Bulletin*, *128*(5), 825. doi: 10.1037/0033-2909.128.5.825

Stice, E., & Bearman, S. K. (2001). Body-image and eating disturbances prospectively predict increases in depressive symptoms in adolescent girls: A growth curve analysis. *Developmental Psychology*, *37*(5), 597. doi: 10.1037/0012-1649.37.5.597

Stice, E., & Shaw, H. (2003) Prospective relations of body image, eating, and affective disturbances to smoking onset in adolescent girls: How Virginia slims. *Journal of Consulting and Clinical Psychology*, *71*, 129–135. doi: 10.1037/0022-006X.71.1.128

Stice, E., & Whitenton, K. (2002). Risk factors for body dissatisfaction in adolescent girls: A longitudinal investigation. *Developmental Psychology*, *38*(5), 669. doi: 10.1037/0012-1649.38.5.669

Swami, V., Gray, M., & Furnham, A. (2006). The female nude in Rubens: Disconfirmatory evidence of the waist-to-hip ratio hypothesis of female physical attractiveness. *Imagination, Cognition and Personality*, *26*(1), 139–147. doi: 10.2190/R11X-5752-V164-4240

Thompson, J. K., Heinberg, L. J., Altabe, M., & Tantleff-Dunn, S. (1999). *Exacting beauty: Theory, assessment, and treatment of body image disturbance.* Washington, DC: American Psychological Association.

Thompson, J. K., Schaefer, L., & Menzel, J. (2012). Internalization of thin-ideal and muscular-ideal. In *Encyclopedia of body image and human appearance* (pp. 499–504). Amsterdam, Netherlands: Elsevier. doi: 10.1007/s11199-017-0886-0

Thompson, J. K., & Stice, E. (2001). Thin-ideal internalization: Mounting evidence for a new risk factor for body-image disturbance and eating pathology. *Current Directions in Psychological Science*, *10*(5), 181–183. doi: 10.1111/1467-8721.00144

Tiggemann, M., & Miller, J. (2010). The Internet and adolescent girls' weight satisfaction and drive for thinness. *Sex Roles*, *63*, 79–90. doi: 10.1007/s11199-010-9789-z

Tiggemann, M., & Zaccardo, M. (2015). "Exercise to be fit not skinny": The effect of fitspiration imagery on women's body image. *Body Image*, *15*, 61–67. doi: 10.1016/j. bodyim.2015.06.003

Tiggemann, M., & Zaccardo, M. (2016). 'Strong is the new skinny': A content analysis of #fitspiration images on Instagram. *Journal of Health Psychology*, *23*(8), 1003–1011. doi: 10.1177/1359105316639436

Valla, J. M., Ceci, S. J., & Williams, W. M. (2011). The accuracy of inferences about criminality based on facial appearance. *Journal of Social, Evolutionary, and Cultural Psychology, 5*(1), 66. doi: 10.1037/h0099274

Van Der Donk, J., Hunfeld, J. A. M., Passchier, J., Knegt-Junk, K. J., & Nieboer, C. (1994). Quality of life and maladjustment associated with hair loss in women with alopecia androgenetica. *Social Science & Medicine, 38*(1), 159–163. doi: 10.1016/0277-9536(94)90311-5

Waddell, T. F., & Ivory, J. D. (2015). It's not easy trying to be one of the guys: The effect of avatar attractiveness, avatar sex, and user sex on the success of help-seeking requests in an online game. *Journal of Broadcasting & Electronic Media, 59*(1), 112–129. doi: 10.1080/08838151.2014.998221

Wade, T. J., & Bielitz, S. (2005). The differential effect of skin color on attractiveness, personality evaluations, and perceived life success of African Americans. *Journal of Black Psychology, 31*(3), 215–236. doi: 10.1177/00957984052778341

Watson, H. J., Joyce, T., French, E., Willan, V., Kane, R. T., Tanner-Smith, E. E., ... & Egan, S. J. (2016). Prevention of eating disorders: A systematic review of randomized, controlled trials. *International Journal of Eating Disorders, 49*(9), 833–862. doi: 10.1002/eat.22577

9 *Media Stereotypes of Class and Socioeconomic Status*

REBECCA ANN LIND
University of Illinois at Chicago

> Class will always be a site of struggle, as it encompasses interests, power and privilege.
>
> (Skeggs, 2004, p. 44)

Despite Beverley Skeggs' claim about the constancy and underlying nature of class struggles (and thus the real constraints or opportunities linked to one's class position), we are not always willing to acknowledge class. Many authors (e.g., Bullock, Wych, & Williams, 2001; Paulson & O'Guinn, 2018) have noted that even in the face of clear class stratification in the United States we imagine ours is a classless society or even that the vast majority of Americans is middle class. The powerful ideology of the so-called American Dream—a belief, commonly held and widely represented in the media, that with hard work and determination, anyone can succeed—belies the limitations and privileges associated with class positions. We rarely even speak of class, although Deery and Press (2017, p. 3) argue that:

> class matters because, quite simply, it still marks and consolidates power, which means that it also affects the fundamentals of life and death. For each of us, our class position affects how we will live and how long we will live, how we will be cared for and educated, how we will interact with the law, and what experiences and pleasures are open to us. To a large degree, class still determines geographic and social location: where we live, where we go to college, where we go on vacation. It affects how we speak and who listens.

But what is class, and how does it differ from socioeconomic status (SES)? Many influential scholars, from Karl Marx, to Max Weber, to Pierre Bourdieu, among others, have theorized class; a discussion of the conceptual similarities and differences in their work—or even their individual contributions—is well beyond the scope of this chapter. Here, we acknowledge the value of seeing class positions as relational and as reflecting an accumulation of economic, cultural, social, and symbolic capital: "Social class is defined as social stratification resulting from the unequal distribution of wealth, power, and prestige" (Sen & Sen, 2016, p. 129; emphasis removed). Although both social class and SES are based on social, cultural, and economic backgrounds, some scholars believe one's SES may be more variable because it is based on one's current situation, whereas class is more fixed over generations (Rubin et al., 2014).

The stratification of classes and SES reveals, quite simply, that some of us have more than others of what society deems valuable—in many cases, much more. Indeed, "The United States is the most highly stratified society in the industrialized world" (Mantsios, 2007, p. 636), and Census Bureau data show that income inequality in the US in 2019 was at its highest level ever (Telford, 2019).

Therefore, issues of class and SES are linked to power, affecting all aspects of our lives. Real-world trends indicate that disparities are increasing, even though many of us believe we live in an egalitarian society. Mantsios (2007) argues that we continue to hold such beliefs because of how the media portray (or don't portray) inequities. This chapter looks at media representations of class and SES across the 20th and 21st Centuries, considering also the effects of stereotypical representations.

Representations and Stereotypes of Class and Socioeconomic Status

Scholarly interest in the mediated representation of class and SES has a long and rich history, ranging across many disciplines (sociology, psychology, anthropology, economics, marketing—and of course, media studies and communication) and all types of content (comic books, films, radio, television, music, newspapers, textbooks, cookbooks, and more). Excellent contributions have been made by researchers across the social scientific, critical-cultural, and humanist paradigms.

The multiplicity of disciplines interested in issues of class/SES is matched by an acknowledgment of the multiple connections between class/SES and other relevant variables. Most scholars recognize that class positions do not exist in a vacuum; as Skeggs and Wood argue: "Gender, race and sexuality amalgamate in all class definitions" (2011, p. 13). Although some scholars focus exclusively on class/SES, many acknowledge and address the intersection of class, race, gender, and so forth. Some class stereotypes, such as the welfare mother and poor White trash, cannot even exist apart from their relationship with gender or race. Thus readers of this chapter will see some conceptual overlap with this book's chapters on race/ethnicity and gender.

Given the variety and richness of the traditions and paradigms informing studies of class, scholars consider a vast number of stereotypes. At the core, most stereotypical media content can be tied to the idea of *symbolic annihilation* (Gerbner, 1972; Gerbner & Gross, 1976; Tuchman, 1978). This concept assumes both that the media offer symbolic (rather than literal) representations of society and that to be represented in the media is in itself a form of power. In the symbolic representation of a society, media can either exalt or disparage certain social groups. Tuchman (1978) focused on the representation of women, but the concept is applicable to other socially-constructed groups including those based on social class. She argued that through the mechanisms of omission, condemnation, and trivialization, the media reflect a social world in which women are consistently devalued. Women are underrepresented in the media, and when they are represented, they may be incompetent, function effectively only when they remain within the confines of normative gender roles, be evaluated primarily on their appearance, and so forth; if so, they have been symbolically annihilated. The concept is instructive: when considering representations of people in certain classes or SES, we should question not only the use of stereotypes but also the extent to which such individuals are even portrayed. If certain social classes are not represented, audiences might infer that the group does not exist, does not matter, or is not valuable.

The following sections consider entrenched representations and stereotypes in the 20th and 21st Centuries, although some analyses cross this convenient but artificial boundary. The following sections also cross boundaries in that what seems to be presented as a single stereotype may at times be expanded to consider related stereotypes.

20th Century Representations and Stereotypes

Symbolic annihilation is evident in the varied stereotypes of class/SES in the 20th Century, especially in mediated representations of the poor and the working class. Both the working class and the poor have been and continue to be relatively nonexistent in the media. When portrayed, the working class was often shown to be deserving of their place in society. Whether they are authoritarian, tasteless, irresponsible, backwards, buffoons, or exhibit other shortcomings, they fail to adhere to middle-class expectations (Butsch, 2017; DeFleur, 1964; Kendall, 2011; Lipsitz, 1988; Opler, 2003; Skeggs, 2004). Despite this, scholars have noted that the working class tends to be portrayed as content, even happy, in both TV content (Thomas & Callahan, 1982) and advertising (Paulson & O'Guinn, 2012), and that poor and working-class hardships are minimized (Streib, Ayala, & Wixted, 2016). The poor, when portrayed, are stereotyped in numerous ways; African Americans are overrepresented, and the media often blame the poor, rather than social structures, for poverty (Entman, 1995; Katz, 2013). The middle class, on the other hand, is *not* omitted, trivialized, or condemned. The middle class is progressive, good; it is normative, typical, the yardstick against which all others are compared (Kendall, 2011; Mantsios, 2007; Skeggs, 2004; Streib et al., 2016). Those who do not measure up are deviant, and in many ways presented as an "other."

Working-class men as buffoons. Richard Butsch found that working-class families appeared in only 14% of television sitcoms between 1946 and 2000 (Butsch, 2003). Besides this absence, "the stock character of the ineffectual, even buffoonish working class man has persisted as the dominant image" (2003, p. 32). This stereotype can be found in shows such as *The Honeymooners* (1950s), *The Flintstones* (1960s), *All in the Family* (1970s), and *The Simpsons* (1980s–present).

Butsch highlighted just how thoroughly these working-class men are marked as failures by comparing their representation to the far more favorable depictions of not only middle-class men, but also their own wives. In this way, Butsch acknowledged the intersection of class and gender. These working-class buffoons fail to live up to masculine expectations. In essence they become feminized, rendered powerless. Berk (1977) posited that comedy based on the flaws of the past, noting that viewers accept these class stereotypes whereas they "would not tolerate a comparable racial stereotype" (p. 29). Thus, the intersection of race, class, and so forth explicates our understanding of class positions.

Scholars explain that some form of adjustment may be needed when people hold contradictory social positions (Baron, 1989, Butsch, 1992; Scott, 1988). Butsch (1992) is indebted to the work of Scott (1988) and Baron (1989) on the gender coding of social class and the ability for gender to establish class status. At times, individuals might hold contradictory class positions; as a simple example including only two positions, consider that a White woman is simultaneously less powerful (than men) and more powerful (than people of color). A working-class man such as those represented in the sitcoms analyzed by Butsch holds the contradictory positions of being more powerful than women but less powerful than the middle or upper classes. This and other contradictions (based on any of the multitude of intersections of race, gender, sexuality, class, and so forth) can be resolved by undercutting the higher status position. The symbolic coding of the working-class man might, for example, de-masculinize him by "applying descriptors that contradict the culturally accepted definition of masculine" (Butsch, 1992, p. 387). The incompetent, irresponsible male buffoon in working class sitcoms, who is inferior to his wife and even to his children, is in this way feminized. The process "not only devalues them as men but also uses gender to establish their subordinate class status" (p. 387).

Organized labor as negative. Labor unions, clearly associated with the working class, are often stereotyped, as Puette (1992) found in an expansive analysis of both entertainment and journalism. Across film, television, and print media, Puette found that labor unions are shown as corrupt entities which protect lazy workers and harm our nation's ability to compete because they demand exorbitant wages. They are shown as a relic of the past which is no longer needed. Puette argued that news coverage is biased against organized labor. As an example of the portrayal of organized labor in films (and public/media industry response to those portrayals), Puette (1992) discussed two 1954 films about unions: *Salt of the Earth* and *On The Waterfront*. Although Puette considered both films outstanding, he noted that they generated significantly different responses. The former, which "portrayed a clean, worker-inspired union ... was viciously attacked" and remains relatively unseen, whereas the latter, "a film that chose to look at the seamy side of the movement was given awards and the widest possible release" (p. 21).

The poor as invisible, racialized, and undeserving. This set of stereotypes reflects multiple factors. The most frequent stereotype of the poor is that they do not exist. News media explicitly address poverty in only a small percentage of stories (Entman, 1995; Iyengar,1990). When poverty is addressed, the coverage tends to overrepresent people of color, especially African Americans (Clawson & Trice, 2000; Entman, 1995; Gilens, 1996; Iyengar, 1990). Thus, we see the intersection of race and class/SES. The media also tend to focus on people whose poverty is implicitly or explicitly due to their own behaviors and moral deficiencies—the so-called undeserving poor (Katz, 2013; Kelly, 2010; Kendall, 2011; Rose & Baumgartner, 2013). Perceived deficiencies include drinking, laziness, bearing children out of wedlock (at worst being a "welfare mother" which is an unmistakably gendered deficiency often tied to race), and so forth. The undeserving poor will not do what it takes to lift themselves out of poverty, unlike the deserving poor who are deemed morally upstanding and are at least trying to rise to society's expectations. Considerations of whether the poor are deserving or undeserving necessarily focus attention on the individual and usually frame poverty as an individual problem, rather than a structural or societal problem (Bullock et al., 2001; Entman, 1995; Gilens, 1996; Iyengar, 1990), reinforcing the myth of the American Dream.

The normativity of the middle class. In both news and entertainment, audiences encounter the middle (and upper-middle) classes almost exclusively. In shows such as *Father Knows Best* (1950s), *The Brady Bunch* (1960s–1970s), *Happy Days* (1970s–1980s), and *The Cosby Show* (1980s–1990s), the middle class was viewers' appropriate role model, successful at home and in the workplace. On such shows, characters enacted "the presumed middle-class values of honesty, integrity, and hard work, all believed to enable people to get ahead in life and solve problems as they arose" (Kendall, 2011, p. 179). According to Butsch (2003), "the domestic situation comedy population has been persistently and overwhelmingly middle class, predominantly successful professionals" (p. 390). Butsch argued that this pattern reinforces the normativity of middle class success and encourages labeling unsuccessful working-class men "deviants who are responsible for their own failure" (p. 390). Further, the preponderance of middle class families in domestic sitcoms exists even though the genre affords great flexibility for portraying social classes. Butsch (1992) noted that some genres, such as the detective series, are rooted in occupation and hence social class is relatively more restricted in those genres than in sitcoms (Butsch, 1992).

The wealthy are fascinating; they are benevolent—except when they're not. Mantsios (2007) argued that our culture holds the myths that "the wealthy are fascinating and benevolent" and that "the wealthy include a few bad apples" (p. 641). Our fascination with the upper class—at times focusing on conspicuous consumption and extravagance—has been fed by journalism (society pages, profiles of business leaders, gossip columns) and entertainment (*Dallas* [1970s–1990s], *Lifestyles of the Rich and Famous* [1980s–1990s], and *Beverly Hills, 90210* [1990s]). Such content both reinforces the American Dream and allows audiences "to gawk at [the] excesses" (Mantsios, 2007, p. 640). Coverage of major fundraising events or charitable donations highlights the generosity of the upper class. The wealthy are largely presented positively, and "the media assures us that wealth and power are benevolent. One person's capital accumulation is presumed to be good for all" (Mantsios, 2007, p. 640). Further, accumulating significant wealth is often portrayed as the result of an individual's hard work, creativity, intelligence. In the process, just as when poor people are blamed for their own poverty, social structures and systemic inequities providing advantages to the upper class are not considered; in America, you can make it if you try.

Yet members of the upper class do at times misbehave. When they do, the media have tended to focus "on the individual scoundrel rather than on harm done by many people or established corporate practices" and as a result "media audiences typically view the problem as one of individual, rather than corporate, abuse" (Kendall, 2011, p. 55). The social structures are not questioned; they are in fact reinforced.

21st Century Representations and Stereotypes

For several decades leading into the turn of the century, academic interest had trended away from studying class; Deery and Press (2017) explained that researchers had turned their focus to individualization and identity politics (with greater attention to gender, race, and sexuality). Callier (2014) noted that social class had been "long out of fashion in the critically informed discourse analysis of US society" (p. 582), a gap which Henry and Caldwell (2008) said had lasted 30 years in the field of marketing. Yet, by 1994, Golding had voiced a rising concern that researchers "must reconnect with wider questions of social inequality, power, and process" (1994, p. 461), and, as Taylor (2007) put it, we have seen a "resurgence of interest in class across disciplines" (p. 4).

When considering class/SES in media content in the new century, there is no doubt that the stereotypes of the 20th Century remain alive and well. Each of the stereotypes mentioned in the previous section can be found today, although some have evolved. Symbolic annihilation continues. Through the process of undercutting and feminizing described above, the symbolic coding of people inhabiting contradictory social positions continues to prioritize the dominant social positions: the straight, White, Christian, middle- to upper-class, well-educated male. Thus, the (gendered, raced, and so forth) middle class is still presented as normative (Bishop, 2008; Butsch, 2017; Callier, 2014; Jakobsson & Stiernstedt, 2018a, 2018b; Stiernstedt & Jakobsson, 2018). We are still fascinated with wealth and extravagence and dysfunction (*Gossip Girl* [2000s–2010s], *The OC* [2000s], *Keeping Up With The Kardashians* [2000s-present], *Succession* [2010s–present]); journalism still presents the actions of wealthy individuals who behave badly as individual actions, not reflecting societal structures. Again, we cannot consider all stereotypes; below is a discussion of the softening of the working-class male buffoon stereotype, the reemergence of the working-class hero, and the racialized poor and working class.

The softening of the working-class buffoon. This change is occurring at a time in which the situations presented in situation comedies have become much more complex and the families more varied. Richard Butsch, whose work on 20th Century sitcoms was discussed above, extended his analysis through 2016. Although the total number of TV sitcoms decreased, Butsch (2017) found that occupational classes are less distinctly isolated in the 21st Century sitcom, and representations of the working class have become relatively more common and slightly more varied. The male head-of-household is less likely to be a buffoon than he was before. Indeed, sitcom households are no longer always headed by straight married White men; the nontraditional family is becoming more typical in sitcoms (e.g., *Modern Family* [2000s-present]). Still, although the stereotype of the working-class man as buffoon has, in some ways, softened, Butsch (2017) presented *The Family Guy* and *The King of Queens* (both of which began right before the turn of the century but extended well into the 2000s [*King of Queens*] and even the 2020s [*Family Guy*]) as forms of *Flintstones* (1960s) revivals.

Working-class heroes. The 21st Century saw the resurgence of an earlier stereotype, what Skeggs (2004, p. 97) called "the heroic industrial working-class man." However, industrial and manufacturing work has largely been overtaken by service work, and the new heroic stereotype takes two very different forms. The first is a direct result of the 9/11 terrorist attacks; Kendall (2011) argues that "no event in U.S. history did more to popularize the image of working-class heroes and victims" (p. 137). Firefighters, police officers, emergency medical technicians, and members of other labor unions who lost their lives in the aftermath of the attacks were presented as heroes and praised for their sacrifice. Providing a counterpoint to the stereotype of unions and union workers as selfish, greedy, and corrupt, the media began sharing inspirational stories about the heroic actions of these individuals and groups. These union workers—usually male—were framed as worthy of the highest praise and emulation. Similarly, according to Kendall (2011), the media presented as heroic the workers and volunteers involved in responding to natural and other disasters such as Hurricane Katrina or the BP Deepwater Horizon oil spill.

The second form of the working-class hero stereotype appears in a subset of the reality television genre. These programs, such as *Dirty Jobs* (2000s–2010s), *American Chopper* (2000s–present), *Duck Dynasty* (2010s), *Deadliest Catch* (2000s–present), and *Ice Road Truckers* (2000s–2010s), focus on working-class men following manly pursuits (Carroll, 2008; Kendall, 2011; Kirby, 2013; O'Sullivan, 2016). The activities are decidedly masculine—especially when they are dangerous—and these individuals are presented as "real men." Clearly this stereotype is gendered, demonstrating to all that this rough-and-tumble, potentially hazardous world is the province of neither women nor non-hypermasculine men. In some cases, the men who do not fit into this world are diminished, in essence feminized. This stereotype is also largely raced, especially when the men involved embrace the label or identity of "redneck."

The racialized poor and working class. This set of 21st Century stereotypes reveals that the stereotypes of the poor discussed previously are still evident (Kelly, 2010; Larsen & Dejgaard, 2013; Rose & Baumgartner, 2013; Tihelkova, 2015). In addition, a particularly powerful racialization—invoking Whiteness—is evident in representations of both the poor and the working class, largely on reality shows.

Barton and Davis (2016) found that the portrayals of poor and working class people in reality TV were linked to stereotypes reflecting whether the people deserved help. Over time, poor and marginalized people have become increasingly denigrated and blamed for their own fate. Other scholars have also noted that reality shows tend to represent the working class negatively and the middle to upper classes positively (Fairclough, 2004; Matheson, 2007; Palmer, 2004).

As in other media content, class stereotypes in the reality genre frequently intersect with raced and gendered stereotypes. Shugart (2006) argued that reality court programs (she analyzed *Judge Judy, Judge Joe Brown, Divorce Court*, all of which began in the late 1990s and maintained a strong presence into the 21st Century, with *Judge Judy* and *Divorce Court* still on the air in the 2020s) serve a disciplinary function, especially when the working class or the poor are people of color, who are depicted as "requiring considerable disciplinary force" (p. 97). The shows construct "those individuals as representing a significant moral and implicitly criminal threat" (p. 97). Most shows highlighting physical transformations (e.g., *Extreme Makeover* (2000s) and *The Swan* (2000s) present makeovers of women who fail to measure up to gendered and classed expectations. As Franco (2008, pp. 482–483) put it, "the underlying normative gender and class regimes of extreme bodily transformations are echoed ... across a broad range of reality formats that find women lacking in all departments." Some shows, such as *Undercover Boss* (2010s-present), might feature the deserving poor or hardworking honest worker, but in the process labor relations are personalized and distorted; concrete issues in the workplace such as sexism, racism, wages, health-care benefits, and the like are ignored (Aho, 2016). *Undercover Boss*, according to Aho, "showcases well-meaning bosses and hardworking individuals" and not "the wrongdoings of executives within a capitalist system that is based on power imbalances favoring exploitation and inequality" (p. 94).

We also see, in the reality genre and beyond, a clear invocation of the race-based stereotypes of White trash and rednecks. The redneck identity "strongly represents masculinity and whiteness ... This identity is unabashedly white, but opposed to middle- and upper-class whiteness" (Morris,

2008, p. 741). Pruitt (2016) described the redneck identity as "a badge of pride and honor among many working class and rural Americans" (p. 294) and, thus, quite distinct from White trash. To be redneck is to perform a life-style orientation that is White, rural (usually Southern), and "authentically" (and hegemonically) masculine (O'Sullivan, 2016). O'Sullivan (2016) wrote that hegemonic masculinity in the US is marked by "race (whiteness), region (rural/South), and a relatively subordinate, vaguely working-class identity that masquerades as rugged individualism" (p. 377). The masculinized red-neck identity is, on *Duck Dynasty* (2010s), advanced as the polar opposite of the feminized so-called yuppie man who transgresses masculinized gender rules by cooking, failing to hunt, and so forth (O'Sullivan, 2016). Still, not all rednecks are men, as evidenced by the wives and children of these dominant men and shows such as *Here Comes Honey Boo Boo* (2010s) (Owen, 2016).

In some cases, what may be seen as overly forceful or even aggressive pride in one's redneck identity might reveal an unstated fear about the relative insecurity of one's own social or economic position. Davies (2010) studied a set of jokes evolving from popular comedian Jeff Foxworthy's "You might be a redneck" line. The "you might be White trash" jokes functioned to estab-lish a hierarchy in which White trash is designated as a lower social category than the rednecks making the jokes. The jokes present rednecks' social val-ues as positive, but White trash were "poor, stupid, reckless, dirty, toothless, homophobic, alcoholic, addicted to tobacco in various forms, and violent" (Davis, 2010, p. 195).

Unlike "redneck," the term "White trash" explicitly draws attention to the otherwise invisible normativity of Whiteness, highlighting that norms have been broken. White trash fail to follow cultural expectations and, in the media, are punished for their transgressions by being denigrated and humil-iated (Lockyer, 2010; Loughnan, Haslam, Sutton, & Spencer, 2014; Pini & Previte, 2013; Raisborough, Frith, & Klein, 2012). To Wray (2006), the con-cept of White trash expresses fundamental tensions and deep contradictions. It simultaneously evokes cleanliness and filth, and in the process "names a people whose very existence seems to threaten the symbolic and social order" (p. 2). It creates and recreates what Wilson (2002) called "an underlying structure of attitudes and assumptions materially prejudicial to those to whom it is applied" (p. 399).

Effects of Stereotypical Representations of Class and Socioeconomic Status

The predominant line of research examining the effects of class/SES-related stereotypes is the work related to images of poverty and the poor. Iyengar's (1990) analysis revealed that TV news framed the issue of poverty in one of two ways: episodic framing (stories that focused on particular individuals and their personal experiences) and thematic framing (impersonal stories that focused on general trends, facts and figures, or public policy matters). Besides revealing the dominance of the episodic frame (reinforcing the stereotype and essentially blaming the victim), Iyengar also showed how these frames correlate with people's attributions of responsibility for poverty. In an experiment using multiple news stories with episodic and thematic frames, Iyengar's subjects were significantly more likely to hold individuals responsible for poverty (and society less responsible) when exposed to episodically-framed stories than to thematically-framed stories. Further, subjects responded differently to the specific types of individuals featured in the stories using episodic frames. Although Iyengar's research was not designed specifically to test the direct effects of stereotypical representations, it does show that how the poor are portrayed can indeed affect viewers' perceptions about the causes of and solutions for poverty.

If media framing and stereotypical representations of class/SES can affect people's attitudes and beliefs, the next step is to see whether those attitudes and beliefs can influence policy. The results of Hannah and Cafferty's (2006) experiment "suggest that the media's coverage of poverty is likely undermining the public's willingness to help the poor" (p. 3011). Without addressing stereotypes per se, Abril, Binder, Nan, Nevar, & Rojas's (2014) experiment provided evidence that different ways of framing stories about poverty affect people's willingness to support public policies to eliminate child poverty. Perceiving social class as controllable (thus associating poverty with individuals), "has direct implications for the kinds of economic and social policies that are supported by the public" (Williams, 2009, p. 42). Bullock, Williams, and Limbert (2003) found that people who attributed poverty to individual causes favored restrictive welfare policies, whereas those who attributed poverty to structural causes supported progressive welfare policies. Using an innovative new measure called the Government Generosity Index, Rose and Baumgartner (2013) found that "the tone of media coverage can predict government spending on the poor" (p. 41) and, ultimately, that "the portrayal of the poor as either deserving or lazy drives public policy" (p. 22).

Apart from studies related to media coverage of poverty, there is almost no empirical research demonstrating the effects of mediated representations of class/SES. Pennell's (2014) experiment using clips from the reality show *Teen*

Mom (2000s–present) documented both the impact of class representations on class-related beliefs and the intersectional impact of class and gender on gender-related beliefs. She found that representations of working-class teen parents generated more favorable attitudes about working-class people, although the working class moms were deemed less responsible than middle-class parents. The relationship between the parents' social class and subjects' attitudes and beliefs was moderated by identification, homophily, and parasocial interaction. Finally, in an experiment involving a so-called slut-shaming post on social media, Papp, Erchull, Liss, Waaland-Kreutzer, and Godfrey (2017) discovered that social class and clothing affected subjects' perceptions of both the "slut" and the "shamer."

Directions for Future Research

Many scholars in many disciplines have used many approaches to study mediated representations of class and SES. The question of social class is inherently complex, and researchers always need to delimit their investigations. Thus, on one level, suggestions for further research could be specific to a discipline or even a discipline's subfield. However, on another level, scholars should be wary of overly-restrictive parameters when studying the literature and theory related to their research. Because of the complexity of social class, and its inevitable confluence with other socially-constructed phenomena such as race, gender, sexuality, and so forth, scholars should be encouraged to cross boundaries and break down barriers. We should acknowledge and be informed by the diversity of perspectives being brought to the study of class.

Researchers should work toward a greater understanding of the psychological mechanisms underpinning responses to media content—and they should do so because of what results from those responses. For example, as Hannah and Cafferty (2006) note, "The importance of causal attributions lies in their influence on eliciting helping behavior" (p. 2996).

Scholars should also continue to work on various models to describe, explain, or predict class-relevant media content and the responses thereto, such as in the work of Hannah and Cafferty (2006), Behm-Morawitz, Miller, and Lewallen (2018), and Ramasubramanian (2011, whose work on race is directly applicable to social class). These studies make important contributions.

Of particular interest is Behm-Morawitz, Miller, and Lewallen's (2018) model for quantitatively identifying representations of social class, which includes occupation, financial security, and material possessions. Perhaps this model could be expanded to explicitly incorporate Bourdieu's (1977, 1984) multiple forms of capital: economic, symbolic, cultural and social. Although economic positions clearly matter, a model folding in the additional forms of capital could facilitate a richer, more contextualized, and more relational understanding of social class even in the quantitative realm.

Class Dismissed?

We have a long way to go before we can say that our mediated representations of class and SES are no longer rooted in stereotypes and no longer symbolically annihilate the working class and the poor, or present the bulk of society as an imagined middle class. Given the impact of the portrayal of class/SES on individuals and policy, we must continue to pay close attention to these issues. As Gamson, Croteau, Hoynes, & Sasson (1992, p. 374) wrote:

> We walk around with media-generated images of the world, using them to construct meaning about political and social issues. The lens through which we receive these images is not neutral but evinces the power and point of view of the political and economic elites who operate and focus it. And the special genius of this system is to make the whole process seem so normal and natural that the very art of social construction is invisible.

Class is not dismissed. Continued research (and activism) is needed to make visible the processes involved in the social construction of our reality, the power held by the media and other elites in that process, and the complex interrelationships among class, gender, race, sexuality, and other facets of our multidimensional selves.

References

Abril, E. P., Binder, A. R., Nan, X., Nevar, P. M., & Rojas, H. (2014). Persuasion and affect in the framing of poverty: An experiment on goal framing. *Signo y Pensamiento, 33*(65), 50–68. doi: 10.11144/Javeriana.SYP33-65.pafp.

Aho, T. (2016). Reality TV and its audiences reconsidered: Class and poverty in *Undercover Boss* (CBS). In S. Lemke & W. Schniedermann (Eds.), *Class divisions in serial television* (pp. 89–117). London, UK: Palgrave Macmillan.

Baron, A. (1989). Questions of gender: Deskilling and demasculinization in the U.S. printing industry 1830–1915. *Gender and History, 1,* 178–199.

Barton, A., & Davis, H. (2016). From empowering the shameful to shaming the empowered: Shifting depictions of the poor in "reality TV". *Crime Media Culture, 14*(2), 191–211.

Behm-Morawitz, E., Miller, B. M., & Lewallen, J. (2018) A model for quantitatively analyzing representations of social class in screen media, *Communication Research Reports, 35,* 210–221. doi: 10.1080/08824096.2018.1428544

Berk, L. M. (1977). The great middle American dream machine. *Journal of Communication*, *27*(3), 27–31.

Bishop, R. (2008). From a distance: Marginalization of the poor in television ads for Goodwill Industries. *Journal of Poverty*, *12*, 411–431. doi: 10.1080/10875540802350096

Bourdieu, P. (1977). *Outline of a theory of practice*. Cambridge, UK: Cambridge University Press.

Bourdieu, P. (1984). *Distinction: A social critique of the judgement of taste* (R. Nice, Trans.). Cambridge, MA.: Harvard University Press

Bullock, H. E, Williams, W. R., & Limbert, W. M. (2003). Predicting support for policies: The impact of attributions and beliefs about inequality. *Journal of Poverty*, *7*, 35–56. doi: 10.1300/J134v07n03_03

Bullock, H. E., Wyche, K. F., & Williams, W. R. (2001). Media images of the poor. *Journal of Social Issues*, *57*, 229–246.

Butsch, R. (1992). Class and gender in four decades of television situation comedy: Plus ça change. *Critical Studies in Mass Communication*, *9*, 387–399. doi: 10.1080/15295039209366841

Butsch, R. (2003). A half century of class and gender in American TV sitcoms. *Cercles*, *8*, 16–34.

Butsch, R. (2017). Class and gender through seven decades of American television sitcoms. In J. Deery & A. Press, (Eds.), *Media and class: TV, film, and digital culture* (pp. 38–52). New York, NY: Routledge.

Callier, P. (2014). Class as a semiotic resource in consumer advertising: Markedness, heteroglossia, and commodity temporalities. *Discourse & Society*, *25*, 581–599. doi: 10.1177/0957926514536829

Carroll, H. (2008). Men's soaps: Automotive television programming and contemporary working-class masculinities. *Television & New Media*, *9*, 263–283. doi: 10.1177/1527476408315495

Clawson, R. A., & Trice, R. (2000). Poverty as we know it: Media portrayals of the poor. *Public Opinion Quarterly*, *64*, 53–64.

Davies, C. E. (2010). Joking as boundary negotiation among "good old boys": "White trash" as a social category at the bottom of the Southern working class in Alabama. *Humor*, *23*(2), 179–200. doi: 10.1515/HUMR.2010.009

Deery, J., & Press, A. (2017). Introduction: Studying media and class. In J. Deery & A. Press, (Eds.), *Media and class: TV, film, and digital culture* (pp. 1–17). New York, NY: Routledge.

DeFleur, M. L. (1964). Occupational roles as portrayed on television. *Public Opinion Quarterly*, *28*(1), 57–74.

Entman, R. M. (1995). Television, democratic theory and the visual construction of poverty. *Research in Political Sociology*, *7*, 139–159.

Fairclough, K. (2004), Women's work? *Wife Swap* and the reality problem. *Feminist Media Studies*, *4*, 344–347.

Franco, J. (2008). *Extreme Makeover:* The politics of gender, class, and cultural identity. *Television & New Media, 9,* 471–486. doi: 10.1177/1527476408323339

Gamson, W. A., Croteau, D., Hoynes, W., & Sasson, T. (1992). Media images and the social construction of reality. *Annual Review of Sociology, 18,* 373–393.

Gerbner, G. (1972). Violence in television drama: Trends and symbolic functions. In G. A. Comstock & E. A. Rubenstein (Eds.), *Media content and control, Television and social behavior* (Vol. 1, pp. 28–127). Washington, DC: U.S. Government Printing Office.

Gerbner, G., & Gross, L. (1976). Living with television. *Journal of Communication, 26*(2), 172–199.

Gilens, M. (1996). Race and poverty in America: Public misperceptions and the American news media. *Public Opinion Quarterly, 60,* 515–541.

Golding, P. (1994). Telling stories: Sociology, journalism, and the informed citizen. *European Journal of Communication, 9,* 461–484.

Hannah, G., & Cafferty, T. P. (2006). Attribute and responsibility framing effects in television news coverage of poverty. *Journal of Applied Social Psychology, 36,* 2993–3014. doi: 10.1111/j.0021-9029.2006.00139.x

Henry, P., & Caldwell, M. (2008). Spinning the proverbial wheel?: Social class and marketing. *Marketing Theory, 8,* 387–405. doi: 10.1177/1470593108096542

Iyengar, S. (1990). Framing responsibility for political issues: The case of poverty. *Political Behavior, 12,* 19–40.

Jakobsson, P., & Stiernstedt, F. (2018a). Naturalizing social class as a moral category on Swedish mainstream television. *Nordicom Review, 39,* 81–94. doi: 10.2478/nor-2018-0003

Jakobsson, P., & Stiernstedt, F. (2018b). Voice, silence and social class on television. *European Journal of Communication, 33,* 522–539. doi: 10.1177/0267323118784819

Katz, M. B. (2013). *The undeserving poor: America's enduring confrontation with poverty: Fully updated and revised* (2nd ed.). Oxford, UK: Oxford University Press.

Kelly, M. (2010). Regulating the reproduction and mothering of poor women: The controlling image of the welfare mother in television news coverage of welfare reform. *Journal of Poverty, 14,* 76–96. doi: 10.1080/10875540903489447

Kendall, D. (2011). *Framing class: Media representations of wealth and poverty in America.* Lanham, MD: Rowman & Littlefield.

Kirby, L. A. (2013). Cowboys of the high seas: Representations of working-class masculinity on *Deadliest Catch. The Journal of Popular Culture, 46,* 109–118.

Larsen, C. A., & Dejgaard, T. E. (2013) The institutional logic of images of the poor and welfare recipients: A comparative study of British, Swedish and Danish newspapers. *Journal of European Social Policy, 23,* 287–299. doi: 10.1177/0958928713480068

Lipsitz, G. (1988). The meaning of memory: Family, class and ethnicity in early network television programs. *Camera Obscura, 6*(1), 78–117.

Lockyer, S. (2010). Dynamics of social class contempt in contemporary British television comedy. *Social Semiotics, 20*(2), 121–138. doi: 10.1080/10350330903565758

Loughnan, S., Haslam, N., Sutton, R. M., & Spencer, B. (2014). Dehumanization and social class: Animality in the stereotypes of "white trash," "chavs," and "bogans". *Social Psychology*, *45*(1), 54–61. doi: 10.1027/1864-9335/a000159

Mantsios, G. (2007). Media magic: Making class invisible. In P. S. Rothenberg (Ed.), *Race, class, and gender in the United States: An integrated study* (7th ed., pp. 636–644). New York, NY: Worth Publishers.

Matheson, S. A. (2007). The cultural politics of *Wife Swap*: Taste, lifestyle media, and the American family. *Film & History: An Interdisciplinary Journal of Film and Television Studies*, *37*(2), 33–47. doi: 10.1353/flm.2007.0057

Morris, E. W. (2008). "Rednecks," "Rutters," and "Rithmetic": Social class, masculinity, and schooling in a rural context. *Gender & Society*, *22*, 728–751.

O'Sullivan, S. E. M. (2016). Playing "Redneck": White masculinity and working-class performance on *Duck Dynasty*. *The Journal of Popular Culture*, *49*, 367–384. doi: 10.1111/jpcu.12403

Opler, D. (2003). Between the "other" classes: *The Nanny* and the ideological creation of American middle class content. *Cercles*, *8*, 68–77.

Owen, D. (2016). "Hillbillies," "welfare queens," and "teen moms": American media's class distinctions. In S. Lemke & W. Schniedermann (Eds.), *Class divisions in serial television* (pp. 47–87). London, UK: Palgrave Macmillan.

Palmer, G. (2004). "The new you": Class and transforming in lifestyle television. In S. Holmes and D. Jermyn (Eds.), *Understanding reality TV* (pp. 173–190). New York, NY: Routledge.

Papp, L. J., Erchull, M. J., Liss, M., Waaland-Kreutzer, L., & Godfrey, H. (2017). Slut-shaming on Facebook: Do social class or clothing affect perceived acceptability? *Gender Issues*, *34*, 240–257. doi: 10.1007/s12147-016-9180-7

Paulson, E. L., & O'Guinn, T. C. (2012). Working-class cast: Images of the working class in advertising, 1950–2010. *The Annals of the American Academy of Political and Social Science*, *644*(1), 50–69. doi: 10.1177/0002716212453133

Paulson, E. L., & O'Guinn, T. C. (2018). Marketing social class and ideology in post-World-War-Two American print advertising. *Journal of Macromarketing*, *38*(1), 7–28. doi: 10.1177/0276146717733788

Pennell, H. (2014). *Gendered and classed stereotyping: The effects of viewing* Teen Mom (Unpublished doctoral dissertation). University of Missouri, Columbia.

Pini, B., & Previte, J. (2013). Gender, class and sexuality in contemporary Australia: Representations of the boganette. *Australian Feminist Studies*, *28*(78), 348–363. doi: 10.1080/08164649.2013.857385

Pruitt, L. R. (2016). Welfare queens and White trash. *Southern California Interdisciplinary Law Journal*, *25*(2), 289–310.

Puette, W. J. (1992). *Through jaundiced eyes: How the media view organized labor*. Ithaca, NY: ILR Press.

Raisborough, J., Frith, H., & Klein, O. (2012). Media and class-making: What lessons are learnt when a celebrity chav dies? *Sociology*, *47*(2), 251–266. doi: 10.1177/0038038512444813

Ramasubramanian, S. (2011). The impact of stereotypical versus counterstereotypical media exemplars on racial attitudes, causal attributions, and support for affirmative action. *Communication Research, 38*, 497–516. doi: 10.1177/0093650210384854

Rose, M., & Baumgartner, F. R. (2013). Framing the poor: Media coverage and U.S. poverty policy, 1960–2008. *Policy Studies Journal, 41*(1), 22–53. https://doi-org.proxy.cc.uic.edu/10.1111/psj.12001

Rubin, M., Denson, N., Kilpatrick, S., Matthews, K. E., Stehlik, T., & Zyngier, D. (2014). "I Am Working-Class": Subjective self-definition as a missing measure of social class and socioeconomic status in higher education research. *Educational Researcher, 43*(4), 196–200. doi: 10.3102/0013189X14528373

Scott, J. (1988). *Gender and the politics of history.* New York, NY: Columbia University Press.

Sen, A. F., & Sen, Y. F. (2016). Media representation of class issues in Turkey: A review on media coverage of work-related rights. In J. Servaes & T. Oyedemi (Eds.), *Social inequalities, media, and communication: Theory and roots* (pp. 125–145). Lanham, MD: Rowman & Littlefield.

Shugart, H. A. (2006). Ruling class: Disciplining class, race, and ethnicity in television reality court shows. *The Howard Journal of Communications, 17*, 79–100. doi: 10.1080/10646170600656839

Skeggs, B. (2004). *Class, self, culture.* London, UK: Routledge.

Skeggs, B., & Wood, H. (2011) Introduction: Real class. In B. Skeggs & H. Wood, (Eds.), *Reality television and class.* London, UK: Palgrave Macmillan.

Stiernstedt, F., & Jakobsson, P. (2018). Ghettos and gated communities in the social landscape of television: Representations of class in 1982 and 2015. In D. O'Neill & M. Wayne (Eds.), *Considering class: Theory, culture and the media in the 21st century* (pp. 255–272). Leiden: Brill.

Streib, J., Ayala, M., & Wixted, C. (2016): Benign inequality: Frames of poverty and social class inequality in children's movies. *Journal of Poverty, 21*, 1–19. doi: 10.1080/10875549.2015.1112870

Taylor, Y. (2007). *Working-class lesbian life: Classed outsiders.* Basingstoke, UK: Palgrave Macmillan.

Telford, T. (2019, September 26). Income inequality in America is the highest it's been since Census Bureau started tracking it, data shows. *The Washington Post.* Retrieved from https://www.washingtonpost.com/business/2019/09/26/income-inequality-america-highest-its-been-since-census-started-tracking-it-data-show/

Thomas, S., & Callahan, B. P. (1982). Allocating happiness: TV families and social class. *Journal of Communication, 32*(3), 184–190. doi: 10.1111/j.1460-2466.1982.tb02510.x

Tihelkova, A. (2015). Framing the "Scroungers": The re-emergence of the stereotype of the undeserving poor and its reflection in the British press. *Brno Studies in English, 41*(2), 121–139. doi: 10.5817/BSE2015-2-8

Tuchman, G. (1978). Introduction: The symbolic annihilation of women by the mass media. In G. Tuchman, A. K. Daniels, & J. Benet (Eds.), *Hearth and home: Images of women in the mass media* (pp. 3–38). Oxford, UK: Oxford University Press.

Williams, W. R. (2009). Struggling with poverty: Implications for theory and policy of increasing research on social class-based stigma. *Analyses of Social Issues and Public Policy*, 9(1), 37–56.

Wilson, J. Z. (2002). Invisible racism: The language and ontology of "White Trash". *Critique of Anthropology*, 22(4), 387–401. doi: 10.1177/0308275X020220040101

Wray, M. (2006). *Not quite white: White trash and the boundaries of whiteness*. Durham, NC: Duke University Press.

10 Coming Out in Primetime: Stereotypes of LGBTQ Communities

Leigh M. Moscowitz
University of South Carolina

In March of 2016, The CW's cult hit *The 100* (2014–present) shocked audiences with the sudden and seemingly random death of a beloved queer female character, Lexa, played by Alycia Debnam-Carey. Set in a post-apocalyptic world nearly 100 years after a nuclear holocaust, the series followed the lives of the few remaining survivors who led their own clans of people through an increasingly treacherous and uninhabitable world. The CW hit was lauded by LGBTQ (lesbian, gay, bisexual and transgender, queer) audiences who celebrated the "fierce, unconventional portrayals of female strength, power and relationships" (Snarker, 2016, para. 6). Fans of the show applauded the positive representations of Clarke Griffin (played by Eliza Taylor), the series' leading role and one of the few bisexual female characters on television at the time. That was until Lexa, Clarke's on-again, off-again female lover, was killed by a stray bullet intended for Clarke. The show not only abruptly killed off a queer female heroine but put an end to the short-lived same-sex love affair central to the plot.

Lexa's death sparked outrage among LGBTQ fans of the show. Her high-profile killing marked a total of four lesbian or bisexual female character deaths on television that month alone. With a total of only 28 lesbian or bisexual female characters on television that season, the loss of four in such a short time span generated controversy (Townsend, 2016). Fans of *The 100* took to social media in outrage, bringing renewed attention to the long-standing trope that has plagued queer representation in media for decades: Bury Your Gays. The Bury Your Gays stereotype acknowledges the higher number of queer characters on television, but argues LGBTQ content is often written in—and quickly written out of—mainstream media storylines to appeal to progressive audiences and profit off of LGBTQ representation (Bridges, 2018; Waggoner,

2018). Queer characters and plots are typically used to advance heterosexual storylines and then quickly discarded, leaving queer couples together on screen for only a short time, their romances often ending in tragedy. As Bridges (2018) put it, "queer characters are disproportionately more likely to die on-screen—often violently—than their straight counterparts" (p. 122) and in particular, queer women most often fall victim to this trope. The LGBTQ website Autostraddle went as far as to create an infographic of queer female deaths on television, dubbing it a "graveyard of dead queer women" (Hogan, 2016). Of the 383 lesbian or bisexual female characters to ever appear on American scripted television since 1976, the site claims, 95 of them have died.

After Lexa's death on *The 100*, queer fans launched a campaign to bring renewed attention to the Bury Your Gays trope, pressuring media producers to put an end to it by demonstrating the real-world costs of this dangerous framing for queer youth. The media watchdog group GLAAD (formerly Gay & Lesbian Alliance Against Defamation) reported an increase in this trope during the 2016–2017 season, highlighting over 25 queer female victims who died (Townsend, 2016). The activism surrounding Lexa's death and other similar fates also spurred a major fundraising campaign for The Trevor Project, the nation's leading LGBTQ suicide prevention organization, and forced *The 100*'s show creator Jason Rothenberg to apologize to viewers, acknowledging fans' "real emotional trauma" (Wigler, 2016, para. 4).

The story of a queer fan favorite's sudden death in a popular television series and forceful social media response highlights many of the contradictions surrounding LGBTQ representations in the contemporary media landscape. While there are more varied and nuanced representations than ever before, historic and dangerous anti-gay stereotypes persist and new problematic tropes emerge. Admittedly, the sheer volume of LGBTQ representations has vastly increased across film, television, streaming services and in social media. For example, before her untimely death, *The 100*'s Lexa was one of 70 LGBTQ characters across scripted broadcast during the 2016–2017 season, accounting for 7.8% of the total number of characters on TV (Townsend, 2016). By 2019, that number had more than doubled. GLAAD's report showed that for 2019–2020, a record number of 90 LGBTQ characters appeared on prime-time scripted television, accounting for 10.2% of the total (up from 8.8% during the 2018–2019; GLAAD, 2019–2020). However, even as more queer characters appeared on screen, "gay characters were nearly always punished within the narrative for their transgression via death, suicide, loneliness, and/or misery" (Bridges, 2018, p. 116), sparking an "LGBT Fans Deserve Better" movement to counter and reshape LGBTQ narratives (Hogan, 2016).

The 2010s have seen the historic prevalence of, as well as great critical and commercial success for, queer-themed programming—including hit dramas like *Pose* (FX), *Killing Eve* (BBC America), and the reboot of *The L Word: Generation Q* (Showtime); comedies like *Modern Family* (ABC) and *Grace & Frankie* (Netflix); reality television such as the revival of *Queer Eye* (Netflix), *Ru Paul's Drag Race* (Logo TV), and *I Am Jazz* (TLC); and The CW featuring the first lead female superhero on network TV in *Batwoman*. Several of these performances have received industry accolades, including Emmy Awards for Eric Stonestreet in *Modern Family*, Billy Porter in *Pose* (the first time an openly gay Black man has won lead actor for a drama), and Ru Paul as best reality host, which he won four years in a row. At the box office, cinematic hits such as *Boy Erased* (2018), *Moonlight* (2016) and *Love, Simon* (2018) drew critical acclaim. These big screen moments exist alongside expanding visibility on small screens as well, with the growth of LGBTQ online safe spaces and popular queer-identified YouTubers.

These growing and more varied LGBTQ representations have evolved against a backdrop of advancing, yet contested, civil rights battles such as marriage equality, expanded rights to serve in the military, and hate crime protections. Nevertheless, verbal and physical attacks against LGBTQ people are on the rise. The FBI reports an increase in hate crimes against LGBTQ people in the past three years, with Black transgender women being the most targeted (Hauck, 2019). Moreover, for the first time in years, public polling data shows that young Americans may be growing *less* tolerant toward LGBTQ people, not more, as the percentage of young people saying they were comfortable interacting with a LGBTQ person has fallen from 53% in 2017 to 45% in 2018 (Miller, 2019). Despite the gains in media visibility, the terrain for LGBTQ people is contradictory at best.

This chapter examines the complex issues surrounding LGBTQ representations in media by first examining the history of invisibility of queer representation followed by the dangerous, anti-gay stereotypes that emerged when gay and lesbian people first began to appear in the media. Next, I explore the relative explosion of gay-themed media from the mid-1990s into this contemporary era, highlighting the stereotypes and tropes that mark the current media landscape. I conclude by highlighting the potential impact of these stereotypes for LGBTQ communities as well as for non-gay audiences, before charting future directions for media scholars, fans and activists alike.

Not Seen, Not Heard: The Erasure of LGBTQ People and Emergence of Historic Stereotypes

The sheer volume and variability of LGBTQ representations across today's mediascape is a monumental shift from the invisibility that has historically marked these communities (Gross, 2001; Walters, 2001a). After all, it was not until the late 1990s when Ellen DeGeneres emerged as the first leading lesbian character on mainstream television in the ABC sitcom *Ellen* (1994–1998). These moments of early visibility were celebrated as groundbreaking because images of the LGBTQ community in the media, consistent with other marginalized groups, were virtually nonexistent a mere half century ago, as chronicled in the 1995 documentary *The Celluloid Closet*. Invisibility in the media was eventually replaced with a host of anti-gay representations of LGBTQ people as sick victims, predatory villains, predatory perverts, dangerous criminals, laughable buffoons, queer radicals, and the "antithesis" of wholesome, American family values (Alwood, 1996; Gross, 2001; Walters, 2001a).

The absence of gay-themed narratives during this period of invisibility led to queer audiences developing a long-standing practice that continues today: actively re-reading or interpreting storylines and relationships otherwise coded "straight" as queer. In fact, Hollywood production codes of the 1930s, 1940s and 1950s (known as the Hays Code) forbid any act of "sex perversion," which included same-sex relations, romances or characters. The only way for LGBTQ audiences to "see themselves" on screen, then, was through active queer readings (Rappaport, 1997), an earlier form of "fan fiction" popular online today. While not explicit, early films included homoerotic overtones and scenes, prevalent in the classic American Western genre. The strategy of queer readings continued well into the 1980s even after gay and lesbian characters began to appear on television, reimagining same-sex friendships as romantic relationships like Cagney and Lacey, Lucille Ball and Ethel Vance, Kirk and Spock on *Star Trek*, Peppermint Patty and Lucy from *The Peanuts*, and DC Comics's Batman and Robin (Sender, Jhally, & Griffith, 1998).

Like early film and television, gay issues were considered "unfit to print" 60 years ago by America's widely read newspapers and magazines. When representations did begin to emerge, they perpetuated a host of anti-gay stereotypes to be feared and scorned (Alwood, 1996). Beginning in the 1940s, gay identity was characterized as a threat to national security, as army regulations forbid gay recruits from serving in World War II (Bennet, 2000). In the 1950s, "homosexuality became synonymous with communism" during McCarthy-era concerns over communists and "perverts" infiltrating top government agencies (Gross & Woods, 1999, citing a report in the *New York Times*, April 19, 1950).

It was not until the 1960s that the first gay people—exclusively men—appeared on television in the form of documentaries under the medical sickness model (Sender et al., 1998). With the growth of gay activism, a part of the larger civil rights movement of the 1960s and 1970s, it became harder to pretend gay people did not exist. The 1967 hour-long documentary "The Homosexual," hosted by CBS's Mike Wallace, represented one of the first television appearances by gay men, presented as an ominous and threatening exposé: "Homosexuality is in fact a mental illness which has reached epidemiological proportions," Wallace warned (1967 CBS reports: "The Homosexual"). The men interviewed were hidden behind potted plants or shown only partially, their faces and voices disguised, as they confessed their "sickness" and "immaturity" to television audiences (Gross & Woods, 1999, p. 350). These representations placed gay men as exhibits on display for presumably straight audiences to see for their own eyes that such an "epidemic" was, in fact, real.

In the late 1960s and early 1970s, the gay liberation movement began to change the face of LGBTQ visibility. The 1969 Stonewall riots protesting police harassment during the raid of the Stonewall Inn in Greenwich Village, New York, are considered by many the launch of the modern gay rights movement. Media representation became a defining logic of the movement. Nevertheless, while these events were hard to ignore, *The New York Times* buried coverage of the riots in a brief article on page 33, while the *New York Post* sensationalized the protests with the headline "Homo Nest Raided! Queen Bees Stinging Mad" (Alwood, 1996). From trivializing the Stonewall riots, to underreporting the numbers at gay rights marches by relying on "official" police estimates rather than those of organizers, mainstream news organizations have historically disparaged and marginalized gay activist efforts (Alwood, 1996; Gross & Woods, 1999).

It was not until 1973 that the American Psychological Association removed homosexuality from its list of mental disorders—but it was 1972 that the first television drama featured a gay storyline. *That Certain Summer*, a made-for-TV movie aired on ABC, featured a young teen who discovers his father is gay and included scenes where he meets his dad's romantic partner. Thought to be sympathetic and unapologetic with gay issues at the time, the drama still depicted gay life as difficult and full of strife (Gross, 2001).

The growing popularity of disco music in the 1970s gave increased visibility not only to Black and Hispanic artists but to sexual non-conformists as well. However, conservative backlash soon followed, charging LGBTQ people were "taking over the media," destroying communities, and dissolving the nuclear family. In 1977, Anita Bryant's hateful "Save the Children" campaign successfully overturned an equal rights ordinance that would have protected gays and lesbians from discrimination in housing and employment. A mother, celebrity singer and former Miss America, she became an important face of the Christian right and garnered considerable media coverage. However, the majority of mainstream newspapers and magazines were hesitant to cover any gay issues, resulting in a vast imbalance. The little reporting that did exist portrayed gay activism as a threat, a politically powerful interest taking over the nuclear family and putting American values at risk.

For example, the 1980 CBS special documentary report entitled "Gay Power, Gay Politics" has been widely criticized for its exaggeration, distortion, inaccuracies, and blatant disregard for journalistic standards (Sender et al., 1998). As Harry Reasoner narrates, to someone of his generation, the notion is "preposterous—equal rights for homosexuals?" Filmed focusing on San Francisco's gay subcultures with "dangerous and promiscuous gay sexual activity," he questions, for a group intending to "further their special interests" how "this challenge to traditional values will provoke far more hostility and controversy" nationwide (as cited in Sender et al., 1998).

The 1980s marked the beginning of narratives surrounding the AIDS crisis in popular media and news. Initially, the mainstream press ignored the story because they did not think it mattered to their (White, heterosexual) media audiences. As historian Edward Alwood says in the documentary *Off the Straight & Narrow*, AIDS was thought to only affect "the three H's': Haitians, hemophiliacs and homosexuals," marginalized groups and sexual subcultures (Sender et al., 1998). Rock Hudson's death in 1985, with his celebrity status, brought mainstream attention to the AIDS crisis. However, the LGBTQ community soon became defined solely by the disease, as false reporting constructed AIDS as a "gay plague" and the historic roles of victim and villain reemerged. Victim narratives tended to focus on family dramas such as *An Early Frost* (NBC, 1995), *In the Gloaming* (HBO, 1997) and *Our Sons* (ABC, 1991) in which sympathetic gay characters evoke pity from audiences. The nuclear family is forced to confront their child's homosexuality only to lose the child to the AIDS virus. Starring in the villain role, stories of bisexual and gay men as predatory AIDS carriers proved popular. For example, NBC's 1998 *Midnight Caller* centered on a bisexual man who is knowingly HIV positive and "infects" dozens of others as some sort of sexual serial killer. News narratives focused on promiscuity and gay male bathhouses, spreading a false understanding of AIDS transmission and implying that gay men brought it on themselves.

Alongside these narratives were stories of the "blameless" or "innocent victims" of the crisis, well-meaning White heterosexuals who were unfairly "infected" (like Kimberly Bergalis, the young woman who died at 23, one of six patients who claimed she "contracted" HIV from her dentist). In entertainment and in news reports, HIV and AIDS were seen as almost exclusively affecting White, middle-upper class gay men, although one-quarter of HIV+ people were African American or Latino. Indeed, HBO's documentary film *And the Band Played On* was one of the only media narratives to showcase how widespread the epidemic was, as well as to highlight the community's role in fighting for better research, medical treatments and social services.

By the late 1980s, there were still very few recurring characters on mainstream television, and the few lesbian characters that did appear would parachute in for an episode or two to present a "problem" for the heterosexual lead characters. In largely one-off storylines, episodes of popular shows like *Designing Women* and *The Golden Girls* would bring in a lesbian character to reassure heterosexual audiences that their favorite recurring characters were, indeed, straight ("I like you, just not in that way"; Sender et al., 1998). In the 1990s, however, gay and lesbian narratives became more central in the media landscape, moving from decades of limited visibility to that of public spectacle (Walters, 2001a).

Visibility in the Mainstream: Contemporary Stereotypes of LGBTQ Communities

In the 1990s, LGBTQ representation reached "the era of the visible" (Walters, 2001b., p. 338; see also Becker, 2006; Gross, 2001; Streitmatter, 2008). Lesbian and gay characters appeared with more regularity on shows like *Friends* and *Melrose Place*. ABC's *Rosanne*, for example, featured Nancy Bartlett (played by Sandra Bernhart) as Rosanne's friend, who came out as lesbian—and later bisexual—after her husband leaves her. In one episode, Rosanne accompanies Nancy to a gay bar, where she is kissed by Nancy's girlfriend, Sharon (played by Marielle Hemingway). As one of the first lesbian kisses on primetime, the program generated controversy before it even aired. ABC threatened to pull the episode, fearing backlash from viewers, conservative groups and sponsors. After pressure from the show's producer and Barr herself, ABC did air the episode in March of 1994—and even promoted it as "the lesbian kiss episode" to draw controversy and boost ratings (Gross, 2001). This episode and other similar ratings stunts often used lesbian characters and the one-off same-sex kiss to titillate audiences and draw higher viewership, especially during sweeps periods.

It wasn't until the late 1990s that mainstream network programs like *Ellen* and *Will & Grace* offered more varied, consistent and gay-centered representations than in the past. Like other marginalized groups, these programs situated gayness within the "safe and familiar popular culture conventions" of the situation comedy (Battles & Hilton-Murrow, 2002, p. 87). Gay lives were "written into a straight television world," with representations largely crafted to appeal to a heterosexual culture (Kates, 1999). For example, critics celebrated Ellen DeGeneres's coming out in 1997 as a watershed moment for gay and lesbian representation. Her coming out, however, had to abide by certain rules: physical contact with another woman was rarely shown, and her coming out was considered personal and thus separate from any sort of LGBTQ political movement. Ellen Morgan comes out in a straight world, her gayness presented as something for her heterosexual family and friends to reconcile.

Toward the end of the program's run, Ellen was allowed to have a romantic life, but even then a same-sex kiss came with disclaimers warning the episode included "adult content." The lack of physical affection allowed between same-sex couples was a systemic double-standard that permeated the 1990s and into the 2000s, especially on the networks and in mainstream films. While opposite-sex couples were routinely shown in sexually provocative kisses, embraces and encounters, same-sex affection was rarely allowed. Even holding hands was considered controversial, and the same-sex kiss became "a symbolic battleground" (Sender et al., 1998) in which local affiliates would threaten to pull episodes and advertising sponsors boycotted programs (as was the case with *Roseanne*). Even still, only lesbian couples were allowed affection in the mainstream, never gay men. ABC pulled *Ellen* from the air in 1998, citing declining ratings and increased pressure from conservative groups about the program's content.

About one year after Ellen's cancellation, NBC aired *Will & Grace* (1998–2006, recently rebooted from 2017–2020), featuring a gay male lawyer and his best friend, a heterosexual female interior designer, as the title characters. The series was considered ground breaking as it showcased not one, but two gay male leads, who performed gay identity in differing ways—Will presented as more masculine, serious, and "straight," while Jack was presented as stereotypically feminine, flighty, and campy. The series offered a sort of queer family formation, in that Will and Grace act almost as a married couple and parents to the more infantilized, queer characters of Jack and Karen. Critics have noted how this "gay" series operated along heterosocial pairings; the male/female couplings of Will and Grace, and of Jack and Karen, were key to the show's logics (Battles & Hilton-Murrow, 2002).

In addition, consider the extent to which these boundary-breaking narratives have taken place in almost exclusively White, upper-class worlds. These representations perpetuated images of the community within a narrow range of gender, race, class, and sexual conformity. To be gay in the media, until very recently, has been defined as young, White, and wealthy—and oftentimes male. To be seen, in other words, one must meet, as scholar Lisa Henderson puts it, the "class markers of queer worth" (as cited in Sender et al., 1998) tied to Whiteness and high social economic class. Diversity, in other words, has been unidimensional. Interestingly, reality television, including talk shows, have been spaces where more gay people of color have emerged (though oftentimes sensationalized and as objects of scorn and ridicule). For example, one of first non-White queer people representations was Pedro Zhmora, a gay man of color with HIV, who appeared on MTV's *The Real World* (1993–1994).

Representations, however, continued to evolve. The 2000s saw the development of what some have dubbed "the new queer aesthetic on television" (Keller & Stratyner, 2006), the media industry's embrace of sexually provocative, "edgy" programming designed to appeal to young, trendy audiences. In short, "the love that dared not speak its name" became "a commercialized love that never shuts up" (Skover & Testy, 2002). No longer written into straight media narratives, stories now feature queer-centered worlds (Sender, 2006). The growth of subscription cable channels like HBO and Showtime, as well as the introduction of Logo, a network that promised "all gay, all the time," meant that producers no longer needed to be concerned with reaching the largest audiences, but rather, the most loyal. Programs like HBO's *Sex and the City*, Showtime's *The L Word*, and Showtime's *Queer as Folk* played by different rules than those of the more "sterilized" world of network television (Keller & Stratyner, 2006), featuring more adventurous, explicit and graphic same-sex scenes.

While marketers use the allure of gay culture to appeal to progressive audiences, scholars have warned that media narratives may be sending the inaccurate message that "the battle has been won" and homophobia is no longer relevant (Becker, 2006; Walters, 2001a). These media narratives were unfolding in a culture where LGBTQ people faced personal harm and political attack. The battles over same-sex marriage rights were waging, the federal Defense of Marriage Act (DOMA) had yet to be repealed, and conservative backlash was explosive. In headline news, stories and images of gay and lesbian couples getting married, often in defiance of laws established by the state, were seen once again seen as a threat to the nuclear family—and to the institution of marriage as a whole. In terms of the larger media landscape, GLAAD estimated that

"LGBT characters represent[ed] less than 2% of all characters on the broadcast networks" in 2005 (GLAAD, 2005).

This paradox points to the potentially dangerous downside of increased media visibility: that it is often mistaken as a "false substitute" for cultural acceptance and inclusivity (Walters, 2001a; see also Dow, 2001; Gross, 2001). Media narratives may end up celebrating a "post-gay" era, presuming civil rights victories have been granted and equality achieved. What results is a culture eager to consume "the *images* of gay life but all too reluctant to embrace the *realities* of gay identities" (Walters, 2001a, p. 10).

Despite the increased and more varied visibility that has marked the 2000s, harmful stereotypes and tropes of LGBTQ people have persisted. As the introduction to this chapter recounts, the "Bury your Gays" (BYG) trope highlighted by queer fans and activist organizations like GLAAD point to a dangerous trend—the high number of bisexual and lesbian TV characters who are killed off, silenced or otherwise written out of storylines. While this trope has a long history, dating back to the 1970s in some contexts (though it was not referred to at BYG), it appears to have witnessed a revival lately, targeting female characters more than male ones. The 2015–2016 and 2016–2017 television seasons were particularly deadly for queer women characters. As Megan Townsend, GLAAD's director of entertainment research, said, "since the beginning of 2015, we've lost more than 50 queer women on television—often in violent ways that benefit somebody else's story rather than anything contributing to that character's own arc" (Brabaw, 2018, para. 2). Other controversial queer deaths from this time period, in addition to the previously mentioned *The 100's* Lexi, include Kira from *The Magicians*, Denise from *The Walking Dead*, Nora and Mary Louise from *The Vampire Diaries*, and Poussey from *Orange Is the New Black*. As explored more in the next section, with arguably so few queer female characters on television, the erasure of the ones who do exist sends a dangerous messages to fans—and to LGBTQ youth in particular.

Another struggle LGBTQ communities still face is a lack of diversity. The overall story here is certainly one of substantial progress, but there is more work to be done to represent the community more fully and accurately. Along the lines of race and gender, media narratives are improving. Whereas in the recent past, you could count on one hand recurring queer characters of color, now LGBTQ people of color outnumber White LGBTQ people on broadcast (GLAAD, 2019). In addition, LGBTQ women outnumbered men on broadcast scripted series in the 2018–2019 season for the first time.

Transgender characters, once virtually nonexistent in the mediascape a few years ago, are also more visible than ever before with more varied plotlines. For the 2019–2020 season, 38 regular or recurring characters were transgender across all platforms, including 12 transgender men, 21 transgender women and five non-binary characters (GLAAD, 2019). However, critics warn of the "ghettoization" of transgender characters as they are often segregated into only a few specific programs. Only two current shows—*Pose* and *The L Word: Generation Q*—make up more than one-quarter of trans characters on television (Wolfe & Ries, 2019). If even one of those shows is canceled, representation falls off dramatically. The problem of ghettoization reflects the larger realities of audience fragmentation—the dissolution of the once mass media audience into smaller and more targeted niche audiences. In the 1990s, a show like *Ellen* was canceled for dropping to 12 million viewers, while in the 2010s, a program like *Pose* gets renewed with slightly over one million viewers. Simply put, audiences are less likely to "stumble upon" LGBTQ-themed programming unless they are specifically seeking it out.

These narratives surrounding transgender people in media often fall into the medicalized or biological model, the full humanity of a person being overshadowed by trying to "fit in" to the "wrong body" or prove they are in the right one. Transgender characters are thus often forced into hyper-performing their masculinity of femininity. Historic victim/villain stereotypes still permeate transgender representation, casting trans characters as tragic victims of violence and death like in the film *Boys Don't Cry*. Predatory psychopathic serial killers have a long history in media narratives, like Buffalo Bill in *Silence of the Lambs* (1991) who is shown in the film identifying as a woman, a deranged murderer who kidnaps and skins women. A ten-year study of trans characters on television found that they were portrayed as victims 40 percent of the time, as killers or villains 20 percent, and as sex workers 20 percent (Victims or Villains, 2019). In our current media landscape, crime dramas like *Law & Order* (1990–2010), *CSI* (2000–2015), *NCIS* (2003–), and *The Closer* (2005–2012) often depict trans characters as victims of violence, sexual assault, and murder (Reitz, 2017). Even for acclaimed dramas like the show *Transparent* and the film *The Danish Girl*, queer critics argue that media producers cast heterosexual men (Jeffrey Tambor and Eddie Redmayne, respectively) in the starring roles, a practice known as "Transface," denying the experience of a trans actress to play the part (Reynolds, 2015).

Likewise, stories containing bisexual characters are also on the rise, constituting 126 characters across all television platforms, compared to near invisibility several years ago. Bisexuality was routinely cast as a "phase" confined to young people uncertain or confused about their sexuality. Bisexuality has also been stereotyped as a step into homosexuality, or for non-committed people who want to hop from one meaningless relationship to the next. A more fluid, bisexual queerness is emerging, however, as some laudable representation has been praised on programs like Pop TV's *Schitt's Creek*, The CW's *Crazy-Ex Girlfriend*, Netflix's *The Politician* and The CW's *Jane the Virgin*. Still, real invisibility exists when it comes to the lack of asexual characters (only one, Netflix's *BoJack Horseman*, which is ending), queer characters with disability or living with HIV, and LGBTQ religious people, who are still rarely seen. As this next section details, these stories and the lack of diverse representation can have powerful effects on audiences.

Our Stories Matter: Effects of LGBTQ Stereotypes

As this volume explores, media narratives—whether in television dramas and comedies, film, social media, or news reports—provide much more than merely entertainment and information. As the cultural storytellers of our time, media producers and journalists create narrative, literary stories that construct our symbolic definitions of reality. Major media organizations and news outlets create and communicate powerful visual narratives and storylines about LGBTQ life and communities—and in doing so, define who is seen, who is heard, and who is not. Mass media and popular culture have historically served as powerful forces for defining and policing the boundaries of gender identity and sexual orientation—what it means, and what it looks like, to be male, female, or non-binary; straight, gay, trans or bi. As this chapter has demonstrated, marginal groups must often follow the rules of a dominant media culture to gain visibility, often mistaken as acceptance.

To not be seen in the media is, to some extent, to not exist at all. And to grow up not seeing images of oneself or one's community can prove devastating. The erasure of marginalized groups in media narratives acts as a form of symbolic annihilation, "a process by which the mass media omit, trivialize, or condemn certain groups that are not socially valued" (Klein & Shiffman, 2009, p. 56; see also Tuchman, 2000; Gerbner & Gross; 1976). Whereas gay and lesbian identity was once considered "the love that dare not speak its name," symbolic annihilation still exists when it comes to the relative absence of asexual representation, the few male transgender representations, the lack of intersections of queer disability, the lack of diversity in socioeconomic class, and, as previously discussed, the killing off or writing off of queer female representation (Millward, Dodd, & Fubara-Manuel, 2017). A major void remains when it comes to queer religious representation, rural or non-urban LGBTQ people, the absence of particular regional representation (i.e., the South; Veline, 2017), and in particular media genres such as big-budget action films, mainstream video games, and men's team sports (Billings & Moscowitz, 2018).

While research shows more people are coming out (as high as 20 percent of 18–34 year olds identify as LGBTQ, according to the 2017 Accelerating Acceptance report; GLAAD, 2017), and coming out initially at younger ages (on average age 13; Family Acceptance Project, 2015), it does not mean they necessarily come into a supportive environment. According to the latest research from The Trevor Project's national data surveying over 25,000 LGBTQ youth in the United States, 39% say they seriously considered attempting suicide in the past year, with more than half of transgender and non-binary youth saying they did; 2 in 3 LGBTQ youth reported that someone tried to convince them of the viability of "conversion therapy" (to change their sexual orientation or gender identity); and the vast majority, 71% , reported signs of depression and another 71% reported discrimination due to either their sexual orientation or gender identity (The Trevor Project, 2019). According to the Human Rights Campaign, LGBTQ youth are more than twice as likely to be physically assaulted (Growing Up LGBTQ in America, 2020). In particular, for queer youth growing up in areas where there may not be peer, family or community support, places where they may not know others like them, media images and narratives can act as a lifeline. Moreover, media images can reflect a larger cultural recognition of LGBTQ people not just on our screens but in our families, workplaces, schools, churches, and neighborhoods. Psychologists and social workers have recognized strong, diverse and realistic representations "are validating and normalizing for LGBTQ+ youth, and contribute to their identity development and overall well-being" (McInroy, as cited in Shakeri, 2017). Media not only tell stories of people and communities, but help forge our self-identities.

Media messages not only communicate important messages to "ingroup" members, those who identify with a group, but to "outgroup" members as well. Scholars have used parasocial identification theory (specifically the parasocial contact hypothesis) to demonstrate how media messages "influence beliefs about groups with which individuals typically may have little direct social contact" (Schiappa, Gregg, & Hewes, 2006, p. 15). Parasocial identification can explain how fans feel connected to or begin to "see themselves" in specific narratives or characters, how queer women may have felt "real emotional trauma" after losing Lexa on *The 100*, for example, or gay teens may see themselves in a relationship similar to one of Jude and Connor on *The Fosters*. Research shows audiences use media stories to learn about their own communities as well as other groups they may have little-to-no contact with, examining how LGBTQ characters on television, for example, might increase or decrease acceptance or positive or negative attitudes. People who gain a better understanding of communities and issues through positive mediated narratives subsequently report greater acceptance and less negative attitudes.

For LGBTQ representations, however, results are mixed. Some studies showed higher viewing of even one television program like *Will & Grace* can increase parasocial interaction and reduce negative sexual prejudice for those with the lowest degree of social contact (Schiappa et al., 2006, p. 15). Other work has found the contrary—that attitudes toward LGBTQ content are heavily shaped by viewers' gender identity and sexual orientation rather than the content itself. When researchers showed depictions of a gay teen couple on the show *The Fosters*, for example, it generated more positive and hopeful attitudes for LGBTQ identified viewers, but created a "boomerang" effect in heterosexual/cisgender youth, eliciting "disgust" and negative attitudes toward LGBTQ communities (Gillig & Murphy, 2016). An over boomerang effect may help explain why, for the first time in years, public sentiment among young Americans is becoming less tolerant of LGBTQ people even as media representation is at historic highs (Miller, 2019). Still others have found that mainstream narratives and news coverage of LGBTQ issues can play an educational role for outgroup members, teaching people about gender pronouns, gender expression and the diversity of the community.

Put simply, LGBTQ stories matter because the stakes are so high—they impact individuals and communities, and can shape public support and influence policy. As Laverne Cox, most famous for her role as Sophia Burset on the Netflix series *Orange Is the New Black* said, "We've got to tell these stories better because lives are on the line" (as cited in Saraiya, 2017).

Theoretical and Methodological Directions for Future Examination

For media scholars, audiences and fans of queer-themed media, there has arguably never been a more important or compelling time to explore the complex issues surrounding LGBTQ representations in the media. For one, the growth of digital, online and social media has created LGBTQ safe spaces in places where physical or face-to-face ones are difficult to come by. Moreover, the power of social media platforms to create community and connect sexual and gender minorities brings great promise. It has been nearly 11 years since Gray (2009) published her groundbreaking book-length study on queer rural youth, among the first to explore the lives of LGBTQ youth living in small towns and rural communities, studying their off-line interactions and their online media practices. In doing so, she is one of a group of scholars challenging the "metronormativity" (Halberstam, 2005) of queer visibility.

Gray shows the ways in which queer youth, in part, explore and forge their queer identities through online spaces—gaining the tools they use to do the "work" of identity formation. Online spaces can act as a sanctuary for LGBTQ youth—a safe place to forge connections, feel less isolated, and see images and narratives of others who look and sound like them. This is especially true for those who do not have access to off-line communities of support in their families, schools, places of worship or communities. As one example, mother and advocate of a 10-year-old transgender son named Dylan, Vanessa Lee Nic, recently explained to *The Washington Post* how his Instagram account helps bring him a sense of community he would otherwise be lacking in their rural area: "Being 10 and being trans can feel lonely. He doesn't have one trans friend his age in our small town" (Leventry, 2019, para. 9).

Future research will likely continue to examine how emergent digital and social media forms help LGBTQ people navigate their off-line worlds, form community, organize, and provide critiques of cultural, political and mediated homophobia. New scholarship is examining how queer fans organize and respond to problematic topes they see in media narratives, such as the "Bury Your Gays" trope on television, by looking at fan response on Twitter and Tumblr (Waggoner, 2018). Still others have examined how LGBTQ youth curate selfies and other visual images to "navigate inequality, orchestrate identities, and engage civically across digital environments" on social media forms like Tumblr (Wargo, 2017, p. 561) and Instagram. Another exciting scholarly trend is using ethnographic methods, such as participant observation and in-depth interviews, to more fully explore how LGBTQ people are integrating media practices into their lived experiences.

Other interesting areas for further exploration are places that have been historically homophobic and dominated by heterosexual male audiences—genres like the video games (Ruberg & Shaw, 2017), country music (Veline, 2017), and men's professional sports (Billings & Moscowitz, 2018). In these areas and others, progressive strides have been made for greater inclusivity and even more queer production. While the game industry has been thought to be dominated by the views of heterosexual, cisgender men, many women and queer-identified youth engage in games and are pushing for necessary reform. Until very recently, LGBTQ characters were rarely the main actors in gaming narratives, anti-gay slurs were standard, and the few transgender characters who did appear existed only as victims. Several years ago, the advocacy group GLAAD began working with the gaming industry to help reshape narratives and integrate more LGBTQ characters. For example, *Assassin's Creed Odyssey* now allows players to select a wider array of gender identities and pursue a same-sex relationship rather than being forced into a heterosexual romance (following fan backlash, see Romano, 2018). In today's gaming landscape, popular games like *Borderlands, Overwatch, Fallout II, Life is Strange, Sims 4*, and *Last of Us, Part 2* feature queer characters and storylines—largely positive ones. In 2013, the first GaymerCon convention celebrated LGBTQ geek culture, and in 2015, leading scholar of queer game studies, Adrienne Shaw, founded the LGBTQ Video Game Archive. Queer narratives are even more popular in the indie game circuit, and open-source tools like Twine have democratized game creation, allowing virtually anyone to make their own interactive games (Sens, 2015).

Another ongoing theoretical intervention by queer theorists has been to problematize the constructs often tied to the queer experience like "coming out" and "the closet" (Bailey, 2011; Brody, 2016). Coming out, as discussed in the case of *Ellen* and other examples cited in this chapter, is often positioned as fitting in—and oftentimes fitting into a dominant straight culture. In media narratives, coming out is depicted as a rite of passage, and one that is "confession, apology, and rehabilitation rather than a challenge or restructure of power inequalities" (Bailey, 2011, p. 16). Coming out is also often portrayed as a singular, one-time event rather than acknowledging that queer visibility is "a continuous process" that requires "ongoing negotiations" (Kohnen, 2015, p. 15). A term like "the closet" implies hiding, deceit, inauthenticity, and secrecy rather than acknowledging the systemic cultural barriers and strategies of survival queer-identified people face.

Conclusion

The media landscape of the future will hopefully include even more diverse LGBTQ stories across all platforms and contexts. For one, GLAAD is challenging television producers to ensure that 20 percent of recurring characters on primetime scripted broadcast series are LGBTQ by 2025 (GLAAD, 2019). Since most LGBTQ narratives are still largely constructed by heterosexual men (Ryan Murphy being one stand-out exception), audiences, scholars and queer activist groups are calling for more queer representation behind the scenes—as writers, producers, cinematographers, game designers, and the like. As queer scholar Lisa Henderson says, LGBTQ audiences desire and deserve "images not only of us, but also images by us, and images for us" (as cited in Sender et al., 1998). As fans fighting "Bury Your Gays" and other problematic tropes have shown us, LGBTQ fans do indeed deserve better—as do all media audiences.

References

Alwood, E. (1996). *Straight news: Gays, lesbians, and the news media.* New York: Columbia University Press.

Bailey, C. (2011). Coming out as homophobic: Isaiah Washington and the "Grey's Anatomy" scandal. *Communication and Critical/Cultural Studies, 8*(1), 1–21.

Battles, K., & Hilton-Morrow, W. (2002). Gay characters in conventional spaces: Will and Grace and the situation comedy genre. *Critical Studies in Media Communication, 19*(1), 87–106.

Becker, R. (2006). *Gay TV and straight America.* Newark, NJ: Rutgers University Press.

Bennet, L. (2000). Fifty years of prejudice in the media. *Gay and Lesbian Review, 7*(2), 30–35.

Billings, A. C., & Moscowitz, L. (2018). *Media and the coming out of gay male athletes in American team sports.* New York: Peter Lang.

Brabaw, K. (2018, May 22). Courtney's "13 Reasons Why" ending is a huge moment for queer women on TV. *Refinery 29.* Retrieved from https://www.refinery29.com/en-us/2018/05/199864/courtney-crimsen-gay-13-reasons-why-season-2-ending.

Bridges, E. (2018). A genealogy of queerbaiting: Legal codes, production codes, "bury your gays" and "The 100 mess." *The Journal of Fandom Studies, 6*(2), 115–132.

Brody, E. (2016). *The out field: Professional sports and the mediation of gay sexualities* (Unpublished doctoral dissertation). University of Southern California, Los Angeles, CA.

Dow, B. (2001). Ellen, television and the politics of gay and lesbian visibility. *Critical Studies in Mass Communications, 18*(2), 123–140.

Family Acceptance Project. (2015). Coming out at school and well-being in young adulthood. Retrieved from http://familyproject.sfsu.edu.

Gerbner, G., & Gross, L. (1976). Living with television: The violence profile. *Journal of Communication, 26,* 173–199.

Gillig, T., & Murphy, S. (2016). Fostering support for LGBTQ youth? The effects of a gay adolescent media portrayal on young viewers. *International Journal of Communication, 10,* 3823–3850.

GLAAD. (2005). *Where we are on TV 2005–2006.* Retrieved from: https://www.glaad.org/publications/tvreport05?page=8&response_type=embed.

GLAAD. (2018). *Where we are on TV 2018–2019.* Retrieved from: http://glaad.org/files/WWAT/WWAT_GLAAD_2018-2019.pdf.

GLAAD. (2019). *Where we are on TV 2019–2020.* Retrieved from: https://www.glaad.org/whereweareontv19.

Gray, M. L. (2009). *Out in the country: Youth, media, and queer visibility in rural America.* New York: New York University Press.

'Growing Up LGBT in America'. (2020). *Human Rights Campaign.* Retrieved from https://www.hrc.org/youth-report/view-and-share-statistics.

Gross, L. P. (2001). *Up from invisibility: Lesbians, gay men, and the media in America.* New York, NY: Columbia University Press.

Gross, L. P., & Woods, J. D. (1999). *The Columbia reader on lesbians and gay men in media, society, and politics.* New York, NY: Columbia University Press.

Halberstam, J. (2005). *In a queer time and place transgender bodies, subcultural lives.* New York: New York University Press.

Hauck, G. (2019, June 18). Anti-LGBT hate crimes are rising, the FBI says. *USA Today.* Retrieved from https://www.usatoday.com/story/news/2019/06/28/anti-gay-hate-crimes-rise-fbi-says-and-they-likely-undercount/1582614001/.

Hogan, H. (2016, March 25). Autostraddle's ultimate infographic guide to dead lesbian characters on TV. *Autostraddle.* Retried from https://www.autostraddle.com/autostraddles-ultimate-infographic-guide-to-dead-lesbian-tv-characters-332920/.

Kates, S. M. (1999). Making the ad perfectly queer: Marketing "normality" to the gay men's community? *Journal of Advertising, 28*(1), 25–37.

Keller, J. R., & Stratyner, L. (Eds.). (2006). *The new queer aesthetic of television: Essays on recent programming.* Jefferson, NC: McFarland.

Klein, H., & Shiffman, K. S. (2009). Underrepresentation and symbolic annihilation of socially disenfranchised groups ('out groups') in animated cartoons. *The Howard Journal of Communications, 20*(1), 55–72.

Kohnen, M. (2015). *Queer representation, visibility, and race in American film and television: Screening the closet.* New York: Routledge.

Leventry, A. (2019, September 19). The importance of social media when it comes to LGBTQ kids feeling seen. *The Washington Post.* Retrieved from https://www.washingtonpost.com/lifestyle/2019/09/20/importance-social-media-when-it-comes-lgbtq-kids-feeling-seen/.

Miller, S. (2019, June 24). The young are regarded as the most tolerant generation. That's why results of this LGBTQ survey are 'alarming'. *USA Today.* Retrieved from https://www.usatoday.com/story/news/nation/2019/06/24/lgbtq-acceptance-millennials-decline-glaad-survey/1503758001/.

Millward, L., Dodd, J. G., & Fubara-Manuel, I. (2017). *Killing off the lesbians: A symbolic annihilation on film and television.* Jefferson, NC: McFarland.

Rappaport, M. (1997). *The silver screen: Color me lavender.* Couch Potato, NY: Couch Potato Productions.

Reitz, N. (2017). The representation of trans women in film and television. *Cinesthesia, 7*(1). Retrieved from https://scholarworks.gvsu.edu/cine/vol7/iss1/2/.

Reynolds, D. (2015, February 25). Is 'Transface' a problem in Hollywood? *The Advocate.* Retrieved from https://www.advocate.com/arts-entertainment/2015/02/25/transface-problem-hollywood.

Romano, N. (2018, October 9). Ok, Cupid: An ode to same-sex romancing in *Assassin's Creed Odyssey. Entertainment Weekly.* Retrieved from https://ew.com/gaming/2018/10/09/assassins-creed-odyssey-lgbtq/.

Ruberg, B., & Shaw, A. (Eds.). (2017). *Queer game studies*. Minneapolis: University of Minnesota Press.

Saraiya, S. (2017, August 4). Jill Soloway, Laverne Cox talk transgender trends on TV. *Variety*. Retrieved from https://variety.com/2017/tv/news/jill-soloway-laverne-coxtransgender-tv-glaad-1202516445/.

Schiappa, E., Gregg, P. B., & Hewes, D. E. (2006). Can one TV show make a difference?: "Will & Grace" and the parasocial contact hypothesis. *Journal of Homosexuality*, *51*(4), 15–37.

Sender, K. (2006). *Further off the straight and narrow: New gay visibility on television* [Documentary]. United States: Media Education Foundation.

Sender, K., Jhally, S., & Griffith, C. A. (1998). *Off the straight & narrow: Lesbians, gays, bisexuals & television* [Documentary]. United States: Media Education Foundation.

Sens, J. (2015). Queer worldmaking games: A Portland indie experiment. *QED: A Journal in GLBTQ Worldmaking*, *2*(2), 98–107.

Shakeri, S. (2017, June 30). Television has a "bury your gays," queerbaiting, and LGBTQ representation problem. *The Huffington Post*. Retrieved from https://www.huffingtonpost.ca/entry/queerbaiting-bury-your-gays-tv.

Skover, D. M., & Testy, K. Y. (2002). LesBiGay identity as commodity. *California Law Review*, *90*(1), 223–256. doi: 10.2307/3481310

Snarker, D. (2016, March 21). Bury your gays: Why "The 100," "Walking Dead" deaths are problematic. *The Hollywood Reporter*. Retrieved from https://www.hollywoodreporter.com/live-feed/bury-your-gays-why-100-877176.

Streitmatter, R. (2008). *From perverts to fab five: The media's changing depiction of gay men and lesbians*. New York: Taylor & Francis.

The Trevor Project. (2019) National survey on LGBTQ youth mental health. Retrieved from https://www.thetrevorproject.org/survey-2019/.

Townsend, M. (2016, November 3). GLAAD's 'Where We Are on TV' report finds progress in LGBTQ representation on TV, but much work still to be done. Retrieved from https://www.glaad.org/blog/glaads-where-we-are-tv-report-finds-progress-lgbtq-representation-tv-much-work-still-be-done.

Tuchman, G. (2000). The symbolic annihilation of women by the mass media. In L. Crothers and C. Lockhart (Eds.), *Culture and politics* (pp. 150–174). New York: Palgrave Macmillan.

Tzikas, E. (2018). "Bury your gays" trope: How the media kill off LGBTQ characters. *The Global Critical Media Literacy Project*. Retrieved from http://gcml.org/representation-of-lgbtq-characters-through-the-bury-your-gays-trope/.

Veline, L. (2017). *Object of your rejection: The symbolic annihilation and recuperation of queer identities in country music*. Unpublished doctoral dissertation, University of Mississippi.

"Victims or villains: Examining ten years of transgender images on television" (2019). *GLAAD*. Retrieved from https://www.glaad.org/publications/victims-or-villains-examining-ten-years-transgender-images-television.

Waggoner, E. B. (2018). Bury your gays and social media fan response: Television, LGBTQ representation, and communitarian ethics. *Journal of Homosexuality, 65*(13), 1877–1891.

Walters, S. (2001a). *All the rage: The story of gay visibility in America*. Chicago, IL: University of Chicago Press.

Walters, S. (2001b). Take my domestic partner, please: Gays and marriage in the era of the visible. In M. Bernstein & R. Reimann (Eds.), *Queer families, queer politics: Challenging culture and the state* (pp. 338–357). New York, NY: Columbia University Press.

Wargo, J. M. (2017). "Every selfie tells a story...": LGBTQ youth lifestreams and new media narratives as connective identity texts. *New Media & Society, 19*(4), 560–578.

Wigler, J. (2016). "The 100" showrunner responds to Lexa controversy: "I knew it would be emotional". *The Hollywood Reporter*. Retrieved from https://www.hollywoodreporter.com/live-feed/100-showrunner-responds-lexa-controversy-877137.

Wolfe, W., & Ries, B. (2019, November 16). There are more LGBTQ characters on television than ever before. *CNN*. Retrieved from https://www.cnn.com/2019/11/16/entertainment/lgbtq-tv-representation-numbers-trnd/index.html.

11 Stereotypes of Religion: Tired Tropes and New Market Possibilities

STEPHEN J. LIND
Washington & Lee University

In a season two episode of Netflix's makeover show reboot, *Queer Eye* ("God Bless Gay," 2018), the so-called Fab Five stars of the show find themselves not just helping elevate the life and style of a community-serving woman outside of Atlanta, but also confronting some of their own demons and stereotypes about religious communities. Heartfelt conversations are had among the stars and their client about what it means for the church to have fixed views on those who are gay and how many in the LGBTQ+ community likewise have fixed views of organized religion and its followers, seared in by personal trauma and theological dogma. The episode concludes with the woman taking the mic in her predominantly Black southern church during their "homecoming" service, extolling them to accept and love those who are gay, including her son who had only reluctantly decided to return to church. Tears are shed as the cast members in this melodramatically edited yet seemingly authentic group explore the possibility that there is more sameness and love to be found than the stereotypes of both communities might have previously suggested.

It is no small thing that such a religiously-centric episode can exist in mainstream American entertainment media, let alone the turn it marks in depictions of sexuality. The stars of the show themselves would have grown up on entertainment content largely devoid of religious representation, let alone nuanced explorations. Such a lack of representation can be particularly troubling for many viewers and critics alike, given just how prevalent religious identity, practice, and belief are in American culture. According to the Pew Research Center (2019) while 26% of Americans may self-identify as being religious "unaffiliated," nearly a third have said that religion is still important (2015a). Seventy-two percent of Americans self-identify with a religious group—65% Christian and 7% non-Christian faiths.[1] Even if the Pew data indicates that religious self-identification has decreased throughout the 21st Century, the dominance of religious identity is exceptionally high when compared with other modern societies. Even a segment of the unaffiliated appear at least somewhat interested in the notion of a higher power.

Even further, studies show that religion is not just a nominal aspect but is rather an important aspect of Americans' lives. Two-thirds of the total number of religiously affiliated, which amounts to half of the total population, value religion as "very important" in their lives. An additional quarter of the religiously affiliated find religion to be "somewhat" important in their lives. This is born out in personal habits—two-thirds of the religiously affiliated report praying daily, four out of ten read scriptures weekly, and nearly one-third participate in weekly scripture study groups (Pew Research Center, 2015b).

Because of entertainment media's power to reinforce perceptions and to offer exposure to life experience other than one's own, and because of the massive presence of religion across American private and public contexts, it is imperative for scholars, practitioners, and viewers make regular review of the landscape of religion in entertainment media. As will be described below, religious representation in American entertainment media has at times been largely absent from media properties. When present, which may come in waves as the industry zeitgeist shifts, it is rarely a prominent, let alone predictably affirmative, feature of the entertainment property, often fraught with simplistic, stereotypical depictions.

Because Americans consume so much of their entertainment content through television (average of 4 hours and 14 minutes in 2018 of live and time-shifted TV; The Nielsen Company, 2019), because of its breadth, and because of its powerful possible effects, special attention is paid in this chapter to entertainment television portrayals of religious belief, practice, and identity. A variety of perspectives from quantitative studies, reviews of exemplary media moments, and insights from industry practitioners will fill this chapter, intending to give a representative reflection of television's representative role in American entertainment media. This chapter charts out a set of primary stereotypes deployed across television and other media in the 20th century. While these tropes persist into the 21st century, along with the overall lack of religious representation in mainstream broadcast media, this chapter also

---

1 Unaffiliated identification includes: 4% atheist, 5% agnostic, and 17% "nothing in particular." Christian faith identification includes: 43% Protestant, 20% Catholic, 2% Mormon, <1% Orthodox Christian. Non-Christian faith identification includes: 2% Jewish, 1% Muslim, 1% Buddhist, 1% Hindu, and 3% Other World Religions. Numbers do not add up to 100% because of Pew Research Center rounding mechanics.

describes a set of important market evolutions. These changes in the media landscape—even in such a risk-averse industry like television—open new possibilities for representations of religion.

21st Century Religion

Infrequent Religion

Studies of religious frequency across television programming consistently establish the same findings—religious reference on television is rare. Though televangelism (Hadden & Shupe, 1988; Schultze, 2003) and media made by religious groups for religious groups (Schultze & Woods, 2008) have flourished and fallen in idiosyncratic ways since the mid-20th century, mainstream media properties on television tell a different tale. The lack of religion has been true since the early age of the medium. In the 1960s, reference to religion even within Christmas programming was extremely rare, with only 8.6% of programs containing a substantive verbal reference to religion that was not in a song (Lind, 2014). Explicit themes of theology in 1970s and 1980s programming were likewise rare at only 6% (Chesebro, 1991). As the 1990s opened, the same reality of religious omission endures, with only 5.6% of characters on network television being identifiably religiously affiliated (Skill, Robinson, Lyons, & Larson, 1994).

When present, religion on television has strongly tended to be Christian—either Catholic or nondenominationally Protestant (Skill et al., 1994). Judaism is, at times, present (Shandler, 2009), often through secular references, Hanukah recognition, or at times driven by an actor's own identity. Non-Christian faith traditions, or even nuances within Christianity or Judaism, are rarely present. Such an erasure makes any stereotypical or homogenized portrayal that much more important.

Historical Tropes

While aberrations certainly exist in provocative, powerful, and problematic ways, and the following list is certainly not intended to be exhaustive, a set of common tropes has nonetheless dominated the rare references to religious belief and action in American entertainment media. The stereotypical depictions of religious identity and practice are generally Christian (Clarke, 2005), often driven by a sense of simple sweetness or a subversive satire.

Simple Clergy and Unpriestly Priests. One of the most common religious tropes throughout television's history is the clerical character. Priests of Catholic (Skill et al., 1994; Wolff, 1995) or denominationally-undefined orders are perhaps the most ubiquitous overtly religious characters on television. Convenient for wardrobe departments, these characters are often identified by their conventional religious costumes, even if there is no dialogue surrounding their role. Nuns are likewise a common character, typically sporting telltale black and white religious habit comprised of robe and headgear. Examples span the spectrum of prominence, ranging from extras and supporting characters to lead characters like the mild-mannered, Roman Catholic US Army chaplain Father Mulcahy on CBS's *M*A*S*H* to The WB/CW's *7th Heaven* gendered depictions of clerical agency (Maddux, 2010).

As Wolff's (1995) study reminds the critic, even if the character is otherwise narratively compelling, the religious elements of 20th century clerical characters tend to be flat and limited, offering little acknowledgment of the complexity of clerical work and little exploration of spiritual matters. The life of a nun, for example, is reduced, with great comedic effect, to a system of silence and bell-ringing in a 1976 episode of ABC's *Laverne and Shirley* ("A Nun's Story"); the life of the sisterly order is simplified to a series of silly struggles resolvable in under a half hour in ABC's mid-century *The Flying Nun*.

The unpriestly-priest is a common variation on the clerical trope. If not a simple two-dimensional facsimile of a priest, often wearing clerical garb and offering soft-spoken words likely conservatively out-of-touch with the modern age (Wolff, 1995), this version of the stereotype adds an explicitly unorthodox twist to the character. In NBC's mid-1980s *Hell Town*, for example, the lead character, Father Hardstep, is a softhearted ex-con using questionable heavy-handed tactics to improve the quality of his parish. In a classic heart-strung clerical comedic turn, the celibacy of a priest is set against romantic attraction as the stern Dorothy in NBC's *The Golden Girls* develops an attraction for Father Frank Leahy (Terry Hughes, 1987), a forbidden fruit twist that ABC's *Happy Days* had likewise used a few years earlier when Fonzie fell for a girl who turns out to be a nun (Paris, 1981).

Naïve Believer. In a post-WWII culture critical of institutions and wary at times of the appropriateness of whether its polite to talk about religion in public, it is not uncommon for religious characters in entertainment media to be cast as the backward, naïve zealot not yet enlightened by modern sensibilities. Many characters of varying prominence have depicted such a naïve member of a faith community, be they myopic zealots or simple-minded members of the laity. In a 1990s episode of CBS's *Dr. Quinn Medicine Woman* (Terrence O'Hara, 1996), for example, the well-intentioned but occasionally culturally-uninformed Reverend Johnson struggles to understand why the Cheyenne natives might object to obligatory Bible readings and baptism.

Perhaps no character reflects the naïve believer as clearly as Ned Flanders on FOX's *The Simpsons*, a show that has been described as the most religious show on television for its frequent subversive satire of religious belief and practice (Lewis, 2002). Singularly-minded to a series of faults (even if endearing) Flanders and his family have served as an eye-roll-inducing caricature of the Christian right since the show's first season. In an episode titled "Home Sweet Homediddly-Dum-Doodily" (Dietter, 1995), a misunderstanding causes the Simpson children to be fostered by the Flanders. "I don't judge Homer and Marge," says Flanders' wife as the children arrive, "that's for a vengeful God to do." Learning that the children have never been baptized, Ned exclaims "Jeepers H. Crackers!" and breaks out the emergency baptism kit, endeavoring to provide the children a "less Hell-bound family." Viewers are given a comedic sigh of relief when Homer dives in front of the divine baptismal water just before it falls on Bart's unholy head.

Black Gospel Choir. African American spiritual identity has deep historical ties to music, dating back to the Negro spirituals during the age of slavery. On television—which inherited many of its stereotypes and practices of underrepresentation for people of color from the film industry (Pieraccini & Alligood, 2005)—the trope of the gospel singer and choir affords a small amount of racial diversity in religious portrayal, though it does so through a simplified and homogenized view of Black gospel belief and practice. Often cast as joyous females who are part of the larger church community, the Black gospel singer injects a sense of praise and often a fair amount of dancing into select television moments. In the 236th episode of *The Jeffersons*, for example, Florence unselfishly gives her money so that the church choir can travel to its competition in Ohio (Scott, 1984). A few years later on *Family Matters* (O'Keefe, 1991), Aunt Rachel zealously takes over the church choir after the former director leaves to sing backup for ZZ Top. The expectation to be fully part of the community is fulfilled in this episode when main character Steve Urkel goes from struggling to sing the right "Amen!" and "Hallelujah!" to fully confessing his faith in the Lord before the church body. The collective nature of the trope is then solidified as the scene concludes with the choir singing a rousing "A-a-amen!"

Supernaturals as Benevolent or Insidious. Occasionally, supernatural characters appear, though almost never from non-Christian faith perspectives, save for the occult. When they are present, they typically are portrayed at dramatic ends of a good vs. evil spectrum. Angels as actual characters or as verbal references are often invoked with themes of protection or the afterlife, sometimes including their visual iconography of feathered wings or glowing light, and are often the bringers of hope or character betterment. Similar to NBC's 1980s

Highway to Heaven, the hit 1990s CBS series *Touched by an Angel*, for example, centered around the good guidance and surprise angelic reveal of the optimistic Monica, played by Roma Downey, gospel singing Tess, played by Della Reese, and the unassuming angel of death Andrew, played by John Dye.

The trope of the insidious supernatural being has been around for millennia. This can take the form of a verbal reference to the devil or demons. The WB/UPN's *Buffy the Vampire Slayer*, for example, was driven by dark references to demonic forces. Though occasionally they are found to be more complex—such as in the romance between Sarah Michelle Gellar's title character and not one but two different soul-deserving vampires—dominant themes of simplified good vs. evil persist.

The "Act of God" variation is another common and casual religious trope. In such scenarios, an unexpected event occurs in the life of a character, causing them to often look to the heavens and either chastise or thank God. In *The Simpsons* (Susie Dietter, 1995), for example, Reverend Lovejoy laments with open hands to God, "Oh, why do you hate my trains?!" after Marge and Homer accidentally crash through his new model train board. There are, of course, moments when characters do substantively wrestle with questions about the intervention of the divine, like in 1977s on ABC's *Welcome Back Kotter* when Horshack and his classmates question the nature of God (Stuart, 1977), but such scenarios are much less typical.

Otherized Beliefs—Rare Non-Christian Faith and Laughably Dangerous Cults Despite the persistent stereotypical belief that Jews run Hollywood (believed by 47% of the non-Jewish American public in 1964 (Quinley & Glock, 1983, p. xv), portrayals of Jewish or Muslim or Hindu or any other non-Christian faiths have been historically rare, if present at all, in mainstream 20th century American entertainment television. The portrayal may be linked to a unique trait of an actor as in the case of NBC's *Seinfeld* (Johnson, 1994; Krieger, 2003), and is often portrayed as a peculiar anomaly or even dangerous. In a 1978 episode of *Happy Days*, for example, Mrs. Cunningham is relieved to find out that the reason the neighbors do not have a Christmas tree is not because of poor spirit, but rather because they're Jewish, a realization that amuses the studio audience (Jerry Paris, 1978). The 1986 NBC TV movie, *Under Seige* (Roger Young, 1986), then demonstrates the way otherized Islam is offered via the trope of the ever-threatening Muslim (Shaheen, 2000), centering its depiction of Islam around domestic terrorist attacks by "barbarians" from a Muslim nation.

Cults as otherized beliefs are portrayed in rather routine ways, describes David Scott Diffrient (2010), shown as either comically out-there hyperboles or as authoritatively dangerous. In an episode of ABC's *Boy Meets World* (Jeff

McCracken, 1997), a teenage Shawn trades in his own individualized thought for a temporary sense of belonging under the sway of a cultic leader at The Centre. As one viewer's reaction suggests, the stereotypical view of authoritarian otherized belief can meaningfully connect to broader narrative themes, affording characters a natural opportunity for reflection and growth:

> It's understandable that in his teenage years, Shawn would get himself not only into this cult, but debating religion and belief for the first time as he is trying to make meaning of his life. [. . .] I think a lot of teenagers go through a time of questioning and self-doubt and this was a natural course for Shawn. (SARAH, 2013)

Faith in the 21st Century

Limits Remain but Successes Stand Out

A lack of religious portrayals persists across the turn into the new century. In a study of early 2000s entertainment programming, Clarke (2005) found that only 5.8% of primetime characters on network TV could be identified as religious, a stark contrast to the Pew study's 72% of actual Americans. Of that 5.8% Clarke identified, only 2% were found to be engaged in some form of religious behavior as opposed to the 3.8% who were merely nominally religious. In a study of 2013–2014 programming, Cohen and Hetsroni (2019) yet again found that focus on religion was "quite marginal in absolute numbers" (p. 8).

Hollywood critics are largely aware of the limited representation of religion on television. "Often, faith has been relegated to syrupy treatments, [. . .] used as a vehicle for supernatural plots, [. . .] or ignored altogether," commented one *New York Times* assessment (Lyons & Poniewozik, 2016). This recognition often manifests in the form of surprise when a breakout religious success happens and Hollywood seems to "find Jesus" all over again ("Hollywood finds God," 2015; "Hollywood Finds God in Bible Stories Made for the Big Screen," 2014; Smith, 2013).

Religiously charged successes across film and television have been very real. An era of notably religious programs was arguably kicked off when CBS's *Touched by an Angel* began in the mid-1990s, running with tremendous success for nine seasons. "The iconic *Touched by an Angel* might have played heavily on the heartstrings," noted one critic in a retrospective for *Variety*, "but there was always some grit that gave the series an enduring quality that still holds up" (Young, 2016). At its height, the show commanded upwards of 21 million viewers, was in the top ten most-viewed programs on television, was nominated for 11 Emmy Awards, and even produced a spin-off, *Promised Land*. Later, star Roma Downey and husband mega-producer Mark Burnett would produce the television mini-series *The Bible* for cable's History channel with high-profile promotion (Lind, 2013b) and great ratings success (Collins, 2013).

Past successes would justify programming choices from broadcast networks, producing shows like CBS's *Joan of Arcadia*, ABC's *Kevin (Probably) Saves the World*, and CBS's *God Friended Me*, each premised on the modern main character seemingly receiving direct instructions from God. Success of the supernatural juggernaut *Buffy the Vampire Slayer* would propel a whole new generation of shows centered around supernatural baddies like the CW's *Supernatural* and *The Vampire Diaries* and CBS's *Evil*, routinely involving episode moments in which sacred religious rites, roles, and scriptures are invoked.

While the previous era's religious stereotypes persist into the 21st century, the more liberal cultural climate can at times produce significantly more sordid variations on the tropes. The unpriestly priest stereotype, for example, now have corruption and even pedophilia connotations regularly trailing in its wake. While Sally on a 1964 episode of *The Dick Van Dyke Show* (Paris, 1964) insisted on keeping her coat on because she was embarrassed by her lace dress when she was accidentally set up to woo a priest, viewers of 2019s season two of Hulu's *Fleabag* are treated to a much different scenario. The fan-favorite "hot priest," who wryly points out that it is his brother who is the pedophile, develops a romantic relationship with the show's protagonist. The two intensely and graphically discuss faith, sex, and relationships, eventually becoming both emotionally and physically intimate—complete with sexual act outside of the confessional booth (Keating, 2019).

Risk Aversion Amidst New 21st Century Market Possibilities

Popularity Factor. The entertainment industry as a whole, and especially network broadcasting, is largely a risk-averse business, wagering millions of production dollars and advertising buys against content that will stand out without causing an uproar. Despite its widespread American adoption, religion has been largely taboo since the mid-20th Century, raising the specter of risk for its inclusion in any commercial product. Producers often worry that speaking too explicitly to any one faith perspective might alienate another when both groups might have shown up anyway if the program had simply avoided religion altogether. In some instances, like with the *Peanuts* franchise, religious groups naturally gravitate toward properties that they see themselves in (Lind, 2015a). In other instances, even religiously-themed products like *Grey's Anatomy* star Sarah Drew's believer-friendly film *Mom's Night Out* or the more theologically explicit *The Passion of the Christ* may be made with a faith demographic in mind but with the hopes of reaching a wider audience.

The desire to produce content that can reach as wide of a global audience as possible may also mean leaning on marketing to ensure a secular product reaches religious audiences. Such was the case with the *Lord of the Rings* franchise films, for example. "Particularly with larger budget productions, you are looking for that whole four-quadrant, all-inclusive, cover-everyone kind of content," explains Matt Dravitzki, who worked on the films' production and promotion. The studio knew the secular films had potential in evangelical communities, which had long been a fanbase for Tolkien's almost-allegorical fantasy books. "The studio courted the religious media quite intensely," he notes, describing how the content itself made it easier for the marketing department to lean in to relationships with religious press even more than usual. The focus of this unlikely hero story, the good versus evil plot base, and the return of Gandalf from the dead with a glow of light around him, Dravitzki (2019) describes, all made for an authentic marketing appeal to faith-based communities.

This risk-averse content mentality means that some of the most boundary-pushing references to religion could only come, then, from powerhouse shows that already command massive followings. Religious faith may still need to be framed within conflict, often favoring the liberal interpretation, but the storylines could be more substantive, nuanced, and unique. ABC's medical tentpole, *Grey's Anatomy*, for example, was able to test jaw-dropping content in which a faith-filled doctor questions God's providence (Lind, 2015b), Jehovah's Witnesses reject blood transfusions (Lind, 2013a) and in which a lead lesbian character exclaims to her father and his priest, "Jesus is my savior, daddy, not you!" (Phelan, 2009) because the faithful viewers already knew and loved the characters within a formulaic program. CBS's *The Good Wife* made similar handleable waves when they revealed that their beloved protagonist was an atheist. The popularity of the critically-acclaimed show thus paved the way for an interesting and unique conversation between the titular mother about her atheism with her teenage buddingly-evangelical Christian daughter (Lind, 2013c).

Reality TV. In addition to the social capital a popular program can spend in a more liberal cultural era, three modern media evolutions have widened the limits on religions reference—reality television, cable channels, and the streaming platforms. On reality television, the intent to cast diversely identifiable demographics in order to reach a four-quadrant market makes it common for noticeably religious characters to be present. These portrayals have been found to be significantly more positive than the trend toward negativity in scripted programming (Gildemeister, 2006). The genre provides networks more cover than on a typical scripted show for any comments or conduct that might offend certain viewers. Bravo's fashion competition show, *Project Runway*, gave new perspective on sex appeal, for example, when a conservative Muslim designer successfully navigated the show to become runner-up (Clark, 2019); musical competition shows regularly include contestants who grew up singing in church; and the winner of season 25 of CBS's *Survivor*, Denise Stapley, was even able to share her perspective as an atheist in the televised game—a journey that she later shared as a speaker at the American Atheists National Convention.

Cable Opportunities. More than Sunday morning broadcast televangelism ever could, cable allowed for significant religious content expansion through entire networks like Jewish Broadcasting Service, Muslim Bridges TV network, Trinity Broadcasting Network, the Christian Broadcasting Network, and contemporary evangelical Hillsong Channel, each devoted without pretense to religious followers. Even for mainstream programming, the increase in channels meant an increase in content and thus increased opportunities for diverse religious portrayals seeking to draw religious audience interest. TLC, for example, greenlit *All-American Muslim* and A&E, for example, enjoyed massive conservative evangelical support for *Duck Dynasty* (Bailey, 2013), as did TLC through its "quiverful" of Dugger family babies on *19 Kids and Counting* (Mesaros-Winckles, 2010).

Streaming Niche. Perhaps no single change since the allowance for televangelism over airwaves has the possibility to change religious presence in entertainment media more than streaming. Taking cable's niche programming allowances to a new level, streaming giants like Netflix, Hulu, and Amazon opened the door to new approaches to religious portrayal in several important ways. First, as new companies not beholden to FCC censors, the perspectives of executives and writers had fewer institutional legacies or content routines with which to contend. Cultural shifts and cable moves had already begun this opening, allowing for new twists on old tropes, like that of angels. "We all grew up with the idea that angels are God's children looking down on us," noted Todd Slavkin, executive producer on Freeform's *Shadowhunters*. "Now we're taking that archetype and turning it on its head. Now, God's children aren't all that cherubic" (Tomashoff, 2016). In streaming, limits could be pushed even further. This meant that the show *Lucifer*, for example, could explore the sexual character of first-woman Eve tangling with the likably fallen Lucifer Morningstar amidst more foul language once the show was canceled by FOX but then revived by Netflix. The new open, clean-ish slate of streaming could also give allowance to Hulu's *The Handmaid's Tale*, set in a rape-traumatized society built on a perversion of biblical precepts. Even the Archie Comic-turned-ABC-sitcom *Sabrina the Teenage Witch* could be reimagined in this new context as Netflix's *The Chilling Adventures of Sabrina*, featuring a storyline that functionally contends that the Bible is true but that the lovable witch characters are justified in choosing to follow the Dark Lord Satan instead of that certain Nazarene (Jesus).

Second, because of the massive amount of money being invested at the onset of new streaming services, a glut of programming was produced. Not only were massive libraries of titles purchased for syndication, allowing whole new generations to discover and enjoy the likes of *Buffy the Vampire Slayer*, *The Nanny*, or *Touched by an Angel*, but new content was being produced in droves, even explicitly religious content like Netflix's dark reflection on Christianity, *The Family*, or Amazon's pluckily Jewish *The Marvelous Ms. Maisel*. Roma Downey's MGM division, LightWorkers, would even sell *Messiah* to Netflix, a scripted program premised on the scenario of the Messiah's advent occurring in the present-day. "We have a whole new place to sell to," reflected a senior director at LightWorkers. "It's very exciting" (Warnock, 2019).

Finally, the platform logic itself is built on niche viewing, affording the operators the chance to test out content that would have always been too risky in traditional broadcast. Unlike in linear broadcast television in which viewers have severely limited options, viewers in streaming contexts feel a sense of agency, actively sifting through programming to find what they want to watch on-demand. Connecting with a single program can be enough to convince a viewer to subscribe, but disinterest in a given program will simply likely cause the viewer to keep sifting, not unsubscribe.

Streaming's niche logic allowed, for example, for shows like Hulu's *Ramy*, a portrayal of a twenty-something Muslim every-guy living outside of New York City in a post-9/11 world. Even in Netflix's *Messiah*, the allegedly returned Messiah is positioned initially as a Muslim prophet. Of course modern, more diverse portrayals of Muslim identity may at times still reinforce notions of the dangerous other (Alsultany, 2016; Shaheen, 2017), may still run counter to the impacts of persistent negative portrayals in the news media (Saleem, Wojcieszak, Hawkins, Li, & Ramasubramanian, 2019) or may balance the character simply by adding tropes of Whiteness (Halse, 2015). Yet, a business model that can profit from niche programming allows for more character depictions that push back against common depictions. Even further, streaming opened up massive on-demand libraries of thousands of programs and films from around the globe. For the first time, viewers have immediate access, for example, to not only post-theatrical releases of films like Christian drama *God's Not Dead* starring Dean Cain and Kevin Sorbo, but also glossy "Bollywood" films, titles like director Natalie Fuchs' Buddhist exploration film

The Enlightenment, and Gowariker's period drama about a Muslim-Hindu wedding, *Jodhaa Akbar*.

Effects

The effects of repeatedly limited mainstream entertainment messaging are well-documented and explained by decades of studies. In short, repetitive exposure to the same limited messages cultivate in viewers certain perceptions about social reality and result in "the steady entrenchment of mainstream orientations" (Gerbner, Gross, Morgan, & Signorielli, 1986, p. 24). Because Americans spend so much time with entertainment media like television, this means that the mid-century notion that religion is not acceptable to discuss in public is re-enshrined as cultural truth when religion is routinely omitted from entertainment narratives.

Even further, as Gregory describes, these stories we engage for entertainment "we often treat as knowledge" (2009, p. 1). Entertainment portrayals offer a rare opportunity to experience another's perspective on faith. Viewers may be missing out on an opportunity to learn more about alternative perspectives, however, because religious representation is so limited and so rarely portrays divergent or intersectional faith perspectives. They may experience the permission to reflect on one's own beliefs, to hold nuanced views, or to see and appreciate the sameness in another even in the light of diverging faith perspectives.

Future Avenues for Research

Studies of religious representation are few and far between. This makes the next era of research rich in possibilities for scholars, practitioners, and critics alike. Future researchers interested in representations of religion are encouraged to take an "all of the above" approach to artifact content and methodology. They may continue the work exploring representations in news media (Bolce & De Maio, 2008; Borchert, 2002; Schmalzbauer, 2002), for example, or may conduct regular quantitative studies of television or film to track the trends in representation. While most quantitative studies will require large populations, even if genre-specific, in order to ensure a representative sample, given how rare representation has historically been, quantitative studies will remain an essential bedrock of the field. Coding schemes require deliberate operational definitions in order to address the inherent difficulty in codifying what is and is not religion, let alone identifying it on screen. Those coding schemes, though, can range in complexity and focus, assessing religious identity and behaviors along with other demographic features like portrayals of class, race, ethnicity, sexuality, etc. and narrative elements like genre, plot primacy, valence, etc.

Qualitative, journalistic, and rhetorical studies will likewise be critical for robust future understandings of religious representation. In such studies, it is often advantageous to seek not only to incorporate many rich analytical tools developed from literary and film analysis but also to seek to incorporate industry perspectives into the study. Interviews with creators, marketers, consultants, and financers responsible for the material's existence can shed significant light on the ways in which religious portrayals come into existence, allowing for insights into creator intent and industry norms. Such interviews also serve to push back against any stereotypes about cultural attitudes toward religion which may have otherwise biased the analysis unfairly. Similarly, engaging fan studies literature and responsibly incorporating actual viewer perspectives will be invaluable.

Conclusion

Owing, in part, to the industry's tendency towards being risk-averse, mainstream American entertainment programming in the 20th century was routinely absent of overt representations of religious belief and practice. An immense disparity persisted between the quantity of religiously identifiable characters on screen and the number of American viewers who would personally claim a religious identity. Given the effect that such representations—or lack thereof—can have on individual viewers and collective social norms, it may be even more notable that those references to religious faith and practice that did show up on the screen often repeated a tired set of simplistic tropes. This includes simple or scandalous clergy, naïve believers, Black gospel singers, and benevolent or insidious supernatural figures, and minority faith as otherized or dangerous.

At the turn of the century, while those tropes persisted across programming, evolving media sensibilities and the popularization of cable services brought modest but meaningful changes to mainstream representations of religion. The popularity of key programs gave way to the greenlighting of additional religious content while reality television provided a useful stage for incorporating increasingly diverse religious identities on screen. This expansion would then accelerate through the possibilities that streaming services offer viewers. With a business model that circumvented censorship norms, capitalized on the lower-risk proposition of niche programming, and celebrated on-demand access to expansive libraries, the advent of streaming services opened new possibilities for diverse representations of religion.

While it is unlikely that there will ever be parity between screen depiction and American religious life, 21st century viewers, scholars, and practitioners have been given meaningful new content to engage and analyze. The future of religious reference study is thus virtually limitless. Relationships and reactions within vast libraries of archival, syndicated, and newly produced material wait to be explored. The harvest, to borrow a phrase full of religious history, is plenty.

References

Alsultany, E. (2016). Representations of Arabs, Muslims, and Iranians in an era of complex characters and storylines. *Film Criticism*, *40*(1), 1–2.

Bailey, S. P. (2013, August 21). "Duck Dynasty" success thrives on Christian stereotypes. *Religion News Service*. Retrieved from https://religionnews.com/2013/08/21/duck-dynasty-success-thrives-on-christian-stereotypes/.

Bolce, L., & De Maio, G. (2008). A prejudice for the thinking classes: Media exposure, political sophistication, and the anti-Christian fundamentalist. *American Politics Research*, *36*(2), 155–185. https://doi.org/10.1177/1532673X07309601

Borchert, M. G. (2002). The Southern Baptist controversy and the press. In S. M. Hoover & L. Schofield Clark (Eds.), *Practicing religion in the age of the media* (pp. 188–200). New York: Columbia University Press.

Chesebro, J. W. (1991). Communication, values, and popular television series—A seventeen-year assessment. *Communication Quarterly*, *39*(3), 197–225. https://doi.org/10.1080/01463379109369799

Clark, A. (2019, February 13). How project runway star Ayana Ife stitches faith and fashion. *Splinter*. Retrieved from https://splinternews.com/how-project-runway-star-ayana-ife-stitches-faith-and-fa-1832569880.

Clarke, S. H. (2005). Created in whose image? Religious characters on network television. *Journal of Media and Religion*, *4*(3), 137–153. https://doi.org/10.1207/s15328415jmr0403_2

Cohen, Y., & Hetsroni, A. (2019). Monotheism and television: A comparative content analysis of religion in prime-time programming in the USA, Israel, and Turkey. *Atlantic Journal of Communication*, 1–12. https://doi.org/10.1080/15456870.2019.1613405

Collins, S. (2013, March 4). *"The Bible," "Vikings" premieres tell a ratings epic for History*. *Los Angeles Times*. Retrieved from https://www.latimes.com/entertainment/tv/la-xpm-2013-mar-04-la-et-st-the-bible-vikings-premieres-history-ratings-20130304-story.html.

Dietter, S. (1995, October 1). Home sweet home-dum-diddly doodily (Season 7 Episode 3). In *The Simpsons*. FOX.

Diffrient, D. S. (2010). The cult imaginary: Fringe religions and fan cultures on American television. *Historical Journal of Film, Radio and Television, 30*(4), 463–485. https://doi.org/10.1080/01439685.2010.523989

Dravitzki, M. (2019, November 12). [Interview by S. J. Lind].

Gerbner, G., Gross, L., Morgan, M., & Signorielli, N. (1986). Living with television: The dynamics of the cultivation process. In J. Bryant & D. Zillmann (Eds.), *Perspectives on media effects* (pp. 17–40). Mahwah, NJ: Lawrence Erlbaum Associates.

Gildemeister, C. (2006). *Faith in a box: Entertainment television & religion.* Parents Television Council. Retrieved from http://www.parentstv.org/PTC/publications/reports/religionstudy06/main.asp.

"God bless gay". (2018, June 15). In *Queer Eye*. Netflix.

Gregory, M. W. (2009). *Shaped by stories: The ethical power of narratives.* South Bend, IN: University of Notre Dame Press.

Hadden, J. K., & Shupe, A. D. (1988). *Televangelism, power, and politics on God's frontier* (1st ed.). New York: H. Holt.

Halse, R. (2015). Counter-stereotypical images of Muslim characters in the television serial 24: A difference that makes no difference? *Critical Studies in Television, 10*(1), 54–72.

"Hollywood finds God". (2015, January 7). *Premier Christianity.* Retrieved from https://www.premierchristianity.com/Past-Issues/2015/February-2015/Hollywood-finds-God.

"Hollywood finds God in Bible stories made for the big screen." (2014, June 29). *Artcentron.* Retrieved from https://artcentron.com/2014/06/29/hollywood-finds-god-in-bible-stories-made-for-the-big-screen/.

Hughes, T. (1987, February 14). Forgive me, Father (Season 2 Episode 18). In *The Golden Girls*. NBC.

"In U.S., decline of Christianity continues at rapid pace." (2019, October 17). *Pew Research Center's Religion & Public Life Project.* Retrieved from https://www.pewforum.org/2019/10/17/in-u-s-decline-of-christianity-continues-at-rapid-pace/.

Johnson, C. (1994). The schlemiel and the schlimazl in "Seinfeld". *Journal of Popular Film and Television, 22*(3), 116–124. https://doi.org/10.1080/01956051.1994.9943676

Keating, S. (2019, May 20). *Let's talk about that confessional scene in "Fleabag".* BuzzFeed News. Retrieved from https://www.buzzfeednews.com/article/shannonkeating/fleabag-season-2-phoebe-waller-bridge-hot-priest.

Krieger, R. (2003). "Does he actually say the word Jewish?"—Jewish representations in "Seinfeld". *Journal for Cultural Research, 7*(4), 387–404. https://doi.org/10.1080/1479758032000165048

Lewis, T. V. (2002). Religious rhetoric and the comic frame in "The Simpsons". *Journal of Media and Religion, 1*(3), 153–165. https://doi.org/10.1207/S15328415JMR0103_2

Lind, S. J. (2013a, February 1). Good job with :Bad Blood": "Grey's Anatomy" and Jehovah's Witnesses. *ReligiMedia.* Retrieved from https://religimedia.wordpress.

com/2013/02/01/good-job-with-bad-blood-greys-anatomy-and-jehovahs-witnesses/.

Lind, S. J. (2013b, April 2). Sharing #TheBible? High-profile tweets support The History Channel's religious program. *ReligiMedia*. Retrieved from https://religimedia.wordpress.com/2013/04/02/sharing-thebible-high-profile-tweets-support-the-history-channels-religious-program/.

Lind, S. J. (2013c, October 1). "The Good Wife" keeps its faith: More religion coming in season 5? *ReligiMedia*. Retrieved from https://religimedia.wordpress.com/2013/10/01/the-good-wife-keeps-its-faith-more-religion-coming-in-season-5/.

Lind, S. J. (2014). Christmas in the 1960s: "A Charlie Brown Christmas", religion, and the conventions of the television genre. *The Journal of Religion and Popular Culture*, *26*(1), 1–22. https://doi.org/10.3138/jrpc.26.1.1

Lind, S. J. (2015a). *A Charlie Brown Religion: Exploring the spiritual life and work of Charles M. Schulz*. Jackson: University Press of Mississippi.

Lind, S. J. (2015b, February 13). Loss and success on "Grey's". *ReligiMedia*. Retrieved from https://religimedia.wordpress.com/2015/02/13/loss-and-success-on-greys/.

Lyons, M., & Poniewozik, J. (2016, August 24). Where is God on the small screen? *The New York Times*. Retrieved from https://www.nytimes.com/2016/08/28/arts/television/greenleaf-oprah-winfrey-transparent-the-path.html.

Maddux, K. (2010). *The faithful citizen: Popular Christian media and gendered civic identities*. Waco, TX: Baylor University Press.

McCracken, J. (1997, April 25). Cult fiction (Season 4 Episode 21). In *Boy Meets World*. ABC.

Mesaros-Winckles, C. (2010). TLC and the fundamentalist family: A televised quiverfull of babies. *Journal of Religion & Popular Culture*, *22*(3), 170–190.

The Nielsen Company. (2019). *Nielsen total audience report—Q3 2018*.

O'Hara, T. (1996, March 9). Hearts and minds (Season 4 Episode 21). In *Dr. Quinn, Medicine Woman*. CBS.

O'Keefe, J. (1991, December 20). Choir trouble (Season 3 Episode 13). In *Family Matters*. ABC.

Paris, J. (1964, January 22). The life and love of Joe Coogan. In *The Dick Van Dyke Show*. CBS.

Paris, J. (1978, December 19). Christmas time (Season 6 Episode 16). In *Happy Days*. ABC.

Paris, J. (1981, December 1). No, thank you (Season 9 Episode 9). In *Happy Days*. ABC.

Pew Research Center. (2015a, May 12). America's changing religious landscape. *Pew Research Center's Religion & Public Life Project*. Retrieved from https://www.pewforum.org/2015/05/12/americas-changing-religious-landscape/.

Pew Research Center. (2015b, November 3). U.S. public becoming less religious. Retrieved from https://www.pewforum.org/2015/11/03/u-s-public-becoming-less-religious/.

Pew Research Center (2019, October 17). In U.S., decline of Christianity continues at rapid pace. Retrieved from https://www.pewforum.org/2019/10/17/in-u-s- decline-of-christianity-continues-at-rapid-pace/.

Phelan, T. (2009, October 15). Invasion (Season 6 Episode 5). In *Grey's Anatomy*. ABC.

Pieraccini, C., & Alligood, D. L. (2005). *Color television: Fifty years of African American and Latino images on prime-time television*. Atlanta, GA: Kendall/Hunt.

Quinley, H. E., & Glock, C. Y. (1983). *Anti-Semitism in America*. Piscataway, NJ: Transaction Books.

Saleem, M., Wojcieszak, M., Hawkins, I., Li, M., & Ramasubramanian, S. (2019). Social identity threats: How media and discrimination affect Muslim Americans' identification as Americans and trust in the U.S. government. *Journal of Communication*. https://doi.org/10.1093/joc/jqz001

SARAH. (2013, July 10). RE: Boy meets cult: Quick religion on "Boy Meets World" (#TBT) [Comment]. ReligiMedia. Retrieved from: https://religimedia.wordpress.com/2013/02/14/boy-meets-cult-quick-religion-on-boy-meets-world-tbt/#comment-754.

Schmalzbauer, J. (2002). Between objectivity and moral vision: Catholics and Evangelicals in American journalism. In Stewart M. Hoover & Lynn Schofield Clark (Eds.), *Practicing religion in the age of the media* (pp. 165–187). New York: Columbia University Press.

Schultze, Q. J. (2003). *Televangelism and American culture: The business of popular religion*. Eugene, OR: Wipf and Stock Publishers.

Schultze, Q. J., & Woods, R. (Eds.). (2008). *Understanding evangelical media: The changing face of Christian communication*. Downers Grove, IL: IVP Academic.

Scott, O. (1984, December 16). They don't make preachers like him anymore (Season 11 Episode 7). In *The Jeffersons*. CBS.

Shaheen, J. (2000). Hollywood's Muslim Arabs. *The Muslim World*, 90, 22-42.

Shaheen, J. (2017). Strategies to successfully push back against harmful Hollywood stereotypes about Arabs and Muslims, and the work new generations must take on. *Washington Report on Middle East Affairs*, 36(3), 47–51.

Shandler, J. (2009). *Jews, God, and videotape: Religion and media in America*. New York: New York University Press.

Skill, T., Robinson, J. D., Lyons, J. S., & Larson, D. (1994). The portrayal of religion and spirituality on fictional network television. *Review of Religious Research*, 35(3), 251. https://doi.org/10.2307/3511892

Smith, G. (2013, January 18). *Hollywood finds God (again)*. EW.Com. Retrieved from https://ew.com/article/2013/01/18/hollywood-finds-god-again/.

Stuart, M. (1977, December 15). "A Sweathog Christmas" special (Season 3 Episode 15). In *Welcome Back, Kotter*. ABC.

Tomashoff, C. (2016, October 13). From "Touched by an Angel" to "Lucifer": TV's heavenly creatures are evolving. *The Hollywood Reporter*. Retrieved from https://www.hollywoodreporter.com/live-feed/evolution-angels-tv-shows-938103.

U.S. public becoming less religious. (2015). Pew Research Center.

Warnock, K. (2019, May 8). [Interview by S. J. Lind].

Wolff, R. F. (1995). Prime-time television's history of the American church: A critical assessment. *Journal of Communication & Religion, 18*(2), 41–53.

Young,R. (1986, February 9). *Under Seige.* NBC.

Young, S. (2016, August 11). A look back at Roma Downey's famed "Touched by an Angel" role. *Variety.* Retrieved from https://variety.com/2016/tv/spotlight/touched-by-angel-memorable-afterlife-1201834936/.

12 Stereotypes of Immigrants and Refugees

JENNIFER HOEWE
Purdue University

SETH P. MCCULLOCK
Purdue University

Public opinion toward immigrants and refugees in Western countries has been historically negative (Citrin & Sides, 2008; Pettigrew, Wagner, & Christ, 2007), and media coverage is an important source, particularly for the American public, of information about immigrants and refugees (Akdenizli, Dionne, Kaplan, Rosenstiel, & Suro, 2008). Illustrating the divisiveness that has arisen around migration in the United States, a Pew survey conducted in 2018 showed that twice as many Republicans (33%) supported cutting legal immigration when compared to Democrats (16%). Additionally, far more Democrats (86%) than Republicans (48%) indicated feelings of sympathy toward immigrants who entered the United States illegally. It is important to note that these attitudes, among all Americans, have changed in recent years. The Pew Research Center has asked U.S. citizens their opinions of immigrants for more than 20 years, providing evidence of this shifting perspective. In 2016, 59% of respondents saw immigrants as strengthening the country, while 33% saw them as a burden to the country. More than 20 years earlier in 1994, responses were quite the opposite: 31% saw immigrants as strengthening the country, while 63% found them to be a burden to the country (Jones, 2016). While these attitudes illustrate a greater acceptance of immigrants, they also show a strong influence of partisanship. Pew also has recently asked Americans about their attitudes toward refugees (Hartig, 2018). A 2018 survey found that about half of Americans believe the United States has a responsibility to accept refugees. However, between 2017 and 2018, Republicans (including those who lean Republican) became less likely to agree with this sentiment, with support dropping from 35% to 26%; the current number is even lower among conservative Republicans (19%). Support among Democrats and those who lean Democrat held steady around 74% (with liberal Democrats at 85%). These partisan shifts in public opinion may be related to media depictions of immigrants and refugees, which is a possibility that this chapter explores.

A lack of public understanding about the differences between immigrants and refugees in the United States and other countries has led to these groups sharing many common stereotypic labels. Research has shown that immigrants and refugees are often perceived to be threatening (Figgou, Sapountzis, Bozatzis, Gardikiotis, & Pantazis, 2011), as pollutants (Cisneros, 2008), and are frequently both deindividualized and dehumanized by the media (Bleiker, Campbell, Hitchison, Nicholson, 2013; Gale, 2004). The development of stereotypic attitudes among the public represents a significant problem, wielding influence over people's levels of prejudice, behavioral intentions, and immigration policy preferences (Rucker, Murphy, & Quintanilla, 2019). One particular contribution to this conflation is that American news media often use the terms "immigrant" and "refugee" interchangeably (Hoewe, 2018) when there are clear distinctions between the two groups. Based on the AP Stylebook's definition of immigrants and refugees, these groups should be differentiated in media coverage—and thus, research as well. Individuals described as immigrants (or migrants) are moving "from place to place for temporary work or economic advantage" (Associated Press, 2016, p. 238). A refugee is "a person who is forced to leave his or her home or country to escape war, persecution, or natural disaster" (Associated Press, 2016, p. 238). These definitions illustrate important distinctions in the understandings of these individuals and groups of people. These distinctions, however, are not always considered in the formation of media depictions of immigrants and refugees, public understandings of these groups, or research in these areas.

This chapter begins by examining stereotypic representations of immigrants and refugees in the media and how stereotypes and stereotypic attitudes have developed in recent years. Then it considers the effects that exposure to these stereotypes in the media may have on message recipients. Finally, it reviews some theories and methodologies that have been used in the study of immigrant and refugee stereotypes and offers suggestions for future research directions.

How Stereotypes Problematically Represent Immigrants and Refugees

Historically, the U.S. has celebrated those who first made the perilous journey to the new world, with the Statue of Liberty illustrating this openness: "Give me your tired, your poor, your huddled masses yearning to breathe free . . ."

Simultaneously, many Americans have remained suspicious of people from foreign countries who seek refuge or wish to migrate. Part of these feelings stem from uncertainty toward immigrants and refugees as well as beliefs that these individuals represent various forms of danger (e.g., Esses, Medianu, & Lawson, 2013). One contributing factor to these stereotypes is media coverage that may create problematic myths, skewing public perceptions of both immigrants and refugees.

Specifically considering the representation of immigrants, research has identified three mythologies that have been established and perpetuated in media content. These are: (a) the metaphor of immigrants as pollutants (Cisneros, 2008); (b) associating immigrants with the cowboy narrative (Santa Ana, 2016); and (c) the Inanna narrative (Santa Ana, 2016). As Cisneros (2008) found, news media visually frame stories of immigrants and environmental pollutants (such as garbage or toxic waste) in similar ways. Specifically, Cisneros concluded that news organizations often define immigrants in terms of the threats they pose to cultural proliferation (as garbage may leak into its surrounding environment) and by their disadvantaged economic status (as in how waste barrels are often damaged or rusted). Relatedly, Santa Ana (2016) identified how the news perpetuates mythic stories when communicating information about immigrants. One is the narrative of the cowboy as an American archetypical hero. In this narrative, the immigrant is the villain who invades from a foreign land and threatens to bring change to the cowboy's way of life. The other myth is the Inanna narrative, which creates a parallel between the Sumerian goddess, Inanna, with the typical journey that immigrants undergo. This myth connects immigrants to the themes of self-reliance, reduction of autonomy, and personal sacrifice that were central to Inanna's narrative. Such illustrations of immigrants are problematic as they work to dehumanize immigrants by associating them with materials that pose an environmental threat, portray them as "antagonists" to an iconic American character, and communicate that these individuals lack personal autonomy and are reliant upon the kindness of others to achieve their personal ambitions.

Along these lines, much of the prior research examining media portrayals of both refugees and immigrants finds these depictions to be negative and typically inefficient in describing the complexities of these groups of people (e.g., Berry, Garcio-Blanco, & Moore, 2015; Gabrielatos & Baker, 2008; Khosravinik, 2009; Klocker & Dunn, 2003). Furthermore, much of the media coverage of both groups has portrayed them as undesirable, even moving toward dehumanization (Esses et al., 2013). Some of the stereotypes shown within media coverage of immigrants and refugees include that they carry diseases, are terrorists, and attempt to come into new countries through illegal methods (Esses et al., 2013). American news media, *The New York Times* and

The Washington Post in particular, were more likely to conflate immigrants with refugees and also associate them with terrorism when comparted to non-American news media (specifically, *Al Jazeera* and *The Daily Telegraph*) (Hoewe, 2018). Such media outlets also tend not to discuss the beneficial side to migration, such as increases in the diversity of ideas and the diversification of culture (Berry et al., 2015).

Examinations of news media content about migration into the United States have found that it tends to center around two generic frames: one of conflict and one of human interest (e.g., Brader, Valentino, & Suhay, 2008; Figenschou & Thorbjørnsrud, 2015; Parrott, Hoewe, Fan, & Huffman, 2019). Conflict frames focus on some disagreement between two parties, highlighting the division among individuals or groups. These frames may include physical conflict (e.g., arresting immigrants) or political conflict (e.g., debate among politicians). Brader et al. (2008) explained that migration is a topic prone to presentation within conflict frames because it involves the separation of people into groups. The human interest frame, on the other hand, typically includes an immigrant or refugee explaining their own personal experiences. These frames are more likely to focus on the challenges faced by immigrants and refugees, which may evoke empathy from the media consumer (Figenschou & Thorbjørnsrud, 2015). For example, Parrott et al. (2019) examined the Twitter feeds of regional news outlets within all 50 U.S. states. In terms of their visual representation of immigrants (i.e., pictures in the tweets), these news outlets primarily featured two dominant frames in their coverage: (1) the human interest frame, featuring immigrants and refugees as everyday people; or (2) the political frame, showcasing politicians. These representations were then tied to public understanding and interpretation of issues related to migration.

Several studies have found that journalists in the United States are prone to associating immigrants with illegal methods of entry. They tend to focus on stories about individuals from Latin America attempting to cross the U.S/Mexico border without the necessary documentation (e.g., Chavez, Whiteford, & Hoewe, 2010; Farris & Mohamed, 2018). In a content analysis of four elite newspapers' coverage of Mexican immigration, Chavez et al. (2010) found that the most frequently addressed topic was crime. Similarly, Chavez (2001) examined images on U.S. magazine covers and concluded that "Mexican immigration has been represented almost entirely in alarmist imagery" (p. 260). Since there were no positively-framed images of Mexican immigrants, every cover showed these individuals as having "backwardness, peasantness, and lack of modern sophistication" (Chavez, 2001, p. 260). In content analyzing newspaper coverage of Arizona's controversial SB 1070,

Fryberg et al. (2012) found that the coverage area of the newspaper as well as its political bent were instructive in understanding the type of coverage, where national papers focused on threats posed by immigrants but also their civil rights and conservative papers focused primarily on threat concerns.

Outside the United States, researchers have established that different types of media organizations portray immigrants in varying—but mostly negative—ways as well. In a study of Austrian adults, Schmuck and Matthes (2017) found that when the media emphasized a symbolic threat from immigrants (as opposed to an economic one), individuals exerted stronger anti-immigrant attitudes. Jacobs, Meeusen, and d'Haenens (2016) examined Flemish public and commercial news coverage of immigration, finding that while both types of outlets were negative in their coverage, commercial news relied more heavily on sensational coverage. They concluded that public media may, therefore, hold potential as a vehicle for promoting greater tolerance.

Depictions of refugees in media content is similarly problematic, though there is much less available research in this area. For example, visual framing of refugees often depicts them such that they are deindividualized (Bleiker et al., 2013). More specifically, when examining media content focused on refugees, Bleiker et al. (2013) concluded that there was a "distinct lack of images depicting individual asylum seekers with recognizable facial features" (p. 406). As several researchers have argued (e.g., Bleiker et al., 2013; Gale, 2004), this removes the emphasis from refugee migration as a humanitarian issue, instead reinforcing public fears of sovereignty and security. And when refugees are deindividualized, news consumers may be less likely to offer aid or assistance to members of that group (Jenni & Loewenstein, 1997).

The ideological slant of the media outlet is an important consideration in the portrayals of refugees as well. Blumell, Bunce, Cooper, and McDowell (2019) found print and online news media in the United Kingdom depicted refugees in differing ways depending on the ideological leaning of the publication; right-leaning publications focused more on criminality and left-leaning publications were more likely to discuss the victimization of those seeking asylum. In this way, it is important to understand where media consumers are getting their information about both immigrants and refugees.

Effects of Exposure to Immigrant/Refugee Stereotypes

Media depictions can be influential in informing individuals' attitudes toward social groups. Mastro (2003) explained that media content can work as a "symbolic environment through which the process of ingroup—outgroup differentiation can be initiated" (p. 100). News content, in particular, can impact the news consumer's thoughts, emotions, policy opinions, and political party support with regard to immigrants and refugees (e.g., Boomgaarden & Vliegenthart, 2007; Lecheler, Bos, & Vliegenthart, 2015). For example, Hoewe and Ziny (2020) concluded that immigrant groups in the United States have become part of an outgroup for some Americans, in part because of media portrayals and politicians' language surrounding discussions of immigrants and immigration. Moreover, Schemer (2012) found that negative news portrayals of immigrants during a political campaign led to an increase in stereotypic attitudes toward these immigrants among the public, particularly the less informed. However, the author also noted that exposure to positive stereotypes of immigrants brought about less negative outgroup attitudes, suggesting the potential for counter-stereotyping effectiveness (see Chapter 14).

Several other experimental studies have illustrated the influence of media messages about immigrants and/or refugees. Parrott et al. (2019) found that exposure to visually framed messages about immigrants shifted readers' emotional responses. Individuals who saw immigrants framed in terms of politics (i.e., a politician pictured in a tweet about immigration) were more likely to experience negative emotions, which predicted more negative attitudes toward immigrants. Conversely, individuals who saw a tweet framed in terms of human interest (e.g., an immigrant family) were more likely to respond with positive emotions, which predicted more positive attitudes toward immigrants. Also examining visual imagery, Esses et al. (2013) concluded that exposure to editorial cartoons depicting refugees associated with disease encouraged participants to dehumanize refugees, more than when participants saw a message without a reference to disease. Wright and Citrin (2011) had participants look at images of immigration protesters who were waving either a U.S. or Mexican flag. The American participants who saw the American flag showcased at the protest were less upset about the protest. Moreover, Merolla, Ramakrishnan, and Haynes (2013) found that participants who saw immigration policies described as "opportunity to eventually become citizens" as opposed to "amnesty" were more likely to show support for these policies (p. 799).

Recent studies have also discovered that the source of news is important in establishing relationships between media consumption and policy attitudes toward immigrants and refugees. Hoewe, Peacock, Kim, and Barnidge (2020) found that even after controlling for political ideology, Fox News was uniquely related to policy preferences aimed at immigrants and refugees. The study accounted for other news use (including other cable news networks) and only Fox News was related to these attitudes, having a negative influence on consumers' willingness to accept immigrants and refugees into the United States. This research is supported by evidence provided by Gil de Zúñiga, Correa, and

Valenzuela's (2012) study, where conservative Republicans were more likely to watch Fox News and watching Fox News was associated with more negative associations with Mexican immigrants. Viewing that network also encouraged support of more restrictive immigration policies directed specifically at Mexican individuals.

Given the potential for exposure to these stereotypes to be mostly mediated, particularly for refugees, Hoewe, Panek, Peacock, Sherrill, and Wheeler (2018) parsed the differences in Americans' perceptions of immigrants and refugees by using moral foundations theory (Graham et al., 2013) to understand how Americans describe both groups of people. Coupling computer-assisted content analysis (conducted with Linguistic Inquiry and Word Count software) with textual analysis, they found that immigrants were described using language related to loyalty and betrayal, while refugees were understood in terms of care and harm. The overarching stereotypes of these groups of people were as follows: (a) refugees were seen as dirty, poor, experiencing physical and emotional distress, fleeing something, and from the Middle East; and (b) immigrants were described in terms of their skin color, language, and work, as well as being Hispanic, seeking a new life, and as markedly different from respondents themselves. This perspective illustrates the potential for different perceptions of immigrants and refugees despite the media's conflation of these groups and the overlap in Americans' preferences for policies directed at both of these groups of people.

Directions for Future Research in Immigrant/Refugee Stereotyping

Theoretical Directions

Considering the perspectives of social identity theory (Tajfel, 1981, 1982) and group threat (Blumer, 1958), individuals often make judgments about others based on their perceived group-based associations as well as their social distance. These judgments may include considerations of changes to the status quo, particularly if it threatens to change the social status of one's ingroup. In simpler terms, individuals may position themselves in relation to others by situating themselves within some ingroup, which potentially sits opposed to an outgroup. As social distance increases, so does the perceived difference between oneself (and one's ingroup) and the outgroup. Theories related to social distance expect that larger geographic, political, and cultural differences can situate individuals as more distant and, consequently, as outgroups (e.g., Meirick, 2006). The perception of threat, in particular, to the social or economic status quo from some outgroup tends to grow as the number of outgroup members increases (Schlueter & Scheepers, 2010). As the social distance between an individual and an outgroup member increases, the likelihood of stereotyping that outgroup and its members also increases (e.g., Magee & Smith, 2013; Trope & Liberman, 2010).

Social identity theory also states that self-esteem is determined partially through evaluating one's own social groups against outgroups. In the event of an "unfavorable" evaluation, people may seek to leave their group or find ways of achieving more positive distinctiveness (Brown, 2000). Immigrants (and refugees) in a new country are often viewed in negative or derogatory ways by the larger society and may take a variety of positions in the face of devaluation of their group (Liebkind, 1992), which can include disassociating from their ethnic identity to better blend in with the larger society's culture or experiencing feelings of self-devaluation. This possibility represents a future direction of research as studies have yet to consider how to longitudinally examine how social identity threats—mediated and otherwise—adversely influence perceptions of self-esteem in immigrants and refugees. Given the divisive political climate in the U.S., it may be that members of these groups will experience continued threats to their social identities in coming years.

Additionally, framing theory can be conceptualized and analyzed at both a micro- and macro-level, which can prove useful in the study of media effects related to stereotypes of immigrants and refugees. Micro-level framing refers to how individuals cognitively process mass-mediated messages (Scheufele, 1999), while macro-level framing refers to how messages are purposely selected or accentuate specific aspects of a perceived reality (Entman, 1993). Numerous studies have examined how both text and visuals utilize various frames in order to convey information. Particularly relevant to the study of immigrant and refugee stereotyping is the concept of visual framing. Specifically, content analyses have identified visual framing as a mechanism used to represent trauma, natural disasters, and human suffering in the news (Borah, 2009) as well as communicate ideological messages that promote nationalistic sentiments (Parry, 2011). Other content analyses of news media coverage of immigrants and refugees have largely found that the news frames these populations in terms of some potential social threat they pose (Esses et al., 2013). Much of the extant literature on media representation of immigrants and refugees has examined how the news media depicts these populations through framing devices. Therefore, a future direction for research using framing is to examine how differing communicative channels, in addition to mainstream news media, represent immigrants and refugees as well as their effects on media consumers. Given that the current media landscape presents a highly saturated media environment, there may be distinctions in these representations and their effects when considering differences in mediums and sources.

Methodological Directions

Overall, much of the prior literature examining stereotypic portrayals of both refugees and immigrants has used one of several approaches, being: cross-sectional surveys, experimental designs, and/or content analyses. These methodologies have been primarily used to determine factors associated with stereotypic attitudes, to understand the causal effects of stereotypic portrayals on individuals' behaviors, attitudes, and other cognitions, and to examine how immigrants and refugees are portrayed in different communicative channels, respectively. The scope of understanding immigrant and refugee stereotypes is narrowed by primarily using these methodologies. Therefore, this section will advocate for future researchers to make use of other, lesser-used methods, such as qualitative approaches and computer-assisted content and textual analysis.

First, future research in this area should pursue the utilization of qualitative research designs. Qualitative studies on immigrant and refugee stereotypes in the media have sparse representation in the literature compared to quantitative studies. Regarding the use of different qualitative methods, interviewing seems to be the most widely used approach among stereotype researchers (e.g., Midtbøen, 2014), though the use of focus group techniques could also prove instructive. By adopting a qualitative approach, researchers will be able to get a better understanding of an individual's experience and may uncover information that could aid the development of future research—both qualitative and quantitative. Pairing these qualitative approaches with quantitative designs would produce even more meaningful research regarding the content and effects of media coverage of both immigrants and refugees.

Second, computer-assisted content analysis and textual analysis are types of designs that, beyond the content of media, can focus on the underlying ideological and cultural assumptions of some body of content. Recently developed software (e.g., Linguistic Inquiry and Word Count; Pennebaker, Booth, & Francis, 2007) has made it possible to quickly and efficiently analyze large bodies of textual data to determine differences in semantic and cognitive expressions. Such a computer-assisted design coupled with textual analysis could be chosen by media scholars to overcome the common limitations of traditional content analysis, such as manifesting content into quantifiable categories. Meanwhile, textual analysis allows the researcher to discern latent meaning, but also implicit patterns, assumptions, and omissions in media content. Some researchers have already coupled textual analysis methodologies with computer-assisted content analysis to study immigrant and refugee stereotypes (e.g., Hoewe et al., 2018). In particular, Fernández et al. (2013) found that exposure to a news frame on crime resulted in participants using greater amounts of negative affective language related to immigrants. As these authors suggested, negative emotional language use could breed other negative feelings and result in the formation of prejudiced attitudes. The relative methodological flexibility of these types of approaches could help produce more comprehensive research on how the media influences the public's perceptions of immigrants and refugees.

Conclusion

The 2016 U.S. presidential election campaign brought policy related to immigrants and refugees to the forefront of public and media attention. Migration was a central issue for Donald Trump's campaign, including an emphasis on building a wall on the U.S./Mexico border and deporting individuals aided by the DREAM Act. During Trump's administration, several additional policy changes continued to put immigrants and refugees in the spotlight: banning travel from several Muslim-majority countries, punishing sanctuary cities, separating children and parents who illegally cross the U.S./Mexico border, and restricting the number of refugees entering the United States. The campaign and these issues received prominent media coverage. Couple this ongoing debate with consistent research evidence of negative media depictions of immigrants and refugees, and it is not surprising to see an increasingly polarized American public, particularly in terms of their attitudes toward immigrants and refugees. Scholarship should continue to investigate both the portrayals of immigrants and refugees in media content and also how that content influences audiences. As this chapter has illustrated, media coverage of immigrants and refugees, particularly when it relies on stereotypes and political rhetoric, has the power to impact individual attitudes and public opinion toward policy directed at immigrants and refugees.

References

Akdenizli, B., Dionne, E. J., Kaplan, M., Rosenstiel, T., & Suro, R. (2008). *Democracy in the age of new media: A report on the media and the immigration debate*. Washington, DC: The Brookings Institution and the University of Southern California Annenberg School for Communication.
Associated Press. (2016). *The Associated Press Stylebook*. New York: The Associated Press.

Berry, M., Garcia-Blanco, I., & Moore, K. (2015). Press coverage of the refugee and migrant crisis in the EU: A content analysis of five European countries. Retrieved from http://orca.cf.ac.uk/87078/1/UNHCR-%20FINAL%20REPORT.pdf.

Bleiker, R., Campbell, D., Hitchison, E., Nicholson, X. (2013). The visual dehumanisation of refugees. *Australian Journal of Political Science, 48*(4), 398–416. doi: 10.1080/1 0361146.2013.840769

Blumell, L. E., Bunce, M., Cooper, G., & McDowell, C. (2019). Refugee and asylum news coverage in UK print and online media. *Journalism Studies.* Advance online publication. doi: 10.1080/1461670X.2019.1633243

Blumer, H. (1958). Race prejudice as a sense of group position. *Pacific Sociological Review, 1,* 3–7.

Boomgaarden, H. G., & Vliegenthart, R. (2007). Explaining the rise of anti-immigrant parties: The role of news media content. *Electoral Studies, 26*(2), 404–417. doi: 10.1016/j.electstud.2006.10.018

Borah, P. (2009). Comparing visual framing in newspapers: Hurricane Katrina versus tsunami. *Newspaper Research Journal, 30*(1), 50–57.

Brader, T., Valentino, N. A., & Suhay, E. (2008). What triggers public opposition to immigration? Anxiety, group cues, and immigration threat. *American Journal of Political Science, 52*(4), 959–978. doi: 10.1111/j.1540-5907.2008.00353.x

Brown, R. (2000). Social identity theory: Past achievements, current problems and future challenges. *European Journal of Social Psychology, 30*(6), 745–778. doi: 10.1002/ 1099-0992(200011/12)30:6<745::AID-EJSP24>3.0.CO;2-O

Chavez, L. (2001). *Covering immigration: Popular images and the politics of a nation.* Berkeley: University of California Press.

Chavez, M., Whiteford, S., & Hoewe, J. (2010). Reporting on immigration: A content analysis of major U.S. newspapers' coverage of Mexican immigration. *Norteamérica, 5*(2), 111–125.

Cisneros, J. D. (2008). Contaminated communities: The metaphor of "immigrant as pollutant" in media representations of immigration. *Rhetoric & Public Affairs, 11*(4), 569–601. doi: 10.1353/rap.0.0068

Citrin, J., & Sides, J. (2008). Immigration and the imagined community in Europe and the United States. *Political Studies, 56*(1), 33–56. doi: 10.1111/j.1467-9248. 2007.00716.x

Entman, R. (1993). Framing: Toward clarification of a fractured paradigm. *Journal of Communication, 43*(4), 51–58. doi: 10.1111/j.1460-2466.1993.tb01304.x

Esses, V., Medianu, S., & Lawson, A. (2013). Uncertainty, threat, and the role of the media in promoting the dehumanization of immigrants and refugees. *Journal of Social Issues, 69*(3), 518–536. doi: 10.1111/josi.12027

Farris, E. M., & Mohamed, H. S. (2018). Picturing immigration: How the media criminalizes immigrants. *Politics, Groups, and Identities, 6*(4), 814–824. doi: 10.1080/215 65503.2018.1484375

Fernández, I., Igartua, J. J., Moral, F., Palacios, E., Acosta, T., & Muñoz, D. (2013). Language use depending on news frame and immigrant origin. *International Journal of Psychology*, *48*(5), 772–784. doi: 10.1080/00207594.2012.723803

Figenschou, T. U., & Thorbjørnsrud, K. (2015). Faces of an invisible population: Human interest framing of irregular immigration news in the United States, France, and Norway. *American Behavioral Scientist*, *59*(7), 783–801. doi: 10.1177/000276421 5573256

Figgou, L., Sapountzis, A., Bozatzis, N., Gardikiotis, A., & Pantazis, P. (2011). Constructing the stereotype of immigrants' criminality: Accounts of fear and risk in talk about immigration to Greece. *Journal of Community & Applied Social Psychology*, *21*, 164–177. doi: 10.1002/casp.1073

Fryberg, S. A., Stephens, N. M., Covarrubias, R., Markus, H. R., Carter, E. D., Laiduc, G. A., & Salido, A. J. (2012). How the media frames the immigration debate: The critical role of location and politics. *Analyses of Social Issues and Public Policy*, *12*(1), 96–112. doi: 10.1111/j.1530-2415.2011.01259.x

Gabrielatos, C., & Baker, P. (2008). Fleeing, sneaking, flooding: A corpus analysis of discursive constructions of refugees and asylum seekers in the UK press, 1996–2005. *Journal of English Linguistics*, *36*(1), 5–38. doi: 10.1177/0075424207311247

Gale, P. (2004). The refugee crisis and fear: Populist politics and media discourse. *Journal of Sociology*, *40*, 321–340. doi: 10.1177/1440783304048378

Gil de Zúñiga, H., Correa, T., & Valenzuela, S. (2012). Selective exposure to cable news and immigration in the US: The relationship between Fox News, CNN, and attitudes toward Mexican immigrants. *Journal of Broadcasting & Electronic Media*, *56*(4), 597–615. doi: 10.1080/08838151.2012.732138

Graham, J., Haidt, J., Koleva, S., Motyl, M., Iyer, R., Wojcik, S. P., & Ditto, P. H. (2013). Moral foundations theory: The pragmatic validity of moral pluralism. *Advances in Experimental Social Psychology*, *47*, 55–130. doi: 10.1016/B978-0-12-407236-7.00002-4

Hartig, H. (2018, May 24). Republicans turn more negative toward refugees as number admitted to U.S. plummets. Retrieved from https://www.pewresearch.org/fact-tank/2018/05/24/republicans-turn-more-negative-toward-refugees-as-number-admitted-to-u-s-plummets/.

Hoewe, J. (2018). Coverage of a crisis: The effects of international news portrayals of refugees and misuse of the term "immigrant." *American Behavioral Scientist*, *62*(4), 478–492. doi: 10.1177/0002764218759579

Hoewe, J., Panek, E., Peacock, C., Sherrill, L. A., & Wheeler, S. (2018, November). Using moral foundations to assess stereotype formation: Americans' perceptions of immigrants and refugees. Paper presented at the annual meeting of the National Communication Association (NCA), Communication and Social Cognition Division, Salt Lake City.

Hoewe, J., Peacock, C., Kim, B., & Barnidge, M. (2020). The relationship between Fox News use and Americans' policy preferences regarding refugees and immigrants. *International Journal of Communication*, *14*, 2036-2056.

Hoewe, J., & Ziny, M. (2020). Congress and immigration policy: Use of moral language surrounding the Trump presidency. *President Trump's first term: The year in C-SPAN Archives research* (pp. 103–128). West Lafayette: Purdue University Press. Available at: https://docs.lib.purdue.edu/ccse/vol5/iss1/1

Jacobs, L., Meeusen, C., & d'Haenens, L. (2016). News coverage and attitudes on immigration: Public and commercial television news compared. *European Journal of Communication, 31*(6), 642–660. doi: 10.1177/0267323116669456

Jenni, K., & Loewenstein, G. (1997). Explaining the identifiable victim effect. *Journal of Risk and Uncertainty, 14*(3), 235–257. doi: 10.1023/A:1007740225484

Jones, B. (2016, Apr. 15). Americans' views of immigrants marked by widening partisan, generational divides. Retrieved from http://www.pewresearch.org/fact-tank/2016/04/15/americans-views-of-immigrants-marked-by-widening-partisan-generational-divides/.

Khosravinik, M. (2009). The representation of refugees, asylum seekers and immigrants in British newspapers during the Balkan conflict (1999) and the British general election (2005). *Discourse & Society, 20*(4), 477–498. doi: 10.1177/0957926509104024

Klocker, N., & Dunn, K. M. (2003). Who's driving the asylum debate: newspaper and government representations of asylum seekers. *Media International Australia, 109*(1), 71–92. doi: 10.1177/1329878X0310900109

Lecheler, S., Bos, L., & Vliegenthart, R. (2015). The mediating role of emotions: News framing effects on opinions about immigration. *Journalism & Mass Communication Quarterly, 92*(4), 812–838. doi: 10.1177/1077699015596338

Liebkind, K. (1992). Ethnic identity–Challenging the boundaries of social psychology. In G. M. Breakwell (Ed.), *The social psychology of identity and the self concept* (pp. 147–186). London: Surrey University Press.

Magee, J. C., & Smith, P. K. (2013). The social distance theory of power. *Personality and Social Psychology Review, 17*(2), 158–186. doi: 10.1177/1088868312472732

Mastro, D. E. (2003). A social identity approach to understanding the impact of television messages. *Communication Monographs, 70*(2), 98–113. doi: 10.1080/0363775032000133764

Meirick, P. C. (2006). Media schemas, perceived effects, and person perceptions. *Journalism & Mass Communication Quarterly, 83*(3), 632–649. doi: 10.1177/107769900608300310

Merolla, J., Ramakrishnan, S. K., & Haynes, C. (2013). "Illegal," "undocumented," or "unauthorized": Equivalency frames, issue frames, and public opinion on immigration. *Perspectives on Politics, 11*(3), 789–807. doi: 10.1017/S1537592713002077

Midtbøen, A. H. (2014). The invisible second generation? Statistical discrimination and immigrant stereotypes in employment processes in Norway. *Journal of Ethnic and Migration Studies, 40*(10), 1657–1675. doi: 10.1080/1369183X.2013.847784

Parrott, S., Hoewe, J., Fan, M., & Huffman, K. (2019). Visual framing and its influence on emotions and attitudes: Portrayals of immigrants and refugees in U.S. news media.

Journal of Broadcasting & Electronic Media, 63(4), 677–697. doi: 10.1080/088381 51.2019.1681860

Parry, K. (2011). Images of liberation? Visual framing, humanitarianism and British press photography during the 2003 Iraq invasion. *Media, Culture & Society, 33*(8), 1185–1201. doi: 10.1177/0163443711418274

Pennebaker, J. W., Booth, R. E., & Francis, M. E. (2007). *Linguistic inquiry and word count: LIWC(2007)—Operator's manual.* Austin, TX: LIWC.net.

Pettigrew, T. F., Wagner, U., & Christ, O. (2007). Who opposes immigration? Comparing German with North American findings. *Du Bois Review: Social Science Research on Race, 4*(1), 19–39. doi: 10.1017/S1742058X07070038

Pew Research Center. (2018). Shifting public views on legal immigration into the U.S. Retrieved from http://assets.pewresearch.org/wp-content/uploads/sites/5/2018/06/02164131/06-28-2018-Immigration-release.pdf.

Ramasubramanian, S. (2007). Media-based strategies to reduce racial stereotypes activated by news stories. *Journalism & Mass Communication Quarterly, 84*(2), 249–264. doi: 10.1177/107769900708400204

Rucker, J. M., Murphy, M. C., & Quintanilla, V. D. (2019). The immigrant labeling effect: The role of immigrant group labels in prejudice against noncitizens. *Group Processes & Intergroup Relations.* Advance online publication. doi: 10.1177/1368430218818744

Santa Ana, O. (2016). The cowboy and the goddess: Television news mythmaking about immigrants. *Discourse & Society, 27*(1), 95–117. doi: 10.1177/0957926515605962

Schemer, C. (2012). The influence of news media on stereotypic attitudes toward immigrants in a political campaign. *Journal of Communication, 62,* 739–757. doi: 10.1111/j.1460-2466.2012.01672.x

Scheufele, D. A. (1999). Framing as a theory of media effects. *Journal of Communication, 49*(1), 103–122. doi: 10.1111/j.1460-2466.1999.tb02784.x

Schlueter, E., & Scheepers, P. (2010). The relationship between outgroup size and anti-outgroup attitudes: A theoretical synthesis and empirical test of group threat- and intergroup contact theory. *Social Science Research, 39,* 285–295. doi: 10.1016/j.ssresearch.2009.07.006

Schmuck, D., & Matthes, J. (2017). Effects of economic and symbolic threat appeals in right-wing populist advertising on anti-immigrant attitudes: The impact of textual and visual appeals. *Political Communication, 34*(4), 607–626. doi: 10.1080/10584609.2017.1316807

Tajfel, H. (1981). *Human groups and social categories: Studies in social psychology.* Cambridge: Cambridge University Press.

Tajfel, H. (1982). Social psychology of intergroup relations. *Annual Review of Psychology, 33,* 1–39. doi: 10.1146/annurev.ps.33.020182.00024

Trope, Y., & Liberman, N. (2010). Construal-level theory of psychological distance. *Psychological Review, 117*(2), 440–463. doi: 10.1037/a0020319

Wright, M., & Citrin, J. (2011). Saved by the stars and stripes? Images of protest, salience of threat, and immigration attitudes. *American Politics Research, 39*(2), 323–343. doi: 10.1177/1532673X10388140

13 Media Stereotypes of Mental Illness: Nurturing and Mitigating Stigma

SCOTT PARROTT
University of Alabama

In an early episode of the popular American television program *Criminal Minds*, a former physicist turned psychiatric patient is accompanying his therapist on a train ride to Dallas, Texas, for a conference in which he will appear as an example of the medical progress against severe psychosis. Things take a turn for the worse, though, when the patient (Dr. Theodore Bryar) experiences hallucinations brought about by his schizophrenia, represented for visual purposes by a darkly clad man whispering in his ear. As the train hurtles across Texas, the situation devolves. Egged on by his hallucination, Bryar steals a firearm, murders a security guard, and holds innocent strangers hostage as FBI investigators wonder aloud what they should do about this "psychotic."

The character of Dr. Theodore Bryar embodies a common stereotype that associates mental illness with violent, unpredictable behavior. Meanwhile, the delusion-begets-murder plotline represents a script that has been all too common in American mass media content, including *Criminal Minds*, a television program that has regularly reached millions of viewers in its 14-season existence. Indeed, Bryar is one of three characters whose schizophrenia triggered hallucinations and violent attacks against strangers during just the first season of the program. If trends persist, this single show would feature a veritable football team of schizophrenia-based characters each wreaking mayhem on society.

As described in this chapter, stereotypes about mental illness are prevalent in mass media content, including television, movies, and news, which is problematic because the media serve as a primary source of information concerning mental illness for many Americans (Wahl, 2003a). Given the inaccurate and stereotypical nature of media content about mental illness, people are often misinformed concerning what it means to live with mental illness. Exposure to stereotypes about mental illness can nurture the stigmatization of mental illness (e.g., Corrigan, Powell, & Michaels, 2013), which can then affect the self-esteem of people who experience mental illness (Link, Struening, Neese-Todd, Asmussen, & Phelan, 2001), lead people to avoid seeking treatment for fear of being labeled mentally ill (Corrigan, 2004), inform attitudes concerning the likelihood of success with mental health treatment (Stuart, 2006), and affect public support for legislative policies such as community-based mental health care (Wahl, 2003a).

Nevertheless, modern media content suggests reasons for optimism. Following decades of homogenous, stereotypical representations, researchers are reporting that entertainment and news content are beginning to provide audiences more nuanced representations of illnesses (e.g., Corrigan et al., 2005; Gwarjanski & Parrott, 2018). Further, there is budding evidence concerning the role mass media can play in nurturing healthy and prosocial attitudes and discussion related to mental health (e.g., McKeever, 2015).

An estimated one in five adults in the United States lives with mental illness (National Institute of Mental Health, 2019a). The most common of these illnesses is depression, which affects about 17.3 million adults in the United States and involves symptoms such as a loss of interest, pervasive sadness, and problems with sleep, concentration, and self-worth (National Institute of Mental Health, 2019b). Less common disorders include the aforementioned schizophrenia, a potentially debilitating illness in which a person can lose touch with reality, be unable to think and communicate clearly, and/or experience deficits in emotional, cognitive, or behavioral experiences (National Institute of Mental Health, 2019c). Causes and treatment vary by disorder and the individual, and the severity of illness influences the extent to which a person can live a typical life.

Not all mental illness is chronic and many illnesses are treatable. With treatment, mental illness may remit or be well-managed to the point where it does not functionally interfere with daily life. In general, treatment for mental illness can involve medication, therapy, and other approaches. The United States has witnessed a transition from institutionalized to community-based care, underscoring the importance of public attitudes in the successful delivery of mental health care (Klin & Lemish, 2008). Despite the prevalence of mental illness, members of the public often endorse stereotypes concerning mental illness, including perceptions of incompetence, character weakness, and dangerousness (Rüsch, Angermeyer, & Corrigan, 2005). Mental health professionals describe this stigma as a barrier to mental health treatment, in part because people may avoid seeking treatment for fear of being labeled "mentally ill" and experiencing subsequent stereotypes and prejudice (see Klin & Lemish, 2008). Critics contend the mass media both reflect and perpetuate stereotypes (Klin & Lemish, 2008), contributing to the stigmatization of mental illness through messages associating mental illness with violence and social undesirability, misinformation about the causes, symptoms, and treatment of illnesses, and the use of derogatory language. This chapter reviews the history of scholarship concerning media representations of mental illness, including long-standing stereotypes associated with mental illness, the (slowly) improving representation of mental health in the American mass media, and the role of mass media exposure in the perpetuation and mitigation of the stigma associated with mental illness.

Mental Illness Stereotypes in the Media: Early Studies

Entertainment

Perhaps the earliest studies of mass media content concerning mental illness came in the late 1950s (e.g., Nunnally, 1957). George Gerbner, who would eventually develop cultivation theory, studied the records of 1950s television network censors who determined whether films should be limited to adult viewing, considered family friendly, or altered before airing (Gerbner, 1959). Gerbner found 5 films involving themes of mental illness passed through a network censor's desk in 1951. By 1957, the figure climbed to 170, which he described as representative of censors' concern over the potential exploitation of people with mental illness. He wrote that censors (p. 296): "deplored the indiscriminate use of such terms as crazy, idiot, moron, and the frequent dramatic association of mental illness, psychologists, psychiatrists with comic, violent, or eerie situations." The findings reverberate 60 years later. Indeed, researchers have described the mental illness/violence stereotype as prevalent in the television world of the 1960s, 1970s, and 1980s (Signorielli, 1989), 1990s (Diefenbach, 1997), 2000s (Diefenbach & West, 2007), and 2010s (Parrott & Parrott, 2015).

Beyond violence, characters labeled mentally ill have traditionally contributed little to the fictional world of American television, rarely appearing in positive personal relationships, holding down steady employment, or demonstrating an ability to positively contribute to society. For example, Wahl and Roth's research team examined 385 prime-time television programs on five major networks in Washington D.C. during the 1980s. They found that three out of four characters who were labeled mentally ill had no family connections, and half had no profession. Characters labeled mentally ill were described as dangerous, frightening, confused, and unpredictable (Wahl & Roth, 1982).

A longitudinal study from the Cultural Indicators Project found comparable results across decades. Compared to real-world proportions, people with mental illness were underrepresented in 1,215 television programs airing between 1969 and 1985 (Signorielli, 1989). When characters with mental illness did appear, they were depicted in predominantly negative terms: they were victims and perpetrators of violence, unlikely to be employed, and more likely to be described as failures. Three out of four characters described as mentally ill attempted to hurt or kill others, and three out of four suffered violence themselves. The representation oversimplifies and exaggerates reality, in which the association between mental illness and violence is complex, involving factors such as substance abuse and socioeconomics, and people with mental illness are more likely to harm themselves than others (e.g., Stuart, 2003). Signorielli (p. 329) concluded that, "The presentation of a character as mentally ill is a decision that is made to serve very specific dramatic needs. Unfortunately, on television, these dramatic needs result in overemphasizing the negative and stigmatized images of the mentally ill, such as violence, bizarre behavior and failure."

News

In addition to television and film, news coverage of mental illness has been problematic. First, journalists rarely interview people who experience mental illness, instead turning to family, law enforcement officers, and other "official" sources (Wahl, Wood, & Richards, 2002). Second, news stories communicate inaccurate information concerning the causes, symptoms, and treatment of mental illness (Stuart, 2006). Finally, much like television and film, news stories frequently associate mental illness with violent and unpredictable behavior (Wahl et al., 2002).

First, source selection in news stories can be problematic because it implicitly strips people with mental illness of agency, suggesting they cannot speak or care for themselves. An additional consequence involves contact, or the lack thereof. Positive contact between social ingroups and outgroups represents an effective method for challenging stereotypes, prejudice, and discrimination (Pettigrew & Tropp, 2008). Media effects researchers have documented such prosocial benefits from contact via media content, a phenomenon described as parasocial contact (Schiappa, Gregg, & Hewes, 2005). When news stories lack sources who have personally experienced mental illness, audience members are deprived of an opportunity for this potentially positive parasocial contact.

Second, assuming that many Americans learn about mental illness primarily through the media, the inclusion of inaccurate information concerning the onset of mental illness and its symptoms, duration, causes, and treatment potential is particularly disconcerting to mental health researchers and advocates as misrepresentations may inform public understanding of who (or what) is to blame for mental illness, whether treatment can be effective, and what an illness actually involves. For example, American film has represented schizophrenia as an illness in which a person has multiple personalities, as illustrated in the controversial comedy *Me, Myself, and Irene,* in which comedian Jim Carrey plays a state trooper who has been diagnosed with "a split personality," or, as another character puts it, as "a schizo."

Like television and film, news stories have traditionally provided audiences a narrow representation of mental illness, one in which violent, criminal, and unpredictable behavior were the focus. Journalists often cover stories involving crime and mental illness. Less prevalent are stories highlighting the humanity of people who experience mental illness, such as stories in which a person describes his/her experiences with mental illness, treatment, and/or recovery.

To illustrate these three areas, a study by Wahl et al. (2002) examined 600 articles that were published in the *New York Times, Washington Post, Boston Globe, Los Angeles Times, St. Louis Post Dispatch,* and *St. Petersburg Times* during 1989 (n=300) and 1999 (n=300). Most newspaper articles from 1999 discussed mental illness in generic terms, using the umbrella term "mental illness." When journalists discussed specific disorders, they seldom described symptoms, courses, or outcomes of the illness. Dangerousness emerged as the most prevalent theme in both 1989 and 1999, appearing in one out of every four newspaper stories involving mental illness during the latter year. These stories often appeared under sensationalized headlines, such as "Escaped Killer from Mental Hospital is Shot, Apprehended." Mental health consumers and their families were rarely interviewed by journalists.

Modern Representations

Over the decades, stereotypes concerning mental illness have persisted in entertainment and news content, and mental health advocates continue to express concern regarding the use of mental health-related terms as slang. As the section below illustrates, stereotypes associating violence and mental illness remain prevalent in entertainment and news content. Nevertheless, the 21st Century has brought gradual change in the media landscape, such that audiences are beginning to more often encounter well-rounded representations of what it means to live with a mental illness.

Entertainment

Several of the concerns expressed by researchers before 2000 remain prevalent in American entertainment. For example, the results of a study by Parrott and Parrott (2015) echo findings of research conducted by Signorielli nearly two decades earlier. Examining the representation of mental illness in 65 episodes of crime-based television programming airing on American television between 2010 and 2013, the study found that characters labeled as mentally ill were more likely than other characters to perpetuate violence, reinforcing stereotypes. They also stood greater likelihood of being victimized by violence. While characters with mental illness appeared with family or friends, the relationships were often negative, involving mistreatment.

Comparable results emerged in a cultivation study conducted by Diefenbach and West (2007), who examined 84 hours of television programming from April 2003, representing one week of prime-time shows on the major networks: ABC, CBS, Fox, and NBC. Television characters with mental illness were more likely to perpetuate crime than people with mental illness in the real world, with 37% of TV characters perpetrating violence compared to a conservative real-world estimate of 4%. They also were more likely to commit crimes than characters who were not described as living with mental illness. Overall, characters with mental illness had a low quality of life and negative impact on society.

In addition to television representations, feature films perpetuate misinformation concerning mental illness. Owen (2012) described Hollywood representations of schizophrenia as misleading after studying 41 movies between 1990 and 2010 that featured characters with schizophrenia. Reinforcing previous findings, characters with schizophrenia often perpetuated violence against themselves or others, and the films rarely provided discussion concerning the causes of schizophrenia.

Research suggests that American audiences are exposed to such inaccurate representations from an early age. When Wahl and colleagues (2007) examined 269 hours of children's television programming, they found that characters with mental illness were most often treated with fear and exclusion by other characters because they appeared aggressive and threatening. As was the case with adult content, mental illness appeared to be an easy explanation for villainous behavior, a finding that is especially problematic because exposure to these messages could leave a formative impression on children.

Despite the lingering presence of stereotypes, U.S. television and film has also begun to include more nuanced representations of mental illness. 2001 saw the release of the film *A Beautiful Mind*, in which actor Russell Crowe portrays Nobel Prize-winning mathematician John Forbes Nash Jr. The movie documents Nash's experience with schizophrenia, including his early symptoms, his troubling—and at times, violent—behavior fueled by delusions, and his recovery with the assistance of his wife, Alicia. While the movie does associate severe mental illness with violent and unpredictable behavior, it has generally been described as a positive representation of mental illness because it afforded audience members a more complex and ultimately human representation of what it means to live with mental illness. Indeed, educators in psychiatry use the movie as a teaching tool for lay and professional audiences because it demonstrates a range of symptoms and provides hope for recovery (Rosenstock, 2003), despite criticisms that the film glossed over or ignored parts of Nash's life, such as his divorce.

Modern viewers of American television have also encountered more rounded representations of people experiencing mental illness. The television series *Monk* introduced millions of viewers to the character of Adrian Monk, a detective who has obsessive compulsive disorder. The series ran for 8 seasons, at times setting viewership records for cable television dramas while winning eight Emmy Awards. Similarly, the television series *Perception* engaged audiences in the life of Dr. Daniel Pierce, a neuropsychiatrist with schizophrenia who partnered with the FBI to solve cases in the drama that aired between 2012 and 2015. Both of these characters were employed in socially respected occupations and were also successful, enjoying personal relationships with friends and romantic partners. They experienced lows because of their illnesses, but they also lived well-rounded lives.

While the programs were generally well received, they could be described as representative of another stereotype concerning mental illness, one associating madness with genius (e.g., Angermeyer & Matschinger, 2004). For example, critics contended *A Beautiful Mind* linked schizophrenia and Nash's mathematical genius, while Monk and Pierce's experiences helped them solve crimes. The question whether creative genius and psychopathology are associated continues to generate debate (e.g., Simonton, 2017).

News

Since the 2000s, journalists in the United States have adopted new guidelines for reporting on mental illness. The Associated Press Stylebook, which guides American reporting and writing, implemented recommendations for the use of words related to mental illness (Associated Press, 2013), the avoidance of slang, and guidance that journalists "not assume that mental illness is a factor in a violent crime" (2013, para. 12). In addition, the World Health Organization issued guidelines for news coverage of suicide to avoid sensationalized treatment and negative effects of exposure to stories about suicide, which have been shown to nurture the so-called Werther effect, when people die by suicide after encountering stories of someone else doing so.

Recent studies of news content suggest media presentations of mental illness have improved in some areas. In the Wahl et al. (2002) study, stories from 1999 compared to 1989 were more likely to share information on where people can find help for mental health, and the percentage of positive articles increased (from 11% to 17%). In a study by Corrigan and colleagues (2005), increased attention to mental health advocacy and decreased attention to stories of violence were present in U.S. newspapers (though the violence stereotype remained prevalent). The study also found that news stories were shifting blame for mental illness from the individual to environmental and genetic causes, a positive shift. While stereotypes about schizophrenia remain prevalent in traditional news outlets (e.g., *New York Times*), stories published on digital native sites (e.g., *Buzzfeed*) often included interviews with people living with schizophrenia (Gwarjanski & Parrott, 2018). The study found that readers were more likely to share personal experiences with mental illness beneath stories that did not perpetuate stereotypes about mental illness.

In addition to stereotypes, researchers have examined how news media attribute responsibility for mental illness and recommend treatment. For example, Zhang, Jin, Stewart and Porter (2016) analyzed how U.S. print and broadcast news outlets framed depression through the assignation of individual versus social responsibility. The study, which examined news content from 1980 to 2012, found that news outlets most often attributed the cause of depression to individual factors (e.g., genetics, personality) rather than social factors (e.g., poverty, access to mental health care). News outlets most often placed problem-solving responsibilities on individuals rather than society, although researchers did note that journalists increasingly referenced societal-level solutions as the 30-year period progressed.

Slopen, Watson, Gracia, and Corrigan (2007) sought to determine whether news organizations cover mental illness differently in stories related to children compared to adults. The researchers analyzed the representation of mental illness in 1,252 articles published by major U.S. newspapers (i.e., >250,000 circulation). Stories involving adults were more likely to represent stereotypes, focusing on an association between mental illness and themes of dangerousness and crime. Articles concerning children were more likely to adopt a feature-style approach, involving themes related to the causes of mental illness, treatment, and criticisms of the mental health system in the United States.

Media and Language

In addition to news and entertainment, commenters have expressed concern over the use of jargon in media content that could stigmatize mental illness and/or offend people who experience mental illness. While less common today, advertisements once employed terms such as "nuts" and "insane" to describe products and clearance deals (Wahl, 2003b). In entertainment programming, nearly half of the children's television shows examined by Wahl and colleagues (2007) used terms related to mental illness, and most often in derogatory ways, with characters calling one another "demented," "nuts," "psycho," and "completely insane." Comparable results emerged in a study by Lawson and Fouts (2004), who examined mental health-related references in 34 Disney animated films, finding that 85% of the films contained verbal reference to mental illness. References were most often used to insult others, with "crazy," "mad" "madness," and "nut" being most prevalent.

Professional media organizations are recommending content creators avoid the use of mental health terms as slang. In its 2013 guidelines, the Associated Press discouraged reporters from using slang such as "insane," or "deranged," as well as terms that connote pity, such as "suffers from" or "victim of." Mental health advocates recommend the use of "people first" language, describing someone as a person with schizophrenia rather than a schizophrenic. Despite the recommendations, researchers continue to explore modern misuse of terms related to mental illness. A line of research by Pavelko and Myrick (2015, 2016) described the trivializing use of mental health terms as prevalent on social media, such as someone declaring themselves "so OCD" for preferring a clean room.

Exposure Effects

Mental health advocates have long expressed concern over media stereotypes of mental illness, primarily because of the role of media content in the perpetuation of the stigma attached to mental illness. Despite the concern, research has largely focused on content rather than the effects of media exposure on audience members' attitudes toward people with mental illness (Granello, Pauley, & Carmichael, 1999; Klin & Lemish, 2008).

Media Exposure and Stigmatization

While investigating effects from stereotypical media exposure, researchers have focused on two areas of stigma: public stigma and personal stigma. Public stigma involves social attitudes and behavior related to mental illness, while personal stigma occurs when an individual internalizes stereotypes, prejudice, and discriminatory treatment, experiencing decreases in self-esteem and personal efficacy (Rüsch et al., 2005). Each will be discussed in the subsequent sections.

Public Stigma

Research suggests that the stigmatization of mental illness is indeed associated with exposure to media stereotypes (e.g., Chan & Yanos, 2016; Dietrich, Heider, Matschinger, & Angermeyer, 2006; Granello et al., 1999). Studies have been conducted using both experimental designs that illustrate short-term effects and surveys that suggest an association between long-term media exposure and attitudes related to mental health. For example, Dietrich and colleagues (2006) exposed high school students to newspaper articles that either (a) associated mental illness with violent crime or (b) provided educational information about mental illness. Participants who read the stereotypical story subsequently reported greater likelihood of describing a person with mental illness as violent and dangerous, an indicator of either stereotypes or prejudice. Conversely, participants who encountered the informative article used terms like "violent" and "dangerous" less frequently.

Comparable results emerged in an experiment by Chan and Yanos (2018), who exposed 172 participants to an article in which a violent event occurred, including one article in which the perpetrator was described as having schizophrenia. Participants were more likely to blame schizophrenia for causing the attack in the condition, with the effect lingering during a follow-up questionnaire one week following exposure.

In relation to more general, long-term exposure, Granello et al. (1999) surveyed college students (n=99) to examine the relationship between media exposure and attitudes toward people with mental illness. Electronic media were described as a primary source of information about mental illness for one in three respondents. Students who primarily received their information about mental illness from these electronic media reported less tolerant attitudes toward people with mental illness than people who received their information from print media, classes, or direct experience.

In a cultivation-based study, Diefenbach and West (2007) conducted a telephone survey with 419 respondents in the United States to examine the relationship between television exposure and attitudes toward people with mental illness. The study documented an association between heavy television viewing and perceptions that locating mental health services within a residential neighborhood would be a bad idea.

Personal Stigma

While effects on public attitudes are documented, less empirical attention has been afforded to how exposure to media stereotypes affect people who have personally experienced mental illness and what they think about media representations of mental illness.

Following a mass shooting at Virginia Tech University, Hoffner and colleagues (2017) surveyed people who personally experienced mental illness, knew family members with mental illness, or had no experience with mental illness to see how they thought other people's attitudes were affected by news coverage of the shooting in which 32 people died. During that coverage, news organizations released excerpts of the shooter's video manifesto and focused on the shooter's history of mental illness. When respondents had personal experience with mental illness, they anticipated that other people's attitudes were negatively affected by the news. In turn, they expressed less likelihood of seeking social connections in the wake of the shooting.

Hoffner and Cohen (2018) sought to determine how people with obsessive compulsive disorder (OCD) perceived *Monk*, the television program in which the main character, a detective, has OCD. Through interviews with 44 people, Hoffner and Cohen found mixed results: some people considered the representation of OCD as counter-stereotypical on the show, while others said it actually reinforced stereotypes. Some considered the character's career as evidence that people with mental illness can be successful, while other respondents considered the character's awkward social interactions and focus on cleanliness as stereotypical.

Positive Effects

A growing body of research has examined how exposure to media messages concerning mental illness may nurture healthy attitudes and behavior by decreasing stigma. Research suggests video-based interventions are effective in reducing stigmatizing attitudes toward people with mental illness (e.g., Janoušková et al., 2017), and recent research highlights the potential of parasocial contact in challenging stereotypes (e.g., McKeever, 2015).

Audiences often develop relationships with media characters, including athletes, actors, musicians, and others with whom they identify despite never having personally met. Such parasocial relationships present an opportunity to counter stereotypes about mental illness, challenge stigma, and encourage help-seeking behavior. For example, the actor and comedian Robin Williams died by suicide in 2014. Researchers discovered that people who strongly identified with Williams experienced strong emotional reactions and subsequently sought out information about suicide, depression, and stigma (Dillman Carpentier & Parrott, 2016). Similarly, respondents who reported parasocial attachment to Williams subsequently shared information via social media about clinical depression, suicide prevention and substance abuse treatment (Cohen & Hoffner, 2016). Similarly, Hoffner (2019) examined fan reaction to the death of actress Carrie Fisher, who played Princess Leia in *Star Wars* and worked as an advocate for mental health care because of her own experiences with addiction and bipolar disorder. Fans who had stronger parasocial relationships with Fisher reported greater grief upon her death, which, in turn, predicted greater likelihood of sharing information related to mental health via social media (Hoffner, 2019). The results underscore the potential power of health-related information being shared by celebrities in the media, nurturing information-seeking and -sharing by the general public. Similar results emerged in studies related to attitudes. Wong, Lookadoo, and Nisbett (2017) exposed participants to messages in which popular singer Demi Lovato discussed her personal experiences with bipolar disorder. Exposure to the celebrity's disclosure nurtured less desire for social distance and less endorsement of negative stereotypes concerning people with bipolar disorder.

Media actors need not be celebrities to elicit positive outcomes in relation to mental health. Toward this end, an experiment by McKeever (2015) found that participants expressed greater empathy, positive attitudes, and supportive behavior when they were exposed to a media character who was similar to them compared to one who was not. Caputo and Rouner (2011) exposed 137 college students to either a nonfiction or fictional narrative about a person with depression to determine the effects of exposure on social distance. The more relevant viewers considered the narrative, the more they identified with the main character. In turn, the more viewers identified with the character, the less social distancing behavior they exhibited toward people with mental illness.

Research also suggests people are more likely to communicate stories of hope and recovery when news stories focus on counter-stereotypes rather than stereotypes about mental illness. Along these lines, Gwarjanski and Parrott (2018) found that online news stories about schizophrenia were more likely to be accompanied by positive reader comments when the stories themselves communicated counter-stigmatizing messages such as personal anecdotes of treatment and recovery. Conversely, stereotypical news stories associating schizophrenia and violence elicited reader comments to "lock away forever" people with mental illness.

Future Research

A number of areas related to mental illness and media warrant future investigation. It is important scholars answer "Why" when it comes to the creation of media content, tapping into research and theoretical models concerning media processes to explain the reason stereotypes appear in news and entertainment content. For example, gatekeeping theory proposes that a hierarchy of influences determines whether an item makes the news, including factors related to the individual journalist, the organization in which the journalist works, and the culture in which the news outlet operates (Shoemaker & Reese, 2013). Journalists might often associate mental illness and violence in part because of the enduring values of American newsrooms, which focus on conflict, timeliness, and other normative guidelines that would make crime stories more likely to appear than feature stories about mental health treatments. Professional norms might also offer an explanation for the way mental illness is represented in entertainment programming. Script writers operate under strict time constraints, and often they must provide audiences closure by the end of an episode. Mental illness, which many people do not understand, provides a quick way to explain incomprehensible behavior. One could argue that the use of mental illness in entertainment programming nurtures fear; while someone might understand greed as a motivation for crime, mental illness provides a less concrete, more mysterious explanation. Indeed, in one of the only studies to examine processes related to the creation of media content about mental illness, Gerbner (1959) provided a behind-the-scenes look at the censorship of television content related to mental illness. Even in 1959, mental illness represented an "area of 'trouble,'" (p. 294), because writers could exploit people with mental illness for laughs or shock.

In addition to exploring processes, researchers should transition away from the umbrella term "mental illness" when conducting inquiry into content, instead exploring specific illnesses or disorders. American society perceives common illnesses, such as depression, differently than rare and less understood disorders such as schizophrenia. It is likely differences will also emerge in media content itself. Researchers should differentiate among disorders to provide detailed understanding of how the mass media represent schizophrenia, anxiety, depression, bipolar disorder, autism, and other conditions that involve different symptoms, causes, treatments, and public opinion.

There is also opportunity to dedicate greater attention to the potential benefits of exposure to media messages concerning mental illness, rather than focusing research efforts on negative representations and outcomes. As recent research suggests, the mass media might provide audience members behavioral models through which to learn about preventative approaches for mental health, the benefits of pursuing mental health treatment, and other positive outcomes. As audiences gravitate toward online content, including digital native news websites and social media, mental health advocates are afforded greater opportunity to bypass traditional media outlets and share positive, counter-stereotypical information with the public. For example, NBA stars Kevin Love and DeMar DeRozan individually announced in 2018 that they experienced depression. Love discussed his experiences in a first-person essay, while DeRozan engaged with basketball fans via social media. The disclosures elicited positive coverage from news organizations, stories discussing stigma, treatment, and the prevalence of mental illness among professional athletes (Parrott, Billings, Buzzelli, & Towery, 2019).

Finally, the field begs for theoretically-driven research. Much of the exposure-related research has been conducted by researchers who are unfamiliar—or simply do not employ—media effects theory. A number of theories, from social cognitive to parasocial contact, may be used to introduce novel lines of inquiry related to mental illness and the media.

References

Angermeyer, M. C., & Matschinger, H. (2004). The stereotype of schizophrenia and its impact on discrimination against people with schizophrenia: Results from a representative survey in Germany. *Schizophrenia Bulletin, 30*(4), 1049–1061.

Associated Press. (2013). Entry on mental illness is added to AP Stylebook. Retrieved from https://www.ap.org/press-releases/2013/entry-on-mental-illness-is-added-to-ap-stylebook.

Caputo, N. M., & Rouner, D. (2011). Narrative processing of entertainment media and mental illness stigma. *Health Communication, 26*(7), 595–604.

Chan, G., & Yanos, P. T. (2018). Media depictions and the priming of mental illness stigma. *Stigma and Health, 3*(3), 253.

Cohen, E. L., & Hoffner, C. (2016). Finding meaning in a celebrity's death: The relationship between parasocial attachment, grief, and sharing educational health information related to Robin Williams on social network sites. *Computers in Human Behavior, 65*, 643–650.

Corrigan, P. (2004). How stigma interferes with mental health care. *American Psychologist, 59*(7), 614.

Corrigan, P. W., Powell, K. J., & Michaels, P. J. (2013). The effects of news stories on the stigma of mental illness. *The Journal of Nervous and Mental Disease, 201*(3), 179–182.

Corrigan, P. W., Watson, A. C., Gracia, G., Slopen, N., Rasinski, K., & Hall, L. L. (2005). Newspaper stories as measures of structural stigma. *Psychiatric Services, 56*(5), 551–556.

Diefenbach, D. L. (1997). The portrayal of mental illness on prime-time television. *Journal of Community Psychology, 25*(3), 289–302.

Diefenbach, D. L., & West, M. D. (2007). Television and attitudes toward mental health issues: Cultivation analysis and the third-person effect. *Journal of Community Psychology, 35*(2), 181–195.

Dietrich, S., Heider, D., Matschinger, H., & Angermeyer, M. C. (2006). Influence of newspaper reporting on adolescents' attitudes toward people with mental illness. *Social Psychiatry and Psychiatric Epidemiology, 41*(4), 318–322.

Dillman Carpentier, F. R., & Parrott, S. (2016). Young adults' information seeking following celebrity suicide: Considering involvement with the celebrity and emotional distress in health communication strategies. *Health Communication, 31*(11), 1334–1344.

Gerbner, G. (1959). Mental illness on television: A study of censorship. *Journal of Broadcasting & Electronic Media, 3*(4), 293–303.

Granello, D. H., Pauley, P. S., & Carmichael, A. (1999). Relationship of the media to attitudes toward people with mental illness. *The Journal of Humanistic Counseling, Education and Development, 38*(2), 98–110.

Gwarjanski, A. R., & Parrott, S. (2018). Schizophrenia in the news: The role of news frames in shaping online reader dialogue about mental illness. *Health Communication, 33*(8), 954–961.

Hoffner, C. A. (2019). Sharing on social network sites following Carrie Fisher's death: Responses to her mental health advocacy. *Health Communication.* Advance online publication. doi: 10.1080/10410236.2019.1652383

Hoffner, C. A., & Cohen, E. L. (2018). A comedic entertainment portrayal of obsessive–compulsive disorder: Responses by individuals with anxiety disorders. *Stigma and Health, 3*(2), 159.

Hoffner, C. A., Fujioka, Y., Cohen, E. L., & Atwell Seate, A. (2017). Perceived media influence, mental illness, and responses to news coverage of a mass shooting. *Psychology of Popular Media Culture, 6*(2), 159.

Janoušková, M., Tušková, E., Weissová, A., Trančík, P., Pasz, J., Evans-Lacko, S., & Winkler, P. (2017). Can video interventions be used to effectively destigmatize mental illness among young people? A systematic review. *European Psychiatry, 41*, 1–9.

Klin, A., & Lemish, D. (2008). Mental disorders stigma in the media: Review of studies on production, content, and influences. *Journal of Health Communication, 13*(5), 434–449.

Lawson, A., & Fouts, G. (2004). Mental illness in Disney animated films. *The Canadian Journal of Psychiatry, 49*(5), 310–314.

Link, B. G., Struening, E. L., Neese-Todd, S., Asmussen, S., & Phelan, J. C. (2001). Stigma as a barrier to recovery: The consequences of stigma for the self-esteem of people with mental illnesses. *Psychiatric Services, 52*(12), 1621–1626.

McKeever, R. (2015). Vicarious experience: Experimentally testing the effects of empathy for media characters with severe depression and the intervening role of perceived similarity. *Health Communication, 30*(11), 1122–1134.

National Institute of Mental Health. (2019a). Mental illness. Retrieved from https://www.nimh.nih.gov/health/statistics/mental-illness.shtml.

National Institute of Mental Health. (2019b). Major depression. Retrieved from https://www.nimh.nih.gov/health/statistics/major-depression.shtml.

National Institute of Mental Health. (2019c). Schizophrenia. Retrieved from https://www.nimh.nih.gov/health/topics/schizophrenia/index.shtml.

Nunnally, J. (1957). The communication of mental health information: A comparison of the opinions of experts and the public with mass media presentations. *Behavioral Science, 2*(3), 222–230.

Owen, P. R. (2012). Portrayals of schizophrenia by entertainment media: A content analysis of contemporary movies. *Psychiatric Services, 63*(7), 655–659.

Parrott, S., Billings, A. C., Buzzelli, N., & Towery, N. A. (2019). "We all go through it": Media depictions of mental illness disclosures from star athletes DeMar DeRozan and Kevin Love. *Communication & Sport*. Advance online publication. doi: 10.1177/2167479519852605

Parrott, S., & Parrott, C. T. (2015). Law & disorder: The portrayal of mental illness in U.S. crime dramas. *Journal of Broadcasting & Electronic Media, 59*(4), 640–657.

Pavelko, R. L., & Myrick, J. G. (2015). That's so OCD: The effects of disease trivialization via social media on user perceptions and impression formation. *Computers in Human Behavior, 49*, 251–258.

Pavelko, R., & Myrick, J. G. (2016). Tweeting and trivializing: how the trivialization of obsessive–compulsive disorder via social media impacts user perceptions, emotions, and behaviors. *Imagination, Cognition and Personality, 36*(1), 41–63.

Pettigrew, T. F., & Tropp, L. R. (2008). How does intergroup contact reduce prejudice? Meta-analytic tests of three mediators. *European Journal of Social Psychology, 38*(6), 922–934.

Rosenstock, J. (2003). Beyond *A Beautiful Mind*: film choices for teaching schizophrenia. *Academic Psychiatry, 27*(2), 117–122.

Rüsch, N., Angermeyer, M. C., & Corrigan, P. W. (2005). Mental illness stigma: Concepts, consequences, and initiatives to reduce stigma. *European Psychiatry, 20*(8), 529–539.

Schiappa, E., Gregg, P. B., & Hewes, D. E. (2005). The parasocial contact hypothesis. *Communication Monographs, 72*(1), 92–115.

Shoemaker, P. J., & Reese, S. D. (2013). *Mediating the message in the 21st century: A media sociology perspective* (3rd ed.). New York: Routledge.

Signorielli, N. (1989). The stigma of mental illness on television. *Journal of Broadcasting & Electronic Media, 33*(3), 325–331.

Simonton, D. K. (2017). Creative genius and psychopathology: Creativity as positive and negative personality. In G. J. Feist, R. Reiter-Palmon, & J. C. Kaufman (Eds.), *The Cambridge handbook of creativity and personality research* (pp. 235–250). Cambridge: Cambridge University Press.

Slopen, N. B., Watson, A. C., Gracia, G., & Corrigan, P. W. (2007). Age analysis of newspaper coverage of mental illness. *Journal of Health Communication, 12*(1), 3–15.

Stuart, H. (2003). Violence and mental illness: An overview. *World Psychiatry*, *2*(2), 121–124.

Stuart, H. (2006). Media portrayal of mental illness and its treatments. *CNS Drugs*, *20*(2), 99–106.

Wahl, O. E., Wood, A., & Richards, R. (2002). Newspaper coverage of mental illness: Is it changing? *Psychiatric Rehabilitation Skills*, *6*(1), 9–31.

Wahl, O. F. (2003a). News media portrayal of mental illness: Implications for public policy. *American Behavioral Scientist*, *46*(12), 1594–1600.

Wahl, O. F. (2003b). *Media madness: Public images of mental illness* (2nd ed.). New Brunswick, NJ: Rutgers University Press.

Wahl, O., Hanrahan, E., Karl, K., Lasher, E., & Swaye, J. (2007). The depiction of mental illnesses in children's television programs. *Journal of Community Psychology*, *35*(1), 121–133.

Wahl, O. F., & Roth, R. (1982). Television images of mental illness: Results of a metropolitan Washington media watch. *Journal of Broadcasting & Electronic Media*, *26*(2), 599–605.

Wong, N. C., Lookadoo, K. L., & Nisbett, G. S. (2017). "I'm Demi and I have bipolar disorder": Effect of parasocial contact on reducing stigma toward people with bipolar disorder. *Communication Studies*, *68*(3), 314–333.

Zhang, Y., Jin, Y., Stewart, S., & Porter, J. (2016). Framing responsibility for depression: How U.S. news media attribute causal and problem-solving responsibilities when covering a major public health problem. *Journal of Applied Communication Research*, *44*(2), 118–135.

14 Positive Stereotypes and Counter-Stereotypes: Examining Their Effects on Prejudice Reduction and Favorable Intergroup Relations

SRIVIDYA RAMASUBRAMANIAN
Texas A&M University

ASHA WINFIELD
Texas A&M University

EMILY RIEWESTAHL
Texas A&M University

Amidst all the negative stereotypes rightly advanced in the preceding chapters of this book, a look at the positive seems an important and necessary coda to encompass the full picture of media stereotyping as we enter the 2020s. As we navigate a global COVID-19 pandemic, outbreak inequalities, discrimination and stigma (based on various identities such as race, social class, nationality, citizenship, and age) continue to be important to examine and challenge. Yet, we also see new ways of coalition-building, solidarities, and positive intergroup relations during crises. Words, images, media, and communication remain powerful tools for healing and transformation at the individual and societal levels.

A fascinating and important area of research within media stereotyping relates to positive stereotypes, counter-stereotypes, and prejudice reduction. Often when we think of the word "stereotype," we imagine negative words such as "criminal," "violent," "loud," "lazy," "threatening," and so on. However, stereotypes are not positive or negative by definition; rather, they simply are cognitive schemas or representations of groups of people that we hold either individually or collectively within a culture. Some examples of positive stereotypes are when groups of people are generalized as intelligent, athletic, polite, hardworking, or sexy. The bulk of the literature on stereotyping, including media stereotyping, has focused mainly on negative stereotypes and hostile forms of prejudice. It is only more recently, especially in the last two decades or so, that media psychologists have started paying more attention to positive stereotyping effects, counter-stereotypes, subtle forms of prejudice such as paternalism and envy, and focusing on prejudice reduction strategies (Ramasubramanian, 2007, 2010, 2015; Ramasubramanian & Oliver, 2007). This chapter will explain the difference between negative and positive stereotypes, counter-stereotypes and prosocial effects, and strategies for prejudice reduction such as media literacy training and ways to work on changing media misrepresentations and improving intergroup relations.

Although the terms "positive stereotypes" and "counter-stereotypes" may sound similar, they refer to two different concepts. Counter-stereotypes are ideas about a group that challenge or counter widely held cultural beliefs and mental models of a group. For example, *The Cosby Show,* an American sitcom featuring an African American upper-middle class family, is a counter-stereotypical representation of an African American family because it is inconsistent with the widely held beliefs that African Americans cannot be members of the upper-middle class at that time. Positive stereotypes, though, are not the same as counter-stereotypes. They can be understood as broad generalizations about groups by associating positive characteristics, traits, and beliefs with members of a group. Some examples of positive stereotypes that are common within the U.S. mainstream culture are notions such as women are more nurturing caregivers than men, African Americans are more athletic than other racial groups, gay men are more stylish that straight men, Asian Americans are more hardworking as "model minorities" compared to other racial/ethnic minorities, and disabled people are inspiring merely on the basis of their disabilities. While these positive traits and characteristics may seem complimentary, they are still stereotypes, since they are abstractions about entire groups of people, which may or may not apply to individuals. Just as with negative stereotypes, positive stereotypes can also affect expectations, emotions, behaviors, and outcomes at the individual and interpersonal levels. They can also influence interpersonal, institutional and societal outcomes.

Throughout this chapter, we use the words "positive" and "negative" cautiously. Media stigmatization of groups is a dynamic function of changing media contexts, evolving intergroup relations, and ever-dynamic social-political factors. With changing political and social contexts, the same groups that were once deemed positive could be seen at a later point in time as negative, or vice-versa. Cultural stereotypes about groups are also dynamic and change constantly over time and across cultures. For instance, the term "nerd" used to be derogatory a few decades ago but now there is a notion of "nerding out," which is typically unpacked positively, showing that one has passion about something. Similarly, words such as "queer," which was seen as derogatory and offensive in previous generations, is now embraced by LGBTQ+ communities as a positive and inclusive term. A group evaluated as positive in one cultural context might be evaluated as negative in another cultural context. Depending on the sociocultural political climate, stereotypes could also change from negative to positive or vice-versa under one political party, for instance, as compared to another. They are also dynamic in the sense that perceptions of one group influence those of another group. For example, terms such as "positive" and "negative" can sometimes be used by dominant groups to create a false dichotomy between "good" and "bad" minorities. For instance, positive stereotypes such as model minority stereotypes towards Asian Americans have been shown to be used as a way of creating racial hierarchies that reinforce anti-Blackness by pitting them against African Americans and Latino/a/x Americans as a way of justifying social hierarchies (Bonilla-Silva, 2004).

Typically, prejudice too, like stereotypes, has been associated largely with negative feelings such as dislike, discomfort, anger, hate, and fear (Stangor, 2000). However, in this chapter, we will focus on more subtle forms of prejudice such as benevolence, paternalism, envy, and pity. For our purposes, prejudice is about faulty judgments based on insufficient knowledge and often involves some kind of negative evaluation of the group. For instance, research by Glick and Fiske (1996) shows that when women are portrayed using positive stereotypes of being nurturing caregivers, patronizing feelings of benevolence are expressed towards them. Ramasubramanian and Oliver (2007) have also shown that news stories about Asian Indians can activate benevolent prejudice among readers, which are expressed as sympathy and pity. As we will elaborate later in this chapter, positive stereotypes can lead, ironically, at times to *more* prejudice and discrimination.

Towards the end of this chapter, we will examine some research-based theory-driven strategies such as counter-stereotypes, media literacy education, and intergroup dialogues for reducing prejudice and discrimination, especially towards groups that have been historically marginalized in various cultural settings, including within media industries, ownership, and representation. As media users, scholars, educators, artists, content creators, and community members, we could all help in small ways to work toward dismantling social inequalities, reducing hate, and removing injustices in the world around us. We discuss directions for theory and practice, including the need to support alternative, community-based media spaces that could serve as safe spaces for minoritized groups to be heard more fully and to flourish in society.

Historical Representations of Positive Stereotypes and Counter-Stereotypes in the Media

Stereotypes in media typically reflect those disseminated through society: the conventional, formulaic, and oversimplified conceptions, opinions, or beliefs (Means Coleman, 1998) become a part of a script, a storyline, and a character's development. Media narratives play a crucial role inside of identity-making processes and the identity negotiation of stigmatized groups, including the perceptions of self, one's ingroups, and other outgroups. Moreover, stereotypes typically originate from a dominant, hegemonic, elitist, patriarchal, top-down view of minoritized and marginalized groups rather than from those who are othered. Historically, given that media industries and corporations were owned and operated by social elites, mainstream media reflected dominant cultural discourses and values. From radio shows like *Sam N' Henry* (1926–1928), later titled the popular, *Amos 'N' Andy* (Ely, 1991), to the silent motion picture, *The Birth of a Nation* (1915), since the early 1900s, audiences have been exposed to examples of stereotypical portrayals in the media, even racial invisibility. Media producers realized the financial benefit of producing content that could be re-produced easily. This led to the production of stereotypical content based on race, gender, sex, and class in different genres and platforms.

Stigmatized groups pay careful attention to how their groups are represented in mainstream media as it works as a source of information about their status and positionality in society (Fujioka, 2005). There are also examples throughout history of stigmatized groups challenging mainstream stereotypes as well as using avenues such as community media, alternative media, and ethnic media to resist and protest cultural stereotypes of their groups (Ramasubramanian, 2016, 2019). However, social groups such as the poor, prisoners, and indigenous groups such as Native Americans in the U.S., Aboriginal people in Australia, Maori in New Zealand, Romani people in Europe, and adivasis in the Indian subcontinent, continue to be excluded even from so-called alternative media. Such groups are termed "subaltern" populations, without much visibility. Not surprisingly, against such a backdrop of invisibility for certain stigmatized groups, the "first-ever" phenomenon is typically a much celebrated moment in the history of media portrayals of groups since it marks the first time these groups find themselves represented in the media.

Shows such as *I Love Lucy* (1951–1957), which presented miscegenation between a White woman and Cuban man, became extremely popular, arguably the most popular sitcom to date. Miscegenation, or interracial marriage, was illegal in some U.S. states until 1967, making the program one of the first of its kind. Not only in terms of race relations, but also because it continued to challenge gender stereotypes against the backdrop of the standard image of White, heterosexual couples within the American Dream mythology. It attempted to counter the nuclear family presented in other programming during the time, shows like *Leave It to Beaver* (1957–1963), *Beverly Hillbillies* (1962–1971), *Father Knows Best* (1954–1960), *Little House on the Prairie* (1974–1983), *The Honeymooners* (1955–1956), *I Dream of Jeannie* (1965–1970) and *Bewitched* (1964–1972). The image of women and Black America were the first to be stereotyped and the first to introduce counter and positive stereotypes after several decades of one dimensional television and film representations. Years of White actors portraying people of color by applying darker makeup, adopting accents, and appropriating culture, as well as persons without disabilities portraying those with different abilities, were followed by the continuation of stereotypical material and gains in representations into the new millennium.

Such "first-ever" shows, films, ads, or magazine covers are not without criticism. Historically, television shows such as *I Love Lucy* (1951–1957), *The Cosby Show* (1984–1992), *The Oprah Winfrey Show* (1986–2011), or *The Ellen Degeneres Show* (2003–Present) were all significant in terms of increasingly positive portrayals of typically marginalized groups, but often ended up focusing on a token positive role model who often had to work within the limitations of the imagination of the dominant audience members for these shows. Programs from the 1960s to early 2000s like *Facts of Life* (1979–1988), *Different Strokes* (1978–1986), *Designing Women* (1986–1993), *The Power Rangers* (1993–1996), *Clueless* (1995), *Saved by the Bell* (1989), *Blossom* (1990–1995), *Dawson's Creek* (1998–2003), *Seinfeld* (1989–1998), *Full House* (1987–1995), *Friends* (1994–2004), *The Office* (2005–2013), and *Boy Meets World* (1993–2000) were widely popular, but only had one or two people of color in the main cast. Later, programs would feature one character from the LGBT community, followed by people with disabilities. Most characters from marginalized groups were added to mainstream media content as an afterthought or as token characters.

In terms of representations of people with mental health issues, some prominent representations occurred in popular films like *One Flew Over the Cuckoo's Nest* (1975), *Good Will Hunting* (1997), and *Girl Interrupted* (1999). *A Beautiful Mind* (2001) is a true story about John Forbes Nash, Jr., a Nobel Prize-winning mathematician who lived with schizophrenia. *The Soloist* (2009) tells the story of Nathaniel Ayers, a musician who deals with schizophrenia while homeless in Los Angeles. Although these media entertainment programs feature people with disabilities prominently, seemingly positive portrayals often erase the painful past of groups by "making it seem like it wasn't that bad" and this often had negative impacts on the audiences (Jhally & Lewis, 1992). Another example of this phenomenon is seen in the Disney movie, *Pocahontas* (1995). While some might argue it was visibility for Native Americans, critics see the film as erasure, a retelling, and a missed opportunity for a group's truth. Similarly, Jhally and Lewis (1992) point out that programs such as *The Cosby Show* (1984–1992) might appear to be progressive with its presentation of the Black upper-middle class family. However, their study revealed mixed reviews and reception as the presentation of success failed to capture the systemic oppressions Blacks encounter.

Contemporary Representations of Positive/Counter-Stereotypes in the Media

Cultural stereotypes, including those within media spaces, are not static entities but they do fluctuate both gradually and abruptly over time. For instance, socio-political climate and current affairs play a role in shaping how a group's perceptions and cultural stereotypes (both positive and negative) could change. An incident such as the September 11, 2001 terrorist attacks in the U.S. brought fairly invisible groups such as Muslims, Sikhs, and South Asians in the spotlight of U.S. mainstream media and also saw increased hate crimes against these groups (Arora, 2013; Stomer, 2005).

Intersectionality, when taken up together with media examples to better understand identity, complicates and deepens the conversations surrounding stereotypes. For example, religion when taken with race can act as a buffer or modifying variable to explain positive and counter-stereotypes that different racial groups experience. In research by Hayward and Krause (2015), religious identity, affiliations, support and media consumption impact even how African American individuals cope with racial discrimination and their determination to cope with stereotyping. Additionally, if one finds their racial and religious group to be congruent with a media text, they will likely work to match the media representation. On the other hand, as seen in Hayward and Krause, if there is dissonance in the media image and the individual, one may assume self-blame along with other negative coping outcomes.

Another more positive example could be the legalization of gay marriage by the U.S Supreme Court, a major policy accomplishment for marriage equality activists, which could lead to more positive media coverage and publicity for this group. In other words, groups that are invisible otherwise might become more visible in a fairly short period of time. Similarly, their portrayals could also move from negative to positive and vice-versa. The trajectory of media portrayals for each group, therefore, could vary considerably across time and cultures; continuums from invisibility, to negative, to positive portrayals are misnomers.

While many stigmatized groups are often fighting even just for visibility in the media, their representations tend to be uneven, mixed, and contradictory at times, even when they are portrayed in the media. For instance, media representations of Asian Americans range from derisive yellow peril and unassimilated perpetual foreigner to seemingly positive portrayals such as hardworking model minorities or as exotic and subservient (Ono & Pham, 2009; Paek & Shah, 2003; Zhang, 2010). In particular, research shows that contemporary media portrayals focus on the model minority stereotype of this group as being intelligent, polite, and nerdy (Chou & Feagin, 2008; Deo, Lee, Chin, Milman, & Wang Yuen, 2008; Kawaii, 2005). These representations also fail to note that Asian Americans vary vastly in terms of ethnic heritage, cultural values, achievements, education, and income levels in the U.S.

Counter-stereotypes and counter stories offer audiences an opposing narrative contrary to the historical ones they have often consumed through various media texts that position marginalized groups at the margins of society (Delgado, 1989). Counter-storytelling allows for marginalized groups, in particular, to be centered in the narrative presented about their respective group. Counter-stereotypes are not without the recognition of the existence of archaic and contemporary stereotypes. However, they complicate the narrative by allowing for oppositional reading, understanding, perceptions, and points of views. On the other hand, positive stereotypes, though they seem harmless, may affect audience members in negative ways.

An example of counter-narratives appears in shows such as ABC's *Grand Hotel* (2019), where Latino/a/x characters star in the show and are depicted as the owners of a luxury hotel instead of the subservient positions, a typical archetype on primetime television. CW's *Jane the Virgin* (2014–2019), a modern day telenovela, also presents an intersectional look into modern day Latin-American families inside of a hotel management and complicates ideas of motherhood, marriage, education, immigration, unplanned pregnancy, queer relationships, breast cancer, and success (Rose, 2019). These two shows followed ABC's *Ugly Betty* (2006–2010) with America Ferrera and they all present Latin-American communities without the inferiority or hypersexualization tropes. Indeed, the 2010s presented the newest media portrayals and made visible once invisible and denigrated groups of people.

Moving into the 2010s, audiences found racial groups were not the only ones receiving counter narratives in the media, particularly, entertainment media. In line with racial recognition, LGBTQ groups were becoming increasingly more visible in television and film contexts. After Ellen Degeneres used the platform of her own show, *Ellen* (1994–1998), to announce to a live audience that she was gay in 1997, many other programs began to cast and star gay and lesbian characters. MTV's *The Real World* (1992–Present), CBS's *Survivor* (2000–Present), CBS's *Big Brother* (2000–Present) were some of the first to lead the way in the reality television genre. In recent years, fictional depictions are also increasing their queer and transgender media representations: *The L Word* (2004–2009), *Orange is the New Black* (2013–2019), *How to Get Away With Murder* (2014–2020), *Grey's Anatomy* (2004–present), *Black Lightning* (2018–2019), *She's Gotta Have It* (2017–2018), *Master of None* (2015–2017), along with many others on cable networks and streaming services have featured or starred characters that were lesbian, bisexual, queer or transgender. Many more "firsts" in films and television would soon follow the popular culture trend of presenting more inclusive representations. *Brokeback Mountain* (2005), *Moonlight* (2017) and FX's *Pose* (2018–present) gave audiences a deeper look into the lives of gay and transgender men, combating the one-dimensional view of the community. Recently, audiences were privy to shows like Freeform's (formerly ABC Family), *The Fosters* (2013–2018), where more realistic portrayals of modern, multi-talented women working together to support their family of teens were portrayed. With many current programs that center on the inner workings of diverse characters, audiences can choose shows that reflect their nuanced and complex lifestyles more wholly, absent of stereotypes. Even more films are being released that counter the stereotypical tale of identity groups. Recent box office films like *Black Panther* (2018) and *Wonder Woman* (2017) provide audiences with an opportunity to engage with superhero narratives in more culturally-inclusive ways, breaking away from the White male savior trope.

Beyond films, other animated television programs like *South Park* (1997–Present), *The Boondocks* (2005–2014), *Family Guy* (1999–Present), *The Cleveland Show* (2009–2013) use a much more raw, in-your-face, adult comedy version of stereotypes that made the audience aware of their existence. In 2016, Disney Pixar released *Zootopia*, personifying animals to teach its audiences about race and rage. Other animated movies like *Finding Nemo* (2003) and *Finding Dory* (2016) displayed for children the abilities of those with mental illnesses and other abilities. King, Lugo-Lugo, Bloodsworth-Lugo (2010) argued that positive stereotypes in animated films are still stereotypes which present distorted and dehumanizing renderings where values are still at the heart resting within dominant frames, often depicting delusions about difference after racism and sexism (pp. 158–159).

The landscape of primetime television in the last thirty years may appear to be changing with the increase of diverse programming, but some stereotypical images persist (Sink & Mastro, 2016; Tukachinsky, Mastro, & Yarchi, 2015). From race, gender, sex, sexuality, age, political affiliation, and class, there are progressive storytellers and content creators who are committed to more authentic, speculative and creative portrayals. They resist the archetypes and tropes of the past by embracing their own and others' stories that focus on the complexity of characterization, removed from underdeveloped caricatures, and toward the authentic. Because audiences are searching for the authentic in the representation that they see on the screen (Gray, 1995), it forces producers to "come correct." The list of recent and presently running television shows presenting counter-stereotypes through diverse representation in storytelling includes but is not limited to: ABC's *Black-ish* (2014–present; Black identities), ABC's *Fresh Off the Boat* (2015–present; Asian identities); ABC's *Mix-ish* (2019–Present; mixed racial identities), CW's *Jane the Virgin* (2014–2019; Latinx and religious identities); FX's *Pose* (2018; race and gender identities), ABC's *Good Doctor* (2017–present; neurodiversity), ABC's *Grey's Anatomy* (2005-present; race, religion, sex, gender, and immigrant identities), Netflix's *Atypical* (2017–present; neurodiversity), Netflix's *Grace and Frankie* (2015–present; age), NBC's *The Cool Kids* (2018–2019; age), CBS's *The Neighborhood* (2018–present; intercultural relations), Netflix's *Dear White People* (2017–present; race, sexuality, education, class), HBO's *Insecure* (2016-present; race and dating) and *Euphoria* (2019–present; age and drug use), Freeform's *Grown-ish* (2018–present; age, class, and education), and VH1's *RuPaul's Drag Race* (2009–present; race, gender and sexuality). Yet, we note that shows like ABC's *Fresh Off the Boat* (2015–present) present the model minority stereotypes of Asian culture, and Lifetime's *Devious Maids* (2013–2016) depicted the sexualized, subservient trope of Latin women on primetime television along with their nuanced storytelling. Outside of cable television, the use of premium channels and streaming services such as Netflix, HBO, Hulu, Showtime, and Starz have become a platform for counter stories.

Additionally, many media users today learn about contemporary cultural stereotypes (and counter-stereotypes) from sources such as late night television shows, social media, and celebrity news (Arcy & Johnson, 2018; Bennett, 2014; Ramasubramanian, 2015). Contemporary Asian American stand-up comedians such as Hasan Minhaj and Margaret Cho, for instance, have a huge following and are using humor as a way to bring greater attention to socio-political issues affecting their communities through programs such as Minhaj's Netflix show, *Patriot Act with Hasan Minhaj* (2018–present). Social media and new media sources like Twitter and Facebook open up new opportunities for user-generated content that can be more focused and help gain greater visibility for minoritized groups through such means as hashtag activism and visual digital storytelling opportunities such as #UnfairandLovely #WhyIStayed, and #BlackLivesMatter that could help reject mainstream stereotypes by countering its normalcy by drawing attention to important issues such as colorism, domestic violence, police brutality and the like. Given the possibilities of customization, personalization, and niche marketing within many contemporary media types, it is possible to tailor representations to niche audiences, which changes traditional notions of what would be considered mainstream, broadcasting, and a viable program. This is not to say that social media or other newer media technologies are the only media formats to use for media activism or that mere customization makes programming successful or that these forms of media do not contribute to negative stereotypes, misrepresentations, and hateful rhetoric towards marginalized communities. Yet the changing media technology and digital media environment has implications for the spaces where positive and counter-stereotypical storytelling can be expressed or constrained, as the case may be in various contexts.

Unraveling the Negative Effects of Positive Media Stereotypes

Although positive stereotypes may sound complimentary, they often have harmful effects on the stereotyped individual. For example, research suggests that model minority portrayals of Asian Americans might appear to be positive, but they actually reflect increased anti-Asian sentiments, reinforce racial hierarchies and lead to lack of policy support for minority groups (Chou & Feagin, 2008; Kawaii, 2005; Ramasubramanian, 2011). Research shows that Asian Americans are less likely to be considered for top administrative leadership positions and are often ostracized from organizational social networks (Paek & Shah, 2003; Suzuki, 2002). Ramasubramanian (2011) has found empirical support that heavy television viewers internalize positive Asian American television stereotypes, which increases anti-Asian sentiments, symbolic racist attitudes towards Asian Americans, and attributing their failures to internal causes such as lack of social skills.

Models such as the Stereotype Content Model (Fiske, Xu, Cuddy, & Glick, 1999, Fiske, Cuddy, Glick, & Xu, 2002; Glick & Fiske, 2001) from social psychology are significant because they throw light on less studied aspects of prejudice such as benevolent prejudice and envious prejudice, which are explained below, and they are especially relevant to unraveling the complex effects of positive stereotypes. It helps us understand that beyond feelings of pride and admiration expressed toward ingroups and close allies (for example, middle class straight Christians in the U.S.) and downright hostile prejudice such as contempt and hate expressed towards groups evaluated as low on both warmth and competence (such as poor people or Muslims or undocumented immigrants in the U.S.), there are mixed and subtle aspects of prejudice elicited towards other groups. Benevolent prejudice, which includes feelings of pity and sympathy, is expressed toward groups judged as high in warmth but low in competence (such as the elderly, young children, or the disabled). Meanwhile, envious prejudice involves feelings such as envy and jealousy toward groups perceived to be high in competence but low in warmth (such as Asian Americans or Jewish people in the U.S.). Research shows that the portrayals of one minority group can influence the feelings of other minoritized groups along similar dimensions. For instance, Ramasubramanian and Oliver (2007) found that feelings of pity and sympathy are manifestations of benevolent prejudice towards Asian-Indians. They call this phenomenon "comparative media stereotyping," such that reading positive news stories about Asian Indians as model minorities leads to hostile prejudice toward other racial minorities by White audiences.

Another important effect of positive stereotypes are "dovetailing effects" with negative stereotypes. That is, researchers have found that positive stereotypes are often accompanied by underlying subtle negative expectations. Researchers have found that priming positive stereotypes may lead to stereotype threat and negatively affect an individual's performance on a stereotype-related task (Kahalon, Shnabel, & Becker, 2018). They found that women primed with stereotypes about motherhood performed worse on math tests than women who were not primed. These results illustrate the dovetailing effect of the positive stereotype of women's ability to nurture others; it is accompanied by a negative expectation that women have lesser academic ability. Although some may believe that positive stereotypes are harmless, these results indicate that positive stereotypes result in the validation of complementary negative stereotypes (i.e., if women are good at childcare, they are not good at math).

Positive stereotypes are especially damaging because they often come with high expectations, unlike negative stereotypes. Research has shown that most people endorse the positive stereotype that Black people are good at athletics (Devine & Elliot, 1995). These endorsements can lead to performance expectations. When we meet someone who does not fit the stereotype, we are often shocked or confused. These expectancies can lead to damaging effects. Researchers have found that the positive stereotype of Black athleticism can affect career advice and ultimately career decisions (Czopp, 2010). In the study, participants assumed the role of a high school guidance counselor and were given the folders for three students. Their task was to review the files and recommend that the student focus on one area (i.e. sports, business, theatre, schoolwork, etc.) in order to maximize their success. They found that male participants were more likely to recommend that a low academic-achieving Black student focus on sports more than a low academic-achieving White student. Another effect of performance expectations that originate from stereotypes is that marginalized groups can also internalize media messages—both positive and negative. Positive media stereotypes that are internalized as reality by members of a group can also lead to negative effects on them. For instance, Asian Americans have been documented to have increasingly higher rates of mental health and suicide (Kuroki, 2018), in part because they feel that they cannot live up to the expectations of the model minority and are less likely to seek or receive help for such health conditions (Morrison & Downey, 2000; Noh, 2018). Noh found that the model minority stereotype affects Asian women in three unique ways. Firstly, the expectation of success generates stress for the women. Secondly, the expectation of success causes women to blame themselves if they are not able to live up to the expectation. Lastly, the expectation of success partially explains why they are less likely to be provided health resources.

Counter-stereotypical portrayals in the media often include token authority figures holding prestigious positions of power such as political leaders, superstar athletes, judges, and so on. Sometimes there are token representations of characters and media personalities from marginalized groups just to "check the diversity box." Social psychologists have studied the effects of such token counter-stereotypes to find that audience members might continue to hold negative stereotypes about the groups if the positive admirable media character from a marginalized group is seen as atypical (Barden, Maddux, Petty, & Brewer, 2004; Bodenhausen, Schwarz, Bless, & Wänke, 1995; Eagly & Karau, 2002). Ramasubramanian and Martinez (2017) show how media framing of President Obama as the first Black President of the U.S. could lead to reinforcing symbolic racism when framed in a negative light as not living up to expectations.

Token positive celebrities in the media continue to be judged and assessed using majority groups' dominant values, often having to assimilate into them to be taken seriously. For instance, Black actors are often expected to assimilate to Whiteness through their language, attire, hairstyle, and so on, in order to fit into White institutions and spaces. Communication accommodation perspectives (Coover, 2001) have been used to understand how only those counter-stereotypical exemplars that fit in with mainstream values (such as older adults who appear to be youthful, Blacks who assimilate to Whiteness, or queer folks who exhibit heterosexual normative behaviors) are seen as "acceptable" by dominant groups. In such cases, the original mental model about the marginalized groups remains intact because the token representations are not pushing the needle enough in terms of disrupting existing stereotypes.

Research continues to show that positive stereotypes place the stereotyped individual between a rock and a hard place. Researchers have found that racial minorities who choose to speak up when confronted with a positive stereotype are evaluated by others as less favorable when compared to those who confront a negative stereotype or do not confront at all (Alt, Chaney, & Shih, 2019). They found that the perceived offensiveness of the racist remark and perceived evaluations partially mediate the relationship between stereotype expression and intention to confront the perpetrator about positive stereotypes. This case shows that many minorities may choose to bite their tongue when it comes to positive stereotypes, not because they have nothing to say, but because they are aware that they are putting their relationships, reputation, or more on the line if they do speak up.

Moving Towards Counter-Stereotypes, Prejudice Reduction, and Positive Intergroup Relations: Future Directions

An important development within this area of research has been a move towards more practical solutions and action-oriented research that can provide insights on what can be done at the individual, intergroup, and community level in terms of countering, combating, and reducing the harmful effects of both positive and negative stereotypes (Ramasubramanian, 2016, 2019). Media scholars have more recently started examining the role of counter-stereotypes and counter-narratives as ways of challenging mainstream media stereotypes (Ramasubramanian, 2007, 2010, 2015). Here, the word "counter-stereotype" refers to media portrayals and representations that counter, resist, or challenge existing cultural stereotypes.

Although positive stereotypes in the media can cause damage when they are used to categorize others, counter-stereotypical representations in the media can also help minoritized individuals develop a sense of social identity. For instance, if the prevalent cultural stereotype of Black-Americans is that they are violent and criminal, then the counter-stereotype would be portrayals that depict them as law-abiding and peace-loving. Or if a group such as the elderly are portrayed as frail and dependent, a counter-stereotype would be to present them as independent and strong. For instance, researchers found that media representations of gay, lesbian, and bisexual (GLB) individuals serve as role models and sources of inspiration for GLB viewers (Gomillion & Giuliano,

2011). The participants cited the following as influential to their self-realiza-
tion, decision to come out, or feeling about their GLB identity: books, websites, *Ellen DeGeneres, Will and Grace, The L Word*, and *Queer as Folk*.

Studies reveal that exposure to counter-stereotypical in comparison to stereotypical media exemplars have a positive effect on reducing stereotypical
attitudes of majority groups, as well (Bodenhausen et al., 1995; Dasgupta
& Greenwald, 2001; Power, Murphy, & Coover, 1996; Ramasubramanian,
2007, 2011; Ramasubramanian & Oliver, 2007). For instance, experimental
research shows that exposure to admirable media celebrities from marginalized groups can lead to prejudice reduction among majority group members
(Ramasubramanian, 2015), thus making a case for more auspicious portrayals of stigmatized groups through such portrayals. Over the long term, it is
also possible to form parasocial relationships with characters from outgroups
who are admired and likable (Schiappa, Gregg, & Hewes, 2005). Ortiz and
Harwood (2007) have further theorized that mediated parasocial contact is
especially likely to happen if characters from dominant groups model prosocial
behaviors in intergroup portrayals in media stories.

Another possible benefit of counter-stereotypes to the target is "stereotype
boost." Stereotype boost is an improvement in performance that is elicited
by positive stereotypes. Researchers have found that priming Asian identity
improved math performance (Shih, Wout, & Hambarchyan, 2015). But, they
also found that the method of priming stereotypes is incredibly important in
this process. The participants that were primed implicitly performed better
than participants primed explicitly. These results suggest that positive stereotypes can cause stereotype boost or stereotype threat, depending on the way in
which the subjects are primed. Researchers found that priming White identity
for biracial Black-White individuals caused a boost in verbal reasoning performance (Gaither, Remedios, Schultz, & Sommers, 2015). These results suggest
that multiracial people may be able to manage their complex identities in ways
that may counteract the many forms in which multiracial individuals experience double jeopardy.

Another approach towards prejudice reduction has been called "cognitive retraining," and it consists of repeated exposure to counter-stereotypes,
reducing stereotype activation, which is consistent with social learning and
social cognitive theory perspectives from communication (Burns, Monteith,
& Parker, 2017). Research has found that even brief exposure to media featuring counter-stereotypical depictions of outgroup characters can change racial
attitudes (Bodenhausen et al., 1995; Ramasubramanian, 2011). Research has
found a pervasive tendency for people to see members of outgroups as more
similar to each other than ingroup members are to each other (i.e., "they all

look the same" or "all of them act the same"). This tendency is called the outgroup homogeneity effect (Mullen & Hu, 1989). One reason that cognitive retraining or other counter-stereotypic interventions may be effective is that they increase the perceived variability of the outgroup by highlighting the members of the outgroup who do not fit into traditional stereotypes. Researchers have found that increasing an individual's perception of the variability of the outgroup members reduces prejudice and discrimination (Er-rafiy & Brauer, 2013). Researchers have begun to test the effectiveness of self-generated counter-stereotype interventions and have found that they reduce heuristic thinking and decrease the dehumanization of outgroup members (Prati, Vasiljevic, Crisp, & Rubini, 2015).

Less formal interventions can be used in everyday life to work towards reducing the prevalence of positive stereotypes. For example, if a person does not use positive stereotypes, they can still work to reduce the prevalence of these stereotypes by speaking up when they are a bystander. Since research has shown that the targets of positive stereotypes choose not to speak up to avoid jeopardizing their relationship (Alt et al., 2019), it is important for bystanders to voice their feelings and concerns. By speaking up, they are taking the weight off their shoulders by removing the potential cost (lost friendship) to the target. Positive stereotypes are common because most people do not understand the harmful effects that they have. To reduce their prevalence, it is important for people to continue to educate themselves on the effects of positive stereotyping and share what they have learned with others.

In terms of media-based strategies to reduce intergroup prejudice, research by Ramasubramanian (2007) and Ramasubramanian and Oliver (2007) show that a combination of message-based strategies and audience-centered approaches could potentially work together to counter prejudice. That is, when media users are provided with training such as media literacy training, as well as exposed to counter-stereotypical exemplars in the media, the combined effects could work together to create beneficial effects on intergroup attitudes. Therefore, in terms of practical implications, media literacy education continues to be important for diversity education. Along with it, there is a need for mainstream media to actively promote more auspicious and counter-stereotypical stories, characters, and content to help negate the effects of existing stereotypes, both positive and negative. Additionally, research also shows that exposure to mainstream media is much more likely to lead to lower self-esteem and negative self-concept among ethnic minorities as compared to exposure to ethnic media (Ramasubramanian, Doshi, & Saleem, 2017). Therefore, supporting meaningful media produced by smaller, localized ethnic media, be it initiatives such as Latinitas magazine for Latina girls (Sousa

& Ramasubramanian, 2017) or projects such as Question Bridge and East Los High (Ramasubramanian, 2016) that are community-driven and explicitly focused on critical media literacy education, digital storytelling, and anti-prejudice narratives, is another way forward.

Conclusion

At every corner of media portrayals, there are opportunities for positive and counter-stereotypes to be present, though those are not without their negative consequences on members of the different marginalized groups. Counter-narratives and counter-storytelling in social media content also do not work in a vacuum. The effects of such media activism also impact the individual and their willingness to fight back. While counter-frames are designed to fight back and used as a means to survive everyday oppression felt by American society, they continue to be difficult and challenging. Practices such as online misogyny, doxxing, and other toxic environments continue to marginalize and silence minority groups. The lack of funding support and research attention for community-oriented initiatives and small media initiatives that are oriented towards social good are also significant challenges and barriers to overcome. Therefore, as media scholars, educators, and activists committed to social justice and using media for social good, it is important to not just do theoretically excellent and methodologically sound research studies in lab-based settings, but to take such research into the real-life to engage directly with media producers, policymakers, parents, and educators. Nonprofit media initiatives such as GLAAD, the Geena Davis Institute on Gender in Media, Media Rise, Silk Road Rising, and Honor the Treaties are all important to support in terms of broader public engagement, collaboration, and partnerships among academe, media industry, nonprofits, and policymakers.

Acknowledgements

The authors would like to thank undergraduate Texas A&M student, Ms. Olivia Osteen, for her excellent feedback and assistance with proof-reading.

References

Alt, N. P., Chaney, K. E., & Shih, M. J. (2019). "But that was meant to be a compliment!": Evaluative costs of confronting positive racial stereotypes. *Group Processes & Intergroup Relations, 22*(5), 655–672. doi: 10.1177/1368430218756493

Arcy, J., & Johnson, Z. (2018). Intersectional critique and social media activism in Sleepy Hollow fandom. *Transformative Works & Cultures, 26.* Accessible from: http://dx. doi.org/10.3983/twc.2018.1132.

Arora, K. S. (2013). Reflections on the experiences of turbaned Sikh men in the aftermath of 9/11. *Journal for Social Action in Counseling & Psychology, 5*(1), 116–121.

Barden, J., Maddux,W. W., Petty, R. E., & Brewer, M. B. (2004). Contextual moderation of racial bias: The impact of social roles on controlled and automatically activated attitudes. *Journal of Personality and Social Psychology, 87*(1), 5.

Bennett, L. (2014). "If we stick together we can do anything": Lady Gaga fandom, philanthropy and activism through social media. *Celebrity Studies, 5*(1–2), 138–152.

Bodenhausen, G. V., Schwarz, N., Bless, H., & Wänke, M. (1995). Effects of atypical exemplars on racial beliefs: Enlightened racism or generalized appraisals. *Journal of Experimental Social Psychology, 31*(1), 48–63. doi: 10.1006/jesp.1995.1003

Bonilla-Silva, E. (2004). From bi-racial to tri-racial: Towards a new system of racial stratification in the USA. *Ethnic and Racial Studies, 27*(6), 931–950. doi: 10.1080/0141 987042000268530

Burns, M., Monteith, M., & Parker, L. (2017). Training away bias: The differential effects of counter stereotype training and self-regulation on stereotype activation and application. *Journal of Experimental Social Psychology, 73,* 97–110. doi: 10.1016/j. jesp.2017.06.003.

Chou, R., & Feagin, J. R. (2008). *The myth of the model minority: Asian Americans facing racism.* Boulder, CO: Paradigm Publishers.

Coover, G. E. (2001). Television and social identity: Race representation as "White" accommodation. *Journal of Broadcasting & Electronic Media, 45*(3), 413–431.

Czopp, A. M. (2010). Studying is lame when he got game: Racial stereotypes and the discouragement of Black student-athletes from schoolwork. *Social Psychology of Education, 13*(4), 485–498.

Dasgupta, N., & Greenwald, A. G. (2001). On the malleability of automatic attitudes: Combating automatic prejudice with images of admired and disliked individuals. *Journal of Personality and Social Psychology, 81*(5), 800–814. doi: 10.1037/ 0022-3514.81.5.800

Delgado, R. (1989). Storytelling for oppositionists and others: A plea for narrative. *Michigan Law Review, 87*(8), 2411–2441. doi: 10.2307/1289308

Deo, M. E., Lee, J. J., Chin, C. B., Milman, N., & Wang Yuen, N. (2008). Missing in action: "Framing" race on prime-time television. *Social Justice, 35*(2), 145–162.

Devine, P. G., & Elliot, A. J. (1995). Are racial stereotypes really fading? The Princeton trilogy revisited. *Personality and Social Psychology Bulletin, 11,* 1139.

Eagly, A. H., & Karau, S. J. (2002). Role congruity theory of prejudice toward female leaders. *Psychological Review, 109,* 573–598.

Ely, M. P. (1991). *The adventures of Amos 'N' Andy: A social history of an American phenomenon.* Charlottesville: University of Virginia Press.

Er-rafiy, A., & Brauer, M. (2013). Modifying perceived variability: Four laboratory and field experiments show the effectiveness of a ready-to-be-used prejudice intervention. *Journal of Applied Social Psychology, 43*(4), 840–853.

Fiske, S. T., Cuddy, A. J., Glick, P., & Xu, J. (2002). A model of (often mixed) stereotype content: Competence and warmth respectively follow from perceived status and competition. *Journal of Personality and Social Psychology, 82,* 878–902.

Fiske, S. T., Xu, J., Cuddy, A. C., & Glick, P. (1999). (Dis)respecting versus (dis)liking: Status and interdependence predict ambivalent stereotypes of competence and warmth. *Journal of Social Issues, 55,* 473–489.

Fujioka, Y. (2005). Black media images as a perceived threat to African American ethnic identity: Coping responses, perceived public perception, and attitudes towards affirmative action. *Journal of Broadcasting & Electronic Media, 49*(4), 450–467, doi: 10.1207/s15506878jobem4904_6

Gaither, S. E., Remedios, J. D., Schultz, J. R., & Sommers, S. R. (2015). Priming White identity elicits stereotype boost for biracial Black-White individuals. *Group Processes & Intergroup Relations, 18*(6), 778–787. doi: 10.1177/1368430215570504

Glick, P., & Fiske, S. T. (1996). The ambivalent sexism inventory: Differentiating hostile and benevolent sexism. *Journal of Personality and Social Psychology, 70*(3), 491–512. doi: 10.1037/0022-3514.70.3.491

Glick, P., & Fiske, S. T. (2001). An ambivalent alliance: Hostile and benevolent sexism as complementary justifications for gender inequality. *American Psychologist, 56*(2), 109–118. doi: 10.1037/0003-066X.56.2.109

Gomillion, S. C., & Giuliano, T., A. (2011). The influence of media role models on gay, lesbian, and bisexual identity, *Journal of Homosexuality, 58*(3), 330–354. doi: 10.108 0/00918369.2011.546729

Hayward, R. D., & Krause, N. (2015). Religion and strategies for coping with racial discrimination among African Americans and Caribbean Blacks. *International Journal of Stress Management, 22*(1), 70–91. https://doi-org.srv-proxy1.library.tamu.edu/10.1037/a0038637

Jhally, S., & Lewis, J. (1992). *Enlightened racism: The Cosby show, audiences, and the myth of the American dream.* Boulder: Westview Press.

Kahalon, R., Shnabel, N., & Becker, J. C. (2018). Positive stereotypes, negative outcomes: Reminders of the positive components of complementary gender stereotypes impair performance in counter-stereotypical tasks. *The British Journal of Social Psychology, 57*(2), 482–502.

Kawai, Y. (2005). Stereotyping Asian Americans: The dialectic of the model minority and the yellow peril. *Howard Journal of Communications, 16,* 109–130.

Kuroki, Y. (2018). Comparison of suicide rates among Asian Americans in 2000 and 2010. *Omega, 77*(4), 404–411.

Means Coleman, R. R. (1998). *African American viewers and the Black situation comedy: Situating racial humor.* New York: Garland.

Morrison, L. L., & Downey, D. L. (2000). Racial differences in self-disclosure of suicidal ideation and reasons for living: Implications for training. *Cultural Diversity and Ethnic Minority Psychology, 6*(4), 374–386.

Mullen, B., & Hu, L. (1989). Perceptions of ingroup and outgroup variability: A meta-analytic integration. *Basic and Applied Social Psychology, 10*, 233–252.

Noh, E. (2018) Terror as usual: The role of the model minority myth in Asian American women's suicidality. *Women & Therapy, 41*(3–4), 316–338, doi: 10.1080/02703149.2018.1430360

Ono, K. A., & Pham, V. N. (2009). *Asian Americans and the media*. Cambridge, England: Polity.

Ortiz, M., & Harwood, J. (2007). A social cognitive approach to intergroup relationships on television. *Journal of Broadcasting and & Electronic Media, 51*, 615–631.

Paek, H. J., & Shah, H. (2003). Racial ideology, model minorities, and the "not-so-silent partner:" Stereotyping of Asian Americans in U.S. magazine advertising. *Howard Journal of Communications, 14*(4), 225–244.

Power, J. G., Murphy, S. T., & Coover, G. (1996). Priming prejudice: How stereotypes and counter-stereotypes influence attribution of responsibility and credibility among ingroups and outgroups. *Human Communication Research, 23*, 36–58. doi: 10.1111/j.1468-2958.1996.tb00386.x

Prati, F., Vasiljevic, M., Crisp, R. J., & Rubini, M. (2015). Some extended psychological benefits of challenging social stereotypes: Decreased dehumanization and a reduced reliance on heuristic thinking. *Group Processes & Intergroup Relations, 18*(6), 801–816. doi: 10.1177/1368430214567762

Ramasubramanian, S. (2007). Media-based strategies to reduce racial stereotypes activated by news stories. *Journalism & Mass Communication Quarterly, 84*(2), 249–264. doi: 10.1177/107769900708400204

Ramasubramanian, S. (2010). Television viewing, racial attitudes, and policy preferences: Exploring the role of social identity and intergroup emotions in influencing support for affirmative action. *Communication Monographs, 77*, 102–120. doi: 10.1080/03637750903514300.

Ramasubramanian, S. (2011). The impact of stereotypical versus counterstereotypical media exemplars on racial attitudes, causal attributions, and support for affirmative action. *Communication Research, 38*(4), 497–516. doi: 10.1177/0093650210384854

Ramasubramanian, S. (2015). Using celebrity news stories to effectively reduce racial/ethnic prejudice. *Journal of Social Issues, 71*, 123–138. doi: 10.1111/josi.12100

Ramasubramanian, S. (2016), Racial/ethnic identity, community-oriented media initiatives, and transmedia storytelling. *The Information Society, 32*(5), 333–342. doi: 10.1080/01972243.2016.1212618

Ramasubramanian, S. (2019). Media inclusion, racial justice, and digital citizenship. In *How public policy impacts racial inequality* (pp. 56–75). Baton Rouge, LA: LSU Press.

Ramasubramanian, S., Doshi, M. J., & Saleem, M. (2017). Mainstream versus ethnic media: How they shape ethnic pride and self-esteem among ethnic minority audiences. *International Journal of Communication, 11*, 1879–1899.

Ramasubramanian, S., & Martinez, A. (2017). News framing of Obama, racialized scrutiny, and symbolic racism. *Howard Journal of Communication*, *28*(1), 36–54. doi: 10.1080/10646175.2016.1235519

Ramasubramanian, S., & Oliver, M. B. (2007). Activating and suppressing hostile and benevolent racism: Evidence for comparative media stereotyping. *Media Psychology*, *9*(3), 623–646. doi: 10.1080/15213260701283244

Rodino-Colocino, M. (2014). #YesAllWomen: Intersectional mobilization against sexual assault is radical (again). *Feminist Media Studies*, *14*(6), 1113–1115.

Rose, N. (2019). Modern melodrama: How the American Telenovela *Jane the Virgin* updates the sentimental novel. *The Journal of Popular Culture*, *52*(5), 1081–1100. doi: 10.1111/jpcu.12849

Schiappa, E., Gregg, P. B., & Hewes, D. E. (2005). The parasocial contact hypothesis. *Communication Monographs*, *72*(1), 92–115. doi: 10.1080/0363775052000 342544

Shih, M., Wout, D. A., & Hambarchyan, M.(2015). Predicting performance outcomes from the manner of stereotype activation and stereotype content. *Asian American Journal of Psychology. 6*(2), 117–124. https://doi.org/10.1037/a0037707

Sink, A., & Mastro, D. (2016). Depictions of gender on primetime television: A Quantitative content analysis. *Mass Communication and Society*, *20*(1), 3–22. doi: 10.1080/15205436.2016.1212243

Sousa, A., & Ramasubramanian, S. (2017). Challenging gender and racial stereotypes in online spaces: Alternative storytelling among Latino/a youth in the U.S. In D. Lemish & M. Götz (Eds.), *Beyond the stereotypes—Images of boys and girls, and their consequences* (pp. 75–83). Gothenburg, Sweden: Nordicom Press.

Stangor, C. (Ed.). (2000). Key readings in social psychology. In *Stereotypes and prejudice: Essential readings*. Psychology Press, Philadelphia, PA.

Stromer, M. (2005). Combating hate crimes against Sikhs: A multi-tentacled approach. *Journal of Gender Race and Justice, 9,* 739.

Suzuki, B. H. (2002). Revisiting the model minority stereotype: Implications for student affairs practice and higher education. *New Directions for Student Services, 2002,* 21–32. doi: 10.1002/ss.36

Tukachinsky, R., Mastro, D., & Yarchi, M. (2015). Documenting portrayals of race/ethnicity on primetime television over a 20-year span and their association with national-level racial/ethnic attitudes. *Journal of Social Issues, 71*(1), 17–38. doi: 10.1111/josi.12094

Zhang, Q. (2010). Asian Americans beyond the model minority stereotype: The nerdy and the left out. *Journal of International and Intercultural Communication, 3*(1), 20–37.

List of Contributors

Editor Bios

Andrew C. Billings (Ph.D., Indiana University) is the Ronald Reagan Chair of Broadcasting in the Department of Journalism & Creative Media at the University of Alabama. His research focuses on media content and effects, often in the area of sport.

Scott Parrott (Ph.D., University of North Carolina) is an associate professor in the Department of Journalism & Creative Media at the University of Alabama. His research focuses on media content and effects, often involving questions related to mental health.

Contributor Bios

Cory L. Armstrong (Ph.D., University of Wisconsin) is Professor and Chair of the Department of Journalism & Creative Media at the University of Alabama. Her research interests include micro- and macro-influences on news content, gender diversity and media, and weather-related media messages.

Sharon E. Baldinelli (M.P.H., University of Florida) is a doctoral student in the College of Communication & Information Sciences at the University of Alabama. Her research interests focus on health communication and information.

Elizabeth Behm-Morawitz (Ph.D., University of Arizona) is an Associate Professor in the Department of Communication and Associate Dean in the Graduate School at the University of Missouri. Her research interests focus on media stereotyping, often as it relates to race, gender, self-concept, and health in the contexts of entertainment, news, and interactive media.

Jenna Campagna (M.A., Boston College) is a fourth year Ph.D. candidate in the Counseling Psychology program at Northeastern University and a member of the Applied Psychology Program for Eating and Appearance Research (APPEAR). Her research with APPEAR investigates the role of traditional and social media in the development of body image concerns in young women and mothers, particularly during pregnancy and the postpartum period.

Kevin N. Do (B.A., University of San Diego) is a doctoral student at the University of California, Santa Barbara. His research examines the portrayal of racial/ethnic minorities on traditional and new media and how exposure may affect one's self-concept, psychological-well being, and intergroup communication, primarily among Asian Americans.

Travis L. Dixon (Ph.D., University of California, Santa Barbara) is Professor of Communication at the University of Illinois at Urbana-Champaign. He is an internationally recognized expert whose research focuses on the effects of mediated stereotypes.

Andrea Figueroa-Caballero (Ph.D., University of California, Santa Barbara) is an assistant professor in the Department of Communication at the University of Missouri-Columbia. Her research focuses on the intersection of media effects and intergroup processes.

Rhonda Gibson (Ph.D., University of Alabama) is a professor in the Hussman School of Journalism and Media at the University of North Carolina at Chapel Hill. Her most recent research focuses on media portrayals of LGBTQ+-related topics and the influence of these portrayals on individual perceptions and public conversations.

Jennifer Hoewe (Ph.D., Penn State University) is an assistant professor within the Brian Lamb School of Communication at Purdue University. Her research focuses on the depictions and effects of stereotypes and identity as influenced by media consumption and political orientations.

Rebecca Ann Lind (Ph.D., University of Minnesota) is associate professor and director of undergraduate studies in the Department of Communication at the University of Illinois at Chicago. Her research interests include race, gender, class and media; new media studies; media ethics; journalism; and audiences.

Stephen J. Lind (Ph.D., Clemson University) is an associate professor of business at Washington and Lee University. His research explores the intersections of faith, entertainment, and industry. He is the author of *A Charlie Brown Religion: Exploring the Spiritual Life and Works of Charles M. Schulz.*

Dana Mastro (Ph.D., Michigan State University) is a Professor of Communication at the University of California, Santa Barbara. Her research documents depictions of Latinos in English and Spanish language U.S. media and empirically examines the range of intergroup and identity-based outcomes associated with exposure to these portrayals.

Sharon R. Mazzarella (Ph.D., University of Illinois at Urbana-Champaign) is Professor of Communication Studies at James Madison University. Her research focuses on news media constructions of girls and girlhoods.

Seth P. McCullock (M.A., University of Connecticut) is a doctoral student in the Brian Lamb School of Communication at Purdue University. His research focuses on health communication and message design.

Leigh M. Moscowitz (Ph.D., Indiana University) is an associate professor in the School of Journalism and Mass Communication at the University of South Carolina. Her research examines representations of gender, sexuality, race, and class in media and popular culture.

Srividya Ramasubramanian (Ph.D., Penn State University) is Presidential Impact Fellow and Professor of Communication at Texas A&M University. Her research focuses on critical media effects, prejudice reduction, intergroup communication, social justice, difficult dialogues, and media literacy.

Emily Riewestahl (B.A., Xavier University of Louisiana) is a doctoral student in the Department of Communication at Texas A&M University with a focus on media, culture, and identity. Her research explores representations of race and gender in entertainment media and how they affect attitudes towards outgroups, social identity, and selective exposure.

Rachel F. Rodgers, (Ph.D., Université de Toulouse) is an associate professor in the Department of Applied Psychology at Northeastern University, Boston. Her research focuses on media content and effects, as related mainly to body image and body change behaviors, including disordered eating behaviors.

Melinda Sevilla (B.A., University of San Diego) is a master's student of Mediated Communication & Technology in the Department of Communication at the University of Illinois at Urbana-Champaign. She studies stereotypes and new technology environments.

Jennifer Stevens Aubrey (Ph.D., University of Michigan) is an associate professor of communication at the University of Arizona. Her research focuses on media effects on emotional, mental, and physical health in young people.

Jacob R. Thompson (M.A., University of Texas at Austin) is a Roy H. Park Doctoral Fellow at the University of North Carolina at Chapel Hill's Hussman School of Media and Journalism. His research focuses on the role of identity in shaping media effects.

Amanda N. Tolbert (M.A., University of Texas at Dallas) is a doctoral student of Mediated Communication & Technology in the Department of Communication at the University of Illinois at Urbana-Champaign. She studies political polarization and stereotyping.

Kristopher R. Weeks (M.A., Montclair State University) is a doctoral candidate in Communication at the University of Illinois at Urbana-Champaign. He primarily investigates the intersections of minority media representations, interracial violence, audience affect, and audience perceptions of criminal justice.

Asha S. Winfield (M.A., University of Houston) is a doctoral student in the Department of Communication at Texas A&M University with a concentration on media, culture, and identity. Her more recent research focuses on Black media representations, the storytelling of Black content creators, and the audience reception of those stories and depictions.

Kun Yan (M.A., University of Arizona) is a doctoral student in communication at the University of Arizona.

Index

of stigmatized groups 57–58
on television 265
women's role in 80–81
Cox, Laverne 198
Craig, C. 95
Crazy-Ex Girlfriend (television) 195–96
creative genius 245
Crenshaw, Kimberlé 144
crime 103–4
  by African Americans C5.S3295–96,
    97, 102, 103
  hate 113
  Latinos depicted in media on 113,
    116–17
  media's depictions of 95
  mental illness and 245–46
  in video games 102
Criminal Minds (television) 239
critical media literacy 155–56
Critical Race Theory 144
cross-cultural stereotypes 19
Croteau, D. 179
crowdsourcing 61–62
Crowe, Russell 244–45
CSI (television) 195
cultivation theory 26, 38, 93, 152, 241
cults 210–11
cultural construct 135
cultural stereotypes 258–59, 262,
  269–70
cultural values 1–2

The Danish Girl (film) 195
data collection 44–46
Davies, C. E. 176
Davies, P. G. 80
Davis, H. 175
Davis, M. 63
Deadliest Catch (television) 174
death penalty 102
Debnam-Carey, Alycia 185
Deery, J. 167, 173
Defense of Marriage Act (DOMA)
  193–94
DeGeneres, Ellen 188, 192, 263–64
depression 246
DeRozan, DeMar 251–52

Designing Women (television) 191
Devine, P. G. 23–24
d'Haenens, L. 227
The Dick Van Dyke Show (television) 212
Diefenbach, D. L. 244, 248–49
Dietrich, S. 248
Diffrient, David Scott 210–11
digital content 41, 46–47, 142–43
Dill, J. 118
Dill, K. E. 56, 102–3, 118
Dirty Jobs (television) 174
disabilities 42, 47–48
discrimination 46, 157, 158, 197
Disney films 247
diversity 194
Dixon, Travis L. 9, 97, 100, 101, 102
  local news analysis by 95–96
  social media use from 60–61
  young people in news and 139
Do, Kevin N. 9
documentary 1, 188, 189, 190–91
DOMA. *See* Defense of Marriage Act
Döring, N. 60–61
Downey, Roma 209–10, 211–12
Draper, N. R. A. 142–43
Dravitzki, Matt 213
Drew, Sarah 212
Driesmans, K. 82–83
Dr. Quinn Medicine Woman (television)
  208
Duck Dynasty (television) 174, 175–76,
  214
Dukes, K. N. 103–4
Duong, H. T. 42–43
Duvall, S. S. 141–42
Dye, John 209–10

An Early Frost (television) 190
East Asian 19
eating disorders 158
Eggermont, S. 82–83
electromyography (EMG) 62–63
Ellen (television) 188, 192, 194–95,
  200, 263–64
EMG. *See* electromyography
emotional responses 122
empathy 55

Gerbner, G. 5, 26, 38, 93, 241, 251
Gibson, Rhonda 8
Gil de Zúñiga, H. 228–29
Gilens, M. 99–100
Giles, H. 121
Girl Interrupted (film) 261–62
girls 140–41, 151–52
"Girls in Crisis" (Billings) 140–41
Giroux, H. A. 135–36, 137–38
Givens, S. B. 104
GLAAD. *See* Gay and Lesbian Alliance
    Against Defamation
Glascock, J. 85–86, 97
Glaubke, C. 118
GLB. *See* gay, lesbian, and bisexual
Glick, P. 259
Godfrey, H. 177–78
God Friended Me (television) 212
God's Not Dead (film) 215–16
Goffman, Erving 24, 39
The Golden Girls (television) 191, 208
Golding, P. 173
The Good Wife (television) 213
Good Will Hunting (film) 261–62
Gosin, M. 101
gospel choirs 209
Grace & Frankie (television) 187
Gracia, G. 246
Grady, J. 143–44
Granello, D. H. 248
Grau, S. L. 43–44
Gray, M. L. 198–99
Gregory, M. W. 216
Grey's Anatomy (television) 212, 213
Grimm, J. 101
Gross, L. 26, 93
Grossberg, L. 137
Gunn, Sakia 140
gun violence 25
Gwarjanski, A. R. 6, 41, 42, 48–49, 250

Hall, W. 57
The Handmaid's Tale (television) 214–15
Hannah, G. 177, 178
happiness 150–51
Happy Days (television) 172, 208, 210
Hardin, B. 42

Hardin, M. 41–42
Harwood, J. 270
hate crimes 113
Haynes, C. 228
Hays Code 188
Hayward, R. D. 262
hegemonic masculinity 38
Hell Town (television) 208
Hemingway, Mariel 191
Henderson, Lisa 193, 200
Henry, P. 173
Here Comes Honey Boo Boo (television)
    175–76
heterosexuality 199–200
Hetsroni, A. 211
Higgins, E. T. 23
Highway to Heaven (television) 209–10
Hinman, N. G. 59
Hoewe, Jennifer 10, 227–29
Hoffner, C. A. 249
Holloway, Natalee 141–42
homophobia 62–63, 193–94, 199–200
"The Homosexual" (documentary) 189
homosexuality 188–89, 195–96
The Honeymooners (television) 170,
    260–61
hormone cortisol 125–26
Horton, D. 20–21
Hoskin, R. A. 62–63
Hoynes, W. 179
Hoyt, C. 80–81, 85
Hudson, Rock 190
Hull, K. 41
human coding 48
Hunter, S. B. 63
Hurricane Katrina 103
Huston, A. C. 80
hypermasculinity 75–76, 83–84, 101,
    150–51

I Am Jazz (television) 187
IAT. *See* Implicit Association Test
Ice Road Truckers (television) 174
idealization 82
Ifel, Gwen 141–42
I Love Lucy (television) 260–61
immersive media 59–60

Lightning Source UK Ltd.
Milton Keynes UK
UKHW021839070922
408495UK00009B/2128